Caribbean Chapters Publishing Inc. is committed to publishing works of quality and integrity.
In that spirit, we are proud to offer this book to our readers; however, the story, the experiences, and the words are the author's alone.

This is a work of non-fiction.
The events are portrayed to the best of Philip V. Nicholl's memory. While all the stories in this book are true, some identifying details have been changed to protect
the privacy of the people involved.

The conversations in the book all come from the author's recollections, though they are not written to represent word-for-word transcripts.
The author has retold them in a way that evokes the feeling and meaning of what was said, and in all instances the essence of the dialogue is accurate.

Copyright © 2016, Philip V. Nicholls.
All rights reserved.

This publication may not be reproduced, in whole or in part, by any means including photocopying or any information storage or retrieval system, without the specific and prior written permission of the author.

This book is sold subject to the condition that it shall not, by way of trade or otherwise, be re-sold, hired out, or otherwise circulated without the author's prior consent in any form of binding or cover other than that in which it is published and without a similar condition including this condition being imposed on the subsequent purchaser.

FEBRUARY, 2016

Caribbean Chapters Publishing Inc.
P.O. Box 8050, Oistins, Christ Church, Barbados
www.caribbeanchapters.co

Edited by Carol A. Pitt
Illustrations by Jeremy Alleyne

ISBN (paperback): 978-153-0235-18-6

*To my parents,
who made me what I am...*

*to my children,
who will finally know
what was worrying Daddy...*

*to Auntie Marcelle,
in the hope that one day
the truth will out...*

*and to the clients
who have suffered.*

Table of Contents

1. In Jail 1
2. Early Start 12
3. The 'Mother Country' 28
4. Call to the Bar: Joining Cottle Catford 40
5. Early Years at Cottle Catford 50
6. Marriage and Family 58
7. Captain! The Ship is Sinking! 69
8. Time to Jump Ship 82
9. I Dun With That 93
10. It's All Coming Back to Me Now 104
11. Court 113
12. Vernon Smith 133
13. 151/152 of 2004: Cottle Catford and Co. vs Delvina Watson 143
14. 1612/1613 of 2005: Nicholls vs Griffith and Watson 152
15. The Death of a Friend 175
16. Final Resting Place 202
    Photo Plates 217
17. Philip Nicholls and Associates 224
18. Court of Appeal 243

19	Still Married to Cottle	262
20	Trying to Recover the Money Yet Again	284
21	Annus Horribilis 2014	306
22	Coping With Stress and Disappointments	317
23	Pickwick Cricket Club	329
24	A Cricket Umpire	347
25	The Barbados Cricket Association	355
26	Cricket and the Law	377
27	Banks and Other Financial Institutions	400
28	Kingsland Estates	420
29	I Did What Was Right	440
30	Requiem, Repast and Resurrection	456
	Epilogue	464
	Appendices	469
	About the Author	515

Acknowledgements

IN ANY STORY that covers the better part of fifty years there will undoubtedly be persons who have assisted me or extended kindness to me or even played an integral part in several chapters of my life that I may have overlooked. To all of them I issue a sincere apology and state it was not deliberate.

Still I must acknowledge a core of professional individuals including: Julie Harris Hill, Charmaine Delice-Hunte, Marguerite Knight Williams, Edmund Hinkson, Dawn Shields Searle, Yvette Lemonias Seale, Taneisha Evans, Alicia Nicholls, Elliott Mottley Q.C., Andrew Pilgrim Q.C., Walter Scott Q.C., Sir Hugh Rawlins Q.C., Carlisle Forde and Orson Simpson; friends such as Allan and Penny Smith, Shernell Cole, Andrew Sealy, Suleiman Nana, John Blackman, Gary Peters and Rowenia Warner; and last but not least, work colleagues Shatara Ramsey, Maxine Babb and Frederick Cyrus, who have stood by me and carried me at times when I was down and full of despair.

As ever I accept full responsibility for all that is written, none of which would have been possible without the pushing and tireless editing by my publisher Carol Pitt. I also hereby acknowledge the intuitive and valuable contribution of Jeremy Alleyne in the form of the outstanding illustrations at the start of each chapter.

Finally, I cannot put into words the support both material and otherwise that my parents and brothers have given me over this time. I can never repay them, but that I know is the last thing they would want.

Author's Note

AS MY TROUBLES at Cottle Catford resulted from the failure of my former partners to honour their agreement, the toll on me was only too evident to my close friends. Several of them, especially those who were not attorneys, were incredulous about what was transpiring in our legal system, as no one doubted that the money was owed. However, it was my friend Yvette Lemonias Seale who first said to me "Philip I hope you are chronicling these happenings to write about them."

I did not keep a diary of things as they happened, but as many of the things played out in court and elsewhere, there was a paper trail to follow. After Yvette's exhortation the late Stephen Alleyne also made the suggestion, but it was only when I was staying briefly at an apartment owned by Marcelle Smith, who recently so tragically met her death, that I started writing at her urgings. She often said to me "you need to tell your story… you need to expose Vernon for what he has done." As I began writing it became cathartic for me, and I let out a lot of my frustration and pain at what has transpired and the failings of not only the judicial system, but many of the participants in the system who have let me down. That anger has dissipated through several drafts, many of which I know could never have been published, but allowed me to let off some steam.

The late Francis 'Woodie' Blackman, who served the university for years, once told me you never distribute a letter written when you are angry. Though I have breached in the past, nearly all of my text has been rewritten and vetted to take care of my anger which is still evident. My story chronicles what has happened to Cottle Catford and by extension to my life. It is my story. I take full responsibility for it.

Foreword

I WAS GLAD to respond positively to the request of my son Philip Nicholls to write this foreword to his book. For while his request might be regarded as unusual, he says that no one (his great friend Stephen Alleyne having died in 2007) knows better than I do the challenges which he has faced in his professional life. He also felt that someone like me with over fifty years of legal experience in the Barbados and regional public services would be able to offer a non-partisan perspective on what he has faced in his battle because I have not been an active participant in the Barbados legal system for nearly four decades.

Philip starts his story with the day his world came crashing down when he was arrested for something that others bear total responsibility for legally, and more importantly, morally. He then takes us through his early education, secondary, tertiary and finally his entry into the workplace. As parents, both my wife and I were proud of not only his achievements, but those of his brothers. Both he and Stephen have on their own charted careers akin to those with which I was intimately involved, while my third son Christopher is now able to use his medical qualifications to help Philip with the inevitable effect on his health that the events over the last fifteen years have caused.

As such it has been heartrending, as I have watched how a promising legal career as well as one of service through his voluntary work with several organizations like the Barbados Cricket Association have become but a footnote because of the struggles that he has faced with the disintegration of a long-standing law firm. This has been occasioned in part by the scandalous conduct of his former partners. It has been all the more difficult to witness how such conduct has been, if not championed, allowed to go unpunished by the efforts of one person in particular, once viewed by me as a friend.

The several attempts by Philip at preventing the collapse of Cottle Catford and Co. are spoken of with the clarity and feeling of one who has lived through it. The desperation he has experienced during that time and since, not to mention the stress he was under, comes through clearly in his story. I have marveled at how he has recollected and written about what transpired bearing in mind that when he joined Cottle Catford as a bright-eyed youngster in 1987, the last thing on his mind would have been the need to chronicle what was taking place.

He describes the pain of betrayal by his partners and the apparent indifference to his problems of those in the legal profession and the wider community who might reasonably have been expected to come to his assistance, since many of them had benefitted in the past from work sent their way by Cottle or by the services Cottle had provided them for years.

Instead, he was left on his own to bear the full responsibility for the financial morass, caused in the main by the exploitation of the lax financial practices in the firm which depended on the honesty of those involved, something which his partners apparently did not possess. For him and indeed for me the unkindest cut has been the sense of betrayal that he has felt at the manipulation by persons who should have known better of a legal system that he joined, and the failure of those responsible for administering justice to be firm enough to end the abuses which still continue.

In this context, it would be remiss of me not to comment on the ease and speed with which Philip was arrested and charged with theft from a client and engaging in money laundering at the instigation of the then president of the Bar. This speed must be compared with the delay by the police who made repeated requests for adjournments to allow for them to be in a position to comply with the requirements that an accused be made aware of the reasons for the charges he is facing.

As such, after ten appearances over twenty-two months, the presiding magistrate dismissed the charges for want of prosecution when this evidence could not be presented. This appears to be a clear failure on the part of those in the DPP's office who advised the police to proceed with the charges brought against Philip.

Philip's reputation was seriously damaged, which, given the facts of the meltdown of Cottle, is a gross miscarriage of justice. His legal practice has been decimated and his ability to travel restricted because of what I can say as a former chairman of the Anti-Money Laundering Authority is a ridiculous policy apparently being peddled by the office of the DPP, which in so doing fails to recognize that the situation that Philip faced was never the genesis of what constitutes money laundering under the legislation that he was charged, with its links to the financing of terrorism.

As chairman of that authority, I had pointed out on several occasions at meetings at which the DPP was present, that the pressure by the OECD and its sidekick the Financial Action Task Force on countries like Barbados to amend their anti-money laundering legislation to permit money laundering charges to be attached to any case of theft of money, was a device by the OECD to increase the number of Money Laundering cases occurring in Barbados and other Caribbean countries, and thereby provide the OECD with the evidence to press for the closing down of the Offshore Financial Centres based in such countries. This was also intended by the OECD to divert attention from the real centres of money laundering in London, New York, Miami, Zurich and Luxembourg where more significant money laundering transactions take place daily than in Caribbean Offshore Financial Centres annually.

Surely it will be a travesty of justice if those who initiated the charges against him were not made to pay through the same legal system for actions taken for what now appears to be an attempt to deflect attention from the defalcations of his partners, one of whom had a professional relationship with the person whose written letter to the Commissioner of Police instigated the charges.

It is often said that one of the hardest things that any parent can do is to bury a child. While Philip has not at this time succumbed to physical death, I have had to watch many times helplessly the torment of another kind of death, as he has endured day-by-day setbacks and situations that would make a lesser man fold. It has impacted on his family life, and his three daughters will no doubt be better able to understand what they were too young to appreciate previously.

Hopefully his writing will be of help to young attorneys who might otherwise fall into the same trap he did.

Sir Neville Nicholls
Retired President of Caribbean Development Bank
Barbados, 2016

1

In Jail

TUESDAY OCTOBER 29th 2013 started like any other day, but by the time day ended I was incarcerated in a grubby cell at Central Police Station where the en-suite facilities reminded me of those that persons on the local club cricket circuit encountered every weekend at the hundreds of grounds that adorned the island. At least a player, spectator, or whoever, had the choice of using another facility. Now for the first time in my life I did not, and I was livid at what life had done to me after the decade-old battle. Fighting to do what I perceived was right, I would say, had come back not so much to haunt me — that would suggest that I did something wrong — but certainly the chickens had now come home to roost where Cottle Catford (Cottle) was concerned.

I had joined Cottle as a bright-eyed youngster in January of 1987, becoming one of the youngest partners at a major law firm in the island on January 1st 1992. But now the few words of wisdom uttered to me in December 1991 by one of my mentors — the late Freddie Hutchinson Q.C. — that he hoped my acceptance of partnership was not a mistake, certainly rang hollow.

Even today, the 6th of July 2014, as I finally put pen to paper, or to be more accurate punch the keys of my laptop after much encouragement to chronicle my story, I may not be physically in jail, but for all intents and purposes my life is a daily torment. I wrestle with my inability to repay clients and meet other routine financial commitments as I drown in the debt hanging over my head because of the defalcations of my two former partners Allan Watson and Joyce Griffith in not settling their dues to the Cottle Catford partnership that ended in December 2002. Their refusal in spite of a court judgment has been emboldened by the unscrupulous, erratic and callous antics of a man who for some time has boasted to all and sundry about to his intentions to cause me ruin.

His attack on me was born of a vendetta, in his warped mind, arising over twenty years ago as a result of the affairs of the Barbados Cricket Association (BCA). It is a sad commentary on him as a human being, and to think that I once referred to Vernon Smith as 'Uncle' as a mark of respect makes me want to puke. In my mind, just like any other criminal, he should be charged with aiding and abetting Allan and Delvina Watson and Joyce Griffith in the fleecing of the Client's Accounts of Cottle Catford.

When I think of how this person who has caused me much harm and my family much pain was a man who went to this school with my father and uncle, both scholars from Kolij, I wonder where the school failed in producing human beings who could set aside their desire to have their point of view upheld at all times, however irrational and illogical their position might be. Even though he may be an extreme case as will be evident throughout this story, any contempt that I hold for this poor excuse for a human is nothing compared to the contempt and disdain I have for our legal system that has allowed itself to be used and abused by him in his quest to absolve my former partners from their responsibility in repaying the money they have embezzled from the clients of Cottle. What I witnessed over the last decade has so disgusted me that I am ashamed to call myself an attorney-at-law, because this profession, once deemed to be noble, has a serious cancer eating out its core.

It was October 29th and I had just returned home from taking my eldest child Carissa to Community College and the twins Anya and Edaynah to Combermere. Though they had been at the school for only six weeks, they were already displaying that Combermere spirit — the feeling that this 'Waterford University' is the greatest institution in the world, something that has eaten at the core of all proud Old Harrisonians, as I was, and even though my school undoubtedly had the better record academically, as I grew older I came to appreciate that Combermere cultivated among their students a sense of belonging that 'Kolij' never did, and they supported and looked out for the welfare of anyone who went through those gates even after leaving school.

My office was at that time situated at home. My secretary Shatara Ramsey, one of the half dozen people who has remained loyal to me through many events, often with delayed pay, informed me that there were people walking around the house. I was working from home because I could no longer afford the previous office I had occupied, and while searching for new premises I soon had persons even junior to me indicate that they did not wish to be associated with me as if I had become some sort of pariah. The perception was that I was the cause of the Cottle meltdown, but as I would learn, this was a rumor being fuelled by those with no goodwill towards me.

Shatara spoke through one of the windows and asked a well-dressed young man what he wanted, and he stated that he wished to speak to me, so I went to the front door to be greeted by three men and a woman who indicated that they had a warrant to search "these premises" and wanted to question me about a matter.

I asked for what purpose, and they stated that it was in connection with a client named Connor. I invited them in, looked at the warrant, and advised them that the records they were seeking were not present there, and if any such records were available, they were in storage on my father's property, which the warrant did not cover. I added that there was however a file I had on the matter, and if they wanted I would provide it to prevent them from rifling through all my legal documents. They said they would take it. Sergeant Trevor Howard indicated to me that I should accompany them to the station for questioning, and I stated I was not going anywhere to answer questions I could answer right there. He replied that he would have to place me under arrest, to which I said: "Be my guest."

I told them I would need to dress and two of the men followed to watch me dress, and we left. At this time I advised my secretary to cancel a couple of appointments that I had, to make a call to my father and to three attorneys informing them of what had happened, and to contact the lady who had looked after my children from the age of three months to ask her to pick them up from school. My ex-wife was out of the island at the time. I suspected that even though it was before 10 am, it would be a long day.

Upon leaving the house I indicated to the officers that the car they came for me in was much too small for me to sit in the back given my hip problem, and therefore I was allowed to sit in the front while three sat in the back. We drove off to District 'A' Police Station, arriving there around ten.

After the usual formalities of checking in, I was asked to sit on a bench while a room was made available for questioning. This took nearly two hours. It quickly became evident that there was no intention of laying any charges so that I could attend court for bail that evening, so I indicated to one of the officers that I needed to make a call to check on the arrangements for the pickup of my children. A phone was made available, but I requested my cell phone to get the number that I wished to call. Though I was well aware of the number, I wanted to check my messages, as I was sure that news of my arrest had been spreading. A young detective of no more than thirty, in response to my request, said words to the effect that prisoners could not use their cell phones. Not deterred, I said to him in a somewhat contemptuous tone of voice that there is a difference between using the cell phone and extracting a phone number therefrom to allow me to make a call that I am entitled by law to make, and that his records would show I had made none since being there.

His response was that if I wanted to be difficult, he would deem me a risk and could have me strip-searched. My response was: "Risk to whom?" and I asked him if he did not think that the government already had to pay the Jamaican Shanique Myrie enough money for "foolishness like that", and that his idle threat, which no doubt he was accustomed making routinely to persons brought there, meant nothing to me.

Our voices became raised as I told him that I was an attorney, and from his looks for longer than he was alive, and that he was talking abject nonsense about me being a threat, as prior to my coming to the station two of the arresting officers had watched me dress, saw everything that had been placed in my pockets which he now had, so the 'risk' tag was nonsense. I continued with words to the effect that they had arrested me before ten stating that they wanted to question me; it was approaching midday and they still had not begun. My 11 year old daughters were expecting me to pick them up by three and as it seemed clear that I would not be in a position so to do, I needed as any reasonable parent would to make alternative arrangements for their collection.

He suggested that they would send someone to the school to pick them up. I fixed a look of pure derision on him and thought that I should ask what was the minimum level of intelligence needed to join the force, but before I could frame it in a manner that would not later be considered worthy of a criminal charge for insulting an officer, a female inspector came out of her office and asked what was the noise about. I explained my request to her and she instructed that my phone be given to me.

While searching for the number of Lucy Philip, the lady who looked after the twins, especially from 3 months after their birth, I noticed several messages from a number of people expressing concern that everything would be okay, in addition to about 20 missed calls. I did not reach Lucy by phone, so I called Shatara, who advised that she had spoken to everyone I requested her to, and that arrangements for the children had already been made. She also indicated—which relieved me a lot—that arrangements had been made for someone to stay with them in the house that night and that she would wait there until Lucy had arrived, and that someone from Elliott Mottley's office had called to say that he was arranging for young Romain Marshall to come to the station.

With that settled, I could focus on figuring out why I was there. A client, Connor, whom one of the attorneys, Kynara Roett, had worked for while she was employed at Cottle back in 2007/8, had not received the money due from the sale of his property. There was no question that the money was due from Cottle. The simple fact was that at the time Cottle's accounts were and had for some time prior been seriously in deficit because of the amounts due from my former partners since 2002 (see Appendix One).

Now on October 29th 2013 that seemed irrelevant. The debt to the client had been admitted in a civil action that had been brought by Hastings Attorneys. Several civil measures had been attempted to recover the debt, but the simple fact was that I was no longer able to source the funds as I had been doing for the last decade to settle the debts of Cottle. This fact had been stated forcefully to Barry Gale (see Appendix Two), who was the driving force behind the civil action, but his attitude was that he could not care less about the reasons. As he had been in association with Allan Watson, one of my former partners for about five years, we had come to high words about his part in the proceedings. So as I sat there I pondered that Gale had made good on his threat to have me imprisoned. My eyes were burning with anger and hatred for the bastard.

The police started questioning me at about midday. By then I had indicated that my attorney was on his way to the station, but all of a sudden they were now ready to start. The same inspector who intervened with respect to the cell phone knocked on the door of the interview room, came in and asked Howard for a word. I could hear her dressing him down with words to the effect that I had indicated that my attorney was coming, that I myself was an attorney and he needed to play this by the book. I really found the situation to be hilarious, because they were breaching ever rule with respect to my rights by starting to question me, but I was going along and quite frankly was sorry that the inspector stopped them, but she no doubt smelt a rat.

While we continued to wait on Marshall's arrival lunch time was approaching, and another officer entered the room and stated that since I had declared that I was a diabetic while being booked into the station and had been there for nearly three hours, would I like something to eat.

I could not resist the chance to mischievously reply: "filet mignon with caramelised sweet potato would go down well… I can give you the number for Champers who do a good steak and you can collect it if we cannot go." Sgt. Howard smiled and said "Ask a stupid question…" and I finished: "…you will get a stupid answer." I was in no mood to eat, but told them to go across to one of the shops and buy some biscuits and a drink using the money I had turned in, which they did after signing for it. I did not actually eat until about nine o'clock that night when my friend Sulieman Nana brought me a sandwich at Central Police Station.

After the arrival of young Romain Marshall from Elliott Mottley's chambers, the questioning began. I had never met him before, which was becoming the norm at the bar with the number of young lawyers coming in. I believe Romain was more nervous than I was at the time. Howard himself was almost deferential in his questioning. I soon became irritated and advised him not to insult me by asking if I was aware of documents, some of which bore my signature or were letters written to me or from me. These documents were all part and parcel of the civil litigation brought by the estate of the client, and it was apparent that they had the entire file on the matter, and this file had not been given to them by a lay person, but was an attorney's file.

I therefore paid rapt attention every time they opened the file to retrieve a document they wanted to ask about until I saw something that had piqued my interest. It was a letter addressed to the Commissioner of Police from the then president of the Bar Association Barry Gale, on the letterhead of Hastings Attorneys. I kept gazing surreptitiously at the file while answering their questions, during which time I was reading the letter upside down. When I had finished I said to them that the late Freddie Clarke Q.C. had about twenty years prior advised me that whenever you are in a meeting you need to take advantage of whatever you can to do a good job for your client—that people sitting across the table from you are often careless in leaving their files open, so learn to read upside down. That advice had now come in handy and I said as follows:

"Instead of asking me foolishness about documents you know have my signature, why don't you show me the letter that Gale sent you?" This was met by a sheepish smile.

Clearly taken aback, they tried to fob off my question by responding nervously that they thought Gale and I were friends. My response was that I was not friends with "that bitch" and "…you want another charge to add? Here is the vernacular of what Gale is. He is a f…ing red-neck bitch who think he white. Take that down and add using indecent language to any charges you want to bring." To be truthful, I described his qualities in far more colourful language, but as not only my female children but my mother will probably read this, I will spare the details.

After being informed that I was going to be charged with theft and money laundering, a charge that they said was on the specific instructions of the Director of Public Prosecutions, I was momentarily stunned. I thought to myself: *What has that asshole come up with? Surely Charles, who knows the situation surrounding Cottle, could not be such a dickhead as to level a money laundering charge.* I then shrugged and said "Do as you have been instructed…" and I mused that his ego was far in advance of his commonsense, so anything was possible.

At the end of the interview I was asked to sign my statement and, acting on the advice of Mr. Mottley transmitted through young Marshall, I informed them that I had not written it, that they had made notes of what I said, and so I was not signing anything other than the documents they showed me which were already known to me. Of course the letter from Gale was not produced and remained unproduced until Inspector White was summoned by Magistrate Bannister 18 months later to ask why it was taking so long to procure discovery. At that time I was presented with the 'statements made by me' and they bore little resemblance to what I said, which given the several complaints of other accused in our system, did not surprise me.

It became evident to me that the process was being delayed so that it was impossible for me to be brought before a magistrate to be granted bail that day, a common tactic by the police. Both Andrew Sealy and Sulieman (Solly) Nana had arrived at the station to accompany me to court to stand as sureties, but after a while Marshall told them to leave, as it was clear the process was being delayed.

This had become clear to me from a conversation with Inspector Jefferson Clarke, who was apparently leading the investigation into the matter but did not appear to have one clue about the history of Cottle, as he simply spoke about other monies owing, seeming to have come to the conclusion that all I had been doing was relieving clients of their money. After listening to him I said: "Let me draw you a simple illustration. See that car in the car park? How much do you estimate it does on a full tank? Let's say 400 kms. If you siphon off half the tank before the car leaves, will it still do the 400?" He said no. I said "Well, there is Cottle." He said nothing, and I determined it was useless speaking with him, as it was clear that he had been fed a line that I was responsible and that was that. As events were later to show, I had judged him right.

Around 4 pm I was taken from District 'A' to Central for the formalities of being fingerprinted, photographed and booked. I found this very demeaning, but I was kept in the best spirits I could possibly be by several of the officers who knew me from cricket and kept saying I was being given a bum rap. Many said they expected me to get Police Bail, even as I was too late to appear before a magistrate. I was aware of the practicalities of Police bail, as in 1992 I had obtained same for a sports photographer working on the cricket on a charge of lewd behavior towards a woman in a night club at 3 in the morning. And he was not even Barbadian.

As the evening wore on it became obvious that this would not happen, and I was told: "it appears someone has it in for you" because all the inspectors who could authorize this were suddenly not willing to, one or two even coming to explain that as it was Clarke's case, they didn't want to go behind his back because he had not approved it, and was suddenly unavailable. By this time, as evening drew in and shifts changed, more and more officers who I knew from cricket saw me there and asked what was going on. I overheard many saying "…this is nonsense… everyone know on the street his partners carry away the money, so who doing this?" Many were apologetic, but I said to them "Listen, do your job, don't worry about me."

When it became clear that I would be spending the night, I advised the duty sergeant that I needed to sleep with a CPAP machine to lessen the risk of having a heart attack, as I suffered from sleep apnea. My friend Solly was asked to collect it from my house, which he brought along with some toiletries and books to read, all packed by Carissa, and a sandwich to eat. I was then taken to the cell for the night after some officers had rigged up a connection to allow the machine to work.

During an uncomfortable night I was visited virtually every hour, no doubt to see if I was okay, but I spent most of the night recording my thoughts on paper that I had asked for. In the morning after a shower and breakfast of a ham cutter and juice, I was visited by Errol Niles before my appearance in court. I was told by Romain that the police would not be objecting to bail, and that Solly and Andrew Sealy had arrived to stand surety.

I was escorted to court without cuffs, or indeed without being held, much to the disappointment of those who wanted to see my picture in the next day's newspaper thus restrained. That picture was never published, and now for the first time I thank my friend from cricket Louis Linton, who is a probation officer. He appealed to the photographer not to publish the picture, saying that everyone knew I was holding the can for my partners, and to be decent about it.

I returned home at about midday to deal with the many missed calls and messages from all over the world, as news of my arrest had predictably made headline news. To this day I have had nothing but support from friends, colleagues and indeed clients. It has warmed me. I even received a call that night from the prime minister expressing his concern about the long battle I had engaged in through the courts to get my partners to pay their due, but still, nearly two years later, nothing has changed.

Early Start

MY PRIMARY SCHOOL education was at Merrivale Preparatory School, known to all as Mrs. Carrington's school. I am sure that my brothers and I were destined for that school, as in her early teaching career Ms. Inniss, as she was then known, had taught a couple of young boys at St. Giles who later went on to be island scholars, namely my father Neville and Uncle Courtney.

Mrs. Carrington, or Auntie Avis as I have always known her even when she was dispensing that strap that modern day educationists frown on but which many of us have been no worse for tasting, is still alive now, well into her 90s, as is her sister the former headmistress of St. Michael's school, Dan Inniss. My connection to Auntie Avis extended to my early professional career, as her late husband Vere, a former Registrar of the Supreme Court, became a consultant at Cottle Catford after his retirement from the public service. He had retired from the firm by the time I joined in January 1987, but I remember that on my first day at work he visited to wish me well on his behalf and that of Auntie Avis. Up until his death in 1994 he was always a phone call away when I needed advice.

At Merrivale I formed many friendships, many of which have remained lifelong. One of these was with Stephen Alleyne, who tragically died in October 2007 at the age of 47. Stephen's loss was devastating to me, as he was the only one who at that time really knew the seven years of hell that I was going through with Cottle, which hell has now stretched to 14 years. Our friendship grew through the years, especially during our tenure as president and secretary of the BCA between 1999 and 2005, a fact that some resented and tried to put asunder. I include later in this book my tribute paid to him at his funeral at Kensington Oval in 2007. Though I know it was said in jest, I was touched that one of our friends, at the viewing of his body at his beloved Empire the day before his funeral, would remark that we were "as close friends as two men could be and remain men."

Other close friends from Merrivale were Andrew Sealy, Joseph Steinbok, Paul Niles, Michelle Lashley (who later became pediatrician to my twins), Devina O'Brien, Angelica Hewitt, Gillian Alleyne, Sheri Alleyne, David Wickham (his early death in a motorcycle accident was also a great loss), Peter Craig, who sadly died young from natural causes, David Harrison, Peter Nanton, Glenn Roach, Allan Smith, Derek Daniel, David Neblett, David Harrison Jane Brathwaite, and Philip Tudor. We have all moved on, many with successful careers both here and abroad, but we all benefitted from the excellent schooling at that institution. Mrs. Carrington's contribution to her charges and education in general in Barbados was recognized some years back with a gala celebration at the Lloyd Erskine Sandiford Centre. One of her charges, Mia Mottley, then Minister of Education, was the featured speaker.

During this time my passion for cricket—which was, sadly, always more than my ability—developed, and Stephen Alleyne and I used to live and dream it. Like any true-blooded West Indian, we dreamed of representing the West Indies and had to satisfy ourselves with a role in administration in later life when it was clear that our dreams were really not practical. As there was no organized primary school cricket in those days, we had to content ourselves with playing on the hill at school, opposite 4th Avenue Belleville, or at cricket birthday parties at the Garrison Savannah.

From Merrivale I moved on to Harrison College in 1971. Stephen and Andrew had preceded me the year before, and my brothers were to eventually join me at Kolij. At Kolij I met up with persons who were also to become lifelong friends, guys such as Edmund Hinkson, Solly Nana, Frank Belgrave, Gary Peters, John Blackman, George Alleyne, Adrian Cummings, David Commissiong, Hughie McClean, Llewellyn Rock and Reuben Bailey (the latter two both sadly deceased shortly after entering the world of work). In Sixth Form we were joined by young ladies, mostly from St. Michaels and Foundation, schools which had no Sixth Form at that time, namely Barenda Brewster (sadly also deceased in 1994 after a ten year battle with lupus), Roslyn Lynch, Glenda Gittens (who I had not seen in years until my twin daughters entered Combermere in 2013 and she was their year head), Valerie Whittaker, Deborah Hart, Sophie Harper, Antoinette Clarke, Betty June Austin and Julie Williams.

That Upper Sixth Arts Form, maybe because it had some vibrant discussions, not only amongst us but with anyone who ventured into it, produced five attorneys. I still recall one particular discussion with Ralph Walker on the merits and demerits of Combermere over Harrison College, with most of us questioning his sanity for his views that he would move heaven and earth to ensure that any son of his did not end up at Kolij, as Combermere was a more rounded school. At the time he was a leading educator in the Ministry of Education, so as proud defenders of our school the argument was fierce, and it is more than ironic that I recently relived these discussions with him, having been reacquainted with him through his son-in-law Roland Holder.

My interest in cricket led to friendships with guys like Curtis Campbell, Caesar Haynes (now a pilot with LIAT), Hattan Callender, Earle Yearwood, Richard Jeffers, Graham Bethell, Richard Armstrong, Edward Ince, Andrew 'Sprite' Daniel of Weisers, Mark Sealy, Peter

Rochester, Casper Jemmott (now a pastor), Michael Phillips, Trevor Gittens, Mark John, David Bynoe, Ronnie Griffith, Chris Coyle, Hendy Forde, Stephen Goddard, Sammy Worrell, Dwight Edghill, Erwin Bowen, and Anthony Wood and Adriel Brathwaite (both later to be MPs for the same constituency in St. Philip, but on opposite sides of the political fence). Orlando Greene, a Combermerian and former Olympic athlete, was our Games Master at the time.

Already, however, those early days were seeing auditions for our future interests. Those present at our many summer limes that included robust playing of road tennis will remember well David Comissiong's mortification that some of us could be supporting 'imperialist' nations at the 1978 World Cup when African nations and Brazil were playing. The court sessions used to be held every lunch time in the assembly hall, where every transgression from liking the wrong girl to making '0' on the weekend were prosecuted with ferocity by the number of lawyers that emanated from that Upper Six Arts Form and by many others who went into other fields of endeavor.

The only headmaster I knew at Harrison College was the legendary Albert 'Tank' Williams, who sadly died last year, and who I was able to interact with but not influence in my last year at school as head boy. I can still picture the moment when I put forward a request from the Sixth Form for a graduation ceremony with him responding with raised eyebrows and saying: "Aw… Please I am sorry that is an American concept; no useful purpose." End of conversation.

It makes me smile today when I read of children graduating from kindergarden school, but then a lot has changed in our education system over the years. I am not convinced that all is for the good, and remain one who supports reasonable corporal punishment. I recall our earlier petrification with being summoned to Tank's chambers or to be accompanied on that walk to the Retreat with a fatherly hand around your shoulders, often not much higher than you, by Mr. E. W. 'Heads' Marshall. You knew a flogging was imminent, and despite his size he still could wield a harsh cane. My knowledge of these smackings came from other reports, as I managed to evade such a fate at Kolij. Contrary to the growing opposition to corporal punishment by parents of late, I knew that any flogging would be greeted by another on my return home, after which I would be asked what I had done wrong. Both Stephen and I used to talk about this shared concern of the bias of our parents when a teacher had determined that we had done wrong.

I have fond memories of the many teachers, all of whom helped to shape me into the person I was to become; teachers like Mr. Lionel Gittens, Captain Maurice Hutt, Mr. Fanny Fields, Mr. Ralph Jemmott, Mr. Frank Blackman, Ms. Gloria Yarde, Mr. Anthony Walrond, Mr. Bill Snowdon, Mr. Mike Chapman, Mr. Stowell, Mr. Wiltshire, Mr. Gordon Belle, Mr. Carmichael, Reverend Jones, Mrs. Pilgrim, Mrs. Wapinski, Ms. Alleyne, Mrs. Boyce, Mrs. Procope, and last but by no means least Mr. Orlando Greene, and Mr. Maynard who believe it or not was still there up until earlier this year as Deputy Headmaster before moving on to a richly deserved headship at St. Leonard's Boys.

I look back at my time at Harrison College with fondness. I always found myself thrust into some form of responsibility, being Form Captain on several occasions and later House Captain in my first year of Upper Sixth, and then Head Boy during my final year. Reuben Bayley was my deputy and we developed a close relationship, though coming from vastly different backgrounds. Reuben was an excellent sportsman, excelling at the Carifta Games, winning gold in several middle distance events, and it was a monumental shock when he collapsed and died while playing football one evening in the prime of his life at the BET pasture at the young age of 30. Reuben had never been sick a day in his life, and his death from an aneurism took many of us long to recover from.

I now better appreciate why some of my former fellow students don't share the fondness of my memories at Kolij. Yes, there was an emphasis on academics, but many extra-curricular activities were available at the school. Plays were regularly produced under the guidance of Mr. Chapman, one of the many recruits that headmaster Williams brought in from the UK at the time, while the music department's recordings of classical, contemporary and their own music under the late Janice Millington were simply awesome.

Looking back now, one recognizes that there was in existence an elitist system that perhaps I was too cloistered to appreciate at the time, or perhaps my detractors might say I was a part of that. I just didn't appreciate a notion I have always frowned at, but a system did exist in which if you were from more humble circumstances than others, you may have felt that different standards were applied to you. As one advanced in school and did not spend all lunch hours on the playing field, it became quite apparent that boys tended to congregate in different spots with persons whose appearance and background was similar to their own.

I have, certainly since leaving school, admired how Combermere for example has been the leader in setting up vibrant alumni associations, not only in Barbados but in the wider Caribbean diaspora, be it New York, Toronto or London while Kolij, having managed to get a comparable alumni up and running, has not attracted the support of past students. No doubt Ralph Walker is smiling at this admission as well as the fact that my twin daughters who now attend that rival institution have already let me know that it is the best school in Barbados.

I have to accept that I under-achieved at school. I was never at the very top of the class, but was certainly above average. I had all the usual boyhood dreams of being a pilot or a firefighter, and really don't think I made up my mind that I wanted to do law until I was in the Sixth Form. I never had a liking for Sciences, and in fact was placed in the Language/Humanities stream from Fourth Form along with persons like Edmund Hinkson, Frank Belgrave and John Blackman. It seemed funny at the time, but our Fifth Form had the unheard of record of an entire form bar one (Hughie McClean spoiled the record) of failing our Biology 'O' Level Exam, which drew the ire of not only the goodly Tank, but our several parents.

After repeating Sixth Form with the sole intention of improving my grades to get into the Law Faculty, I was joined in my repeat year in Sixth Form by my brother Stephen, and as murmurings started to circulate of the possibility of the Nicholls boys emulating what my father and uncle did in 1951, I decided to put an end to that. One morning, on one of my daily visits to Mr. Williams, I advised him that I thought it best to drop one of my subjects and concentrate on the other two. He agreed, and so my classmate Reuben was left to break the news to the teacher, who just happened to be my mother. Latin was split between HC with Mr. Wiltshire and QC with her. The ride home that evening was particularly uncomfortable, but I pointed out to her that this was the only logical thing to do. I didn't like the subject, and having passed it at 'O' Level, my 'A' Level result was an F, to which my father in a lecture to me expressed his displeasure by pointing out that I had spent two years 'disimproving', if that is a word.

My first desire at school for a career choice, other than the dream of scoring a hundred at Lords, was to be a pilot. I was informed after I started wearing glasses that a lack of twenty/twenty natural vision ruled me out. It was during my third form year at school or rather the summer of 1975 that my eyesight started failing, though I didn't realize it until I returned to school for fourth form and could not make out the blackboard. That partially explained why I could not get a run in the Ronald Tree competition that summer after finishing on a high with Mark Sealy the year before. After Under-15 level I got left behind by my contemporaries, not only because of my failing eyesight but also my weight gain, which earned me the nickname 'Lumpy 2', following on 'Lumpy 1', the name for Stephen Greaves after a TV character I think from a series named *Leave it to Beaver*. With the departure of Stephen from school I had the name outright, and some of my casual acquaintances from school and on the cricket field still gently call me Lumpy because they know of no other name as one told me as recently when we bumped into each other in October of 2015.

I recall one day being in the Magistrate's Court and a young man who was known to be a difficult case at school with regard to behavior when I was head boy was brought into court by prison officers and placed on the bench for the accused. After a while I noticed he was signaling to me, as I had not recognized him at first, and when I went over he addressed me as 'Mr. Lumpy' which brought great hilarity to the prison officers when he said he must show some respect because we were no longer students. As he explained he really did not know my name, as many school boys are known by their nicknames, and he insisted he had shown respect by placing 'Mr.' before it.

I went on to captain both the Second XI and the First XI at school, but was never in contention for any youth representation for Combined School XI, far less Barbados. I recall with fondness the camaraderie of those days and indeed the outright scurrility that was sometimes stated. During one game Orlando Greene joined a batsman at the crease who shall remain nameless, when another character who went on to be Manager of a leading Bank in the island rose from his seat in the Pavilion and screamed at the top of his voice that you should never bat with "a man that horn* you". No sooner than he said it the unidentified batsman got out, only to be greeted on his way back to the pavilion with the words: "You idiot... no one knew I was talking about you."

I subsequently entered the faculty of Law at the Cave Hill Campus of the University of the West Indies (UWI) in 1980 with Barenda Brewster from that Kolij Sixth Form. The two of us were study partners from school. She also dabbled with cutting my hair, and it is fair to say that she became the sister to me that I never had. Barenda and I were from the same school, but our first year had just five Barbadians — the two of us, and Glenda Medford, Carol Ann Smith and Sheridan

Reece, all of whom were from Queen's College. There were three other students from Barbados, all direct entrants doing the first two years combined. These were Grantley Watson who was later to be Commissioner of Police, Tyrone Estwick, later to be a member of the Erskine Sandiford Cabinet but now deceased, and Philip Pilgrim. Another direct entrant who was to become a lasting friend was Arlene Maxwell from Jamaica, though she has been resident in the USA for the last thirty years, and Kenny Anthony who needs no introduction as the current Prime Minister of St. Lucia. I remember our current Prime Minister Freundel Stuart as an active reader and philosopher at UWI, primarily because I saw him a lot as he studied in the same section of the library that Barenda did.

In that first year I was joined by a Jamaican lass by the name of Yvette Faye Dunwell Lemonias, to which we had to add Seale when she got married shortly thereafter. We have remained firm friends to date. I can only, as the young people say, SMH (shake my head) upon reading as I am writing this that 56 attorneys were admitted to the bar this October 2014 and in 2015 another 51. How times have changed.

That class of 1983, entrance in 1980, contained the Myers boys from Trinidad, Ronnie and David, and produced two First Class Honours candidates, Kenny and Yvette, but it was widely reported that Yvette's was in a different category. I say without fear of contradiction that Yvette was easily the top student amongst us and the best legal mind I have studied with.

That period of time saw all manner of Caribbean social life debated at Cave Hill, including the Grenada Revolution with students like Terrest Sylvester from Grenada, now sadly deceased, strident in her views on the rebel West Indies tour of apartheid South Africa. This I recall led to heated discussion with some of my Jamaican friends, in particular my girlfriend at the time Joan Charles, now a judge in Trinidad, who was particularly upset with me for not condemning the many Barbadians that took part in the rebel tour.

I took the view that from my somewhat privileged perspective I was in no position to condemn men for taking a decision that I would never be faced with. It was seen as a cop-out by some. My view was that my parents were always able to put food on my table, I was getting an education that would allow me to do the same for my family (little did I know what the future held for me), and I therefore felt I could not justifiably condemn others who went to a country that was the pariah of the world.

Looking back now I realize how little I knew at that time of the struggle in South Africa, and I have subsequently come to the conclusion that my stance was wrong. This change, ironically, really only materialized when I entered the University of Manchester in the UK in 1985 when university politics soon came my way. On arriving there I looked across from my room and saw a Barclays Bank and went to open an account, and was nearly lynched by some African students picketing outside who gave me a crash course on the involvement of Barclays in apartheid in South Africa. Seeing that I had left home having interned at Cottle Catford, and that its major client was Barclays, I was very sheepish about being hyper-critical, but hastily agreed to open my account at Nat West to avoid confrontation. Welcome to student politics. I don't think I endeared myself to the African students with my apparent ignorance of the situation.

Prior to the UK I spent two years at Norman Manley Law School (NMLS) in Jamaica. How I ended up there along with about a dozen other Eastern Caribbean Students was a story in itself. I, like all others entering Law School in 1983, had submitted an application to the Hugh Wooding Law School (HWLS) in Trinidad. At the time a new school was being built to replace the cramped conditions of the original school, but there was considerable doubt that it would finish in time to open in September 1983, and it was suggested by my father that I should submit an application for NMLS. I thus submitted said application on the last day possible—I think it was in January—and forgot about it.

During the summer of 1983 I received a call—no emails, WhatsApp, BBM in those days—from my friend David Myers in Trinidad saying he was going to Jamaica, or had been told he would have to report to Jamaica if he wanted a place that year. It then dawned on me that I might be in the same boat, as it soon transpired that anyone who had applied to both places was being accepted for Jamaica, even Trinidadians. I dismissed his warnings that I had to go as well, but soon got what at the time was the dreaded news that I had to go.

I was at the time facing another problem which was the start of my foray into interpersonal relations with the fairer sex. I had not advised Joan that I had made an application to Jamaica, because quite frankly I thought nothing would come of it, and now I had to man up. I have faced worse problems since then, including Patrick Patterson in the nets at Kensington Club in Jamaica, but at the time her anger was quite frightening. To digress, I remember returning home in the summer of 1984 and speaking of this man, Patrick Patterson, who bowled like the wind, only to be dismissed as not knowing what fast bowling was like. Shortly thereafter I must admit to chuckling in Jamaica when I listened to him terrorizing regional batsmen, including those from Barbados.

At NMLS, a situation arose that while David was in Jamaica, his brother Ronnie was in Trinidad, he having not made the application for Jamaica, so it was an anomaly that Trinidadians, despite there being the Hugh Wooding Law School, were being sent to Jamaica. The foreign group excluding the Bahamian and Belizean students who regularly went to NMLS during the period 1983 to 1985 consisted of myself, Cappy Greenidge, Philip Pilgrim, Errol Niles and Herbie Arthur from Barbados, David, Penny Carballo, Camille Robinson and Suzanne Charles from Trinidad, Stephen Fraser, Vejah Singh, Carole James from Guyana, Alberton Richlieu, Hugh Rawlins, Gail Royer and Mark Williams from St. Lucia, St. Kitts, Dominica and St. Vincent,

Eleneth Kentish from Antigua and a number of Bahamian students such as Willie Moss, Andrew Thompson and Gregory Rawlins. We were thus transported to Jamaica and found ourselves at the feet of Aubrey Fraser, the eminent Caribbean jurist who was principal of the school at the time, to continue what he called that great experiment in Caribbean integration.

At the beginning of this sojourn it is fair to say that many of us were livid at being forced to Jamaica, as we argued as good future lawyers that our rights under the relevant legislation which determined how places at the law schools were to be determined by residence had been breached. However, after much gnashing of teeth, we extracted a concession from Mr. Fraser that if we wanted we could get a transfer to HWLS at the end of the year. In the end only two of us took up the offer to change over, such was the extent of our enjoyment of student life in Jamaica. The NMLS is situated in the heart of the Mona Campus and though we were not considered UWI students, all the facilities of the campus were available to us. Even then Mona was akin to a community in itself, something that of late has become even more apparent, as you could remain within the confines of the campus and have all your personal needs attended to.

With that we settled down into Jamaican life and received much help from people like Wally Scott, Andrea Rattray, Chester Henlin, Dougie Thompson and Arlene Maxwell in doing so. We became fully involved in the Law School and enjoyed our year. Jamaica is by far the biggest of the English-speaking Caribbean islands and has several natural amenities that we in Barbados do not have. With the help of all the above and also because of the number of foreign students, we attempted to arrange excursions at least twice a month that took us as all over the country.

David and I, along with Allan Smith who was studying at Mona, joined Kensington Cricket Club and toured all over the island playing matches, and have made lasting friendships as a result. Just prior to our leaving in the summer of 1984, we were involved in a game with Lucas, a local derby, as the two clubs are but a six-hit away. While batting at the non-striker's end, David was given out, handled the ball after the bowler requested that he return it to him. Not *au fait* with this guy's *modus operandi* (Serrao was his name), he did just that, and as soon as he picked it up an appeal was made and David given out and the match degenerated after that.

On the final day David caught Serrao close in and gave him a send-off that would have attracted any match referee today, and after a close victory I think we won, and a riot amongst the rival spectators ensued. As the club captain at the time, the former Jamaica and West Indies batsman Basil Williams who has just recently passed, said it had to be Myers or Nicholls that did that, as no Jamaican would have fallen for a standard Serrao trick—interesting times on the field and off.

Years later when entering the George Headley stand at Sabina to watch a Test I was hailed by the said Serrao, and we had a friendly reminiscence of the incident. Playing club cricket certainly introduced us to everyday life in Jamaica. Some of our teammates arrived in BMWs, while others used to borrow bus fare from us students to get home. Our captain was one of the BMW drivers and he never went anywhere without his trusty firearm which he kept in a pouch. That was my first close up inspection, and as far as my memory goes my only inspection of a firearm. It puzzles me thinking of this when I view the obsession in the United States, a supposedly civilized society, with this need to be armed and the arguments about right to bear arms.

One of our protectors that day when the disturbance started was David Bernard (Sr.), a teammate at the time who has subsequently had a distinguished career as a trainer for the Jamaican cricket team. I was reunited with him a few years ago when I got a call from my cricket club, Pickwick, where Jamaica were playing a first class game in Barbados. He as trainer along with his son Dave Bernard (Jr) and Darren Powell, both former West Indies players but youngsters while I was at the club, had recognized my picture which was hanging in the club house as a past president of the club. They asked to contact me and after receiving a message from the BCA, I eventually met up with them over dinner which allowed me to catch up with much of my past at the club when I was in Jamaica between 1984 and 1985.

Though we had fond memories of our first year in Jamaica after exams in 1984, both David and I left, but determined to move closer to home by transferring to Law School in Trinidad. Back home for the summer of 1984, some stories of HWLS began to emerge that seemed totally contrary to the family atmosphere at NMLS where judges like Justice Rowe, Carey who sadly has recently passed; Harrison and Panton were welcoming and helpful. To these judicial titans I must add Denis Morrison, now himself a Court of Appeal judge in Jamaica, who was easily the best lecturer I've ever had in my student career, and who made the subject of Evidence seem alive while he lectured us.

No matter if Dennis scheduled a class at 2 am, it would be full, and one female student who shall remain nameless was heard to say that the prize for evidence should be a weekend for two with Dennis, to which the men said "suppose a man wins?" only to be met with a look of derision when she said "He would be an idiot, which he clearly is not, if he allowed a man to win."

I remember Justice Carey with fondness. When the marked copy of my first Family Law assignment was returned, I was mortified to see that I had been awarded a 'C' upgrade from a 'D'. I therefore took up his offer of attending his chambers to query the grade, and with my sidekick David in tow, journeyed by minibus—an experience in itself—downtown to query it.

After being ushered into his chambers, Justice Carey asked what my problem was, and I said "Sir, I feel my grade was too low" and I proceeded to explain why. Justice Carey listened, looked at me, and when I finished passed me my script and said that if I can show him all that I have said was in my essay, he would give me an 'A' immediately.

With the help of David I frantically searched my essay, and after being unable to find same, said with unreserved embarrassment: "Sir, thank you for the C" and retreated gratefully.

Still he would stop for me and others at the corner in Liguena where students seeking a ride to campus in the morning hung out, and the ability to interact with him and other judges demystified their office to many of us, and on many of those rides he would start with "Young Nicholls have the essays improved?" Just being able to talk to him and other judges informally assisted me tremendously in my development, and I have always made it a point to try and pass on what I have learnt to anyone junior who might seek my advice just as was done to me.

So as the return date for the second year approached, I started thinking I should go back. I did not know that David was thinking the same, so when I called him to say I was doing this, I heard him breathe a sigh of relief and say: "I didn't know how to tell you." In fact only Suzanne, Penny and Carol transferred. My next call was to Joan, who understandably was not pleased, and my decision probably ended any chance of our relationship going further.

Our return to NMLS was met with much leg pulling, and we had to eat crow for a while, but we were able to resume our final journey to become attorneys under the guidance of Aubrey Fraser. His subsequent murder saddened us, all the more shocking that his wife was one of the accused. She was later acquitted, but the thought of this matronly woman having something to do with his death was incomprehensible to many of us students who had been entertained by them both to Sunday brunch at their residence on more than one occasion.

I have returned to Jamaica more times than I care to remember since graduating in 1985. I regard it as my second home and have maintained many of the friendships that I started then and that I have developed with other students who have been in my classes over the years and are now established practitioners in their own country. The country has often been portrayed as a violent one, but other than an occasion when someone attempted to pick my pocket downtown, I have so far never encountered trouble. It is the only country that I would consider living in, and who knows, it may well become so. I have had more practical help from friends at the bar there in my view than in Barbados, something that has saddened me, and it was a pleasure to return on the 25th anniversary of our graduation in 2010 to make acquaintances with many members of the class whom I had not seen since graduation. Time has certainly flown so much so that two of my friends have given me watching briefs over their children who have recently come to Barbados to study.

Graduation occurred in early October of 1985, just days before I left for England to pursue my Masters. That was a new adventure.

The 'Mother Country'

PRIOR TO MY arrival in the United Kingdom in October of 1985 to study for my Masters, I had visited the UK on three occasions, but never for more than a couple of weeks. There is nothing like living for an extended period in a country to allow you to really get to know it and its people intimately. I have named this chapter 'The Mother Country' which will no doubt have some up in arms because of the view that the motherland has to be somewhere in Africa and not the United Kingdom. Whatever one's views on the subject are, I have always taken the more practical position that our ties with the UK, whatever the reason, have been far greater than those with Africa. To say so in no way means that I am unfamiliar with or am overlooking the horrors of the middle passage that was inflicted on my ancestors and the cultural linkages that we have with Africa.

Over the ensuing sixteen months after my arrival in October of 1985 I pursued and subsequently obtained a Masters in International Business Law at Victoria University of Manchester.

My home away from home was situated at the Moberly Tower on Oxford Road, a postgraduate residence for males only that boasted of students from over 50 different nationalities, the predominant nationality being Hong Kongers. Close behind them were African students from several countries. This cosmopolitan gathering led to many opportunities at both breakfast and dinner to interact with and learn about the cultures and customs of various countries, many of which I would never visit.

As I got settled into life a pattern, a pattern of dining with the same persons was established, and I can honestly say that seldom did I interact with the other African students. It was not for a lack of trying, but it soon became clear to me and indeed the other West Indians there that we were looked down upon by those from what others regarded as the 'mother country'. Having done West Indian History to 'A' levels, I was aware of the treatment of the African slaves brought to the Caribbean, but I will admit that my knowledge of Africa was limited. I did not increase this knowledge greatly in Manchester from my fellow African students, as I had little interaction with them, even though two of them were on my course. Our conversations tended to be very perfunctory and I was left with the feeling that they felt I was coming from an inferior place, an attitude that soon began to annoy me. However, I did glean far more information and understanding of the apartheid state of South Africa from the many protests and lectures that were held on campus. It appeared to me that virtually every building I entered bore some reference to Nelson Mandela, a far cry from what I had left at the two university campuses that I had been associated with.

After I returned to Barbados in 1987 I witnessed the growing movement for increased ties with Africa—something no rational person could be opposed to—by some persons, prominent among them was my old school colleague and cousin David Comissiong. I have always felt that much of the 'Back to Africa' movement was born out of a utopian idea of what we as a race have lost by being transported from the land of our birth. However, to me the connections with Africa have long been severed, and what I saw during my brief sojourn to a sporting conference in South Africa in 2008 or 2009 did not leave me with a burning desire to return. While like all societies we have problems from my reading and the news reporting (admittedly some with an overt Western bias), I am of the view that Barbadians really live in a little paradise and we must do all in our power to keep it that way.

My early days in Manchester were made easier by my meeting a Trinidadian student doing a Doctorate in medicine, who became my closest friend at university and who to this date has remained a true friend. Dr. Andre Douen is now a Stroke Specialist at a leading Canadian Hospital and has been to Barbados on several occasions to lecture not only to doctors in a similar field here, but as recently as October 2015 to give a public lecture on strokes. I would not attempt to try and explain his specialties, but the fact that Dr. Raymond Massay and Dr. David Corbin, both respected as leaders in their field, speak highly of him is enough for me to understand that he is a leader in his field. It must have bemused many doctors and medical students, not knowing of our connection, to see me attending one of his early morning lectures at the Queen Elizabeth Hospital a few years ago.

While sharing summer digs in Manchester in 1986 which were self-catering, he tried to convince me without much success that the skin on the chicken was not the best part as I was fond of saying, but contained many harmful fats. My recent health challenges have meant that many of the problems and drug treatments prescribed by physicians to prevent the onset of a stroke I have become only too familiar with, and may well have been avoided if I had paid more attention to his cooking lessons.

Having been in Manchester the year prior to my arrival, Andre was able to show me the essential areas of the university and city. He is a man that believes in the gym, a fondness which was never replicated by me, especially when we had to walk back through the cold campus after a session to our residences. We, along with other Barbadians at Manchester at the time, Gregory Hazzard and David Jean Marie to name two, and Steve Louis from St. Lucia, did sample many of the concerts put on by international musicians that came our way while we were there, not to mention visits to Manchester City and Manchester United, the latter whose fortunes I have identified with more since leaving.

I still vividly recall returning from a Third World concert in the wee hours of the morning waiting at the bus stop for the hourly night service in the biting February wind chill factor of below zero, and swearing that if I ever heard anyone in Barbados complaining of the cold again I would do them some bodily harm. Feeling cold may be relative, but Barbados can never be classified as cold when the temperature seldom ever dips below 75°F at night.

Attendance at a football game is an experience in itself. We usually went in a group for security reasons, and were joined by other students, but were still taken aback by the volley of abuse hurled at Black players at the time. One of the games we went to was to see John Barnes playing for Watford at City's ground which was within walking distance of the university. He scored in the game, and as Paul Keens-Douglas would say, 'who tell him do that?' Seated with the City supporters, we dared not show our appreciation for his skill. I of course was supporting him because his sister Tracey had been a student with me at UWI and NMLS. The kindest words said to him that night was that he was a wanker.

Another interesting experience occurred as we explored the city. A group of us ventured into a bar and settled in for the usual pint when, on surveying the scene, I asked of my fellow pub crawlers whether they noticed anything strange about the bar. It was packed, but had not one single woman in it. It then dawned on us that we had stumbled into a gay bar in the centre of Manchester, from which we made a hasty retreat, casting suspicious looks at Andre who had taken us there amidst claims from him that he did not know of its reputation.

This episode was but a forerunner to an encounter I had with an English student. My own remembrance of her was that she was a young pretty white English girl studying to be a nurse. I was in the

Students' Union one day when she approached me to ask whether I was a foreign student, and if so, whether I intended to vote in the upcoming guild elections. She indicated that she was running for overseas student rep, and would be grateful if I could vote for her. Up to that point I'd had little interest in the elections, which by and large were dominated by eccentrics and persons auditioning for every post available; typical student politics.

The young lady kindly provided me with her manifesto, and to her credit pointed out on the student notice board that she had two opponents. After I'd read her manifesto and looked at her two opponents in less than a minute, I said "I will vote for you." She queried what had made my mind up so quickly, as I could not have read their manifestos, and I said that from a cursory glance at her opponents, I did not want them representing me because both declared they were members of the Lesbian-Gay Society, a society that I had no connection with nor could I identify with even though I knew of some of my fellow students including one from Trinidad (not Andre) who were gay.

I was taken aback when she said that she was surprised that I, a black student, would display such a discriminating attitude, and we engaged in a heated conversation for over 30 minutes about whether my views were discriminatory or not. I was at a loss to see how the question of racial discrimination could be tied up with the question of gay rights. Years later it still mystifies me how this had somehow become accepted, particularly in American politics, where the two are placed on the same level by no less a person than President Obama, whom I admire greatly. While I will never subscribe to active or passive discrimination of someone with an alternative lifestyle or to the treatment meted out in some countries of hounding such persons out and putting them to death, I am at a loss to understand how this can be taken further to mean that you have a divine right to marry, which no version of the Bible let alone the Koran comes near to suggesting.

My point to my friend was that where I came from no such places like Gay/Lesbian clubs existed in the open, and unlike now it was not something that was advertised in public. We agreed to disagree, shook hands, and I ended by saying "Look, you can have my vote if you want it, as I need not vote… it's up to you." No prizes for guessing what occurred; a future politician no doubt.

As I met up with my fellow students on the course—one individual from Uganda, one from Angola, and two from Australia—we came under the tutelage of Professors Margot Brazier and David Milman, who became instrumental in our academic lives that year and who I have still kept in contact with. I believe we were the first intake of students doing the course in International Business Law. Some of our lectures were with the students in the third year of their LLB. Interacting with them in class library and socially made me appreciate even more the excellent grounding that I was given at Cave Hill, knowledge which I took for granted when reading for my LL.B and which clearly they did not have at the same stage.

For example, unless a decision in the Privy Council went contrary to what the House of Lords had ruled on a point of law, such as in the Law of Foreseeability to establish Negligence in the Wagon Mound cases, they basically were ignorant to the existence of that set of jurisprudence which of course those coming from the Caribbean knew. In many respects their education was very insular, and it reminded me somewhat of History taught at school where we learnt all about the English monarchy in addition to West Indian history. Our diet in that respect may not have been right, but at least we learnt more.

In my opinion the standard of the LLB course at Cave Hill was higher than that which the undergraduate faced in Manchester, and I was indeed proud to be singled out by a guest lecturer one day—I think she was Professor White—as coming from an institution whose marking of student papers in her words "was as tough if not tougher than any university she was associated with." Given that she had been an external examiner for UWI for many years, she was well placed to make this comment.

Being a class of five, in effect four as the Australian male student was simply working on a dissertation while his female counterpart read for her degree with the three of us, it meant that much of our taught seminars consisted of only the lecturer and the four students. There was no place to hide and it was tough, but it was a rewarding experience.

I found Manchester to be a far more friendly and personal city than London, though a cold and dreary place at times, and as the first winter that I was there gave way to spring and summer, I saw more and more of it and indeed its surrounding cities. It was a completely different experience than what little Cave Hill or NMLS had afforded me. After all, the student body of the university then totaled at least 20,000, and with other tertiary institutions around, as many as 50,000 students were in the city during term time.

Besides trips to London to spend time with Allan Smith who was studying there, I made side trips to Scotland to visit my friend Stephen Alleyne, who introduced me to aromatic crispy duck, a necessity every time I return to England, and for which I am eternally grateful. Gary Peters also studied in Scotland at the time, and the two of them showed me around Edinburgh, which struck me as an extremely clean city compared to the two that I was familiar with—Manchester and London.

A group of us travelled to Birmingham where we met up with Kenny Anthony and Dr. David Corbin, both doing I think doctoral work in Birmingham while there to attend a cricket game involving many West Indian players at Edgbaston, but sadly it was ruined by rain. It was to become ironic for me that David at the time had a very young daughter who I remember running all over the place with her siblings and who was twenty years later to work with me as my secretary while studying law at Cave Hill. "Getting old," I tell myself.

Other cities that I visited while at Manchester were Cambridge to see fellow UWI students Yvette Lemonias Seale, now vice-president of the Caribbean Development Bank, and Winston Anderson, now a judge at the Caribbean Court of Justice, and also to visit the haunts of my father while he was a student in the fifties. Having visited Cambridge I was compelled to visit Oxford, my mother's *alma mater* and where David Myers was now in residence on a Rhodes scholarship. In the last three months that I was in Manchester my brother Christopher came to study at Leeds and we used to interchange weekends with one another as the two cities were just an hour apart by coach.

Life on campus was clearly different. While at home I had little time for campus politics, but I became aware of more and more social causes maybe because the Student Union was a few hundred yards away from my residence and it offered a place to watch TV in down times. One of these was the Free Mandela Movement, and I learnt more about the conditions in South Africa and about the man Mandela in my first few months in Manchester than at home. You had no choice. There was a Mandela walk, building, park, and room, so one had to.

My love for cricket saw me turning out for the university team and touring Denmark with them, where I experienced a game ending after midnight in high summer, still in clear light. That was the summer of 1986 and the hand of God goal that Diego Maradonna scored to defeat England at the World Cup, which I witnessed from somewhere in Denmark, but still recall the agony on the face of my fellow students. Back in the United Kingdom I played every weekend with a group of West Indians named Hulme West Indians in Alexandra Park. I sometimes went down to Lancashire to watch games where Patrick Patterson was playing. He was a member of the Kensington Club I joined in Jamaica. I was always amazed when I saw some of what we would refer to as the 'dibbly dob', medium pacers playing on the county circuit, and then I went to my weekend games to see fellas of West Indian descent giving the batsman the hurry-up who appeared far better prospects. They all had the same story—they got invited to trials, but no more. I have always held to the view that England, unlike in football, has never fully tapped the talent available in the West Indian and Asian community to strengthen their cricket teams.

I have lost touch with many of the guys with whom I shared many a weekend, although one turned up in my office at Cottle in the early 90s to see a colleague, and it was only after I walked past him several times that it clicked that I knew him from somewhere and we eventually figured it out. Another teammate I once met when I boarded a bus on a trip back to Manchester years later and was routinely handing him the fare when he said "hello Philip", much to my astonishment. We breached the rules of not talking to the driver while the bus was in motion (other than in an emergency) while catching up on old times on that journey.

One of our fond memories was when a team of us seven West Indians beat a full team of 11 English players in a league game. The rules of the competition were that whoever was there within thirty minutes of the toss was the number you played with. Four of our guys had not shown on the Saturday, but instead of forfeiting the game we played, batting, bowling and fielding with the seven, much to the embarrassment of the other side when it was reported in the local press.

Though Old Trafford became a frequent port of call, so frequent that I became a member, I was itching to travel down to London for my first visit to Lords, which I did at a Cup Final with Lancashire. Lords is a magical place whether you are a player — which I never came close to — or just a lover of cricket. There is no other place like it. Every time I walked through those gates I shivered, but never more than in the late 90s when I visited the ground and who should come sauntering in but Sir Vivian Richards, to greet me with the conviviality of one who had rubbed shoulders with him in the BCA boardroom. I swear that I had requests for autographs by the crowd around after he left, no doubt feeling that having not got the great man's signature, mine must have been worth something, as he deigned to speak to me.

My course was scheduled to me for one year, but it became evident that I would never complete my thesis by the end of the summer, so I spent an additional term writing up; no classes, much of the time in the library. There was no internet in those days for students. If your library did not have the book you wanted it was brought in on loan for a week. Coming from UWI where you could photocopy everything, it was strange to see copyright laws enforced strictly whereby you could only photocopy seven pages at a time, and then must miss a page, so that required some ingenuity to get around.

Two significant events happened during this time. A relationship developed between myself and a young British girl of West Indian background named Beverley, whom I had met while she had a weekend job at my hall of residence. I learnt that she was studying 'A' level law at polytechnic, and arranged to assist her by getting her into the library to use its facilities. Very often I would go off to cricket practice and come back to find her still at work. When I visited her home, her mother's cooking, which was typically Jamaican, was a far cry from the bland staple diet on Hall.

During our courtship, before our eventual marriage in September 1990, Beverley at times would come over to the park where we played which was near to her residence to watch my games, something which our daughters many years later were to learn with disbelief, given that she really has never developed an appreciation for the game. In one game I took five wickets and was being congratulated as we came off the field, only to hear her ask "What was all the fuss about?" Her visits stopped, however, when some elderly West Indian spectators once asked her why she was there a Sunday instead of at home "cooking somebody food."

In my memory her ire at this statement was only matched years later when I passed on to her a message from a client of mine, Bentley Greaves, who was then on death row. Beverley was doing in-service training with Jack Husbands around 1992 when they visited another prisoner on death row. As I was told the story, as she and Jack were going down to the cells—in those days you went onto the actual row to meet with a client who had already been condemned—there were a number of cat calls, as women were not too often seen on the row. A few weeks later I went to see Bentley, and as I was leaving he said "Mr. Nicholls I would like you to pass on to your wife the apologies of the guys up here for the comments made to her. We didn't know she was your property." It was a good thing when I delivered the message that he was locked away, as she was not amused to be classified as property.

Sometime in late 1986 I came down with a rash on my skin which itched me a lot. After riding it out for a few days I went to the campus medical doctor who prescribed some cream and advised me to ensure that my wardrobe was properly washed in case I had picked up an infection in the communal wash facilities. When I visited the doctor I was taken aback by his questioning as to whether I was gay, and really could not fathom the reason.

When the rash did not ease I went back to the doctor. On this occasion I had dug up a jersey that I had not worn for months. It was a Cockspur jersey. On the previous occasion I was wearing a Mount Gay tee shirt and that probably settled in his mind that I was a closet gay, as he would not accept any explanation that these jerseys represented famous rums in Barbados. When I later recounted this story to Dr. Oscar Jordan on return to Barbados, he could not help laughing, but it was no joking matter because I was immediately sent off to hospital in an ambulance suspected with an infectious disease.

Quite frankly, I was bewildered as to why, as it appeared to me that I was being treated in an infectious disease hospital, which was confirmed by my friend Andre when he visited me and confided in me that they were checking to see whether I contracted AIDS. I blew my top, indicating I didn't have "any blasted AIDS" and that this stereotyping of a young, single black man as either being promiscuous or living a dangerous lifestyle was wrong. Within a couple of days all the tests were negative, to which I said "I could have told you", and I was no longer of interest medically to the hospital.

The antibiotics that I was given soon cleared up the rash, and it was determined that I had contracted hepatitis B, most probably from food poisoning, and I was sent on my way. That was to have a profound effect, as four years later Dr. Massay was to trace back that what I had contracted had resulted in a sero-negative arthritis that attacked and ate away the cartilage between my hip bones, the result of which has been that my hip has frozen in a manner that does not allow my leg to fully rotate. I can no longer ride a bike, as I can't make the full circle and have been left with a permanent limp. Dr. Massay concluded that once they determined I did not have AIDS, no close attention was paid and the effects of the eating away of the cartilage went undetected until it was too late.

After Christmas 1986 it was time to pack up and head back to a new adventure — back home.

Call to the Bar: Joining Cottle Catford

I TOOK A break from my sojourn in Manchester for the Christmas celebration of 1985 to be called to the bar in the New Year. As I was away studying I had missed the general call of those in my class in October of 1985. I was called before Chief Justice Sir William Douglas in January of 1986. I was introduced to the bar by two of my father's closest friends, Asquith Philips Q.C., who died in 1991, and Oliver Browne Q.C., a former Solicitor General who remained a consultant with Carrington and Sealy until early in 2015.

Besides my parents, my uncles Courtney and Harry and their wives Angela and Paulette along with my brothers Stephen and Christopher were in attendance. I have always regretted that my Aunt Marina with whom I lived while studying in Jamaica along with her husband Harold and daughters Nickie and Jackie were unable to attend. My time at #2 Ottawa Avenue was a home away from home, and was a virtual continuation of home life, this time with two sisters and not two brothers. Sadly none of them live in Jamaica anymore, so trips there don't rekindle the memories like if you were going back home.

I remember little of what was said on the morning of my call, other than Sir Douglas' charge that I follow in the footsteps of my father, who though he was at that time the vice-president of the Caribbean Development Bank, had distinguished himself, as I am often reminded, as a legal draftsman. I am sure if and when he proofreads this text it will be significantly altered for syntax, etc. But it was in drafting legislation that he specialized. He also spent much time travelling with the late national hero Errol Barrow as the negotiations for the setting up of CARIFTA and the Caribbean Development Bank took place.

My call in January 1986 was the end of a five-year sojourn into the law, but even then I was well aware that I now had to learn the law, something Daddy always drove into me. My early interest in the law was obviously sparked by my father and some seminal TV programs like *Rumpole at the Bailey* and *Crimes of Passion*. Today there are several legal shows parading on TV and one has to be at pains to point out to the uninitiated that the American gloss of the legal profession is far removed from the everyday slog we go through. Certainly the money on offer is in no way comparable.

Our early family residence was at the Garrison Barracks, now part of the Defence Force headquarters, which at that time in the sixties were accommodation to many public officers who were in the Attorney General's department in the early stages of their careers, but would go on to become legal luminaries. Persons such as Sir Clifford Husbands, who acted as Chief Justice on several occasions before becoming Governor General of Barbados, Oliver Browne, John Husbands and Carlisle Payne, the latter two now both deceased, having served as High Court justices. Our flat was sandwiched between that of Oliver Browne's family and that of Sir Clifford's family, so it's not hard to fathom where the inspiration came for me for a career in law.

Having decided that Law was for me, prior to entering the Faculty of Law at Cave Hill in September of 1980, my father arranged with his solicitor Freddie Hutchinson Q.C. for me to have a summer job as a clerk at Cottle to get an introduction not only into working life, but the practice of law. My association with the firm thus started from the summer of 1980, and if you discount part-time teaching stints at UWI, it is the only place I've ever worked until I closed it in 2009.

I returned to work in Cottle's legal clerical department every summer during my studies at UWI and at NMLS. The magnitude of the firm could be seen then in the number of clerks, which at one point were as many as ten, including persons such as Ronald Graham (that terror of Ronald Tree batsmen), Sherlock Wall, Stephen Thompson, Roger Moore and Fredrick Cyrus. These guys showed me the ropes, both expected and unexpected, but the grounding I got at the time with day-to-day interactions with persons in the registry served me in good stead in the future. I was always grateful for this when I observed the attitudes of some young attorneys to not only registry staff, but support staff around them, as despite whatever degree you have, nothing beats experience. I have always been fond of saying that British Airways does not give the top graduate from Flight School a seat in the cockpit of one of their jumbo jets. You start at the bottom.

It is somewhat ironic that now, 35 years after these events, I have been forced by circumstances to return to doing what I did then because of the meltdown of my practice, but I have always maintained that I would never ask someone to do something that I was not willing to do myself.

After being called to the bar, I returned to Manchester to complete my course of study before coming back to Barbados early in 1987, and immediately started work with Cottle. Though Mr. Hutchinson was my prime contact initially at Cottle, I was assigned to work with Mr. Joseph Coleridge Armstrong Q.C., known to all as Joey, but something I never uttered to his face and still to this day refer to him as Mr. Armstrong. I am grateful for the grounding he gave me and the doors to Corporate Barbados that he opened to me to at the time.

I later heard the statement among the many misinformed statements about the meltdown at Cottle which were generally made either without knowledge or by persons seeking to advance their own agendas that I was gifted a job because of my father. I wish to indicate that while my father was instrumental in getting me placed in a summer job (something he may now regret), he never had anything further to do with my employment with Cottle. I arranged all my later placements by calling on Mr. Hutchinson to enquire whether it was possible, and I know from statements from Mr. Hutchinson that my work ethic while working as a clerk, which was never going to be my final call, earned me 'Brownie points'.

That was not difficult to do, because you worked at your own pace in handing in assignments, and I can still recall the statements of admonishment from one or two who showed me the ropes that I was "working too fast" in returning assignments, as this would cause problems for them after I left. I later used these experiences to tell all clerks working with me that I knew the system, and there was not much that they could get up to that I didn't know, although later a combination of Sulieman Benn, Ryan Austin and Tino Best, the first two of whom worked for me as legal clerks, seriously challenged that belief because of the escapades they got up to when instructed to park my car less than a half mile from my office (I subsequently found that it had done thirty miles). I was later contacted by the police who said "Nick... Ryan Austin does not have a license...," something he assured me he did, "...just warn him to get one."

At the time that I joined Cottle the partners, in addition to the aforementioned Hutchinson and Armstrong who I considered to be my principal mentors in the legal profession as both took me under their wings, were Rudolph Hinkson and Allan St. C. Watson. I joined as an associate, with the other associates at the time being Joyce Griffith and Laureen Waterman.

While I did not work directly under Mr. Hutchinson, he was always there for advice. It was he who first gave me the opportunity to work in my summer holidays and when I decided after completing Law

School in 1985 to go to further my studies in Manchester. He stated that he had hoped I would be coming on as soon as possible, but he would welcome me when I returned. I was always grateful to him for this, and in the last few years before he died I kept his office exactly how he had left it when he had last used it around 2003 until he died, letting him know it was there to use whenever he wanted. It was only after his death that I began the process of disposing of the years of precedents with respect to land transactions that he had accumulated.

Mr. Hinkson was the father of my close friend from school, Eddie Hinkson, who later became the best man at my wedding in 1990. I was always made to feel welcome by him around the firm, as I was a frequent visitor to his house. A die-hard supporter of the BLP, he would adjourn from his office every Tuesday afternoon to the House of Assembly to listen to the debates live, and his demeanour on return to office the next day would very much be dependent on which party was in office at the time.

During the campaigning for the 1981 election held while both Eddie and I were in the law faculty I let slip when I picked up Eddie that we were going to attend a DLP meeting and I was fearful he would not let Eddie back in, as he viewed such attendance as if it was heresy. It was regrettable that ill heath in the last few years of his life and his subsequent death meant that he was unaware of his son's entry into active politics and his election as a Member of Parliament for St. James North representing his beloved BLP.

My early years of practice at Cottle were as junior to Mr. Armstrong, and I will forever remain grateful to him for all the knowledge that he passed on to me. One of the things that I have learnt from him and tried to pass on to younger attorneys was his saying that you never change a man's work for style, only do so it if it is wrong. I have always viewed with annoyance how some attorneys, while perusing documents you have prepared, feel compelled to change them. As I often pointed out, changing the description of the property to be sold from within the body of the conveyance to a schedule of the conveyance is simply a matter of style. Change it if it is wrong, not because you prefer it done your way, as by doing so you are suggesting that there should be a robotic way of doing things, which, if correct, would obviate the need for the profession.

Mr. Armstrong had a memory like an elephant, and when you thought he had forgotten something he had requested you to check, he would drop in when you were at lunch, invariably to discuss cricket, and on his way out of the clerk's office say in that famous drawl "don't forget that matter I asked you about." He was a great lover of cricket, steadfast in his belief that Sir Everton Weekes was the greatest batsman he had ever seen, and I have no doubt that he played a behind-the-scenes role in his capacity as an honorary vice-president of the BCA in my being recommended to serve on the board in 1988.

When one received a letter from Mr. Armstrong it was a work of art and he kept both his secretaries Jill Johnson and Kathy Gardner fully occupied as they took turns sitting in a chair strategically placed to his left. The chair was positioned slightly behind his desk as he reclined in his chair with his feet outstretched on his desk, while he dictated his various missives. That chair, which I have warmed on many occasions, was also utilized by many persons as he went over documents that he was advising them on.

Often when he finished dictating to his secretaries he would send for me and say "Child, sit down in this chair and see if we can work this out." One never felt insulted by the description, as often despite many demanding matters he was working on he would break to regale you with some story from times past. That chair has become seared into my memory.

In those early days I was exposed to working with giants of the legal profession such as Jack Dear Q.C., Sir Harold St. John Q.C., and Sir Henry Forde Q.C., all through their association with Joey Armstrong, who without doubt was the leading commercial lawyer in Barbados and had a list of corporate clients that quite frankly was unimaginable.

I have special memories of my interaction with all three gentlemen. Jack Dear of Gabby immortalization in his calypso *Jack*, was a larger-than-life figure who ensured that any juniors working with him were adequately compensated. I recall a time when an issue affecting a number of insurance companies for whom Cottle worked had to go before the courts. Not surprisingly, I had to coordinate the filing of documents that he and Sir Henry were working on. One day I received a call from Mr. Dear to state that the tax man was calling soon, and would I be kind enough to arrange for his fees to be paid. Not having a clue what these should be, I stated that I would talk with Mr. Armstrong to ascertain what the clients should be charged when he interrupted me in horror by saying "Mr. Armstrong knows of many things, but charging fees is not one of them."

I was then summoned over to his chambers for him to review what was being done and after he said "…there are four insurance companies in the matter for whom we are acting, so that is $25,000 per company." He continued: "Thirty for me. Thirty for Henry." He paused and said, "No, young Nicholls you are a junior. Forty for me, forty for Henry and twenty for Cottle." I submitted the bill to the clients and it was paid without a murmur.

When I subsequently sent his cheque over, he called to say "come to the top of the class." He was not greedy, but just believed he should be paid a proper fee for his expertise. Sadly, I didn't learn this art enough. I recall that I had worked on an opinion in another matter, and was asked by the client for him to review it. I therefore took it for him. He went home, reviewed it and called me to collect it the next day, and I found scribbled at the end "I agree" $5,000. It was settled without a murmur. A larger-than-life figure in more ways than one.

Most of my interaction with Sir Harold came in relation to the Kingsland Estates saga and sale of the shares in the company litigation that is still ongoing today. I found him to have a very sharp and analytical brain which allowed him to grasp quickly whatever problem you were seeking advice on. Suffice it to say that his assessment that the family warfare that Kingsland has become and which has been fought in the courts in Barbados, UK, Toronto Canada and now Florida would never end until all the current protagonists are dead, seems somewhat prophetic given that we are into the second decade of the legal battles surrounding that company. It was always a source of great sadness to me that I was not on the island when he called at my office as he did with many others with whom he had worked a few months prior to his death, which he appeared to know was drawing even closer. Though he was a former prime minister you would never have known that from the way he dealt with you as if you were on par principally because you were a member of the profession.

Much of my interaction with Sir Henry came when he was the opposition leader, and because of this it often meant me journeying to his constituency office in Hastings to discuss legal matters with him. Often he would be returning the many messages that had been brought up from his legal office and he gave me a piece of advice I have always tried to follow: "Philip I return all my phone calls. It may not be today or tomorrow or until next week, but once you call and leave a message, whoever you are, I will call you back."

At that time Cottle had a number of legal secretaries, who to be fair would in this day and age be classified as either paralegals or executive assistants, as they were more than simply typists. Persons such as Jill Johnson, Kathy Gardner, Evelyn Maughn, Gail Wall, Harriett Holder, Janice Wallboom and Anne Gayle were available to lend their experience to anyone wishing to avail themselves of it. All of them helped me without complaint to find my feet in the profession.

Anne Gayle would have become a distinguished attorney if the opportunities for study now present to all were available to her when she was a young married woman raising a family. Instead she became the contact person for Barclays Bank within Cottle, and I am not ashamed to say that on many occasions, even years after I was called, I would seek her opinion on how to proceed in a matter. Two stories illustrate her worth and respect.

An attorney, now a senior Q.C., was known to have this stricture that he does not talk to secretaries on the phone. He once explained to me that this decision by him was borne out of frustration that attorneys would have their secretaries call him and he would be hanging on forever waiting for them to come to the phone. He felt that if you were calling an attorney then you should do it yourself.

One day a matter was to be completed and his input was needed, but the attorney dealing with the matter at Cottle was not in office, so he was not called. He later came over to the office to enquire about the delay, and was told by Mrs. Gayle that she had not called him because he does not speak to secretaries, whereupon he said she should have, because she is among two or three secretaries in legal firms that that stricture did not apply to.

I also recall another senior attorney storming into Mr. Armstrong's office to complain that Mrs. Gayle had had the temerity to send back his document marked as wrong without even presenting it to him, to which Mr. Armstrong replied without batting his eyelid that if Mrs. Gayle says it's wrong, it is wrong and therefore do it over.

Mrs. Gayle is an avid supporter of the Barbados Labour Party and had always said that she had little time for the politics of David Thompson, whom I think she viewed as a young upstart at the time. That was until the day, a few months after he was called to the bar, she was very impressed by his humility as he came over to her office and said "Mrs. Gayle, I understand you are the contact for Barclays, and I would like you to go through some of the things that you do for them in preparing documents, as I need to learn." It was humility that other young attorneys failed to display, some of whom worked at Cottle, and as such did not endear them to her. She was an astute judge of character and indeed of a person's behavior. When both Ryan Austin and Sulieman Benn were clerking with Cottle, Ryan had got the jump start on his cricket career, but it was Anne who said to me at the time that Benn was going to be the far better cricketer than Ryan once he could control his temper. Prophetic words indeed.

The characteristic that most of the individuals I have referred to shared was that they were not afraid of hard work. All were hard taskmasters, but fair, and I owe each a debt of gratitude.

Early Years at Cottle Catford

FROM 1987 TO 1991 I was employed as an associate attorney at Cottle Catford and Co. I was assigned to Mr. Joseph Armstrong Q.C. ('Joey'), the senior partner at the time. He was already a legend in the profession by the time I joined the firm. He arrived at the office most days by 7:00 am, was gone by 4:00, and usually ate the lunch that Mrs. Armstrong packed for him at his desk with his ever present flask of warm beverage.

I have learnt a lot from Joey.

I don't know what he would have made of this instantaneous society, though I am sure he would have coped, for in his day the quickest way to contact him from overseas was via telex to Cottle's major client Barclays Bank in the days before fax machines, emails, etc. I can vividly recall several times clients calling to press for something to be completed, and Joey saying "rush work is not good work; if you want it done so quick find someone else." Of course they never did. While he embraced the use of technology, he did not think that he himself must be proficient at it and many a time he would bring a document for you to copy with the words "child do me a favor… you know I can't operate that thingamajig… please help me…"

Mr. Armstrong retired before I was admitted to partnership, and though he was a consultant for a few years thereafter, failing health reduced his time in the office. During the last year of his life his secretary Kathleen used to stop by his house on the way into the office to get the day's work and return it for his approval. On occasion I would travel to his house to discuss matters with him, but usually it was on the telephone—the instrument ringing, that unmistakable voice on the other end saying, "Armstrong here. Where are we now with…?" As his energy was slowly drained from him we learnt that we would soon have to fend for ourselves.

My last meeting with him before he died in 1994 was when I took to him a video of the 1975 World Cup triumph of the West Indies team, which Mrs. Armstrong later told me he enjoyed tremendously. He was an avid follower of the sport, but no one could convince him that he had seen a better batsman than Sir Everton Weekes. He would just raise his hands in supplication when discussing the greats of batting—Sobers, Worrell, Walcott, Richards, young Lara—and simply say "Not better than Everton…" but add the caveat "…only saw Headley once or twice but never in his prime, and I never saw Bradman. But Everton said he was better than him so he must have been."

I learned this from Mr. Armstrong—that you should always seek to discuss matters outside the realm of work with your staff members. Not only did it cut the ice, but for that moment everyone else was on par. There was absolutely no need for him to entertain us clerks in discussions outside of work, but regularly during the 1984 West Indies tour of England he would spend up to an hour talking about the happenings of the day's play. As a West Indian, he was extremely proud of the team's achievements.

I believe it was Sir Henry Forde who, in paying tribute to him in a sitting of the high court after he died, said one of the saddest things with his passing is that it has happened before we as a race have learnt how to preserve the knowledge of someone before they pass, because his knowledge of the law was like an encyclopedia. Mr. Armstrong introduced me to Corporate Barbados. I do not think there was a company of any worth that he was not in some way connected to and often when we went to meetings, when he spoke on any matter, that was that.

The Society With Restricted Liability Legislation which provides vehicles of a hybrid nature whereby they possess some characteristics of a company as well as characteristics of unincorporated associations such as a partnership so that certain tax concessions available to partnerships in the USA in particular were available, came into force sometime after he had finished practice. Long before that, however, he had devised various amendments to the Articles of Incorporation of companies registered here and wanting to take advantage of these concessions whilst being incorporated here, but operating in the US for tax purposes. These amendments to its articles as crafted by him were accepted by the authorities overseas to constitute the entities being considered as partnerships for their purposes.

Next in line to Mr. Armstrong was Mr. Frederick St. Clair Hutchinson. He was my first contact with Cottle Catford, as he had worked for my parents when they purchased their present home in 1976. Mr. Hutchinson was fastidious, extremely neat and organised. His routine was different from Mr. Armstrong in that he did not come in much before 11:00 am, preferring to work from home, but he often stayed in office until after dark. Mr. Hutchinson's specialty was conveyancing and mortgages, and he handled the legal work for many of the developments that sprung up in Barbados over the years he was in practice, as well as being the principal attorney dealing with mortgages for the Barbados Mutual. He loved to follow precedents and helped create many of the standard form conveyances that were in use during his time and for a long time after. Unlike Mr. Armstrong, who did not believe in changing a man's work unless it is wrong, Mr. Hutchinson, if it was a matter he was dealing with, it had to follow one of his precedents.

As I have struggled over the last five years to dispose of the records of Cottle Catford, seeing wherever possible that the numerous deeds are returned to their correct owners or answering queries from numerous attorneys seeking information from the records of the firm, the easiest tasks I have in accommodating these requests, and this includes matters that I may have worked on, is when the attorney in question was Mr. Hutchinson. It is still possible to examine the books of housing developments he kept in which were noted the date he forwarded documents of title to the attorneys representing buyers and ultimately where and when the final conveyance ended up. Many times I have simply photocopied the book, when especially First Caribbean tries to convince persons that the deeds are still in the possession of Cottle Catford, rather than lost by them when Barclays and CIBC merged.

Like Mr. Armstrong, Mr. Hutchinson was an avid sportsman. His family name is synonymous with the Carlton Club. Mr. Armstrong was a former president of Wanderers Cricket Club. Mr. Hutchinson, in addition to being an avid race horse fan and owner, was also an internationally accredited football referee. He always jokingly said that he turned down the opportunity to purchase the horse 'Bentom' and then suffered in silence as it turned out to be a champion horse now owned by one of his clients.

I well remember the occasion Mr. Armstrong called me to his office and told me to handle a transaction. He said "Mr. Hutchinson is working for the purchaser, so you have to draw the agreement..." then with a twinkle in his eye he added: "No matter what you prepare, he will change it." Colleagues of mine who began their practice around the time I did used to say they would smile when they saw that Mr. Hutchinson was working for the buyer or the lending institution, because they then could sit back and draw an easy fee, as he would do all the work.

Early in my career I said to Mr. Hutchinson that the routine that he went through with these sales would drive me mad. I am not disciplined enough to be going over the same thing over and over again in the sale of a development, and I am of the view that this is why I was attached with Mr. Armstrong for the type of work he did. Mr. Hutchinson did, however, give me an early lesson in making sure you dotted your I's and crossed your T's when dealing with a sale.

I was working for the purchaser of land—one of his clients—and the matter, a routine one, was done and dusted when one day the purchaser, a woman in her fifties who always dressed in her Sunday best to come into the office, turned up unannounced after the sale was completed and presented a water bill that was marked due for disconnection. I was perplexed. I said "…but you just bought land. What water you talking about?"

She informed me that she did go up to the land and found that there was a water connection, which apparently was being used by workmen from other buildings nearby. Water is a charge on land, so she, or more pertinently the vendor, was liable. I had forgotten to requisition on it, and the vendor had by this time left the island. I went with my tail between my legs to Mr. Hutchinson and explained the situation, offering to pay it out of my salary, as the firm now had to pay it. He would not hear of it, saying it was a genuine error and adding "You will never make that mistake again…"

I never made that error again, but the manner in which he dealt with me that day, as I was petrified at my mistake, taught me a more lasting lesson that I remembered more than twenty years later when one of my employees offered to repay $600 that went missing under her watch and I refused, telling her "No. It is clear that someone else took it."

It was another five years before I found out by chance who had taken the money.

The other two partners when I joined the firm were Allan St. Clair Watson and Samuel Rudolph Hinkson. Like Mr. Armstrong, Mr.

Watson, though technically old enough to be my grandfather, more realistically was of the generation of my father, and as I did not know him before joining Cottle, I referred to him as Mr. Watson. Suffice to say that at present I have dropped the 'Mr.' and simply call him 'that bastard Watson'. Unlike the other two he had no interest in sports, though he was an avid computer enthusiast and was able to write the accounting programs that allowed Cottle to get a head start in having its accounts computerized. It was a source of complete annoyance to me during the years of litigation hearing him challenge the authenticity of the in-house accounts, because these accounts were produced from a system he created.

Rudolph Hinkson was the other partner. My great school friend Eddie is his son, so I knew him long before I joined the firm, and he did all to welcome me to the firm and to make me feel comfortable therein. A traditionalist by nature, he yearned for the days when the rotary phones would return rather than these instruments that he was confronted with. His loyal secretary for many years, Harriet Holder, would often say she would have to go into his office to transfer a call to him, as he always disconnected it as he fought with the instrument.

There were two other associates with the firm when I joined, namely Laureen Waterman and Joyce Griffith. In all there were seven attorneys, each with a secretary, two with two, plus an accounts department of four, half a dozen clerks, a para-legal in the form of Sherlock Wall, two messengers and two ladies who kept the office clean and organized lunch for a total staff of thirty. Grace Maynard was my first secretary, and her sister Golde worked in the accounts. Both ladies had worked at the firm for a long time when I had to take the decision to retire them, and even though I ensured that they got their full pension rights from Life of Barbados by paying up a year's contributions, for some reason they seem to have held it against me these last half a dozen years and we are no longer on speaking terms.

Though many of the personages changed, I inherited most of this number when I took over the running of the firm in 2003, and it is a sad reflection on what has transpired that today I now only employ two persons.

Those early days as I look back were carefree. The problems, if any, were not mine. At the end of the year all staff used to get a substantial bonus besides being generally well paid. I recall the days when the accounts department would advise around November not to write up any more fees, as the partners wanted to defer the income to the next financial year. The annual Christmas party for staff and their families spared no expense, and was held at all the best hotels and restaurants of the day, one of the last of which was on the Bajan Queen in 2005 that sadly saw Mr. Hutchinson falling ill on board and it was so serious that the Coast Guard had to come and take him to shore in one of their speed crafts to get urgent medical attention.

At the time I did not appreciate it, but the seeds were being sown for trouble later on. The staff was aging, and productivity was never a measure for the bonus you received, because if it was, some would get none. The work atmosphere was very relaxed and by and large persons enjoyed coming to work. In some respects, the adage that lawyers are not good businessmen applied. I recall for instance simple things like maximizing your tax entitlements by taking as allowance emoluments rather than as strict salary, and some energy saving and other measures, were slow to be introduced.

At the end of 1991 Mr. Hinkson came to my office and to the office of Joyce Griffith and asked us to come to the partners' meeting that was in progress.

This we did and Mr. Armstrong advised that he was retiring from the partnership at the end of the year, and that the remaining partners had decided to admit the two of us to partnership, which we of course accepted. To this day I recall the statement to me by Mr. Hutchinson as he shook my hand. He said: "I hope you are not making a mistake by becoming a partner."

I have often reflected on his words. Did he know something? Or was he just typically being cautious? I have concluded that it was the latter, but as it has turned out, it was to become the worst decision of my life.

Marriage and Family

BEVERLEY AND I were married by Dean Harold Crichlow at the St. Michael's Cathedral on Saturday September 15th 1990. Eddie Hinkson was my best man, while her twin sister Sheila was her maid of honour, with her other two sisters bridesmaids. My brothers Stephen and Christopher were the other groomsmen. Our wedding was originally due to take place in Manchester on September 1st, her mother's birthday, but contrary to what my friend Stephen Alleyne said in his toast to us at the actual ceremony, the change was not because of my cold feet, but because of illness.

I had been advised against travelling to the United Kingdom at the time. Sometime in August I had been struck down by such excruciating pain in my hip radiating down my legs that at times I was immobile. I now know that the pain I was experiencing was as a result of a silent attack of sero-negative arthritis that was destroying the cartilage between my right hip joint. It had been for the previous four years from my illness towards the end of my student days in Manchester at work on my hip joint, and has now left me with a permanent limp.

Shortly after returning home from umpiring a local Division One Game, I had experienced worsening pain in my leg and hip, and by the next day not only was umpiring out of the question, but I was soon admitted to hospital, so excruciating was the pain. I can still feel the sharp pangs of pain that shot through my leg every time the ambulance hit a pot hole on the journey to hospital.

Dr. Winston Seale, I am sure, must have thought I was a great malingerer, because one week I was in such excruciating pain that I could scarcely move and the other I was pleading to be released from hospital and moving with complete freedom. He however was eventually able to diagnose from viewing x-rays taken over a period of a couple of months that the hip joint where the ligaments were supposed to be was narrowing as the cartilage that provided a buffer between the bones rubbing against one another was being eaten away by the arthritis. The rubbing together of the bones without the cartilage as a buffer was what was causing the pain.

Dr. Seale stated that there was little that could be done until the joints fused, and then the bones would not rub against one another, a process that lasted another couple of years, my pain being alleviated by all manner of painkillers in the interim. I was thus advised against travelling at that stage until the process settled some more. The cause of the arthritis was later traced by Dr. Massy when he obtained the records from the hospital that treated me in Manchester in 1986 as the side effect of the hepatitis B that I had contracted from improperly cooked food was not treated amid the initial thoughts that I may have contracted HIV. Regrettably it was too late to sue by then, a fact that highly annoyed me when I thought of the way that I was questioned and the disbelieving looks at my responses.

At times when the pain returned I was virtually unable to walk, and because of this it was considered unwise for me to travel, as standing for periods of more than fifteen minutes at a time caused extreme discomfort and the switch was made for the ceremony to take place in Barbados. Unfortunately, no one saw it fit to inform the Dean to keep it short!

After a week's honeymoon at an all-inclusive resort in St. Lucia near the airport where we appeared to be the only non-American couple, we returned to start the reality of married life. Beverley's family had stayed for a while after the wedding, and after they left with the usual 'thank you' etc., kept Beverley busy until it was soon time for us to travel to England in December for the reception that was supposed to follow the wedding there in September. Looking back now, it was not until our return in January that it really struck Beverley that her life had completely changed with her move to Barbados, as she had no family here.

In particular her twin sister was not here. They talked on the phone virtually every day, which was my introduction, as I only had brothers, to this phenomenon of 'female speak'. This was the time when there were none of the telecommunication packages for overseas calls as they had today, so I really had little choice but to just bite my lip and pay the bill. I realised that other than my friend Barenda and my father's younger half-sister Peggy, Beverley did not know anyone in Barbados with whom she could talk and socialize. One of two of her girlfriends came out to visit her, but outside of that her life revolved around mine, something I did not fully appreciate at the time, especially as it related to social interests. Beverley had come from an all-female household where when sports was broadcast on TV it meant you changed the channel, so that was never a shared hobby, and as at that time the offerings of CBC were limited to just three channels, boredom and restlessness soon set in.

Matters reached a head during the West Indies/Australia test match in 1991 when Gordon Greenidge was in the midst of scoring his double hundred. Beverley called me at the boardroom on the Saturday afternoon to say she was bored and wanted to go to the beach. My reaction at first was one of incredulity, that this was the major test match day. Nevertheless I still took time from it to go to Brandon's beach.

Beverley really was never interested in cricket, which she felt was a competing wife for my attention during our marriage, and over time began to resent it. She never came to the many cricketing functions that I was invited to attend, saying they were boring. On one of the few occasions that she did come to Kensington, I was reintroducing her to Sir Clyde Walcott with the words "you must remember Sir Clyde" and she responded "Oh… the man from the boat", referring to the boat cruise for the English team in 1990 that she had attended with me. I nearly died from embarrassment, but Sir Clyde just laughed and said it was a first for him.

In the summer of 1991 Beverley went off to England a few weeks before me, and I later joined her there for my holiday. We returned home towards the latter half of August and within two weeks an event occurred that on reflection has cast a shadow over our married life forever. On the morning of September 1st, her mother's birthday, while we were still asleep, the phone rang and all I could hear was screaming in the background as one of her sisters asked to speak to her. The news was that her twin sister had just been found hanging in her apartment.

Needless to say this shocked my whole family as well, and Beverley was inconsolable. As twins, Sheila and Beverley shared a lot together. I was grateful to Dr. Adrian Lorde, who I knew fairly well as he was one of the physicians involved with providing medical services at Kensington. He readily agreed to see her as it was a Sunday, and prescribed sedatives for her, and within two days we were back in England.

I was unprepared for the firestorm that I walked into. When we arrived back in Manchester there was seething anger among her family and friends with a feeling that the police were somehow covering up the true cause of her death.

After returning from the funeral Beverley was due to enter Law School in Jamaica at the time and the professional advice given to me was that she should proceed, as to be home alone would compound her grief. I found myself travelling to Jamaica virtually every four to six weeks when she was there. Both Beverley and I underwent counselling during her time in Jamaica. Indirectly, Beverley blamed herself, for many times she would be calling Sheila to tell her where we had been because in 1991 we had been to Toronto and then on to Mexico where the CDB was having its annual Board of Governors Meeting. All this time, apparently, Sheila's relationship was deteriorating and becoming more difficult.

The next two years were difficult as Beverley mourned, and to be frank, as I had never lost at that time anyone close to me, I did not appreciate what she was going through.

As Beverley started working after being called to the bar in 1993, she developed a greater network of friends along with her colleagues from Law School. Still the loss of Sheila had an effect on her and in my opinion continues to have an effect, and for periods of time she returned to the United Kingdom to be with her family. Carissa was born in 1997 in the United Kingdom and time has certainly flown, as she is now an adult. It also is a measure of the length of the problem that I have faced, in that her abiding memory of anything related to Cottle is of my being upset about it.

I missed her birth, as described earlier, and so was determined when the twins Anya and Edaynah were born in 2002 that I would be present. The birth of the twins was an event in itself. The date for their birth was set, so I had arrived in England well in time and accompanied Beverley to the hospital. I had to dress up with surgical garb and was told to remain seated by her head, as too many fathers who wanted to witness the actual birth had themselves ended up being patients themselves after passing out. I was not brave enough to test that, so I told the doctors I would accept their advice.

Anya was the first to be born and I was invited to a room adjoining the delivery room as they checked her over. Thus I was able to hold her before Beverley did. When she was being cleaned—this was within a few seconds of her birth—I saw one of the nurses attempting to insert some implement into her mouth and enquired why. I was told it was to clear her airwaves because she is not breathing.

Totally incredulous, I said "slap her," and was dumfounded when I was told that it was against the child's human rights to do this, so they were proceeding this way. In typical Bajan parlance, I told them "human rights s..., so you prefer the child to die? You people carrying this human rights thing too far. She is my child. I will slap her and deal with any jackass who wants to say I am being cruel." I guess Anya for the first time heard my raised voice and started to cry on her own. As I told the nurses, I had received a hard slap myself, and it had done me nothing. By this time Edaynah had been delivered, but other than looking bluish, was crying already. Beverley was then reunited with them both as they were placed on either side of her while being checked by the nursing staff. My abiding memory is of her just shaking all the time as the effects of the epidural wore off.

Beverley stayed in hospital for one week after the birth—which was not unusual in the UK for multiple births, I was told—to allow her to get some rest at night, especially when the nurses would take the babies in the night. My brother Christopher who was working in the UK at the time became the first person from my family to see them when he visited at the hospital. He keeps reminding them of that when he claims certain parental rights over them.

Around the time of the twins' birth Victoria 'Posh' Beckham, wife of David Beckham, was in the same hospital. I can't recall if it was to give birth to one of their children at the time, but there was a mad media scrum to get on to the ward and security was extremely tight. After being stopped for the third time and questioned what I was doing there, I let the guards know to remember me as one of the few people who genuinely could not care less about the Beckhams, as I had come to the hospital to visit my children and wife, and certainly was not smuggling any camera in to get photos for the papers. I believe they got the message because I was never stopped again.

When Beverley was ready to leave the hospital with the twins I was warned in advance that they would not be allowed to leave the ward unless strapped into a car seat, and a nurse would accompany us to the car to see that I knew how to fix them properly in the car. This was my start of buying things in double. My thoughts turned immediately to home as I pondered that if that restriction was applied, many children would grow up in the hospital.

I returned home after a few weeks.

Carissa, who was already in the UK for some time, stayed to complete her year at school. She was five at the time, and I remain convinced that the year out of the school system in Barbados meant she was always catching up thereafter, as on reflection she should have been put in the six year group in the UK.

My first order of business on return home was to secure some form of help for when all three children returned with Beverley, as the support system of her mother and sisters would not be there. I could not see my brothers—who up to now have no children as far as I know—pitching in, and with the help of Yolanda Alleyne I was able to interview three persons and eventually employed Lucy Phillip, who in effect became part of the family afterwards. Lucy, a St. Lucian by birth, had lived here most of her life, but has only recently got her Barbadian citizenship. She accompanied us on many family holidays overseas and became very close to all three girls.

Lucy was a great help to us both, as by this time with Carissa in school and the twins demanding double attention, it was quite exhausting. We learnt one trick that I passed on to other couples I found out were having twins, including my fellow Pickwick member Adrian Griffith, the former West Indies opening batsman, and that was: always feed both at the same time. Even if one was sleeping, wake them up and feed one with the other, otherwise you spend all your time doing that. I would like to think that by now I had become an expert in changing nappies. You never forget, as I found out recently when a friend's young child needed changing and her mother was indisposed.

During this time many persons used to meet me in the supermarket shopping and express admiration, but I was quick to tell them that if I had to choose between shopping and trying to deal with meal time and bath time day after day, it was a no-brainer. This is where Lucy's help was so crucial, and she bonded with all the girls, especially when Beverley went back out to work. Unlike with Carissa, the twins never went to preschool, as Lucy looked after them and stimulated them with the various early education materials. One drawback of not going to preschool is that they were not exposed to the germs normally transmitted from child to child, so when they joined school we seemed to be at FMH clinic every week.

One incident with Lucy stood out. She had raised her sister's child as her own. Her sister had died from an asthma attack, and so she is well aware of the perils. One of the children one day had started wheezing and she was rushing her down to FMH clinic and had made an illegal right turn on to Forde's Road when she was stopped by a policeman. Despite explaining the situation, he continued to write her a ticket and it gave me great pleasure when she was convicted, reprimanded, and discharged and the officer upbraided for endangering the child's life by delaying her journey instead of assisting her to the hospital. I had deliberately not gone to court, as I did not want to see him, but I conveyed to the court through her attorney what I thought of the officer's actions.

In my opinion Lucy went above and beyond the call of duty. As I was frequently away on business, she frequently eased Beverley's burden with transport to and from school and the obligatory parties that seemed to abound every weekend. At times some persons mistook her for the twins' mother, and I believe this in the end led to the breakup of the relationship between her and Beverley. Contrary to what Beverley said and believed, I never countermanded her instructions behind her back, but where what she was telling Lucy made no legal sense, I saw no reason for her complying.

For instance, the law in Barbados is that children be restrained in car seats or booster seats until 5 years old. In the UK it was much later, and Beverley had opted to insist that the children remain in car seats. We had four car seats, two for my car and two for hers, but for some reason Lucy had to pick them up in her car and Beverley wanted her to come in early to get the seats from her car. I didn't think it was necessary and said so, which she interpreted as countermanding her instructions.

Shortly after that incident in October 2009 I was attending the International Bar Association Conference in Madrid, Spain, when I received a telephone call from Anya (they had no concept at the time that Daddy's cell phone was on roaming) to tell me that Mummy had just sent home Auntie Lucy. On my return to the island Beverley disputed that, saying Lucy had walked off the job. I indicated to her that unknown to her one of the twins had called me, very upset and worried. I spoke with Lucy, trying to persuade her to come back, but she indicated she would not be coming back and it appeared clear to me that the relationship between her and Beverley had broken down.

Later that year it became clear that our relationship was breaking down. Every conversation ended in a shouting match and it was beginning to affect the children. I found myself dreading to come home to find Beverley up, as a fight would ensue which was a departure from the times when I was exasperated to come home and find her sleeping. Having gone to bed with the children, she would then be up at 4:00 am to exercise in the bedroom when I was now trying to sleep.

In any relationship that breaks down no one party can be at fault, and I would be the first to admit that as my troubles at Cottle Catford grew, I became more irritable. I recall my friend Allison Hutson-Daniel, who has been my pharmacist for many years, telling me one day that my countenance and demeanor had changed over the years. At the end of 2009 I'd had enough and decided it was time to leave. It was heartrending for me, and every morning when I was scheduled to do the school run I still returned to take the girls to school. However, as the relationship between us deteriorated further, this soon became impracticable. As I was being prevented from seeing the children, I had to make an application to court for access.

To my mind the ensuing divorce litigation that was filed by Beverley became acrimonious because of her refusal to obey the court orders, and I can say without fair of contradiction that if it was me, a male, I would have been jailed. There is much merit in what MESA has been advocating for the rights of fathers to be recognized.

As I never had any problem with Lucy, after Beverley and I separated, she would come at any opportunity when the children were with me to see them. In 2012 she travelled overseas with me when the twins went with me on holiday. Some people, Beverley included, deemed this excessive, but from my experience unless you have grown up in that society, 10 year old girls in a place like New York cannot cope by themselves with the hustle and bustle of public bathrooms. This I could not help them with, of course.

I recall in Manchester having to request one of the female pool attendants to accompany the twins, then 5, through the female bathroom, as that was how you entered the pool, and they were deemed too old to go through the male bathroom with me. It was necessary to have an older female present while travelling with young girls.

Thus my marriage to Beverley ended more than twenty years after it began. We grew apart, basically, and now I try to focus my attention on my girls. They have all reached an age now when they can freely state with whom they want to reside, and when and they themselves determine when and whom they want to spend time with.

But if I thought my troubles with that marriage were bad, my other marriage, that of my partnership, continues to be a nightmare. As my good friend Eddie has said to the Court of Appeal, this partnership is worse than any marriage. You can surely get out of a marriage, but you can never get out of a partnership, which I have found out to my cost. That is another story.

Captain! The Ship is Sinking!

THE TITLE OF this chapter is from Gypsy's 1986 blockbuster calypso *Captain This Ship Is Sinking*. The lyrics are a parody with respect to the events in the economy of Trinidad and Tobago at the time of writing, and the need for the country's leaders to take urgent corrective actions were erringly relevant to what was happening at Cottle just over a dozen years later. As I again listen to the lyrics, I find so erringly prophetic the symbolic reference throughout the calypso or social commentary to the fact that the great leader of the past was no longer there, and thus the new ones had to step up to the challenge in order to keep the ship afloat.

Though sung in reference to the events in his native homeland, the catchy song soon became associated with the events on the field of play as the 1986 English cricket team was hammered by the West Indies during their tour and suffered a second successive 'Black Wash', losing the series 5-0. David Gower, a fine and stylish player in his own right, was the English Captain in both series, and doesn't deserve to go down in history only for being the one at the head of these thrashings. In a style typical of him, he started his final after-match press conference to the assembled media and millions watching on TV and to rapturous applause by the supporters of the Caribbean team with the refrain:

"Now that the ship has well and truly sunk…"

As a student in the United Kingdom, at the time listening on from afar in a blustery and cold Manchester, I was filled with a sense of pride. Now as I reflect on what has happened over the last nearly twenty-five years, the words of the song—especially the plaintive cries by Gypsy for urgent corrective action—haunt me because I was like a voice in the wilderness crying to my partners to do something tangible in the late 90s.

My professional and personal life has sunk into the proverbial abyss by this decade-long nightmare I have been living.

The tremendous satisfaction from the adrenalin rush that I experienced as a result of our success on the field of play in 1986, albeit only briefly, made me understand the tremendous importance of cricket, not only to those back home, but to the citizens of the wider diaspora. Members of my hall of residence which I have already described as consisting of a melting pot of students who could have held a UN General Assembly, such was the diversity of nations represented, took time at breakfast or in the TV room at night to express their congratulations, though many of them knew nothing of cricket. As most emanated from territories that were once part of the British Empire they identified with the success of a former colony over the UK.

Though it was only on a brief stop in the 'mother country', I was transported back to those ancestors who had left their shores to start lives in what could be a hostile environment, often working under trying and completely alien conditions in a faraway land so that they could remit money to their relatives at home to improve their lot. I never went through the slog of getting up when it was dark and returning home when it was dark during the cold of winter, and I often think that many don't respect the paradise we live in. After all, we complain of being cold at 25°C, so what would we make of -5°C?

Unlike my father I am not an economist, and others more qualified than me have written on what the contribution of nationals of the islands living in the UK and other lands have made to societies in the Caribbean by their remittances. Many families can relate to waiting day after day for that precious letter arriving with pounds or US dollars in them wrapped in foil long before the presence of Western Union made it much easier, safer to transfer money.

In one of my early tutorials in Manchester dealing with International Trade Law, the professor was stating, in explaining the rationale of the Balance of Payment figures, how the figures for the export of goods and services of a country should always be matched by the inflows that the country earns. The components that made up these figures were wide and varied, but he expressed the fact that the money returned from abroad through various central banks always exceeded what went out as reported in the figures, something he was never able to fathom.

Unlike Cave Hill, tutorials consisted mainly of a maximum of four persons, and I indicated to him that the answer was easy: the difference was the money remitted overseas by nationals of other countries living in the UK to relatives back in their homelands. This was done via the post. I was backed up by an African colleague from Uganda that money regularly came home through the post. Professor Lowe was his name, and he was genuinely astounded that people sent money through the post in this manner.

At that time I was transported back to how those early migrants going back to the 50s felt when their team decimated the opposition from the mother country and they could go to work with their heads held high for once instead of facing the constant put-downs as their colleagues would remain silent.

The subsequent poor performances of our team where we now are the subject of the 'White Wash' instead of the 'Black Wash' so proudly claimed by Caribbean people in 1984 and 1986 has made this a somewhat fond memory of the past that any taxi driver in London is quick to let you know is now over. It is something this generation of

West Indies cricketers, in my respectful opinion, has failed to appreciate when considering what it means to represent the West Indies.

Listening on from my student quarters in the Moberly Tower on Oxford Road as I was in the final year of my studies before returning to Barbados and start of my career at Cottle Catford, I could not have imagined that the Gypsy refrain would be applicable to my situation a mere ten years hence.

By this time Mr. Allan C. Watson was at the helm of the three-member partnership. As later events have made me realise, I was fighting an uphill battle in trying to press for corrective action. I was outvoted on every suggestion if the other two did not find it palatable, and while I am in no way suggesting that I had all the answers, in retrospect their narrow self-interest pushed us ultimately over the edge. I was not suggesting radical changes (maybe they were), but what I considered a necessity; not only the need to belt-tighten but to make sacrifices to keep the ship—not the one described by Gypsy as the ship of state, but the ship that was the firm—afloat. I continuously stressed that savings alone would not get us out of the predicament, but changes so as to become more relevant in the modern era were essential.

Change amongst lawyers is always difficult to achieve, and it certainly was non-existent at Cottle. The firm at the time was in a boat that was leaking in the form of increasing overheads, dwindling earnings occasioned by the permanent loss of Mr. Armstrong, the gradual loss of earnings from Mr. Hutchinson firstly because of illness and then retirement, and most importantly a large and ageing support staff. When this was coupled with a mainly young and inexperienced professional outfit, the result, not to be unexpected, was an imbalance between a high wage bill and associated expenses, and dwindling earnings as the clients the firm was attracting not only declined, but the work they brought was not as lucrative as before.

Offhand I can think of half a dozen individuals who had as much as 25 years each with the firm. Only one of these could be classified as fee earning, meaning that the cost of the others and indeed the firm had to be met by income generated by the attorneys. As I grappled with these high support staff incomes in the early 21st century, I remember explaining to one of my accountants around 2008 that if a guy started as a simple clerk in the late 70s and remained with the firm over the next twenty-five years, receiving an annual increase in income on average of $75, his salary after 25 years would then be in excess of many starting attorneys. That clerk was not a fee earner, and so unless the firm increased its income to cover costs such as his, the effect would be only too obvious.

The firm's income during the period 1995 to 2000 was substantially lowered, as Mr. Armstrong and Mr. Hutchinson who regularly earned combined fees of over a million dollars between themselves were no longer there. The fees in total now were struggling to top a million dollars a year, but expenses were growing. Mr. Hutchinson's parting words when he was departing from the partnership around 1998, a warning he delivered in his usual manner halfway on the way out the door but stopping to say one last word, was to "watch those over-drawings and get them in control." Like his musings to me when I was admitted to the partnership in 1991, was he not ever so right?

Mr. Hinkson retired shortly after this, and it struck me that the connection with the traditional past was at an end. Typical of the individual he was, at the last meeting he attended he brought a cheque to settle his over-drawings. More than twelve years after the end of the partnership, the other two have not only failed to clear theirs, but have engaged in all sorts of legal gymnastics to avoid the day of reckoning to do so, including the discredited nonsense of Vernon Smith that the audited accounts must be presented before I could sue. How did Hinkson know what was due when he went? He followed the internal accounts at the time. A traditional, but more importantly an honest and honorable man.

The stark reality facing the firm was apparent to the three partners.

Every meeting started with a scouring of the fees earned for the year and more importantly the expected fees, as the mounting expenses that affected the bottom line meant that the ratio of expenses to dollars earned was rising as high as 80 cents in every dollar earned. The reality of this was that only 20 cents in every dollar was available for distribution between the three partners, so for every dollar the firm earned, you got 6 cents. This inevitably led to the over-drawings growing.

What are over-drawings you may ask?

When I became a partner I was introduced to the system that I am told was in existence for years. At the beginning of each month a deposit was made to your account, and this was listed in the firm's ledgers as your drawings. In effect you thus received your money in advance. From memory the initial amounts of my drawings were in the region of $7500 a month, not excessive given what was paid in other firms, but as my mother often reminded me I started earning within a year of being employed at Cottle more than her, a teacher of nearly thirty years at the time. That is the lot of teachers. They are responsible for all of us professionals, but are distinctly underpaid and their service to the country is borne out of a love for children, not in the hope of any social or monetary advancement.

The theory behind the drawings was that an amount would be paid to you by monthly installments on account of your expected share of the profits which would be determined when the firm's yearly figures were audited and determined in time for tax deadline at the end of April, by the then auditors Price Waterhouse. Once the amount due to you under the partnership agreement—in my case 23%—was determined, you would be credited with the difference at this time, that is, your percentage of the profits less whatever your drawings were. Christmas for partners came around tax time, unlike other employees who would receive their annual bonuses around Christmas. My drawing rose I believe initially from around 23% to 32% when Mr. Hutchinson retired, but it was always the least of the three of us.

Each partner was ascribed an account in the firm's books to which these monthly drawings were charged. In addition to the monthly drawings, any other money that the partner received such as payments for income tax purposes were charged to his account. The firm, however, as part of its running expense, paid for the upkeep of each partner's car including its gas, his or her telephone service—which at the time was his landline—a newspaper subscription, and the fees for membership of a club of his or her desire. I recall my club was Pickwick, and there was some grumbling that Joyce Griffith wanted to charge membership fees for Sandy Lane Golf Club for her husband, as she had never been associated with a club.

For the first two to three years this went well, but then the firm's income dropped with the result that there were no profits to distribute come tax time, as the amounts drawn by each partner had exceeded his/her entitlement share of the profits, hence references to his/her overdrawings. This started creeping in around the year 1995. Technically, when the accounts in 1996 for 1995 were finalized, each partner should have repaid to the firm the amounts that he was overdrawn by, just as he/she would have received a windfall if profits were available to share. That never happened, as it was always anticipated that profits would return to normal levels.

When the figures were audited at the end of some years the profit to be distributed to the partners sometimes amounted to under $50,000 for the year, which was less than some of the associates were making. With the system of drawings, it meant that in some years partners would be overdrawn after about five months simply by receiving their monthly allowance, and by the end of the year this could rise to $100,000, especially if unauthorized drawings were added.

At the time I was of the view that the partners could not draw anything other than the agreed monthly amount, as we clearly were having difficulty with sustaining this. What I did not know at that time was that my other partners were using other means of getting cash from the firm so that I would not notice the increase in their drawings when the monthly figures were examined. Money that should have gone as drawings was often placed under fictitious Client's Accounts, so a cursory glance would suggest that this was an amount due from a client and not one of the partners. It should have been spotted earlier by me, maybe, but there were two members of the accounts department who daily updated the records and must have soon realized that these phantom accounts were just that. As I was to find out later, their silence was borne out of a loyalty to the other two, so it did not come to my attention.

Another trick of Watson's in particular to increase his taking of cash from the firm was as follows. The system was operated at Cottle whereby members of staff could obtain the equivalent of a payday loan by borrowing money from the cashier by signing a simple chit. This was meant for the employees so that when salaries were paid, whatever money was advanced by the cashier was simply deducted.

Unknown to me initially, Watson was in the habit, on Friday afternoons as he was leaving, of borrowing as much as $1,000 from the cashier. In one month he could run up a chit of as much as $5,000 at times. Instead of repaying same from his drawings from the following month, he would simply have a cheque drawn to refund the cashier her float and the amount charged to his drawings. These creeping monthly additions to his overall drawings, which by now were in excess of $400,000, was not readily apparent.

Another unauthorized drawing was to charge expenses incurred at home re overseas calls and gasoline bills to the office. The firm paid for the gasoline for the car for each partner from a designated station. With three partners filling up on average once a week at a cost then of about $100 per tank, this would amount to about $1200 per month. It so happened that one month when he was not in the office, a cheque to pay the bill was brought to me and I queried why it was as high as $2,500, and was astounded to find that all his children filled up at his station, including one working in the accounts department.

They charged the gas they took from the station to him, and he in turn had the firm pay for it. By the time I discovered this, it had been in existence for years. Between these two methods he had increased his monthly drawings by about $5,000 at a time when the agreed monthly figure was already putting all of us in an overdrawn position. My response was to cancel the gas accounts, which did not go down well with his children, as after requesting and examining the bills I noted how they were filling up the cars every three days.

It was only a matter of time before it would come to a head. The auditors, by this time Price Waterhouse Coopers, had in previous years simply indicated that these over-drawings were becoming a worry, as they basically were being financed by the clients' accounts and would have to be repaid. In 1998 the auditors, clearly concerned, addressed a letter to the partners indicating that if the over-drawings were not repaid, they would cease to continue being auditors of the firm, as they had serious doubts about its ability to continue as a going concern. For reasons that I have never had explained to me by PWC, though the letter was addressed to all the partners, only one copy of the letter was delivered and that was to Mr. Watson as senior partner.

Around the time for the audit of the firm's accounts in 1999, as I had not seen the regular appearance of the auditors, I queried of the accounts department if they had not been called. I was told that Mr. Watson had indicated he would arrange it and asked them to remind him. I left the island on business shortly thereafter, and coincidentally was on a trip in Canada where one of the partners from the auditors, Mr. Marryshaw, was in attendance and so I had the opportunity to raise it with him.

He was utterly perplexed when I did, and said to me that as there had been no response from us to the letter sent last year, they assumed that we no longer wished them to carry out the usual audit of the accounts. I asked what letter, as I had never seen one. He arranged on our return to the island for a duplicate to be sent to me. On receipt I entered Mr. Watson's office and asked him if he was aware of this letter. Mr. Watson calmly said "oh yes..." he had forgotten to bring it to our attention, and calmly reached into his top left drawer and took out the original, explaining that it had slipped his mind, but he thought we had received copies.

I am not afraid to say that perhaps for the first time I let him have some choice words that my mother would have been aghast at. It would later turn out to be many choice words, and he in fact complained to Justice Crane Scott that I have abused him in the most filthy language (in some parts of the world he would not have been alive to make the complaint).

To say I was flabbergasted is an understatement. I was virtually speechless, except for the invective that I hurled at him. Eventually, I said: "so what are we going to do?" and for the first time I heard him say there was no legal requirement for the accounts to be audited. After consulting with my father and my friend Stephen Alleyne, I approached Price Waterhouse Coopers to ascertain if the accounts could be done and pleaded that neither Ms. Griffith nor I knew of their demand.

After meeting at their office, PWC were adamant that they could not provide audited accounts without a qualification about their concern about the firm's ability to continue as a going concern, to which I replied if that was made public, we might as well go home. In the end they agreed to produce what were basically management accounts, little more than adjustments to the accounts that were made by the accounts department so as to facilitate us filing income tax returns.

From that event I basically became the *de jure* head of the firm. Watson disappeared. He was seldom in the office, coming in at night and on weekends. Partners' meetings virtually ceased. The minutes of partners' meetings were kept in a red ledger book which the senior partner kept. This book was in his hands, and try as I might in the ensuing years, especially after the partnership had come to an end, he would not return it so that I can have an accurate recollection of the discussions at the time. It was clear to me that urgent corrective action needed to be taken to try and get us back on an even keel. The advice that both Stephen and my father were giving me was that I should not seek finance to clear my over-drawings unless I saw firm and concrete evidence that the other two were doing the same, as it would inject cash into the firm to allow the current situation to continue. It was apparent that no effort at change was being made.

I wrote letter after letter to the other two partners with proposal after proposal as to a way forward. One suggestion, which was something that Rosalind Smith Millar agreed with, was that we needed to move from the present site as one way to manage the horrendous monthly costs. She spent ages looking at sites that would be compatible, but every site was not acceptable. She gave up in the end and her frustration set in and she eventually left.

At the end of 1999 I realized that something drastic had to be done, and therefore proposed that before we came into office in 2000, the three partners should meet at a site outside the office on the first working day for us to strategize how to go forward. Later meetings I had with the planning for the World Cup 2007 made me realize that while the meetings were a correct endeavor, just the three of us without a mediator or a financial planner was a recipe for failure, if not disaster.

I am reminded now that lawyers are not good business people. When this was combined with the facts—that I did not appreciate at the time—that one of my partners, Watson, did not want to change because it would have exposed his shenanigans and the other, Griffith, was too lazy to put in the hard yards, I was beating my head against the proverbial wall. People may find it hard to believe, but I was in the main up until the last year of the partnership still of the belief that both Watson and Griffith genuinely wanted to solve the problem. I am convinced now they were only words said to placate me and I fell victim to the old proverb 'a promise is for a fool to believe'.

The meeting was held at the Accra hotel on the first working day of 2000. For about two hours we had a discussion about initiatives that could be undertaken to not only increase our revenue, but also to reduce our expenses. I indicated that we should consider taking a smaller drawing, but the others indicated that existing commitments made that impracticable for them. It was pointed out that even if we each took a 25% cut, this would still only realize a saving of less than $100,000 a year, so that the real issue was getting our fees up and curtailing other expenses.

One agreement was that we should curtail the hiring of new staff, and that we were not in a position to grant the annual increase. I also proposed and had agreed that the partners would not seek drawings outside of the monthly drawing, and that the accounts department would be so instructed so that they did not feel under pressure in referring the request of one partner to another. The practice had developed of any request by a partner being complied with—the trust principle—but clearly it was being abused.

I recall one year requesting a deposit of $2,500 be paid to my account for prepayment of income tax and $25,000 was deposited. When I enquired why, I was told they thought I had said $25,000. It was clearly an error, but I was taken aback by the fact that the accounts department did not feel the need to refer the request to another partner. Such slack systems contributed to the demise of the firm, and I will have to bear some responsibility for not ensuring it was corrected or improved.

As we were hammering out the Accra accord, the telephone in the room rang. I answered it and told Mr. Watson it was for him. Only able to hear one side of the conversation, it was clear that someone was to come to pick up something from him. The meeting resumed and a few minutes later he said he wanted to raise something. His wife had run into financial difficulties with some business she was running, and he wanted to request a drawing of $50,000 to help her tidy it over.

I honestly thought he was joking after what we had been talking about. When it became clear he was serious, I responded to him by saying: "Mr. Watson we made a loss last year. Today is the first working day, so we have not earned any money yet to take our drawings. How on earth are we going to make a payment of $50,000?" and I ended: "…we haven't been in the office as yet, so there are no cheques here even if we could make the payment."

To my surprise he produced a cheque, and I lost it. I said with expression: "You mean you left the office last week, last year, with a cheque in hand to come to this meeting knowing full well what we were talking about, namely the desperate state of affairs, to ask for an advance for your wife?" I continued: "I will not sully your wife's name to say anything about her, but as you don't need any permission to sign the f…ing cheque that you have brought here, I am not going to be a party to this s… by staying here." Up to that time I had only seen Mrs. Watson in the nearly twenty years I knew her husband on half a dozen occasions. She never came to any staff functions, unlike Mrs. Hutchinson, and as I was later to allude to in letters, she was akin to Lady Macbeth. I started to loathe her, a feeling that has intensified over the years as she clearly viewed the coffers of Cottle as her entitlement.

I left the meeting saying it was a complete and utter waste of time. On my way out, one of his daughters was already in the hotel lobby to collect the cheque.

The ship was floundering, and it was now time to abandon it.

Time to Jump Ship

AFTER THE MEETING at the Accra hotel things just went from bad to worse. It was soon evident to the staff members that the partners were seldom meeting, far less speaking to each other. My solution was to delve into work in the office and in other spheres while I tried to figure out my next move. By this time Stephen was the *de facto* president of the BCA, Sir Conrad the elected president, having died late in 1999 shortly after taking office. As secretary, I was kept busy with BCA affairs which had the obligatory court challenge led by Vernon Smith.

On the sporting front I was also in 2000 to become the first person of colour elected to be president of Pickwick Cricket Club. Interestingly, during one night's drinking session at the bar, that was the subject of much conjecture. As often happens in cricket clubs the effects of liquor can loosen tongues and wild accusations or assertions of facts are made such. One well known member of the club, after leaving an event, was found arguing with a tree that it had moved, as it was not there when he had arrived. As he was heading for his car, many of us would have been rightly blamed for not stopping him if he had not survived the journey.

At the turn of the 21st century I was also the president of the Canada

Barbados Business Association, which made a yearly promotion to Canada for the purpose of promoting the benefits of Canadians doing business in Barbados and utilizing our double taxation treaties with Canada. To put on the annual successful promotion to Canada, monthly, sometimes bi-monthly meetings were held to organize every facet of the trip. Ladies like Carole Bishop, Marietta Carrington and Gale Weithers over the years have given invaluable secretarial assistance with ensuring that the yearly promotions between 1993 and 2001 were a success, but as president, the work now fell to me to coordinate all the efforts and ensure a high quality attendance of professionals from Barbados. The work of the CBBA has to some extent been taken over by the Barbados International Business Association, and after almost ten years of hard slog and countless hours of volunteer work, I have lost it all to the debacle that has befallen me.

During this time I was also chairman of the Disciplinary Committee of the Bar Association. I wrestled long and hard with continuing in this role, as I knew the time bomb that I was sitting under and felt it would be hypocritical of me to seek to be passing judgment of the wrong doings of other attorneys while much was going on in my backyard, so I gave it up. With the fallout that has inevitably happened from the Cottle debacle, it is not unsurprising that I have had to now experience the committee from the other side, a stain on me because as far as I know Watson has never appeared, something that galls me — not that I have not sought the assistance of the bar in this regard, but in truth and in fact the Disciplinary Committee is a toothless tribunal which any attorney worth his salt is able to string out, much to the chagrin of genuinely disaffected clients.

In my last report as Chairman of the Disciplinary Committee I stated that the present structure was virtually toothless and the volume of work too great to be serviced by members on a volunteer basis. I suggested then that retired judges and retired persons in other disciplines be brought on board. That would require legislative change, and some 15 years later nothing has happened, though others have indicated that the present system is in need of reform.

I thus had many distractions to keep me busy, and virtually every weekday afternoon I had some meeting to attend. Many weekends were also taken up, and try as I might to keep Friday nights free for the family, while I was always at home, many times nature took over and I would be asleep early. This understandably led to growing resentment with Beverley, who felt that the raising of Carissa was solely on her shoulders. I was seldom available to take her to the obligatory birthday parties. I tried my level best not to let this happen with the twins. As there were two of them the need for party attendance doubled as they were never kept in the same class.

Though it will no doubt embarrass Carissa by saying this, one of her favorite times when I got home was for her to insist on having a shower with me. No matter if she had recently had one, she had to have a shower with Daddy. Still being small enough to be lifted comfortably by me, she no doubt enjoyed the closeness that the jet sprays from the shower brought. This continued until she was about three, when after one of these showers I handed her to Beverley to dry her and I heard her remarking to her mother how just like Barney the big purple character Daddy was, and Daddy had a tail as well, but it was on the wrong side. Her showers finished after that, and she was reduced to sitting on the ground bawling outside the shower because I would not let her in.

These ventures (not the showering) kept me busy and to some extent provided a distraction from the problems in the office. As no meetings of the partners were being held, the depressing state of the accounts was not in front of you all the time, and so one could pretend it did not exist, but deep down I knew the day of reckoning was around the corner. Some fifteen years on I am not so sure that my partners accepted this, or if they did they were deliberately dishonest in doing anything about it. It is why I, some say unwisely, have not been slow to criticize the judiciary and how they have handled matters related to Cottle, as they have been bent over backwards to accommodate them by extending discretion or the legal presumption of entitlement to representation to persons who have long since displayed no intent to settle their dues.

Price Waterhouse Coopers had not come back to do the audit, which was not a surprise. I found myself personally paying for many of my travel expenses overseas with respect to my travel on business, even though the fees that were earned went into the melting pot and not to me directly. Since I have had access to all the records of the firm, I have discovered how Griffith in particular was receiving some fees privately, or how both were waiving fees for their friends and family. Boy was I naïve.

Sometime in 2000 I discovered what I thought then was as bad as it could get when a credit card bill from Barclays came in for about $40,000. The cumulative limit on the card was $50,000, with each partner having a card on the overall account. There was an agreed protocol for the use of the card, in that it was for associated business expenses overseas or for purchasing items like legal books that were shipped to the office. As in many other things, creeping abuses came in, such as cash withdrawals, which as anyone knows with credit cards like these, attract all sort of fees and interest charges. When Joyce was challenged by me she passed it off as either having forgotten her purse or cheque book, or needed the cash urgently. Watson on the other hand was an avid internet user and soon all manner of charges for membership of various sites began turning up. As these were minor, I didn't notice them. When the bill arrived in accounts it was sent to the respective partner for their approval for payment. However, the creeping misuse of it was starting.

Cash advances tended to be separately noted in the rubric at the head, and so were readily apparent. Looking back, I missed the warning signs and again the words of Mr. Hutchinson came home.

He detested credit cards, and for a long time refused to have one until it was necessitated when travelling overseas for medical expenses. Maybe, in my defence, I can adopt the argument of the gun lobby in the States which I have always found ridiculous—it is not the guns that kill, but the persons who use them—so it was not the existence of the card itself that created the trouble, but by whom and how it was used.

The $40,000 bill astounded me. I had not travelled on business in the month before the bill was issued, and even if I did, I had never come near to making such charges. Every time I did travel I was quick to point out to the accounts department what were personal charges which I paid for myself. When this bill came in, as neither Watson nor Griffith had been out of the island and I was unaware of any purchases for the office, I called Barclays to query it and was astounded to be told that the charges were on the card in the name of Watson.

I approached him and he sheepishly told me that the charges were legitimate. I enquired for what, as he had not recently travelled, whereupon he told me that his wife and grandchildren had recently travelled and he had authorized the use of the card for charges made by her at her hotel in the US. I said words to the effect that "your wife has run up $40,000 in charges to her hotel room and charged these to the firm's credit card, while I recently was away at a conference and because I knew of our financial predicament I had put it on my personal credit card? You can't be serious." As Rosalind Smith Millar would attest, all he would do is give you this blank countenance, saying nothing and probably would still be there if you did not move on or leave.

I really was incredulous. Shortly after this bill arrived, which could have been as much as six weeks after the charges were made, I received a call from a cousin of mine, Lyn Slusher, who was my travel agent with Going Places, indicating that Watson had called her and asked her to issue some tickets for his family which she had done and put to the account of the firm. The bill was now two months outstanding, but she could not reach him. She had authorized the tickets on the firm's account on the basis she knew he was one of my partners, but she needed them to be settled as soon as possible. I pretended to her it was an oversight and I would get it sorted, and went to him. By this time my blood was boiling, as it appeared that there was no end to what could described as the squandermania that was going on.

He blithely indicated that he was just using the same agent that I was in the habit of using, to which I replied "If I did so for personal travel or travel for my family I settled it personally," to which he just stared into space. The bill had to be settled and of course it was another unauthorized drawing for him, as it was charged to his account.

It was inconceivable that if he could not pay this bill of about $5,000 for four airline tickets, that when the time for the payment of the credit card came he would find the resources so to do so when that date arrived. When the due date for payment passed with no payment—the terms of the corporate card was that it be settled in full by the date for payment—the Bank went into any account in the firm that they found money in and took it. This action of the bank was technically speaking illegal, for the account they debited was a Client's Account, but what action could I take?

You can thus imagine my complete and utter bewilderment not to mention anger that I could be charged with money laundering by the DPP when it comes to applying the money laundering statute, especially as he was told on more than one occasion at private functions of the problems that I was facing.

I went into the bank after that, cancelled the credit card account, cut up mine, and informed the other two to turn theirs in within 48 hours or I would be writing the bank putting them on notice that I was not responsible for any charges in the future. I informed my cousin to issue no further tickets on the account I had established with her company, but the damage to the tune of $50,000 had already been done. When this was added to the $50,000 cheque he had written to his wife at the start of the year, it was evident that things could not get better. I was at a loss as to what to do, and bearing in mind the advice I was given not to put any money into the firm until a firm agreement was reached with the other partners about retiring their debits, I was a miserable person to be around.

As a result I wrote a letter to the other partners dated the 30th day of September 2001 (see Appendix Nine) giving three months' notice of my intention to retire from the partnership. I received a subsequent response to the effect that should I withdraw, then before I did so I must pay up all that was charged to me by way of over-drawings. In light of what was to happen later between the two of them, this demand was incredulous.

It soon got out to the staff that I was leaving, and soon many of the professional staff was saying to me privately they would be going with me. Morale by then was very low. However, before the time for my notice to expire something happened which I viewed as a life line.

I received a call in late August 2000 from Mary Mahabir stating that she and Mary Haynes, both partners at Lex Caribbean, would like to meet with me over lunch to discuss a proposal. Barbados is quite small and I have no doubt that they must have heard of my disaffection. I indicated to them that I was going out of the island the next day for a few days, but we agreed to meet the following week when I returned.

While I was away at a conference in Jamaica, paid for by me, I mulled over the various possibilities and determined that I would raise with them the possibility of a merger. To my mind this was perfect; they certainly had a growing client base and greater economy of scale would assist with the expenses. Also by then I was growing exhausted with having to deal with all the non-legal stuff. Readers can thus well imagine how I feel going on nearly 15 years hence.

On Friday September 1st 2000, I met both Mary's for lunch at a South Coast Restaurant. The date was not etched in my memory because it was my former mother-in-law's birthday or my originally scheduled wedding date, but for an incident that occurred while I was awaiting their arrival when I was watching the second day's play of the final test between the West Indies at England from the Oval in London, a date that is easily checked.

After the usual pleasantries the two ladies asked me whether I would be interested in joining the firm as a partner. They prefaced the offer by saying that I probably knew why they were there, and I said I had guessed while away at the conference in Montego Bay, and wanted to make a counter proposal. I briefly indicated to them the problems that I was facing without divulging too much of the nature of the overdrawings, and said if I could get agreement with my partners, would they be interested in merging the firms. They indicated that this was more than what they had discussed, but would discuss it with Peter Boos. Peter was the managing partner of Ernst and Young, and Lex Caribbean was initially very connected with them. It was their vision to become the first truly Caribbean Law Firm with offices in several territories.

Early the next week it so happened that I was at the offices of Ernst and Young for a meeting of the planning committee of the CBBA and Peter asked me to come to his office when we were finished to talk about what I had discussed with the two Mary's, as he liked the idea. This I did, but Peter stunned me by saying "Philip I like the idea of a merger, but on no account is that lazy one being part of it." He was referring to Joyce Griffith, and his opposition was based on the fact that he knew, as did many others, that her work hours of little more than five hours a day (if that much) and none on weekends would not cut it.

After much thought I approached Mr. Watson and outlined what had been offered to me. I indicated to him that I saw this as the only way to solve the problems, especially in relation to our earnings, but indicated I could not see Joyce agreeing to it if she was frozen out. I indicated to him that before discussing it with Joyce I wanted to clear up one or two things with Lex. During our meeting they had indicated that Nigel Camacho in Trinidad would also be joining in. I knew of him, so I decided one weekend to go to Trinidad to see him and explain the problem I was facing with Joyce. He immediately understood my problem and the problem that Joyce was bringing, as she really was not a worker, but typical of those attorneys found in every practice who is content with the lot she has gained in life. Nevertheless he spoke with Peter and an agreement was reached whereby Joyce would be offered at the beginning to be a salaried partner, and if her levels of work and earnings improved, she would be admitted to full partnership.

On that basis I met with her and Watson and was taken aback when Joyce said no. I indicated to her the lengths I had gone to strike a deal to bring her in, and that the two Mary's were willing to meet with her and answer all queries she had. She felt that the offer that was being made to her was only to get her to agree, but once the merger took place she would be thrown out in the cold. I assured her that as far as I was told this was not the intention, but as in life there are no guarantees, but I was sure her continued existence was entirely in her hands, and she could not expect to reap all the benefits without putting in the hard work. Really we had no option but to go ahead, as we were sinking fast.

After her meeting with the two Mary's she agreed to the merger, and negotiations began in earnest. Privately, I indicated to Joyce and Watson that if our accounts in the present state were put on the table no one would agree to a merger, and it was therefore crucial that they arranged finance to repay the over-drawings. I had already made enquires about mine, and stated that I was sure we could have the receivable for Kingsland factored in, which would significantly reduce the amount of cash that would have to be raised.

All of this took place over some months, and soon we were into 2001. Things were moving slowly and Lex were anxious to conclude the matter. Around March of 2001 all the professional staff met at Lex to determine how the merging of different practices could be best achieved (see Appendix Four). There was still one drawback and that was the accounts, which by this time had not been audited for two years. Then out of the blue Watson indicated that he was no longer agreeable to the merger, because having studied the documents he realized that as he was over 65, he could not be a partner. I could not believe what I was now hearing.

Both Stephen and my father were skeptical at this time that Watson was sincere, but I was still prepared to give him the benefit of the doubt. I went back to Mary Mahabir—people must have been tired of seeing me in their offices. I got assurances that Watson would be a consultant and appeared to have smoothed over this problem, so I went back to them. Joyce was now wavering again and I am now convinced that Watson was able to convince her it was a bad idea. Bad because for the two of them they would have had to raise finance before the accounts could be handed over. The matter was dragging on. It was nearly a year since the initial meeting and eventually Lex insisted on an answer and I reluctantly communicated to them that despite all my efforts I was unable to get the other partners to raise the finance necessary to rectify the accounts and I would not even insult them by exchanging them.

I was skeptical about joining on my own, as I was fearful that unless I maintained some measure of vigilance over the draining of the remaining client funds I would suffer in the long run. In the end this has happened, so this is the probably the second biggest mistake of my life, as I should have gone and let the devil take the hindmost.

Many people, Stephen included, have asked me on more times than I care to remember why I didn't just turn my back and leave. I explained firstly to him which reasons he later told me he understood, that my immediate fear was of an implosion within the firm. I believed by this time in late 2001 early 2002 that neither Watson nor Griffith had a concrete plan to manage their deficit. In their minds they felt that there was going to be a fairy godfather to solve the problems, and on many occasions pointed to the money due from Kingsland. Well, as was to be seen, this did not come for four years and was not the amount that they were counting on.

At that time I was convinced that I personally would suffer greatest from a meltdown because of the several public activities that I was involved in. In addition I was keen to avoid a financial meltdown that would have led to much discussion and would have caused embarrassment not only to my father who was by this time president of the CDB, but my brother Stephen who also worked in the financial sector. On reflection I should have jumped because the opprobrium would have been shared between the three partners and not simply fall on me, as has been the case. I hasten to add that I am convinced that Smith has played a part in this by encouraging the other two not to reach any accommodation with me, as it was my headache. This view has been reinforced by the attitude of Gale when he indicated that he cared not what my partners had done.

As I learnt only within the last few weeks of 2014, someone who I knew well and was a leading business figure was of the view that I had gone rogue, as he had no idea that Watson and Griffith were behind the problem, partly because I had kept such a lid on it.

Shortly before his death my friend Stephen said to me "Philip, I will be honest. I did not think this thing would have lasted so long without blowing up in your face." That was in 2007. It took another six years almost to the day of his death, but blow it did. The volcano was smoldering from the year 2000, however.

9

I Dun With That

AFTER IT BECAME apparent that the merger could not go on, I was very despondent. My notice to leave had expired during the negotiations with Lex, and I wondered what to do, as issuing another notice would make no sense if I had determined not to leave and go alone with Lex. From my examination of the accounts to get an idea of what was needed to present accounts that would satisfy potential partners with a merger, I was aware that the financial outlook was looking bleaker and bleaker. This examination by me in retrospect was not done properly. Price Waterhouse had disappeared and the other two had refused to engage someone else, so I was struggling through these accounts as best as I could. What I was using were the cumulative figures; the line items of individual accounts I was not examining.

Nothing, however, could prepare me for the bombshell that was to hit during the fourth quarter of the year 2001. I was working for an Englishman buying one of the townhouses being built by C.O. Williams, and was expecting receipt of a stage payment towards the purchase price in the amount of $250,000. Mr. Hutchinson, who had close links with Sir Charles, had more than once asked whether the funds had come in, as they were to be paid to Sir Charles as soon as they arrived in accordance with the terms of the agreement for sale.

The funds had not yet arrived, and they were late by about two weeks. These were the days before internet banking, etc. Mr. Hutchinson had once told me he shuddered to think what would have happened with Simmons if he had ready access to a computer in his time with respect to internal accounts. I will not even think what it would have meant if internet banking was available to him during this time. Eventually the accounts department advised that money had been received from the UK. It was in the vicinity of about $250,000, so I instructed that it be paid to Sir Charles, or to be more accurate the C.O. Williams Group of Companies.

About a week later around the same time, I received two phone calls from the UK. The first was from a solicitor advising that my client had died, and that his wife, who was now in the process of getting his affairs in order, knew little of the purchase and could I let him have copies of the agreement for sale so that he could advise her as to her best options. He further advised that the client had not sent the money that had been due before he had died that I was expecting. I began to get concerned at this information, as I wondered where the money that I had paid to C.O. Williams had come from. I was shortly to find out.

The accounts department from a Sugar Producers Company in the UK, a client who was one of the legacies of Mr. Armstrong, was the second caller. They called to say that there was a misunderstanding on their part and instead of the billed amount of US $125 for an annual audit letter; they had wired $125,000 US by mistake. He was very nervous as he asked whether I would be kind enough to send it back. I told him "but of course," but the loss on the exchange rate had to be for his account. He could not agree quickly enough to this, so I transferred his call to Ms. Golde Maynard in the accounts department to get the necessary details to obtain the Central Bank permission to send it back to the UK.

After she spoke with him she came into my office and said that the caller told her I had agreed to return the money. I said yes, it was sent to us in error so we could not keep it. She then stunned me by saying if we send it back our client's account will be dangerously low. I said "low? That's impossible." She then reminded me that I had paid out $250,000 thinking it was for the stage payment which we now knew was not coming. If we sent the money back that would be $500,000 that would have been paid.

I said "…we will only be down about $250,000 which we now have to get back from C.O. Williams, so that should not be a problem, so how on earth is this causing a panic?" She continued that the debit accounts currently on the books were over a million dollars, not taking into account the $250,000. I knew that the debit accounts with respect to clients that I was working for were about $50,000, and I was trying as hard as I could to fathom where these million dollars in deficit could have come from.

I was the only partner in the office at the time, so I instructed her to bring me every debit account in the firm. A debit account is an account in deficit because the firm has advanced money on behalf of a client, usually for expenses that are then refunded either when the matter is finished or a request is made for the account to be settled. That in theory is how it works. It has nothing to do with outstanding fees, as the practice always was that fees were written up and transferred to earnings when they were not only paid, but written up in the accounts, hence the early practice of deferring income to another financial year.

It took some time to gather the information, as it required printing of about conservatively 200 accounts on about 500 sheets of paper. I took this home for some bedtime reading. Beverley and Carissa were in the UK at this time as she was in the early stages of carrying the twins.

Only the senior partner was in the habit of being given the list of all the debit accounts in the firm, whereas Joyce Griffith and myself only received the debit accounts we were responsible for. This list would simply have the name and number ascribed to the client in the firm, and the amount in deficit. At partner meetings I would have had my list. What was becoming clearer was that Watson and to an extent Griffith were not reporting on their debit accounts, and as I surmised what was occurring, Watson, who should have seen hers, felt constrained or deliberately did not tackle her about hers, as he had some questionable ones.

I had now gone further than the usual listing in meetings, as I had printed the actual individual accounts to see what they were made up of, in other words every transaction that had formed part of that account. In what was easily then the worst night of my life — my night in jail nearly twelve years later would have superseded it — I came across account number 30559. The number starting the account, three, represented the attorney 'ASW' as responsible for the account, namely Watson. When the computerized accounts were created, ironically by Watson himself, accounts starting with 1 belonged to Armstrong, 2 to Hutchinson, and 3 to Watson.

This account showed that it was in deficit $256,000 plus and that the name of the client was Delvina Watson, et al. Delvina Watson is the wife of Allan Watson. I was flabbergasted. The entries would be akin to a personal chequing account, when one examines the payees. The account indicated transactions over a period of about 17 months dating back to 2000 and continuing to July 2001. I was physically sick, as my life flashed in front of me.

Not only was Watson overdrawn at the time, approaching or in excess of a million dollars, but here now was his wife technically owing another quarter of a million. I felt a sense of betrayal not only by him, but my accounts department, who had processed all those cheques and would have known of the accounts' existence and more pertinently of the fact that the account was in deficit.

It was now pelucidly clear why Watson could not clear up his mess so as to allow for the merger, and why he was cold to the idea of having someone else now that Price Waterhouse Coopers had declined to audit the accounts. This would clearly have been picked up even as the partners had been meeting with the traditional system of debit accounts going to the attorney responsible for same. Other than the senior partner who received all, it would not have come to my attention.

I remember trying to walk from the table I was sitting at in the living room and nearly collapsing. I felt giddy and light-headed. I took some deep breaths and decided to try to drive to FMH and get some attention. This was the time when FMH clinic was open all through the night. However, I could not get the car door open, which in retrospect was a good thing. I realized that I was suffering a panic attack and dragged myself into the TV room. I found a tape of *Crocodile Dundee*, put it on, and can still see the pictures in my mind. I just zoned out and eventually nature took its course and I fell asleep.

The following day I rose early from the couch I had fallen asleep on, got dressed, and went into the office. On my way in I was thinking: *how could this bastard have done this?* All the time we were struggling with not enough earnings he was hiding the extent of his use of money by diverting it to give the appearance of a legitimate client's account. Examination of the account will see that the proceeds from two major loans came into the account, but the spending was way in excess of the amounts borrowed. My anger rose at the thought that the accounts department would not have brought this to my attention.

I arrived in the office, went into the accounts department, and spoke, as the legendary Alfred Pragnell would say: "with expression". I was so loud and animated that a character named Lindsay who used to sell lottery tickets in the alley between the Cottle office and S.Y. Adam, came into the office to ascertain if everything was alright because, as he put it, he had never heard such level of noise nor type of language coming from the premises. To be frank the language was more fit for the alley that separated the buildings, but I didn't care, as my pent up anger for the last two years at the stalling, the misinformation and the outright deceit was reaching boiling point. My wrath was directed at the most junior of the accounts staff, Natalie Watson, Watson's youngest daughter.

I asked her to come to my office and I let her have it. I said: "… your father is out of the island. I don't know where, but you better find him and have him speak to me within the hour." I also said to her: "I have had enough and you are a big woman and I want some straight answers. Does he have a closeted life? Is there another woman? A child out of wedlock demanding support?" I was crazy because the deficit was staggering.

Within an hour he called, and true to form, it was virtually a one-sided conversation. To be frank my anger would not have allowed much on his part, but I was able to extract from him that the deficit was going to be repaid by a loan from Globe Finance, and I could check with Brian Clarke at Clarke and Co. who had received instructions to act in relation to the loan.

I next returned to the accounts department and informed them that if another cheque appeared on this account to further put it in deficit, don't be so drunk as to attempt to come to work the next day. I must have made a compelling case, because that account was never to see another cheque to it since I discovered it. But as I still haven't recovered the funds nearly fifteen years after it was opened, it turns out to be what you call a pyrrhic victory.

I then called Brian Clarke at Clarke and Co. He immediately recognized that I was very agitated, as I told him I didn't want any "BS" about client confidentiality, because "there is a deficit in the accounts of Cottle in the name of the Watsons of about a quarter of a million, and Watson tells me it is to be cleared by a loan through Globe and you are acting for them." He confirmed that he had recently received instructions, but it was in the early stages and he was not sure when it would finish.

After that I began to calm down, but as I look back, I made some fatal errors. I did not insist on handling the transaction so that I would be *au fait* with everything going on. By this time a lot was happening in my life. We were now at the end of 2001 coming into 2002. Beverley was in England carrying the twins, and my mind was distracted elsewhere. Beverley's sister had brought home Carissa for her fifth birthday in early January and the two were spending some time with me before returning to England. By this time Beverley was forbidden from travelling by her doctor.

As 2002 progressed the account was still in deficit, and I could get no straight answer from Watson as to when the deficit would be cleared, so I one day called Brian to follow up. He said Philip "that matter completed and the funds were disbursed." I could not believe my ears. I went to Watson and that sheepish look which I now realise concealed the cynical working of a dishonest mind simply stated 'we needed the money to finish something else'. I almost cried when I said "So what of the money due to the Client's Account?"

Things continued on autopilot until October 11th of that year. The date is etched in my mind because it is my father's birthday. During this period Watson was seldom in office, sneaking in like a thief in the night and leaving written instructions for what work was to be done the next day.

For some reason I decided to stay home on that day, October 11th 2002, probably from lack of sleep as Beverley and the twins had come home in August. Early in the morning I got a call from Joyce Griffith saying that Barclays had called and said if we did not fund our Advances Account which was used to pay salaries and other expenses by close of business, they would return any cheques presented from the next day. I was taken aback, and said "why all of a sudden?" and she said "well I understand the account is $100,000 overdrawn and has been for about a month and we don't have an overdraft agreement." I said "well, their proposed action is not unreasonable."

Technically the account went into overdrawn every day, but was then cleared the next day when transfers were made from the client's account to cover the payments. The transfers that were made would have been from fee income that had been charged when matters were completed and thus transferred to the advance account. The bank knew this was how the accounts operated for years, but by this time the client's account was getting so low that even Golde now was wary of making the transfer, as the fee income had long since been unable to sustain the expenditure of the firm. It was the perfect storm — not enough income to cover the overheads and the Client's Account shrinking because of the high debit accounts.

Joyce asked me whether I would agree to instruct Golde to make the transfers from the Client's Account to cover the Advances Account. She continued that we could cash some separate deposits we held on behalf of clients elsewhere to replenish the clients. I said "Most certainly not," as unless the amounts that we were transferring or cashing were from legitimately charged fees, I was having none of it. I continued that what was needed was that the partners go and get the funds to clear the deficit. My calculation was $35,000 per partner. I indicated to her that I would be in before three with my thirty-five and they should arrange theirs.

Given the state that I am now in, it appears somewhat incredulous that I was able over the phone to arrange an overdraft facility with my primary banker Bank of Nova Scotia. My manager, Mr. Larry Kinch, readily agreed to grant me the facility, so I proceeded into the office with my cheque and met both of them in Mr. Watson's office. I presented them with my cheque and asked "where is yours?" Both looked at me and indicated that they could not come up with the money.

It's difficult to recall exactly what was said now, but surely words were passed and I was now totally exasperated. While we were talking, Barclays called to remind of their ultimatum, and I indicated to the bank that I would be shortly there after 3:00 pm, so please arrange for my admittance via the side door of the Broad Street Branch, which was agreed.

I realized that the game was up as I walked to the bank. With my $35,000 to deposit along with the regular deposit to be made for the day, which was insignificant, we would have been short of the needed $100,000. I decided to make a cheque payable to Barclays for $100,000, and said to the other two on my return "I dun with this. This crap can't continue. You will have my letter of resignation with immediate effect in the morning."

Having paid a cheque for $100,000 but only arranged an overdraft facility for $35,000 my first order of business the next morning was to go into BNS Independence Square and meet with Mr. Kinch. I said to Mr. Kinch: "Look... things changed and I had to make a payment of the full $100,000." I still have the sight of him hitting the roof.

I requested of him help in talking to my partners with respect to them raising funds, and he did talk to both, but after said "From what they are telling me they have no liquid assets." He then said to me "Philip I will cover the cheque, but the full amount has to be cleared within 72 hours, otherwise it will go to head office in Canada and then I am in trouble."

I had only one knight in shining armour, literally, and that was my father, who I approached and obtained from him the $100,000 to settle my overdraft within the stipulated time, after which I went back to the other two and confirmed thus: "I'm finished... I have had enough... I am out of here."

My father has to this day never been repaid this money because, unbelievably, those two said they wanted evidence that I had repaid him my share. I don't know if they were implying that the money was really coming from me, and I was using this as a means to extort it from them, but I had never heard such bullshit in my life. But, as I was to later learn, it followed the pattern of Watson in using money and never repaying same.

One of the most difficult things for me was going to Mr. Hutchinson, who regularly came down to his office now as a consultant, and telling him almost in tears that I had tried and tried, but I could no longer take it and was leaving. He was very upset and said he would try to talk to the other two, and I said to him "Good luck, I have been talking now for nearly two years."

Word soon got out to the staff that I was going. I was approached by the other attorneys on staff that they wished to come with me, and a few days later both Griffith and Watson wrote to me that they would be unable to continue the firm if all the staff left with me. At that point I told them "Well, you have to go. I am not continuing with you two…" and that is how the partnership ended.

Both my father and Stephen cautioned me that it may appear to the outside world as if the firm was disintegrating if we each went our separate ways. This would trigger a run on the Client's Account as persons came for their money, and as I well knew the account could not sustain that. This obvious fact, which I had not thought of, was a conundrum which I thought would best be solved if I offered Mr. Watson to continue on as a consultant. I really had no desire to be around either of them, but this step, on reflection, was not wise. As I thought it through then, Joyce could never be considered a consultant, and perhaps this was the best way. It is clear now that she took it as a slight, but at the time I just wanted to be rid of them.

Thus, thirteen years ago almost exactly to the day, we signed a dissolution agreement on December 31st 2002. I moved Cottle Catford to Warrens while Joyce remained in operation from High Street. Although she was on her own, she never paid a cent towards the running operations of the building, which I undertook for seven months while the winding up of the records on that site took place. Though it was agreed this was to be shared, I have never been refunded the expense and when later Joyce would say that I left her in a lurch, I was fuming. Lurch? The only person left in the lurch was me, as the last thing the two of them did was to sign cheques to one another for $25,000 each, meaning that when I continued the new practice of Cottle I inherited client deficits approaching 4 million, with a net amount of about $25,000 only in the Client's Account. That is another story.

With this background you can well imagine how I felt when accommodation after accommodation was given to them by the courts. Only one judge put her foot down when it came to their delaying tactics, and that was Madam Justice Crane Scott.

10

It's All Coming Back to Me Now

ON LONG FLIGHTS I am not a movie watcher. I usually spend the time catching up on current affairs, which for me is usually cricket magazines, or of late Sports Law Journals which have fascinating articles from around the world of a sporting legal nature. At other times I just like to listen to music. With the proliferation of various devices including phones to store and instantly replay your favourite music, you can always have your personal library close at hand, rather than sifting through the wide and varied offerings on board that have to cater to the divergent tastes of hundreds of your fellow passengers.

Many of us can instantly recall songs that have particular poignancy because of being associated with an important event in your life, such as the song at your wedding or what was popular when you hit the party scene on campus. One song that became very poignant for me is a song by the Canadian Grammy award-winning artiste Celine Dion. While the lyrics speak about a broken personal relationship and the pain and suffering associated with such a break which she paints in that incredible voice of hers, it brings back painful memories of my marriage at Cottle. However, unlike in the song, while Dion speaks of the possibility of the good times being rekindled by a touch or a kiss, for me any such kiss would be a kiss of death.

Within a week of me making it clear that I 'dun with that', Watson and Griffith said that they could not continue on their own, so as the professional staff had indicated, they would be leaving with me. My response was that they had to leave then. I determined that I wanted a change of premises and I thus started a mad scramble to locate new office space. This I eventually found at Warrens Great House, and within two months the move had been made. All hands were on deck in packing up what was needed. Some items were sold to antique collectors. I remember Nicholas Forde, Sir Henry's son, being particularly enthused about Mr. Armstrong's desk which he described as an antique, while Leslie Haynes wished for many of the older books in the library. Many others were sent to the archives, and some to the Law Library. Everything that was needed to continue the practice was moved, with the exception of the office of Joyce Griffith, which was not touched.

The heavy vault door within which was stored all the title deeds and records of the firm going back over 100 years was months later removed after all the contents had been listed when the building was finally sold by the owners. The owners of the building were the estates of two former partners Armstrong and Clarke, and Mr. Hutchinson and Mr. Watson. The practice used to rent the premises from the owners at a nominal fee of $6,000 a month.

Many times since then persons have come to me sent by Joyce Griffith with a story that I have their file, and I have had to impress on them that no files that were in the office of Joyce Griffith were ever touched when the move was made. If title deeds were in the vault, they were with me and I had a record of them, but not any file. All the persons who assisted with the move can testify to that, including two cricketers, one now an established test player—Suleiman Benn—and Ryan Austin, who has also played test cricket briefly but has had an outstanding regional career mainly for the Combined Campuses and

Colleges.

The first item of business was to make a public notice, and one was published on December 31st 2002. Almost immediately I got a call from Joyce Griffith's husband asking me what the hell was going on. As I spoke to him I realized he knew little of the problems we were facing, so I gave him the full story. I was later to be accosted by Joyce berating me for telling her husband and going back on a promise I made that we would be responsible for advising our respective spouses of the troubles. I looked at her as if she were mad, and said "…that was two years ago; if you have not mentioned it to him that's your problem. He asked me some questions and I answered. Any problem you have with him, that's your problem, not mine."

At this time I was wondering who the hell I had been working with for the last ten years. As I write this more than twelve years hence, all I can say is: it's all coming back to me now—the pain, the betrayal, and the heartache it caused. One partner had a spouse who believed, as her subsequent antics were to prove, that she had a divine right to use the funds at Cottle, and the other didn't feel it necessary to advise her husband to the extent that he learnt of the break up when it appeared in the press.

Everything associated with this move was financed by me. A staff of about four remained at High Street to see to the winding up and to assist the several clients who still called there. Griffith, in addition to being allowed to utilize the building rent free, also enjoyed the services of a secretary free of cost, who was paid for from the High Street partnership, but as I have said, their share was never refunded by them and had to be deducted from the income that was collected for the High Street partnership, meaning that even less went to the reduction of the deficit in the accounts.

In the first few weeks of moving to Warrens I met with several of the major clients of the firm, including both Barbados Mutual and Life of Barbados, who were still continuing to act as separate entities, although the latter was taken over by the former, to assure them that the firm was continuing and would continue to provide the services that it had in the past. I had moved quickly to secure the services of Sharon Carter to handle the mortgage portfolio, part of the work done previously by Joyce, and shortly after Julie Harris joined me at Warrens. Pamela Sutherland helped me tremendously at this time by taking much of the administrative nightmare: things like the buying of new stationery and the outfitting of the offices.

The agreement between the partners which subsequently was litigated in court was that all matters not concluded by December 31st 2002, the date of the agreement, would either fall to the new partnership or in the case of Griffith, be for her account if the client stayed with her. To this end I gave her free reign to determine which clients she wanted to keep and she kept all the clients that were listed as hers, other than the institutional clients like Barclays or LOB for whom she may have been acting in a matter.

Matters completed prior to December 31st, but for which payment had not yet been received, would go to the books of the High Street partnership to reduce the deficit when received. Special mention was made of one particular client—Kingsland—but that is a story in itself.

I didn't realize at the time, but I was setting myself up for a loss which I have never been compensated for, and which has added to my misery because of the decision of the Court of Appeal in 2013. For two years, 2003 and 2004, I kept two sets of books. I was determined to do things by the book, accounting for receipt of all income that came in, and any costs that were charged to the High Street accounts. It was thus akin to the unkindest cut of all when these were challenged amid whispers that I was hiding income, especially in the Kingsland matter. By the end of 2004 I determined that the fees coming in for the High Street partnership were virtually at an end, and therefore I stopped keeping separate books.

As I mentioned earlier, Griffith was responsible for her client base.

Within two months my horrors with her started. While the partnership still existed she had begun working for a client of Indian descent—Muslim by faith—who was purchasing property. As quite a few Indian clients had done before, he was purchasing by cash, and paid the full purchase price of approximately $300,000 into Cottle. The sale was not completed prior to the move. This matter was designated as one that she was keeping.

As I looked back after, the income for the fees should have come to the previous partnership, but she apparently did not request payment until early in January of 2003. Griffith was seen descending the stairs at High Street from her office at that time with money stuffed into her handbag, which I later learnt from the client who had come to see me in Warrens was because he had paid approximately $10,000 to cover fees and expenses. It was clear that she delayed billing him until after the partnership ended, although all the work was done prior, so she could keep the fees for herself.

The matter was scheduled to be closed and the purchase price paid to Yearwood and Boyce in early January, and this presented a problem for Griffith. She indicated to the client that she no longer had access to the accounts of Cottle, and that he needed to contact me to get the money paid over. Now here was this woman, knowing well that the accounts had about $25,000, and that she and Watson had taken $50,000 between them as the last thing they did as partners at the end of 2002, sending to me a client to pay $300,000. When the client called, I simply told him that he had misinterpreted what Griffith said, because I did not hold any money for him. This was technically true.

I spoke to Griffith and reminded her that she was well acquainted with the situation, and just as I had borrowed about $500,000 to set up things with my new practice, she needed to do the same to clear this client. After all, she had pocketed the fee. Basil Giles of Yearwood and Boyce was acting for the vendor, and called me almost weekly asking about when the matter would close. I said to Basil that I held no funds for the buyer. I indicated to him that Griffith knew well of the agreement when the partnership came to an end, and "she would have to make the payment to you." I treaded carefully, as at that time many did not know the real reason why the partnership had folded.

To this day I am not sure who came up with the advice to the client, but he turned up in my office in the company of Griffith. He advised he had paid the balance of the purchase price to Yearwood and Boyce, produced a receipt from Cottle for $300,000 issued in November of 2002, and wanted back his money. He muttered that he did not know why things between us were so bad, because he had paid Ms. Griffith the fee in full, and if I had anything to do with it surely she would not be averse to giving me some. One can well imagine how I felt at this time, but I kept a straight face because I still did not want word spreading on the street about the situation at Cottle.

I therefore concluded that the best thing would be to refund him his $300,000 and then watched in amazement when he turned to Griffith and said "you wanted to borrow $100,000?" and wrote a cheque to her for the amount. She could not leave my office quickly enough, because if she had not, I probably would have ended up at Glendairy Prison.

The next week Griffith sent me a cheque for around that amount she received to clear some debit accounts in her name. So in effect she used the money that I borrowed to clear the money she was due the firm, so in effect, I made the payment. I was livid and told her if she ever set foot in my office again, well... This is not fiction. The transcript of 1612/1613, the law suit brought by me against those two, will show that she never denied what was done. So immediately I was on the back foot with my refinancing at Cottle, as this money that I had not bargained for had to be paid out.

My initial plan when I took over the running of Cottle involved a threefold attack to reduce the deficit in the client's account.

1. A hard press to collect in fees that were due, as this would help with the expenses of maintaining High Street.
2. An even harder press to recover the debit accounts such as the ones that Joyce had cleared with the money I borrowed, and the debit account in the name of Delvina Watson.
3. Constant badgering of Griffith and Watson to settle their deficit.

I was aware that although in the books the amounts due to clients was about $4,000,000, not every client wanted or needed their money at once, so I kept a close touch on when matters were closing to ensure that I had funds around to make the payments. At the same time I was trying to ensure that my current practice was continuing and its accounts did not become mixed with the High Street practice.

The effect of the stunt pulled by Griffith was that I soon ran out of cash. But worse still, I was discovering that many of the debit accounts were fictitious, in that they did not belong to real clients. They were phantom accounts created by both Watson and Griffith for money that they used, so this meant this money was not a debt that I would likely collect. It really was another unauthorized drawing on their part.

This, coupled with the stunt pulled by Griffith, started me on the slippery slope. As hard as I tried to separate the practices, I found it was impossible to keep meeting the calls on Cottle High Street without using the resources from Cottle Warrens.

My cause also was not helped by the fact that some of the major clients began reducing their work. In particular, the loss of Barclays or First Caribbean was the worst. I can't recall how long Cottle worked for them. I have seen records when the name of Barclays was Barclays DCO from colonial times. Up to recently I was returning deeds that I recently came across belonging to their properties in Barbados. The firm had been on a retainer and shared that retainer with Sir Henry Forde for as long I knew.

As I had not been advised that the firm's services were not part of their future, I sent the usual request for a retainer in early 2003, just as had been done over the last decade.

This request was met by the most insulting response from a Canadian hatchet man named Mark Strang, who had been sent here to oversee the takeover of the Barclays operation by CIBC. I have always held to the view that it was not so much as a takeover, but a merger. The agreement between the parties was so secret that it was kept from the sight of many people including us at Cottle, which I found objectionable, because I was subsequently required in documents to make certain assertions that I had no way of verifying. I was not prepared to do so, and as such Strang attacked the competency and integrity of the firm, which I took exception to (my letter in response to his remarks is reproduced herein as Appendix Eleven).

By then I was already resigned to the fact that we were no longer featuring in their plans for legal advisors, and therefore over the coming years was very annoyed that we had been summarily dismissed after 100 years of service. They then wanted on many occasions for me to spend time checking my records to advise them what happened in matters. The bank, when I refused to assist them, then took to sending customers whose deeds they could not find to me, saying they were with me. The practice stopped when I photocopied journal entries showing the deeds were delivered to them, and threatened to make my response public if they continued with the harassment. It is fair to say there is a distinctly cool relationship between us at present.

After about nine months at Warrens, the experiment with Mr. Watson came to an end. He had made no effort to pay back any of the funds owed, and one day I had had enough and said "Leave." His daughter was still working with me, but shortly thereafter I said to her: "I am sorry, but your parents leave me with no choice but to sue them to recover the money that they owe me and it is impossible to continue employing you."

Our sojourn at Warrens became short-lived. Certain environmental problems in the building at the time were affecting the mainly female staff members in particular, so another move was necessitated in 2004, this time to Belleville, which became the last resting place of the firm.

Court

"I WILL PUT you in court." It is a refrain that many of us have heard. Barbadians, like citizens of many other nations, have jealously guarded their right of access to the courts and seen it as the fulcrum for settling disputes; for getting satisfaction; for a chance to air their grievances and have their day in court. Like the plebs of Ancient Rome, access was always afforded to the King or his designate for settlement of disputes. In some respects this speaks of our maturity as a nation, as we leave the settling of disputes to a civilized manner rather than seeking to take the law into our own hands. The growing culture of gun violence as a way to settle disputes must therefore be of concern to all law-abiding citizens.

From the man in the street, whether it be a dispute over his boundary marks which mysteriously move every time his neighbor puts out his sheep to graze, to the CEO of the biggest company in the land, or that last family shareholder in a family company who is fighting a hostile takeover of what they regard as the family silverware, they see the easy ability to access the courts as not only a right, but as an essential need so that some normalcy can be resumed in their lives.

This access has been an essential part and strength of our democracy. As such, judges are given virtual appointments for life by the protection afforded them in the constitution. It is only fair that to whom much is given, much is expected. Any senior lawyer worth his salt had far more trappings of success available to him than judges originally did, but over the last five to ten years the lot of judges has deservedly and substantially improved. In addition to the improved emoluments and conditions of service, the physical work surrounds are unrecognizable from when I entered practice.

Sadly, our court system is at present and has for some time been in a total mess, beset by delays and inefficiency which appear to get worse year by year even though or perhaps because more and more lawyers enter the profession. The problems have been well documented and ventilated by many others, including members of parliament who have been moved to express disquiet at the delays in the system as the maxim *'justice delayed is justice denied'* rings true.

My personal view is that until the judiciary takes complete control of the system as it pertains to cases filed before them and holds us lawyers accountable when we are not ready to work, then the practitioners, the dinosaurs among us who like to spin things out for as long as possible and in so doing frustrate the legitimate expectations of litigants, will prevail. All of us at the bar must share some responsibility, and sadly now I have to plead guilty to adopting these practices that play their part in our clogged system, for having detested those tactics for years I have seen how the use of same against me under the guise of good lawyering, has driven me to the verge of bankruptcy.

Someone coined the following phrase some time ago: "When the facts of your case are bad you argue the law, and when the law is against you then you must argue the facts." They never said what to do when the law and facts are against you, but I will offer that you probably retain Vernon Smith, a master at subterfuge and spinning things out and out to prevent the matter coming to a head.

Virtually every judge on the bench at the moment and some now retired have at some point in time dealt with 1612/1613, my case against my former partners which is described in detail later. And this case is not unique to the court system, hence the mess in the system. How does one expect a judge in a four-hour sitting to deal with a list containing as many as 25 cases and at the same time have to deal with matters that are clogging up the system because of the antics of counsel?

While I recognize the right of a defendant to his day in court and the duty of his counsel to fight his case fearlessly, it is really taking the cake and a breach of your ethics as an attorney if, your clients having signed an agreement that money is due by you, you and your counsel continuously dispute that the money is due from you despite previously consenting in the Court of Appeal that upon the accounts of the firm being settled, judgment will be entered for the plaintiff (me).

Part of the problem is that our court system is abused by filings of the most frivolous of contretemps, especially of a sporting nature, taking up productive time that could be better utilized otherwise. Then where the matters are ripe for litigation, one party often just drags their feet whenever it is to their advantage, hoping to make litigants die of frustration.

While there are efforts by the current CJ and AG to lighten the load on the judiciary with introduction of Alternative Dispute Resolution, these are destined for failure until the dinosaurs in our court system are either weeded out or pass out of it by effluxion of time. Such men are not interested in mediation, but in obstruction. On hearing the news that the most recent addition to the attorneys acting for the Watson's was now a trained mediator I did not know if to laugh or cry. How can he be a mediator when he himself can't distinguish between fact and fiction?

It must be of concern to all connected with the justice system—not only our judiciary, but my brothers and sisters at the bar as well—that the highest court in our land, the Caribbean Court of Justice, has seen it fit on more than one occasion to comment adversely on the delay that civil litigants, not to mention those facing criminal charges, especially where the accused is remanded, face in our system.

In more than one case the justices of the Caribbean Court of Justice have tongue-lashed our judges for the delays in delivering judgments, holding to the view that a decision should be delivered in three months as the norm, six months in a case of extreme complexity. It appears to have gone in one ear and out the other. Recently I received judgment which could not be considered complex in eight months, and was told by many that I was lucky. By the same token I have had to endure the Court of Appeal taking seventeen months to deliver a judgment dismissing the appeal of my partners against a judgment I obtained in 2009, and delivered by the sitting Judge Maureen Crane-Scott within a week of hearing, a matter lasting approximately 11 days.

There is still a danger that a non-functioning judicial system can lead to anarchy because persons take matters into their own hands. As a young attorney entering practice in the late 1980s I held no preconceived ideas about what I would find in our courts. Now, after more than 25 years in the system, I loathe it. I dread having to attend court. It is generally a complete waste of time, as seldom does anything productive come of it and to be frank I have nothing to lose by saying that it is as a result of the fact that the majority of our judiciary have not come to grips with the new rules that vest in them rather than the attorneys, the management of court cases.

If some wasted cost orders were flung at some of the perpetually offending attorneys who still revel in practicing by ambush rather than attempting to get the matter ended, the requirement to pull your pocket personally for payment of wasted costs may see the backlog of cases ease tremendously.

The current system is broken.

I know that lawyers like precedent, but being a slave to the past for the sake of not embracing change is not only of no use, but not forward thinking, and a malaise on the whole system. With the entire backlog in the system that we face so dire that the CJ has issued practice directions as to how we are going to clear the horrendous backlog of cases, can someone seriously tell me why the anachronistic system where the courts go on vacation for the entire month of August still continues?

The days have long passed when those in the thick of things, either with the judiciary or senior practitioners, retired to Bathsheba for the month of August. Judges, like all other workers, get their annual vacation—six weeks, I believe—so is there still a need to close all the courts for August? Now in December we have a two-week shutdown as well, as though legal problems take a break at Christmas. It is unbelievable.

Ask any attorney and they can relate how counsel on the other side, well aware of this fact, have staged reasons for adjournments in matters in July, knowing that you would likely not get a date for hearing until November. Now it is not November of the current year, 2015, but one court has been handing out dates in 2017 as a matter of course and I myself as a litigant was mortified to see that a simple matter was adjourned to a date in 2018, as the judge indicated she had no available dates earlier in her diary. I lie not.

The CCJ has hammered over and over the delays in our system that it must by now be an embarrassment to all concerned. It is not fair to leave blame only on the judiciary, as lawyers themselves have played a part as illustrated with Smith, but the broken system must be fixed. In October of 2015 the CCJ said as follows in the case of Walsh Vs Ward and Bjerkham:

> "Regretfully, we are forced to comment once more on the excessive delay that characterizes many cases coming to us from Barbados. These proceedings commenced in 1998, some seventeen years ago, when on the 24th June 1998 a generally

endorsed Writ was filed by Walsh. The substantive hearing in the High Court commenced on the 7th February 2000 and after a three week trial the judge reserved judgment. After several requests for the delivery of the High Court judgment, the trial judge finally gave his decision on 8th June 2005 — more than five years after the substantive hearing. Ward filed his appeal in relation to the High Court judgment on 18th July 2005 and the appeal was eventually heard on the 20th and 21st September 2011. Over a year later the Court of Appeal issued its judgment on the 28th November 2012. This type of delay imposes hardships on the litigants. This is a case where the hardship is obvious. The delay also reflects adversely on the reputation and credibility of the civil justice system as a whole, and reinforces the negative images which the public can have of the way judges and lawyers perform their roles."

On two occasions I have had the opportunity to appear at the Privy Council in London. Situated next door to No. 10 Downing Street, as one would imagine, security is airport-style and this was long before 9/11 ramped up security all over. The whole work ethic of the court was completely different from what I was accustomed to at home, and the contrast all the more in light of the statements above.

The first of these appearances was with respect to the Bentley Greaves appeal to the Privy Council against the dismissal of his appeal of his conviction for the murder of his girlfriend in 1989. My friend Edmund Hinkson and I had represented him at first instance at Court of Appeal and now he was being represented *pro bono* by an English Barrister before the Privy Council.

I was due to be in the UK around the time of the appeal in 1994 and so tied the two together. On the day of the appeal I hailed a taxi from my hotel with my legal briefs in hand for the short drive to the court. As soon as I entered the cab the driver said I could only be going one place dressed as I was, so he drove me there without need for me to inform him of my destination.

I arrived at the court and joined a queue of some of the leading barristers in London waiting to be searched virtually from head to toe, and was surprised when my search was somewhat less intrusive than theirs. I queried why of my lead counsel and he chuckled: "Well, with your garb they are fairly certain who you are, as the IRA have not found any Black recruits as yet!"

But what I found more interesting that morning was that in the robing room a young barrister was seeking compassion and receiving none because of the fact that his senior had come down sick the day before. This, he said, necessitated him being up all night preparing. I said innocently to him: "Would they not grant you an adjournment?" to which one of the seniors bellowed "Adjournment? No way. The illness of your senior is not considered grounds enough for an adjournment. They may give you half an hour if it happened today, but yesterday, no way." I just kept quiet when I remembered some of the grounds that were offered as reasons for adjournments to be granted in Barbados. How many times have juniors appeared in cases to simply ask for an adjournment because their senior is unavailable? I have yet to see or hear the request ever being denied.

Cottle never had a reputation for being involved in litigation, either civil or criminal. During my internship there between 1980 and 1984 while at University and Law School I often went into the magistrate's courts just to listen to cases, as no one from the firm was undertaking such matters. At that time many of the senior advocates of the day would still appear in matters and several of the magistrates were household names. A student could learn a lot just by listening.

After joining Cottle because of the nature of the work the opportunity for me to appear in court was very limited as the firm, after the fusion of the barrister and solicitor professions, had not taken on a barrister. I was later to come to the conclusion when reflecting on the causes of the implosion of Cottle that this lack of foresight by the partners at the time in attracting work that brought substantial fees was one of the reasons why the firm started in the mid-nineties to lose its ground against others, something that eventually proved terminal.

As long and as illustrious as their careers were, I doubt that either Mr. Armstrong or Mr. Hutchinson set foot in a courtroom on more than half a dozen occasions. When I joined the firm I also had no great desire to participate in court work, and my initial forays into court were simple traffic matters appearing more for comfort rather than to challenge, as the clients had breached some minor traffic regulations. There was the wife of a former deceased partner and indeed one or two personal friends of both Armstrong and Hutchinson who had run afoul of the speed limit. In most cases the sight of the court was more traumatic to them than the fact of breaking the traffic laws.

My first initiation into litigation proper in the courts arose because of a request by Captain Peter Short, the long standing president of the BCA, to Mr. Armstrong that I be allowed to assist Harley Moseley Q.C, who was acting for the BCA, in legal action arising out of a game played between Police and St. Catherine. By then I had already joined the board of the BCA. The facts that were before the court, however, had arisen before I had joined the board and the BCA was now facing a challenge to its decision to declare as null and void the result of the game played between Police and St. Catherine.

As a result of its decision the board concluded that the result on the field of play in a game reduced by rain from three days to one was null and void. The result of the match on the field of play meant that BCL, who seemed on course to win the title at the scheduled start of the final series of games in 1987, were at the tape denied their glory, but the board's decision awarded the cup to BCL.

Captain Short requested of Mr. Armstrong that I join Harley to assist him in the court hearing. I recall telling Mr. Armstrong that I was uncomfortable with this, because I believed the actions of the BCA were wrong and that they would lose the case, but he reminded me that was not my call to make. It has always been my view that the BCA approached this case as one of a strictly sporting nature and lost it, as I had indicated privately to Harley, because of the development over the years immediately preceding the decisions of the BCA board of administrative law as it related to sporting organizations when making quasi-judicial decisions. The Board's decision to alter the on-field result was thus struck down for several glaring breaches of natural justice by then Chief Justice Williams.

Lose the case it did, much to the chagrin and embarrassment of my good friend Owen 'Nobby' Estwick, who in his zeal to expose what he clearly felt was skullduggery between the sides (and to be fair the circumstances of what transpired that day didn't smell too good) to prevent his beloved BCL from claiming the title, overstepped the bounds of what is permitted by persons with a vested interest in the matters that they are rendering decisions on.

Nobby was not only a long standing member of the board, but was also president of the BCL, and had brought evidence of the perceived wrongdoings in the game played at St. Catherine to the board, and then, as the judgment said, while he did not participate in the hearing of the complaint and ultimate decision to declare the result of the game null and void with the result that the BCL were the champions, his mere presence in the room offended against the principles of natural justice.

This case was the catalyst for the running to court for every stupid disagreement within the BCA. No prizes for guessing the name of the lawyer who was perched on a horse galloping to the trumpet sounds of his inflated ego in riding to the courts. It used to amaze me that with many serious and pressing issues demanding attention, those attention seekers within the BCA would at every opportunity file an action in court. This continued unabated for many years until Justice Moore put an end to it by simply illustrating that these matters with regard to the BCA filed in courts were premature because they overlooked the rules of the BCA whereby court was a last resort. That route should be followed, rather than running to court as a preemptive strike. It has always been my belief that some members of the judiciary at the time gave too much credence to the clear fishing expeditions that were filed against the BCA. I would hate to think it was because of the publicity that surrounded anything relating to the BCA. Court reports tended to be reserved for criminal cases, but anything that involved the BCA sometimes made not only the back pages, but the front pages of the newspaper, and though it is only my opinion, many should have been thrown out as frivolous and vexatious, as the courts had some serious problems to attend to, not people needing to stoke their egos.

In the first BCA case, then Chief Justice Sir Denys Williams, who sadly has recently left us, issued seminal guidelines for all types of administrative boards to follow. Such boards, when exercising quasi-judicial authority, need not only to be fair and impartial in their deliberations, but just as importantly there must be no appearance of bias and they must give an opportunity to those against whom they intend to exercise any action the right to be heard.

Just as importantly, he struck down as *ultra vires* an ouster clause in the BCA rules that indicated the board was the final arbiter on matters, and as such would oust the jurisdiction of the courts. Sir Denys was very clear that access to the courts for all is a fundamental right that the courts will jealously guard and not allow to be simply denied by an insertion in the rules of any organization.

Outside of BCA matters, my early foray into civil litigation surrounded my dear friend Barenda Brewster, 'Gracie' to her friends. Barenda had been involved in a minor car accident. She was hit from behind while stationery at a traffic light, but because of the anxiety she felt because of the accident, she soon fell ill out of all proportions to the simple accident, and was admitted to hospital where she was subsequently diagnosed with lupus.

As I understood the medical evidence, you are born with such a condition and it may remain latent until some stressful activity in your life triggers it. In Gracie's case it was the car accident, and she instituted suit against the driver. Gracie was herself an attorney. Led by Sir Henry Forde Q.C., the matter was heard before Chief Justice Sir Denys Williams sitting as a first instance judge. He affirmed that the egg shell principle (you take your victim as you find them) enunciated so many years ago in England, was indeed part of our law in Barbados, and it was no defence to say that a normal person would not have had the reaction that she did.

Both of these cases were later reported in the West Indian Law Reports. I found involvement in Barenda's case very difficult, as all the evidence suggested that my friend's life expectancy would be short. I found it hard every day of the trial to listen to these projections, but she was there and never once shied away from commenting on the medical reports and illustrating how it was affecting her. Not only was she a very strong woman, but it was her abiding faith as a member of the Jehovah's Witnesses that sustained her until her death less than three years after the case.

Years later I was to have the same feeling when trying to deal with Stephen Alleyne's estate. After all, it was not simply a name. Every time I picked it up, memories came flooding back and I suppose that at times I pushed it to the bottom of the list of things I was doing. I was subsequently spared the agony when Yolanda, his widow, just turned up unexpectedly one day at my office and simply said "Philip I want you to send Stephen's estate to another lawyer." All I could do was tell her "thank you."

She herself has been an extremely strong woman over these last few years, and often would pop into my office just for a chat. She is an environmental planner by profession, and one of her visits coincided with the day the earthquake struck. I was sitting talking with her and my chair just started shaking, and I was trying to figure out why when she said "Philip we are having an earthquake… get everyone out of the building…" and we just bolted.

Ironically, as I look back on my career, the majority of cases that I was involved in at the beginning were of a criminal nature, as I assisted my friend Edmund Hinkson with his Legal Aid assignments. With him I have appeared in three criminal cases, all murder cases. Nothing can be as traumatic as such a case when the life of your client can literally be in your hands. A stupid error could be the difference between him swinging in the gallows or being acquitted, and you were mentally drained at the end of each day. My involvement brought to my attention how much John Public followed these cases, as everywhere you went someone wanted to speak to you about it.

In the three cases that we dealt with the dreaded pronouncement of death was delivered only to one client with the judge trying to look as close to the grim reaper as possible by donning a black wig. That was to Bentley Greaves in 1988, while St. Clair Lashley was convicted of manslaughter in the 'Uncle Look Up' murder case, but Sherwin Richards was acquitted of the shooting death of a man in Bridgetown.

All three cases have left deep impressions on me. Bentley, though sentenced to death for the killing of his girlfriend in 1987, is now a free man, having first benefited from the Pratt and Morgan Privy Council ruling that if a man is kept on death row for more than five years without execution such length of time is to be considered cruel and inhuman punishment and his sentence should be commuted to life imprisonment. 'Life' in Barbados has been equated with 30 legal years—a legal year is 9 months—and as a result Bentley was released in 2012.

We had always kept in touch, even through his appeal to the Privy Council which I attended in London in 1994, but which was dismissed. The circumstances surrounding his crime were unfortunate, and whilst not condoning domestic violence, I have no fear that he will ever re-offend and have been comfortable with him doing jobs around my office and my parents' home since his release. Bentley is a very intelligent young man who possessed some of the best handwriting I have ever seen, male or female.

St. Clair Lashley was a simple man from whom the police extracted a confession by promising him if he said what happened he could go home (of course the police denied this, but I have seen at first hand that they are not above bending the truth about what occurs in interviews).

As such he told them what he had done and when we visited him in jail he was clearly bemused as to why he was arrested. Clearly undeveloped mentally, he was used by a woman who was in a relationship with him simply to get his money, and when he found out that she had other interests he set fire to the house she was sleeping in. The resulting fire killed the man she was involved with and one of her children, and severely disfigured her. Lack of mental capacity was clearly an issue and the resulting manslaughter conviction was appropriate in all the circumstances. I have never seen him since his trial.

The third murder case involved an accusation that a man, Sherwin Richards, had shot and killed a man in the Orleans. To this day I am not sure of the guilt or innocence of the accused, but as Mr. Armstrong had reminded me, that was not for me. The jury found him not guilty, and as one of the members told me after "we let him go even though the judge tell us to hang him" (not literally of course). Who says lay people are stupid? We felt that the judge, at that time Justice Belgrave, now the Governor General, appeared clearly to be of the view that he was guilty from some of his utterances, which annoyed both Eddie and I and it was with some satisfaction that we greeted the non-guilty verdict.

Richards was a sly fella from the underworld in Barbados. His alibi was that he was at the time of the shooting at home sleeping with his girlfriend. No big deal, you think, but then it transpired that his girlfriend was at the time a 14 year old school girl at St. Michael's. We were faced with a logistical problem. How do you present her as a credible witness, as even though by the time trial came on she might pass for 16, she was clearly young?

She came and she testified, during which both of us were fearful that her youthful features would be given away, and then the jury would hang him for other reasons, namely being a sexual predator. We had hoped to delay her testimony until after the weekend so we could better prepare her for what to expect on the stand, but that didn't play out, as the judge kept saying: "Young Nicholls and Hinkson, you don't think I know what you up to? She testifying today…"

Our fears were soon allayed by her response to the prosecution's request when she took the stand to tell the court what the accused was doing when she said he was home with her with the following words, uttered with a raw Bajan accent: "When a man and a woman does lie down in a bed what do they do?" Total laughter in the court—'case dun'; alibi substantiated.

Those were my only forays into criminal prosecution, although in the late 90s the daughter of a lady who used to work with me had been arrested and charged with stabbing a young man. The family called, and though I was no longer practicing in that area, I went to see her at the police station and interviewed her. It was clear that she had snapped, from what she told me. The guy had been pestering her for sex every time she passed him near to where she lived, but she wasn't interested and she had made it quite clear to him.

He then took to abusing her, saying she felt he was not good enough for her and after one of these occasions she had run in her house, picked up a knife returned and stabbed him. Though injured, his injuries were not life threatening and he had made a full recovery by the time she came on for trial.

When her matter came on in the High Court, I said to her "… look, it's pointless pleading not guilty. I will come and make a plea in mitigation." The case was heard before Justice Waterman, and the late Olton Springer was the prosecutor. He made a song and dance of my presence in the criminal assizes, stating in jest that the court must be honoured that I had paid it the courtesy of coming down into these plain premises from my lofty offices on High Street making all the money at Cottle, to see where "we poor brothers here practice real law." He carried on and on about how I didn't come to 'these places' etc. etc. Even Justice Waterman added his few quips about me being frequently on TV with cricketing matters and that I "have graced their proceedings today." I just listened, and after he had finished I said:

> "My Lord, there is nothing that my learned friend has said that is not true other than the tons of money that I am supposed to be making, although his reasons for stating why I am not seen around these parts may be somewhat fanciful. I would put to your Lordship that if I was so moved as Mr. Springer has said to come down from my lofty perches to pay a transient visit to these surrounds, it must be because I feel that this young lady needs to be helped, and even though she has done wrong, she is deserving of another chance, which will be denied her if she is given a custodial sentence, as this carries a tag for the rest of her life. Her impulsive behavior was wrong and out of all proportion and she regrets her actions and offers her apology. None of us here can place ourselves in her shoes from the perspective of unwarranted sexual advances, and so I urge your Lordship to consider probation."

Springer's countenance changed when the slam dunk he thought he had for a conviction and custodial sentence evaporated when the judge agreed that my client was a fit case for probation.

These criminal trials lasted a few days, a week at maximum, and then it was all over. Though you spent maybe four hours in court, it left you drained. Maybe this adrenalin rush fooled me into thinking that everything would be like this, and shortly as I faced adjournment after adjournment in civil matters, I quickly lost interest in court. How else would one maintain one's sanity far less earn a decent living? Many feel that this lay at the root of the extraordinary and completely wrong protest by Alair Shepherd, Q.C. to a judge in backing her, dropping his pants, and bowing. This action, which was totally lacking of respect to the court, to the profession, to common decency, not to mention to him, is one that I am sure Alair wishes he could erase.

The CCJ has commented not only on the time frame for the delivering of judgments, but the time it takes for the completion of hearing of matters. The Cottle saga is a case in point, as even when the matter was supposedly ended, it has continued on and on. I have already come to terms with the fact that I will suffer severe financial loss from this debacle.

Something that I had feared for some time could be a possibility the longer it took me to recover the money due to Cottle became a reality for me on October 29th 2013 when I was arrested and charged with theft from a client. The money laundering charge I had never foreseen, as in my view—as well as that of many attorneys who expressed surprise to me—the factum of money laundering was not present in this case. Other aspects of the matter, the reasons for the charge and the ridiculousness of them are dealt with elsewhere in this script, but what I want to discuss now is how the court system impacted on me. I was now on the other side of the fence facing a criminal charge, which I strongly disputed as I had a civil judgment that the money missing from the coffers of Cottle was the responsibility of my former partners. A basic tenet of our system guaranteed under our constitution is that once a person is arrested he must within a reasonable time be brought before the courts to answer to his charge. Section 18 of the constitution provides as follows:

> "If any person is charged with a criminal offence then, unless the charge is withdrawn, the case shall be afforded a

fair hearing within a reasonable time by an independent and impartial court established by law."

After my arrest the police were swift to have it announced to the world. It was the lead item on the 5:30 pm radio news and the evening television news at 7:00 pm, and coverage was given to my appearance in court on October 30th. My arrest was transmitted over the air waves, especially the internet, far and wide. Whatever the outcome, the damage to me was irreversible. Yet it took 653 days before the charges were dismissed for want of prosecution, when on the tenth appearance I made in court, the police still were in no position to comply with the strictures of Section 18. But what is more disturbing was that there was a total lack of care as to the effect it was having on me as displayed by the police.

Though the matter was eventually dismissed in August 2015 for want of prosecution, it was evident for quite some time before that the police were not only unable to sustain the charge, but were stalling for reasons best known to them.

The records of the suit 1612/1613 will show that I have paid over two million into the accounts of the firm, just as they will show that with interest and costs, my two partners today owe me in excess of two point five million. The records of suit 151/152, which can be examined by an independent person, not the verbiage spouted by Smith, will reveal that Mrs. Watson owes Cottle nearly half a million. With that in mind, how then can I be charged with stealing over $600,000 from a client, and worse still, being involved in money laundering?

Charge me with being naïve, being an idiot over the Cottle situation, but theft and laundering money? I have no assets left to speak of. It is one of the reasons that I have tremendous anger towards the DPP Charles Leacock whose ridiculous interpretation of the money laundering statutes is that once you are charged with theft, a money laundering charge must follow on the presumption that you have disposed of the money. This charge, more than the theft charge, has spelt the death knell for the offshore practice that I had spent over 20 years cultivating.

I have known Leacock since we were students at Cave Hill. He is also married to one of the young ladies who joined me in our Harrison College Sixth Form. I would describe him as an acquaintance, not a friend, and most of the occasions we met were on social occasions at the house of a mutual friend Edmund Hinkson. On more than one occasion I spoke to him of my predicament, and whilst I am no way suggesting I am above the law or entitled to special consideration, I have always felt it unconscionable that knowing the facts of Cottle, he could authorize that the money laundering charge be laid as I was informed by the police while being interviewed.

Charles has a position as chancellor within the Anglican diocese where he gives advice to the Bishop. He thus must be presumed to know many of the strictures that have biblical references, and I would just point out two. You often reap what you sow, and those in glass houses should not throw stones.

If the theft was so clear, why has it taken the police so long to start a preliminary inquiry? After all, the alleged theft was in 2008, and you are seriously telling me that you don't have all that you need to proceed with the case so that on approximately five occasions that I returned to court in 2014 the police asked for an adjournment on the grounds that they were not ready? What is worse, in a tactic that I have come to understand is very familiar, they introduce piece by piece the evidence that they allegedly have against you so that the magistrate is not tempted to dismiss for want of prosecution, or in my case deliberately went behind the back of Andrew Pilgrim to elicit from Elliott Mottley an adjournment on the premise that discovery would be forthcoming.

On that occasion the police had not told Mottley that Pilgrim informed the court that if the discovery was not forthcoming on that day he would be making an application to dismiss. Mottley was out of the island, and Pilgrim's hands were tied, in that Mottley had granted the request for the adjournment to the inspector in charge of the case, who was then conveniently not in court when the matter came up. That was on September 23rd 2014, and yet when the matter was finally dismissed on August 13th 2015 they still had not complied and were requesting further time.

The antics, and I say so deliberately, of Sgt. Watson, the supposed prosecutor in my matter, I have found incredible. It is my understanding that he has a law degree, and my memory seems to recall seeing him going into the Law Faculty when I was teaching there, but he appears more interested in appearance and posturing akin to his body building physique rather than to getting to the bottom of the matter. Simply to say after eighteen months that the prosecution is not quite ready and to give the court the impression that he does not know why I am complaining about lack of progress in my matter, as it was a recent one, is a disservice to his profession. My matter was eventually dismissed after 653 days, but truthfully even though I may be biased, it should have been dismissed nearly a year ago.

Time after time during the ten times that I returned to court, various reasons were trotted out for the inability to start the case, from the excuse that they have not got the file, to the explanation that they are seeking production orders to gather information, to the story someone from the DPP is vetting the statements from the arresting officers, to the excuse that the person responsible for the actual prosecution is not present in court, while my practice was imploding. The question that I wanted to ask was: Why I was arrested? If there was such a compelling case against me for a matter alleged to have occurred in 2008, why did it take until 2013 to arrest me and then in 2015 it was dismissed because you could not as required by law turn over to me full 'discovery' of the charges I was facing? At times I was of the view that Sgt. Watson had no concept of the maxim *Justice Delayed is Justice Denied*.

When finally in July I was given partial discovery, I was able to vet the letter I had seen upside down when being interviewed in the police station (see Appendix Three). It was written by a snake masquerading as a Q.C. by the name of Barry Gale. He had previously in 2008 written me at Cottle complaining that money due to a client was not forthcoming (see Appendix Two). I had responded admitting it was due stating that I did not have any resources to borrow any more to fund the defalcations of my former partners, but would gladly sign over the money to his client if he would recover same from my former partner who was working in his office for nearly five years.

This was an egregious and deliberate lie by Gale to accuse me in a letter to the police of having taken this money, when he well knew the facts and when one of his partners and employees was acting for Watson in my attempts to recover the funds from him. In doing so he has shown his true colours, and the contempt I feel for him is only slightly less than that I feel for Smith. His time will come. That he did so as well when he was president of the Bar meant that he was completely unfit to lead the organization. Lying by omission, as I understand it, is still lying.

12

Vernon Smith

MY FIRST RECOLLECTION of Vernon Smith, Uncle Vernon to me then, was as the host of an Old Year's party my parents attended, and being too young for the festivities—as it would have been around 1967—my brother Stephen and I were forced to sleep upstairs with his children while the adults rang the new year in down below.

On several occasions at various gatherings of friends, all with children of the same age, he was Uncle Vernon to me. When my brothers and I were children, his wife Dr. Jane Yeo was our paediatrician. As my interest in cricket developed I would have been a wide-eyed youngster at Kensington, taken there with my father to watch regional cricket, and in 1971 to witness my first test match, and he would be in attendance at times amongst the group of men that my father in today's language was 'liming' with (a concept that I have great difficulty envisaging as he has always equated liming with idleness). Since that game in 1971, until the test against New Zealand in 2014, I have not missed a Test Match at Kensington with the exception of three while studying overseas.

I missed the game in 2014 because I had become so disillusioned with life that I dreaded being around people, half of whom genuinely wanted to know of my troubles, but the other half of whom, as I was told by someone that I looked up to, saw me as a dishonest and disgraced lawyer. For that I lay the blame squarely on a group of Q.C.'s who, despite knowing what actually occurred, appear to have made it their life's mission to seek to discredit, harass and embarrass me. Smith has been and continues to be the choir master, but membership of the chorale includes the likes of Barry Gale, Michael Springer, Alwyn Babb and Vonda Pile.

Among that cricket-watching group were men like Sir Clifford Husbands, Algie Symmonds, Oliver Browne and the now deceased Noel Symmonds, Coachie Reid and Justice Colin Williams, and as was the custom of the day I referred to each as 'Uncle' when addressing them. Many long hours were spent after the end of play discussing not only happenings on the field of play, but any other events. I was led to understand that one of the reasons I accompanied my father was that this gave him a good excuse to leave at a decent hour to take me home. It was not only at cricket that I saw Uncle Vernon, but as he and his family were often in the same social circles that my family was in at functions where children attended, we often interacted. One of his closest friends, Justice Colin Williams, was godfather to my brother Stephen.

Shortly after I entered practice in 1987 with Cottle Catford I had reason to go to the offices of Hutchinson and Banfield for closure of a matter at the office of Colin Williams Q.C., as he then was. Upon being ushered into his office I referred to him as Uncle Colin, as he was not only one of my father's friends, but my brother Stephen's godfather, whereupon I was immediately chastised and asked not to refer to him with that title in future in legal circles—call him either Colin or Mr. Williams.

The same instructions were to be given to me a few years later by Vernon Smith, 'VO' as he is known to his friends (even the devil has recruits), when we met in a car park in Bridgetown early one morning shortly after his return to Barbados in 1989, having served as High

Commissioner to London after the Barrow-led DLP was swept back into power in 1986. He welcomed me effusively to the profession, had nothing but praise for Cottle, Mr. Armstrong and Mr. Hutchinson in particular, but said I needed to visit his offices, as he had established the first black firm on the island. I had last seen him in the summer of 1988 when I spent time with his nephew Alan at the residence of the High Commissioner while in London to watch the Lords test between the West Indies and England. I swear that in excess of twenty Barbadian men who were in London to watch the test slept under that roof during that game.

In light of this background, I and others have been perplexed at the vendetta he has carried out against me over the years. Others have surmised why, the late Marcelle Smith on more than one occasion telling me that she was reliably informed that it grew out of Stephen Alleyne and I embarrassing him at meetings of the BCA. I have racked my brain to remember a particular instance, but as he often behaved like a prime jackass at these meetings, it was not too hard to make him look stupid without being deliberate.

After a recent battle in court I attended a meeting of the BCA Rules Committee, still with steam coming out of my ears, and the former Deputy Prime Minister Philip Greaves said to me that he himself just could not understand Smith's relentless actions to delay my recovery of the funds due to Cottle, as Vernon and Neville were in the same Sixth Form. Then he went on: "…but that is Vernon… no one can figure why he does certain things."

Smith's apparent blinkered hatred for me over the last decade has not only caused me untold misery, but also serious financial loss both from the time that I have to spend attending to his incessant filings in court on behalf of my former partners and lately on behalf of Watson's wife, because the longer it has taken me to recover the funds from my former partners the greater is my loss. Understandably, my parents and I have lost what little respect we ever had for him not only as an attorney, but as a man. It saddens me that I ever used the term 'Uncle' to him as a mark of respect, something that I had the opportunity to tell him to his face in court under cross examination when he tried to justify payments he made in a suit later discussed in the next chapter (151/152 of 2004).

As an example of how he has been hell-bent on prolonging my attempts to recover the funds that the courts have ruled are due to me by my former partners, he has now taken, with his sidekick Michael Springer, to filing actions in a suit closed since the decision re the appeal in 1612/1613 was handed down by the Court of Appeal in October of 2013, now seeking to question the judgment entered in September 2009 on behalf of a person not party to the suit. It is the kind of gutter tactic he has employed on several occasions during his legal practice and which the CCJ was moved recently to comment on, but he does so all under the guise of delaying the matter.

My first interactions with Smith, however, were not in law, but in his constant attempts at meetings of the Barbados Cricket Association (BCA) to embarrass the board, at the time led by Captain Peter Short. Short had become entrenched as president during the twenty years he was reelected to the position. His longevity understandably led to some resentment among persons in the BCA aspiring for leadership.

As a young member of the board, first elected in 1987, I was of the view that if it wasn't broken there was no need to fix it. The fact that Short was white, which seemed to upset some, in addition to his longevity, was really of no interest to me at the time, but grumblings that started in his later years of the presidency which coincided with my early years on the board were the start of my introduction to the politics of the BCA.

Smith, an oppositionist by nature, was supportive of any persons who were opposed to Short, and on more than one occasion he was hyper-critical in private to me about the fact that we youngsters on the board, referring to Stephen Alleyne and myself, were somehow in his opinion betraying our heritage by not siding with those who were opposing him.

Smith clearly felt that as we were prepared to follow the same path as Short's lieutenant Cammie Smith in our unwillingness to challenge him or support someone challenging him for the presidency, we were betraying his cause. As I told him then more than once, I did not see or agree that one needed to oppose just for the sake of opposition something that is in his blood stream.

At one stormy Annual General Meeting held at the Old Dover Convention Centre circa 1990, some auditing concerns were highlighted in the Annual Report from the auditors to the members. Smith was at his most bombastic, demanding that the investigative report which had led to the concerns in the Annual Report be laid before the meeting. Short refused this request, and to be fair to him, the auditors had specifically stated that this report was only for the board's attention and was not to be made public without the permission of the auditors.

Smith's antics that day gave me an insight into his later behavior in my legal battles with my former partners as he represented them. Whenever he adopted a position, whatever its legal merit, he stood by it. He railed at the meeting, threatening all manner of retribution on the board if they didn't accede to his request. He suggested to Short that advantage be taken of the presence at the meeting of the then Justice Clifford Husbands, a long standing member, who would surely advise that his threat to visit Coleridge Street if the report was not laid was not fanciful.

Whatever views people had of him, Short was a shrewd man. Anticipating Smith's antics at the meeting, Short had arranged for the prominent attorney Jack Dear Q.C., a member of the BCA but not a particularly active one from the perspective of attendance at annual general meetings, to attend the meeting. Jack took up a position right next to a microphone and after listening to all the verbal barbs being thrown, he announced: "Mr. Chairman, Mr. Chairman may I have a word." He then continued in his own inimitable style "Excuse me for remaining seated, but Mr. Smith is talking absolute nonsense."

Not only the content of what he was saying, but the manner of the delivery of his words brought howls of derisive laughter from the assembled membership, leaving Smith to exit the meeting red-faced to console himself at the bar at the Dover meeting place, where he expounded to whomever would care to listen to him why he disagreed with Jack, but as the calypsonian the Mighty Gabby has so famously said, 'Jack say' was against him.

That incident, I have often thought, was the catalyst for the pest he was to become at the BCA, especially during the time that Stephen Alleyne was president and I was honorary secretary.

My legal battles with Smith however began in the mid-nineties. In 1995 a close friend of mine called me in despair at a time when she was mourning the loss of her friend to state that she had been instructed to get out of her friend's house where she had been resident with him for a number of months after he had suffered a stroke prior to his death. She was issued this instruction by Smith as named executor of the estate within two days of her return to Barbados from the deceased's funeral in his native land, having died in Barbados where he had ended his working life.

My friend had given up her fledging practice as a young attorney (her third career) to come to Barbados take care of her friend after he had fallen ill. She was here for a number of months before the testator suffered another stroke which was fatal, and after attending to his funeral overseas, received this ultimatum from Smith, which greatly upset her.

One thing Smith has never failed to show is his lack of sensitivity. Not only did he seek to eject the woman from the house where she was a guest of the testator (supposedly a close friend of his) for the last few months of his life with just two days' notice, but he subsequently caused her distress and indeed loss in the manner in which he administered the estate.

With an attitude that I was to become more familiar with, Smith even refused to comply with a ruling from the registrar of the Supreme Court in Trinidad as to what was needed to transfer bonds in the estate governed by Trinidad law, arguing that the requirements as stated by the Registrar were unlawful. I recall the call I received from the Registrar expressing her total incredulity that an attorney in Barbados would simply say he does not agree with the registrar in Trinidad as to the law in Trinidad and not comply. His actions forced the beneficiary into unnecessary expensive litigation that, by his delay and refusal, resulted in the value of the bequests left to her being diminished. As I have come to learn, this is a tactic of his, which no doubt fuels his ego because he revels in the inconvenience and pain he causes others. It is typical of his narcissistic behavior. Quite frankly, I have come to the conclusion that he is mad.

It is now ironic to me that at the time, though I was surprised at and disappointed by Smith's actions, I did not share the loathing that the object of his tirades had for him by his actions, as I simply put it down to his typically confrontational and idiosyncratic style. This, when entwined with her own personality of not wanting to back down from a fight, produced an inevitable collision. She had opined at the time that she was dealing with one who has no feelings for others; at one time he is charming and the politest of persons, at other times an irrational lunatic. Over the years, as I have had to endure Smith's antics, I have had to embarrassingly apologize to her. It is now my belief that the ethics he goes by are not those found in renowned texts on Law, but are more along the lines of what Smith wants. In a short word, he is certifiable.

It is clear to me now that Smith, from the end of the Cottle partnership in 2002, was advising Watson and Griffith and in a manner just to delay, delay, delay. By the time the partnership ended his antipathy towards me was well known because of his constant filings of claims against the BCA in the years 1999-2005.

As such, despite a clear acceptance by my former partners in the form of a Dissolution Agreement signed by the three of us in 2002 that they owed the partnership money, he proceeded to make a *cause celebre* of the issue, which in 2013 the Court of Appeal said was really a simple issue, but one which took eight years up to then to get through the legal system.

Smith is and was a past master at these gutter tactics which he continues to exploit today despite the bringing into force of new Civil Procedure Rules to stymie such tactics. He continues to run amok and to do as he pleases because the judiciary on a whole has been weak before him and has unwittingly sanctioned his underhand tactics by not hauling him up for them. By this method he achieves what he wants—to delay and delay so that, as in the Watson case, 14 years after the use of the money by them, it has not been fully repaid. He is also adept at spreading by innuendo aspersions to cast suspicions on others while pretending to be a gentleman of upstanding integrity.

Years previous, while a student in Manchester, I attended a cricket match in Scotland that Stephen Alleyne was playing in when one of his teammates made an observation while waiting to bat that I have always kept with me, and regrettably have seen how it has affected me. He was of the view that there are certain questions that one can never properly answer and gave as an example the following question: 'Are you still beating your wife?' Think of it. Neither a response in the affirmative or negative can help you, as you are damned if you do and damned if you don't. Smith is a master at creating such situations.

Shortly after I took over the running of affairs at Cottle I am told and verily believe that he indicated to persons in the lodge that there were problems at Cottle. As many in Barbados society would attest, prominent persons in society and business are members of the lodge, and while neither my father nor I have been inducted into any of the lodges, we both have friends who are and who informed me of what he had been doing.

Of course persons hearing Smith, a supposedly honourable Q.C., would think given his persona that the problems centered on me, as I was the person in charge of Cottle. It was not generally known at the time that there was a serious deficit in the Clients' Accounts at Cottle because of the failure of my former partners to fund same for moneys attributed to them. Smith knew of this, but he was still prepared to allow this rumour to go abroad as part of his character assassination of me. He of course never mentioned that he was doing his utmost to prevent my recovering this money or that I was battling a bad hand left me by my partners.

I know that I lost clients as a result of his statements, as another close friend who provided secretarial services to several companies I worked for from her private business was told by one of her clients that if she wanted to maintain his account she had to cease connections with me.

It has always galled me how Smith could be so dishonest as to suggest there were problems at Cottle with the clear intention of spreading the view that I was responsible for same when he knew the real score. Your oath as an attorney to represent a client does not extend to deception. While one can represent a client who has pleaded not guilty to murder even though he confesses to you that he has killed the person, by testing the evidence that is presented, you cannot ethically suggest in so doing that he has not killed the deceased, having been privy to the confession. Smith at best seems incapable of understanding this, or at worst conveniently forgets it, as it does not suit the points he is trying to put over.

It is fair to say that he has simply obstructed all my attempts to firstly get judgment to recover the funds. He has now started back up as I try to enforce same to file appeals challenging the judgments all in a process to further delay. It is a tactic he is familiar with doing and I think the last word on the subject of his antics should come from the CCJ in the case of System Sales Ltd. for whom Smith acted and Suttle under the heading 'Interests of Justice', a concept that Smith is unfamiliar with unless it accords with his view of the matter.

> "It was the Court's view that the interests of justice required that the present case must be brought to an end. The present case, the Court pointed out, was filed more than 16 years ago and it would be unconscionable and inconsistent with the overriding objective of the rules of the Court to allow any more time to pass. There had been full consideration of the issues by three levels of court and the applicants (System Sales) failed at each level. In the Court's view there would be no benefit to any of the parties to extend the matter any further.
>
> The Court strongly urges the judiciary in Barbados to adopt practices that prevent the type of delays found in the present case. The Court further commented on the role of the lawyers in creating the delays found in the case. The court was of the view that the conduct of the lawyer's in bringing the present case by way of the wrong process and where there was already a ruling demonstrating that there was no realistic prospect of success fell squarely into the category of improper, unreasonable and negligent conduct.
>
> In concluding the court ordered that the application be dismissed and that the applicant's lawyers (Smith) bear the costs of the application with such costs to be taxed of not agreed. The Court also states that no further applications are to be made in the matter without the permission of the Court."

That sums up in a nutshell what Smith has been up to in my matter. Hopefully one day I will see such a statement applied in my case when finally all the applications to the court are ended.

13

151/152 of 2004: Cottle Catford and Co. vs Delvina Watson

IN CHAPTER 9 I related how I discovered a debit account—No. 30559—in the name of Delvina Watson, et al in the accounts of the firm. The purpose of the account, as I was to be told later, was to facilitate the payment of a deposit on a house at Long Bay, St. Philip being purchased by the Watsons. The amount of the deposit was $34,000. The last entry to the account, which was posted on July 30th 2001, was a payment to Uplands Trading for the rental of a container. With that debit, the account was $259,256.52 overdrawn at the end of July 2001. Other than three transactions related to the purchase of the house, more than 50 transactions were debited to the account over a 20 month period.

I do not recall Mr. Watson ever approaching the partners for permission to make the payment of the ten percent deposit as an advance from the firm, and I certainly know no request was ever made with respect to the several transactions that flowed through the account. If an examination is made of the cheques that were written, one would note that most of them were written in Mr. Watson's handwriting and signed by him. What is significant about that is that two persons were employed by the firm with responsibility for issuing and writing cheques, so by doing this he was making payments that he knew should be queried. It is a sad indictment that neither of the two persons who daily would have processed the cheques that he wrote ever saw it fit to draw it to the attention of the other partners.

The existence of this 'slush fund' made it clear why at the time of the discussion about the merger with Lex, Watson kept refusing all requests by me to have our accounts audited. Not only would this have shown the true financial position of the firm, but more damagingly would have brought the account to light. He was supported by Griffith in his refusal on the grounds that we could not bear the expense, but the motive was now clear.

In light of the clear abuse of the Client Accounts by both Watson and Griffith, a fact known to all, I therefore found it to be the height of hypocrisy for Smith to mount a defense in the subsequent partnership litigation that I was not entitled to sue on the basis that the accounts were not audited, having outvoted me two to one on every occasion that I requested an audit over a period of 18 months between 2000 and 2001. In this regard Leslie Haynes, who was acting for Watson but allowed Smith to make the argument in his most bombastic style, is equally deserving of my scorn. Though he has been very contrite of late as to what has befallen me as a result of the partnership break up, I will always feel extremely let down by his actions or lack thereof. His silence while Smith ranted and frothed at his mouth while making his arguments which were later totally discredited by the Court of Appeal could only be viewed as an acquiescence in what Smith was advocating.

Let me make it clear that I hold no brief against anyone for representing Watson and Griffith. What I find to be hypocritical is to hide behind the coattails of another who is spouting rabid nonsense as the Court of Appeal suggested, and then bail out as soon as the tide starts rising against him because it is clear that he has been manufacturing his positions.

I have always found that aspect of the partnership litigation among the most painful that I have gone through. Two senior attorneys with the all clear evidence from my letters to their clients that I had been asking for an audit, were now seeking to prevent litigation proceeding on the basis that no audit had been done, and insisting that I bear the cost estimated at about $50,000 to have one done before I could proceed. Their argument was that before I could enforce the agreement of December 31st 2002—an agreement that each of their clients, both attorneys of more than 30 years call, had voluntarily signed—this must be done. Even though the suit in this matter was separate from the partnership litigation suit, it was in effect arising from the same facts: the need to recover funds due to the Client's Account.

On May 17th 2000 the loan proceeds of $325,356.50 for the purchase of the house presently owned by the Watsons, and on November 3rd 2000 another loan of $165,408, were paid into the account in question. No other payments were ever made into the account, meaning that the deficit in the account was funded by other clients' money. On May 16th, in anticipation of the loan being received, the balance of purchase price of $281,100 was paid to the vendor's attorney while on May 16th an amount of $20,000 was paid personally by Allan Watson to his wife Delvina.

These transactions had the effect of pushing the account into deficit, as the total money received re the house purchase was $325,100, while the amount paid for the purchase and indeed the $20,000 paid to Delvina Watson amounted to almost $335,000, almost ten thousand dollars more. Watson would have been aware of this almost immediately, as the deposit which had been made in 1999 was never repaid into the account, and thus had to come out of the loan proceeds.

The account was used by the Watsons as though it was a personal chequing account. Even with the proceeds of the second loan of $165,000 received on November 3rd 2000, the account continued to be in deficit and was used primarily over the next eight months to make payments on behalf of the Watsons. Uplands Trading, Barbados Mortgage Finance for one of his daughter's mortgage, Globe Finance, Everson Elcock, Hastings Plaza for rental of space for another daughter, were some of the repeated payments made through the account.

For nearly a year up to the time I discovered the account, the Watsons had benefitted from use of quarter of a million dollars free of any interest charges, and as it has transpired, with no intention to repay it. As I pieced together things it was clear that there were no charges to the account for nearly three months before I discovered it, and it has since struck me that the desperate state of the firm's finances must have been pointed out to him when he last used it, and while that was the reason why I subsequently discovered it, it was sobering to think that but for that, he would have continued on his merry way.

After the High Street partnership ended at the end of 2002, I wrote Mrs. Watson a letter dated June 18th 2003, pointing out the seriousness of the situation and the potential consequences for her husband if the payments were to become public (see Appendix Five). I made this decision to write to her because all attempts by me to get Watson to settle the account had fallen on deaf ears.

I am not certain whether she knew of the exact state of her husband's indebtedness to the firm by reason of his over-drawings or the full extent of this account, as he may have adopted the same stance that Griffith did with her spouse in not informing her. That, however, was not my concern. But from my face-to-face meeting with her in 2003, it was clear to me that she was only interested in what she needed for herself and family and expected her husband to provide it. She appeared to have little concern that this deficit was having a strain on me and from that time I have referred to her as akin to Lady Macbeth. I was taken aback by her statements to me that I was always travelling to England as if I had a large personal debit account, and said to her that other than about two occasions when I travelled on business, all such travel was personal and paid for by me and not from the coffers of Cottle. In any event, it was none of her business.

In the latter half of 2003 the building that the old partnership occupied was sold. Mr. Watson, as one of the owners, was to receive his share of the sale. He had a 25% interest which would have netted him nearly $200,000. The proceeds of the sale were paid into Cottle, but the net amount payable to him amounted to approximately $25,000 because he owed the estate of Joseph Armstrong, one of the co-owners, around $175,000. When Mrs. Armstrong as his executrix called at my office to execute the release of the mortgage that Mr. Armstrong held over Watson's share for the loan he had made to him so as to enable the sale to be completed, she indicated to me that she was relying on me to ensure that the loan amount was settled. She stated that he had been promising for years to settle the debt even after Mr. Armstrong's death, at the time over 8 years.

As I sat there with her it was all coming back to me—his hedging at the suggestions in partners' meetings that we raise finance by using as security his share in the building; he had never mentioned this indebtedness. As I was finding out, Mr. Watson was leading a closeted life and was concealing a part of his personality that I had not up to that time realized existed.

On the 5th day of October 2003 Mr. Watson sent me a letter by fax indicating that his share of the proceeds of the sale were to be paid in a certain manner, with any left over after his instructions to be paid towards the account 30559. This fax was later to become important to me, as by it Watson was indicating that he was personally responsible for certain of the debits in the firm.

These included two debit accounts for his wife's aunt's estate, of which the wife was executrix. There was not enough money to cover these and so I had to file suit in 2006, No. 625, to recover same only for Ivan Alert, then working with Leslie Haynes to defend it saying that neither of them owed Cottle money. I was not pleased with Alert, and told him so. Subsequently he withdrew from the suit and someone else is now representing her in the matter—Vernon Smith—and is attempting to trot out the same arguments that were dismissed by the Court of Appeal in 1612/1613.

There has never been any doubt that the cynical manipulation of the legal system by Watson and Griffith with their standard bearer Vernon Smith has been meant to delay the inevitable, as the paper trail that they owed money was always there. It has been of utmost frustration to me that the law would continue to show itself to be an ass in allowing this. Everyone deserves their day in court, but as that well known cliché states, *justice delayed is justice denied*. For me it has not been so much a delay as that it has come to a shuddering halt.

With no prospect forthcoming of the money being repaid, on January 30th 2004 I issued two writs on behalf of Cottle Catford & Co. against Delvina Watson. Suit No. 151 was for an amount of $168,847.08, the proceeds of 44 cheques paid to the Watsons and children or on their behalf to others, and Suit No. 152 for the amount of $96,300, the proceeds of 9 cheques paid similarly. The two suits were subsequently consolidated to form one action.

On the 19th day of March 2004, judgment was entered in default of filing a defense. The attorney on record in the proceedings at that time was Vernon Smith. As such it can reasonably be presumed that the defendant was admitting that the money was owed, and no issue was taken by him as her attorney as to my right to sue in the name of Cottle. Neither did he oppose the manner in which the suit was done or allege that any of my former partners were entitled to a share in the judgment.

Between the obtaining of the judgment in default in March of 2004 and the partial payment three years later on April 16th 2007, I in association with attorneys working with me at the time, in particular Julie Harris and George Bennett, appeared in court on numerous occasions to try to enforce the judgment. Mrs. Watson was examined as to her means to pay, a writ of *fieri facias* was obtained and levy executed against her car, after which Smith made an *ex parte* application before the then CJ Sir David Simmonds to obtain a stay, and in so doing filed an affidavit that was nothing but a tissue of lies.

These processes took almost three years before an application for committal to prison for failure to pay came before Justice Jackie Cornelius in March of 2007. She indicated to the defendant through her attorney Smith that the plaintiff had obtained a default judgment over three years ago and unless the judgment was settled within 30 days she would be prepared to hear the application for her to be committed to prison in default of payment.

By letter dated April 13th 2007, Smith then pulled a stunt that no sane person could have imagined. He sent me a cheque for $108,491.16 saying it was made up of my 32% of the judgment and interest that I was entitled to. The taxed costs allowed were paid in full. This aspect has always to my mind given a lie to the nonsense that Smith argued that I had no entitlement to sue. He enclosed a receipt for me to sign evidencing payment of my entitlement, which I returned under copy of my letter of April 24th 2007, indicating that as the full amount of the judgment had not been paid, I was not signing same.

Smith subsequently drew and prepared receipts dated April 16th 2007 from Allan Watson and Joyce Griffith indicating receipt of the other 68 per cent. The receipts were signed by them as partners of Cottle Catford, although both had ceased to be partners as of January 1st 2003. These receipts were put on the court file in an unauthorized manner, as a letter dated June 26th 2007 from the then registrar of the Supreme Court Maureen Crane Scott indicated. In particular the receipts bore the 10c stamp that would be issued by a private individual, not the equivalent amount of stamp duty as required for official receipts under the Stamp Act.

Smith's contention that he has maintained to this day—a contention that I am yet to find anyone in agreement with out of all the lawyers and other academics I have discussed it—was that the partners at the time of the debt arising were entitled to receive the repayment of same in proportion to their interest in the partnership. My partnership interest was 32% and the other two between them shared 68%. One such as him who is filled with such bigoted hatred for me must realize the ridiculousness of it.

While there is legal precedent for the view that partners, even when they leave a partnership, are entitled to a share of income of the partnership, such right is related to profits or refund of expenses that they legitimately shared the payment of. In this particular case the amount being paid back or paid was not profit, but a return of money belonging to a Client's Account which, despite all his assertions in court to the contrary, the partners have no personal interest in. It is an account held on trust.

But even if Smith were correct and the partners were entitled to the money, then surely because of his involvement in 1612/1613, as Griffith's attorney he knew that both were being sued for amounts far greater than the amounts he said were paid, and which to this date despite being requested by two different judges, neither he nor the alleged recipients have been able to display the cheque evidencing payment or the account into which the payment was made for which the receipts were allegedly given. I have always held to the view that Smith, by his actions, has become a trustee *de son tort* with respect to the money due to Cottle, and is nothing less than an accessory after the fact with respect to the stealing of the client's money of Cottle by Allan Watson.

Fundamentally there is a more glaring fact to give a lie to the nonsense Smith is arguing. If his argument is followed to its logical conclusion, then he is suggesting that Watson, having taken money in the form of cheques paid to him in his personal name for amounts akin to $80,000, is able to repay this amount and extinguish the debt by receiving from his wife the money to settle the judgment. The height of absurdity could not be greater, and it is a travesty of justice that our courts have allowed this lunacy to be argued for upwards of eight years.

Around the time of the receipts Joyce Griffith and a sidekick of Smith, Michael Springer, also an attorney-at-law, purportedly lent $330,000 to Delvina Watson who granted them a mortgage over property belonging to her. The date of the mortgage was April 20th 2007, but it was not presented for stamp duty and recorded until September 23rd 2008, some 17 months later. It is amazing that Joyce, indebted to me at the time by more than a million dollars and having not paid a cent, could find funds to lend money to Delvina Watson.

The reality is that for upwards of 15 years now, Watson and his wife have had use of about $250,000 of clients' money free of cost. They have not paid any interest (other than for three years between 2004 and 2007, but only on 32% of the judgment awarded) on same, but I who have had to borrow money to replenish the accounts have been paying interest at the rate of 10% per annum to the banks. On the amount that they utilized that equates to about $25,000 a year for the period 2003 to 2007 and then when the credit of the amount paid in 2007 is taken into account, the interest on the balance would equate to about $16,000 a year, an additional $125,000 approximately, to date a total amount of about $250,000 in interest that I have been charged. The letter from Smith and Smith in 2007 illustrates how I am out of pocket even if I recovered every cent, which I have not to date, as the interest awarded on the judgment is way below the amount that I have paid for the money I borrowed to plug the shortfall in Cottle's accounts.

An aspect of the strategy used by Smith and his cohorts has been to bury me with all manner of discoveries and litigation to prolong all matters. All the litigation that I have launched has been with the intention of recovering the money that the Watson and Griffith used. After the partial payment by Smith in April 2007, my attention was turned to what I would call the sister suit, namely 1612/1613 of 2005, the partnership litigation.

14

1612/1613 of 2005: Nicholls vs Griffith and Watson

IN THIS CHAPTER, which is a synopsis of my legal battle against my former partners, I finally write about the most painful episode of my professional life, the repercussions of which have since transcended all aspects of my life.

In earlier chapters I described the events over a period of three to four years that led to the eventual breakup of the Cottle partnership at High Street. The end of the partnership was formalized by a simple agreement that was prepared by me at the last minute when, in the midst of all the moving etc., I realized that not only was there no formal agreement between the three of us about the way forward, but no acknowledgement of indebtedness to the firm's account. As such, on December 31st 2002 a cessation agreement was signed, and given what has transpired since, this was perhaps a slight saving grace. I shudder to imagine what my life would have been like without this document if I had to prove that my partners were indebted to the firm despite the audit accounts from Price Waterhouse Coopers dating back circa 1995 that they were indebted. I had seen and have seen since then termination agreements that would make that document seem like a simple ABC rhyme. However it was based, naively I thought with an element of trust that each party would do what was right. More than a dozen years later it is clear that the other two had no intention of so doing.

On October 4th 2013, in Civil Appeal 22 of 2009, Justice of Appeal Andrew Burgess, in delivering the Judgment of the Court in the appeal brought by my former partners, stated: "This case is essentially a simple breach of contract claim." A simple contract claim for breach of a contract dated October 31st 2002 that took over 8 years from the date of filing to be settled. And despite being settled finally in my favour, now two years on, not a cent has been recovered by me. I am finally summoning up the courage to write about thirteen years of betrayal and the continued assault my persona by three attorneys who seemed to have sworn a blood oath that my destruction is their ultimate aim.

After more than two years of writing and beseeching phone calls on August 16th 2005, I filed suit against Griffith and Watson. I had hoped that one last-ditch effort in April that year when I appealed to Sir Henry Forde Q.C., who for many years was a *de facto* consultant of Cottle Catford, to meet with the three of us to see not so much as a resolution of the dispute, but to impress on the two the need to do what was right and to assist me with the payment of monies due to clients.

I have always remained disappointed that no meeting was ever held, and found it strange when over the years Sir Henry would appear to be surprised when speaking to my father that the matter was not settled. By and large this was the plight that I faced and which Watson exploited—that many in the profession did not want to get involved.

I had for some time been appealing to Sir Henry to meet with the three of us in an attempt to forge a resolution and a meeting was indeed set to take place in April of 2005. Sir Henry sent me an email shortly before the day of the meeting stating that he was forced to postpone the meeting, and as I have said, it was never held. With my writing and asking for meetings, meetings having been scheduled after the filing of proceedings in a hope of finding a resolution. I was more than a little taken aback when nearly eight years after it was suggested to me privately by more than one judge that I took too aggressive an approach to my former partners. Pardon me. I shudder to think if I had been more laid back what would have happened.

At the time of filing the suit I was beside myself as to what to do. I had by that time already borrowed nearly a million dollars to sustain the firm's Client's Accounts and the monthly repayments were already becoming a strain. In addition, I had exhausted all other avenues of getting funds into the accounts, such as chasing down fees due from delinquent clients and recovering money due from clients with debit accounts in the firm, with the result that my cash flow was therefore becoming increasingly perilous at the time. I was and have remained astonished at how the other two, knowing what the debt was doing to me, just simply walked away and would not assist, and as a result have virtually been unscathed by their actions, in my view because of the failure of the judicial system to reign in their dishonesty and that of the attorneys representing them.

As such there was only one source left to fund the deficit—my former partners and Watson's wife Delvina, the story of 151/152. It must be remembered that at the time of the suit the fees eventually paid by Kingsland had not been paid, so I was floundering not only in debt to the banks which required monthly repayments, but still facing several calls from clients who still had money due from Cottle. For me it is the equivalent of an "et tu Brutus" moment that after borrowing all the money up to that time and since that time to sustain an account and to keep the lid on a legal scandal, I would in 2013 be charged with stealing money from that account at the instigation of an attorney (Gale) who knew the facts, and with the authorization of a DPP (Leacock), who also was aware of the circumstances surrounding the missing money in Cottle.

I thus filed suit which at the time was a claim for repayment by my former partners of moneys that I had been forced to pay on behalf of clients whose money was paid into the firm's account at High Street while all three of us were partners, but which was no longer there because of the over-drawings. My initial claim was not for what was due by them as a result of their over-drawings, as this could not be adequately determined until the Kingsland fees were received and hence would have required a finalization of the partnership accounts, but for a simple contribution in the portion of their responsibility as partners for the amounts I had to pay to the clients so affected. The initial claims listed all the clients and the amounts on whose behalf funds were paid.

The claim filed against Griffith was for $430,039.36 and against Watson for $456.102.36, being their respective shares of the amount that I had paid. I myself was responsible for just over $400,000. As I had paid in excess of 1.2 million dollars to clients between the end of the partnership and the filing of the writ, but as I had recovered thus far from them approximately $50,000, I had clearly shouldered all the burden and was paying interest on the money that I had borrowed.

Justice of Appeal Burgess was at pains in his judgement in a lengthy dissection and rejection of the defendant's arguments to point out that I could not start an action for a recovery of debt against my former partners without an account of the partnership being taken, to dispel this nonsense. The genesis of this argument was not surprisingly made by the jackass Smith, who to this day will not accept that the argument which he started has been rejected as out of hand by the Court of Appeal.

What was filed in 2005 was not a claim about a partnership debt, but a claim for breach of contract, an implied contract if there was no express one, that if I was required to pay clients' money due by the former partnership of which you were a member, then you must make a contribution to that payment. It has always been my argument that the taking of the partnership accounts became a red herring in the matter primarily because of the antics of Smith before Cornelius J. It was well known that Smith resented her on two grounds.

Firstly, in keeping with his chauvinistic views because she was a woman; secondly she was young and now had authority over him.

His behavior towards her was very obnoxious at best and downright disrespectful at worst, in a manner that she would have been fully justified in citing him for contempt. My assertions when he was demanding that audited accounts be presented that I had nothing to hide, that these accounts were not audited because I had could not afford to do so, and that I found it somewhat rich that after arguing for years against an audit all of a sudden they now wanted one, were in retrospect used against me when she ruled that unaudited accounts could be presented.

During one of the hearings I was exasperated at the antics that Smith was carrying on within the court and said to the person seated next to me, if memory serves me right it was George Bennett, exactly what I thought of this man in some very graphic language. I was seated to the left of the judge with Smith directly opposite her, and on the one occasion that she attended court in this matter Beverley was seated to the left of Smith, and to the right of the judge. At times Beverley was looking at me quizzically, but it was only when she got home that she told me she could hear everything I was saying to George. It meant that Smith could hear it, which quite frankly I didn't care about, but then it dawned on me that the judge probably heard it as well.

About two days later I was teaching at the university and ran into her, as she was teaching there as well, and I said to her "I am not approaching you on the merits of the case, but I understand you may well have heard some utterances from me in court which contained very unparliamentary language, and I just wanted to offer my apologies, as it was not intended to disrespect you or the court." Her response was along the lines that she had heard, but didn't say anything as she understood my frustration at what was going on as I was facing a situation that was quite frankly unimaginable given who the parties were. The matter ended there, but I was later to learn from other attorneys that Smith was all about telling persons that the judge had allowed me to behave in the most scandalous of ways in the court. That was not unexpected, and is par for course for how he operates.

As my increasingly desperate letters to my former partners showed at the time, I thought it was unconscionable of them to expect me to carry the burden alone. It is clear now that they did not care, and it took me a while to appreciate and face this in part because I was fooled by the persona of Watson. I was not the only one fooled by him. I have lost count of the number of people, both attorneys and others, who have come up to me to express amazement at what he has done. I was livid on three grounds to this order:

1. Since the refusal of Price Waterhouse to carry on auditing the accounts unless the deficits were retired around 1999 I was consistently outvoted by the other two every time I requested an audit of the accounts.
2. It was estimated that the cost of an audit in 2005 would be not less than $50,000 which I could not afford and which they clearly had no incentive to fund.
3. I was not claiming a debt to settle the partnership, but simply to be refunded for money that I had advanced which they were legally obliged to repay; the mere payment of the money was simple enough to trace as I was not trying to establish what their debt to the partnership was.

To continue servicing the clients of Cottle, I had borrowed money, approximately a million dollars at that time. I was incurring costs of about $100,000 a year in interest payments which were not added to my initial claim, and thus the clear breach of contract claim became confused with the issue of the status of the partnership which still at the time of filing could not be settled.

The money that I had borrowed to pay the calls of clients when they arose included an amount of approximately $300,000 to settle a claim made by a client who has continued after the partnership ended with Ms. Griffith as his attorney. My inability to get it back was at the time having severe consequences to me, and I wonder if anyone has thought ten years down the road what this has done to me as I still have not got it back.

It was against this background that on August 16th 2005 I filed suit. With the time lapse necessary to allow for filing of the necessary defenses and other ancillary matters, the matter did not come before Justice Cornelius until March 2006 for interlocutory points to be determined. At this point Vernon Smith stepped in. He was representing Joyce Griffith, while Leslie Haynes represented Allan Watson. During all the arguments Haynes said little, virtually allowing Smith to lead and tagging along in his slipstream. Given the abilities of the two men this was indeed strange, and something when he has later tried to excuse his role in the whole debacle I told him was the equivalent of lying by omission, allowing a known falsehood to spread by not counteracting it. His tactic was to allow Smith to be the aggressor in making the case for the two while he remained behind the scenes representing Watson who was working with him, only to jump ship when he saw that it was sinking. I have always seethed at this. I recognize the right to counsel, but to allow what was transpiring to take place and claim it was not of your doing suggests to me some form of duplicity.

Smith argued that I was unable to bring an action until the accounts of the partnership were settled. At the time I could not fathom why he was making this argument, because I was not suing Griffith and Watson for their dues as partners, but simply for a contribution for the amounts that I had to pay to settle claims for clients who had paid money into the High Street partnership and now wanted it. On and on the arguments went. Unfortunately for me and not for the last time in this saga, Justice Cornelius made a ruling which I was later to regret.

I was insistent that the accounts could not be finalized until the Kingsland fee was received. I was livid that this was now an issue when for the last five years of the partnership the two of them refused my requests to audit the accounts and were now insisting on same as a prerequisite to my instituting an action. It was my opinion that Smith was at his loathsome best in insisting this, and I also had no fondness for Haynes either, who simply sat down and let him make the arguments. The logic of what they were saying was that I would have to carry the burden alone until the accounts were audited. This was ludicrous, but I was not the first and will certainly not be the last to be met by such antics by Smith.

Cornelius ruled that as I indicated I had all the books, that an account should be taken. I had by then determined to get the matter moving. I might as well concede to the production of the accounts. Think again: Smith and Haynes raised another issue. The first issue was whether the accounts were until the end of the partnership or to date of the order. The defendants were insisting to date, that is in 2006, while I was adamant it could not be, as the accounts of the firm were only prepared up to 2002, and I had only kept books for 2003 and 2004. Cornelius went on maternity leave shortly after making the order on 7th March 2006, and this issue as to the exact nature of her order remained outstanding for over a year until she returned to the bench and settled the order in April of 2007 along the lines that I was arguing.

That it took as long as a year was not for want of trying on my part. I have lost count of the times I badgered the Registrar to have the order settled, and was told it had to await the judge's return, to which I naturally replied: so if she died, what? The crap I had to put up with was unbelievable, but neither Smith nor Haynes were prepared to agree to the order, as it has always suited their clients to delay and delay this matter.

After nothing was moving after the order of March 7th 2006, for months I was beside myself with what to do. I got great practical but more importantly moral support during this time when two friends of mine in Trinidad who were both on the bench there, David Myers and Joan Charles, offered to go through everything with me to suggest a way forward.

For them to leave the island when court was sitting involved acquiring of all kinds of permission, so it was decided that I come to Trinidad. Both Stephen Alleyne and Yvette Lemonias assisted in coming with me, and the five of us spent the better part of ten hours closeted in a room in the Hilton Hotel trying to chart a way forward.

Both Stephen and Yvette had flown down on the first flight that morning and returned on the last flight that night, and other than for a break for lunch at TGI Fridays, we didn't leave the room. At that time Stephen was up to his neck with the preparations for the World Cup, and it showed me who my friends were.

At the time we thought nothing of it, but after his sudden death we wondered. When we broke for lunch Stephen said he just needed a ten-minute nap before we left. When we tried to wake him he was out cold and so we left him, went for lunch for about two hours, and brought his back to find him still sleeping. Your body can only take so much.

What is interesting is that at this time in another matter, the infamous 151/152 of 2004, Smith was trying to suggest that the money due from Mrs. Watson was paid back to Mr. Watson in accordance with his share of the partnership, and that in the other matter the accounts of the partnership needed to be audited before I could sue, but it was not the responsibility of Watson and Griffith as they were not in the partnership to pay for same. It was a deceitful argument by a despicable man who was simply trying to throw the whole loss on me and knew well what this delay was doing to me.

In light of the clear tactic by Smith to delay the matter (a tactic that he used in all matters he was involved in where his client benefits from delay) it was not a great surprise that he appealed the order as settled by Justice Cornelius to the Court of Appeal on May 18th 2007. This appeal was heard on December 3rd 2007, five years after the partnership had ended and now two and a half years after I filed suit.

All during this time I alone had borne the cost of trying to keep the firm afloat because of the interest I was repaying to the banks. My life was not only miserable, but at the time I was still in shock, as Stephen's death was less than two months previous. It was he, in a meeting in my office held shortly before his death, that really made me see what I was losing by the payments. He simply said: "Philip whatever you do don't let this kill you as you have a young family." The reality is that the prolonged delay was and continues to cost me more than $100,000 a year in interest payments alone.

I must digress here as I illustrate the wickedness of Smith. He knew well the situation that I was facing and that I was desperately trying to source funds to keep Cottle afloat. My battles with him were not confined to law, because in 2005 Stephen and I were involved in an acrimonious battle for the leadership of the BCA with one of his cohorts Tony Marshall. During the campaign I received an anonymous phone call or rather message on my answer phone warning me that if I continued to oppose Marshall the mess at Cottle would be made public. The only person that I shared this with was Stephen, and he said to me that he would understand if I dropped out of the election race in 2005, but I chose not to do so.

Now he was to show his ugly hand once again. The firm was closing a sale on behalf of a client and Joyce was acting for the purchaser. As the closing date approached I advised the attorney in the firm handling the matter that I would complete the sale. I telephoned Joyce and said: "…you owe me substantially more money than what is due your client, so you settle it and I will deduct it from the amount due." Joyce went to Smith. Unknown to me, the buyer and seller were brothers, and so in regular contact with one another, and after the matter kept me delayed our client started calling and I would tell him that I have no money for Ms. Griffith. He told his brother, the purchaser, what I said whereas Joyce showed her client that she had not received any money, conveniently forgetting to mention to him why I was saying that I owed her no money.

She had gone to Smith for assistance and he promptly directed them to visit the fraud squad and report me. The fraud squad visited my office while I was in hospital and my office manager decided to pay over the money. This I believe was the early genesis of my problems with the fraud squad who opened a file on me, as the impression was being cultivated that I was the bad party. I will never forgive that bastard Smith as long as I live for the damage that he has done to my reputation, and to be frank the best I can hope for him is that he rots in hell. He knows the problems I have faced and yet in his warped mentality has tried to make life far more difficult for me. I have since come to learn that he has pulled this trick on several attorneys, reporting matters to the fraud squad, and I can only surmise being mindful of the libel laws that one must wonder why he is so quick when he is in dispute with an attorney to call in the fraud squad and suggest malpractice on their part. I smell a rat.

When the appeal came on before the Court of Appeal on December 3rd 2007, Smith rose and started a long-winded exposition as to why the order of Justice Cornelius was wrong before president of the court Justice of Appeal Waterman, sitting with Justices of Appeal Williams and Connell. After a few minutes he was stopped by Justice Williams, who had been reading affidavits filed by me, and said words to this effect: "Mr. Smith, is this not a simple issue of money owed by partners to the firm? What I see here is a cry for help from Mr. Nicholls. He has been saddled with all the debt and however elaborate your arguments are, the fact is that when clients come knocking on the door of Cottle Catford, he has to find the money as the other two are no longer there."

He continued: "...as my daughter would say there is no rocket science here. The money has to be found."

Not for the first time when Smith was challenged by someone in authority to whom he felt he must defer, he shut up. He backed down, and shortly after sitting the Court of Appeal, dismissed the appeal and an order 'By Consent' was agreed that the accounts of Cottle Catford would be settled, and once settled, judgment would be entered for me.

What happened next illustrates the deceitfulness of Watson and Griffith. Since the order handed down on 3rd December 2007, it was known to them that judgment would be entered for me once the accounts were settled and hence they proceeded to avoid settling these accounts. A word is necessary about the accounts. These had last been prepared for the year ended 1998 by Price Waterhouse. As they indicated then, unless the partners had retired their indebtedness they were not prepared to provide audit services again. I have already illustrated how all my efforts to get either the deficit retired, or pending the end of the partnership the position verified by an audit failed, the two of them refusing.

What is often overlooked is that there were internal accounts of the partnership. These were prepared by an accounts staff that had 4 full time employees who produced monthly accounts using software sourced and set up by Watson. Every month the accounts were provided and handed to him as senior partner. Thus each partner had a fairly accurate idea of his/her indebtedness. Price Waterhouse, when they came to do the yearly audit, checked over things and applied rules such as depreciation and the various allowances allowed under the Income Tax Act to arrive at the true profit and loss position of the firm.

Shortly after the decision of the Court of Appeal on December 3rd 2007 the three of us met at my office in Belleville to go through all the books of the firms. Truthfully, the only books they should have needed were for the years 2003 and 2004 (I had stopped keeping separate books for the High Street partnership then as in 2003 I had forwarded to them the final accounts for 2002 which were prepared by Golde Maynard who had been working with the firm up to then for over 25 years). No objections had been made prior to 2007. To tidy up matters I had employed Carlisle Forde, then in private practice having for years been a partner with Ernst and Young, to do what PWC were no longer willing to do.

The meeting in 2007 broke up in acrimony. Watson and Griffith clearly had no intention of agreeing with anything, asking for more and more records, many of which they previously had, driving me to frustration, which I let them know in some choice language. Finally I said to them: "...there is nothing you are going to agree to and please appoint an accountant with whom mine would correspond." They appointed Irving Burrowes, ironically a former school mate of mine, who used to be a partner with KPMG, but was now in private practice.

The order of the Court of Appeal was important because it cut through the red tape of me having to establish that the money was owed by saying once the accounts were settled judgment be entered for me. I was to breathe a sigh of relief at the outcome, but that was not the end of my problems. Shortly in the New Year of 2008 after the initial meeting to try and settle the accounts had broken up, I tried to get the verbal order perfected to file in the Court of Appeal. Smith never responded to letters, or simply said he could not remember what the order was. Ivan Alert, who appeared in association with Haynes for Watson in the matter, Smith appearing for Griffith, could not remember also and all my attempts to have the registrar and or the president of the court perfect, it came to nothing. Then the president went on preretirement leave and I was in a bind.

As the ranking member of the court, Justice Williams was approached to perfect the order and he requested that the parties meet with him in his chambers without lawyers at first to try and resolve the issue, my father attending with me. There were several such meetings and nothing could be agreed upon. As the question was the settling of the accounts, both Carlisle Forde and Burrowes attended and were given narrow areas to work on. Then Burrowes was fired by Watson and Griffith (as he was to later tell me because he told them he could find nothing amiss with the accounts of Forde) and it was back to square one.

Watson and Griffith continued stalling that they are not litigators and not sure about the effect of the order which I remind was a consent order, so the lawyers were called back in. They were conveniently absent every time the meetings which were not official court dates due to be heard, until after a year, with his patience running thin, Justice Williams drafted the order and that was that. It took me fourteen months for a consent order issued in December of 2007 to be finally entered on February 19th 2009.

On April 30th of 2009 I made an application to the court for a ruling that pursuant to the order of December 3rd 2007 from the Court of Appeal, the accounts be settled as the parties had failed to agree on same. Madam Justice Crane Scott was assigned to hear the matter. She set about dealing with preliminary matters arising from the order of the Supreme Court when it was first heard on May 15th 2009. I was initially represented by Tariq Khan in association with Julie Harris, one of my associates at Cottle at the time. Not surprisingly Smith, who was representing Griffith, indulged in stalling tactics.

Despite the matter being brought on under a certificate of urgency when it first came on for hearing, he did not show up, sending a message that he was out of the island on holiday. This did not sit well with Madam Justice, who noted that neither he nor any of the defendants had bothered to show up, and Smith had not even had the courtesy of having a junior from his office attend with an excuse. Costs were awarded against them, which of course I have never actually recovered. The rules at the time did not allow for wasted costs to be awarded personally against the attorneys transgressing and causing the delay as it does today, and which the CCJ in 2015 to my glee awarded against Smith for his constant and unreasonable delaying tactics in another matter.

As it had become evident that neither of Watson or Griffith would agree to settle the accounts, Justice Crane Scott set the matter down for hearing and it first came on for hearing on June 2nd 2009. I was now being represented by my friend Eddie Hinkson and Julie Harris, while Smith continued to represent Griffith. The record showed that Leslie Haynes, in association with Ivan Alert, was representing Watson. Alert came on June 2nd 2009, but neither came back after that.

When the matter eventually began on June 2nd 2009, I'd had enough of Smith's antics. He had continued with his nonsensical submissions that I needed to have the accounts audited before we could proceed despite the consent order of the Court of Appeal of December 3rd 2007. After hearing in the morning it was adjourned for lunch and before Smith could leave, I approached him and started to address him, letting him know what species of animal he was. I stood to my full height and size and told him with all the anger my voice could muster that if not for the fact that there was a policeman stationed outside the court, he should be shot. I advanced towards him. It was never my intention to hit him, but I was pulled back by my father who was in court and who told me to "move away from Vernon, he is not worth it."

When the matter came back on for hearing later that day, as I was entering the court, a policeman on duty asked to search my bags. Julie objected that attorneys were not searched and said "why you don't search mine as well?" I was non-plussed at the whole thing, as I had never carried a weapon of any sort in my life. The young officer looked embarrassed, but apparently the jackass (Smith) had made a complaint to the registrar and the police that I had threatened to shoot him. Later that day after court I was approached by the Chief Marshal asking me what I had done to Smith that he was reporting this matter all over the place. I said to him that Smith is just a prime jackass, totally ignorant of the law except when it comes to looking for a technicality to delay a matter and was just grandstanding, because having delayed the matter for nearly four years it was finally going to be heard and bearing in mind the old saying 'when the facts are against you, you argue the Law and when the Law is against you, you argue the facts' he was in a hopeless situation because both the facts and law were against him, so he wanted out.

Smith subsequently wrote the registrar saying he had no choice but to withdraw from the matter as he had been abused and threatened with violence by the plaintiff. He made a song and dance, but as many attorneys have found amusing, my words to him were not an assault which any first year law student would have known. I recall relating the story to the then Deputy Dean of the Law Faculty Jeff Cumberbatch, and as I repeated the words his knees buckled and he contorted in laughter saying "Tuberville and Savage." As I said, first year law students studying the criminal law of assault would have been familiar with this eighteenth century case where it was held in the UK that a person charged with assault was not guilty of assault for saying to another if it were not sessions (court was sitting): "I would run you through with this sword." I have always believed this was above the intelligence of Smith to understand.

I have always been of the belief that Smith was looking for an excuse to get out of the case. Once all the legal issues had been resolved there was nothing to argue. Both Griffith and Watson jumped on the chance to say to the court that they needed time to hire new attorneys, with Griffith suggesting that persons in the profession were so frightened of crossing me they did not want to assist her. The question she should have asked was why it was that two attorneys, one with over thirty years at the bar and the other with forty, could not find representation. Justice Crane Scott declined their request for the matter to be adjourned, saying that what was before her would not be the subject of any intricate legal argument that attorneys of their call, even if they were not practicing litigators, could not handle.

Justice Crane Scott heard the matter often on days, full days that ran to 4 pm on afternoons, after the initial date of hearing on May 27th, June 2nd, 22nd, 23rd 29th, July 13th August 10th, 11th, 18th and 21st and September 10th, 11th and on the 17th when she gave her decisions. On these dates my former partners made some reasonable and several unreasonable requests with respect to the accounts, wishing further details provided. I used to state with exasperation to the court that many of these records being requested were already in their possession from when they were partners of the firm. They challenged everything imaginable, including practices that they were quite happy to live with when they were at the firm. Every single account in the firm was examined either in court or at the offices of Carlisle Forde pursuant to court orders. Julie Harris and my accountant Allison Brewster attended on my behalf. I had no desire to sit in a closeted room with either of them, as I was seething at the betrayal. For three years I had believed that they were genuine in their attempts to settle what was due from them.

Meetings were held, with each to separately go through each account under their name to establish the true status of them. It was clear by this time, that Griffith and Watson were desperately trying to reduce the amount that they would have been held liable to me for. At these meetings all that was due the firm including the deficit accounts in the name of Delvina Watson were painstakingly signed off by them as correct, and yet years later the courts have allowed Mrs. Watson to challenge that these monies were repaid. The attorney positing this argument was Vernon Smith, who had withdrawn in 2009, but in 2014 when I tried to execute the judgments, came back on record this time for Delvina Watson, and when it was pointed out that a previous court had determined this issue, he would say with a straight face that he was unaware of this. The transcript from the 14 days of hearing runs to over 400 pages, but despite all of this, when it was put to them that the figures as presented by Mr. Forde are correct, they refused to agree and as such Justice Crane Scott was forced to make a ruling.

It must be noted here some of the things that were said by both defendants. They first claimed that over-drawings did not mean they were indebted to me, and then Watson stood up in court and said he owed money to the clients, not to me; because he did not tell me repay the clients. He continued that I only did so to keep my good name and that of the firm and should simply have told them there was no money. As such he argued I could not recover it from him. I showed the transcript of his statement to a silk in the UK who, bemused, said if a solicitor in the UK had said that in open court he would not have gone home that night.

The final date of hearing was on September 11th and 6 days later on, on September 17th after 13 days of hearings, Justice Crane Scott delivered her ruling. I have never been able to express my gratitude to Justice Crane Scott for the patience she showed during the 13 days of hearings in systematically going through the tedium of Cottle Catford's accounts (especially when she had to chide me at my outbursts when more and more nonsense was being put forward by my partners in an attempt to delay the matter further). This did not involve any convoluted legal argument, but simply sifting out fact from fiction by two persons bent on delaying matters. That she was able to render her decision so soon, however you look at it, is a credit to her and also suggests that the stance of my partners was without merit. Her clear sentiments in a 25-page judgment that their behavior was unreasonable was one of the reasons I found it so ridiculous when the Court of Appeal, four years after the judgment, would dismiss their appeal, but allow my partners to benefit from this delay by letting all the loss for the interest that amounted over the years fall on me.

Justice Crane Scott's retirement from the bench in Barbados recently in 2015 to take up a position in the judiciary elsewhere in the

Caribbean is a sad loss, as many others have lauded her ability to cut to the heart of the matter. She will be sadly missed.

This is what she said in part of her judgment:

> "Against the background of the Court of Appeal Order and consistently throughout the course of the current hearing, both defendants have participated in the proceedings with a view to ultimately settling the accounts of the former partnership. Furthermore, at the outset when the Court embarked on hearing the current application, all parties had expressly confirmed that it was their understanding that in pursuance of the Court of Appeal Order, judgment would ultimately be entered for the Plaintiff for all amounts shown in the accounts of the former partnership to be owed by the First and Second Defendants.
>
> It having been accepted by all parties that the Plaintiff had by virtue of the Dissolution Agreement assumed responsibility for liquidating amounts owed to clients of the former partnership, it was also clearly understood at the outset that any amounts due to the former partnership by the First and Second Defendants would ultimately be due to the Plaintiff.
>
> The court is also satisfied that both Defendants have clearly accepted and have settled the updated account prepared by accountant, Mr. Carlyle Forde entitled 'Statement of Funds available at December 31st 2002 and funds received and paid after that date' which shows that the bank accounts of the former partnership were in the red and insufficient to enable the Plaintiff to settle the credit balances payable by the former partners to the former clients of the partnership.
>
> On September 11th 2009, both Defendants also accepted and confirmed to the Court that they had examined and settled the account entitled 'Schedule of the Clients of the Former

Partnership other than those shown on the Payments to Clients in 2003 and 2004' prepared by Mr. Carlyle Forde showing that an amount received by the Plaintiff of $1,333,000.00 being legal fees due to the former partnership, was applied by the Plaintiff in settling credit balances amounting to $1,333,071.90- payable by the former partnership to certain clients of the former partnership listed in the said account.

Following the examination by the Defendants of the said Schedule and their acceptance of the list of clients contained therein, the Court is satisfied that the Second Defendant (Watson my emphasis) have conceded that the issues of duplication and objections raised in his affidavit of September 11th 2009 have been explained to his satisfaction.

Given the considerable time and resources which this Court has devoted to hearing of this application in the expectation that the Defendants would, in good faith, have settled the accounts of the former partnership after all reasonable information had been provided to them by the Plaintiff, the Court is of the view that it cannot now be reasonable for the Defendants to refuse to settle the remaining portions of the former partnership accounts relating to their over drawings and essentially resile from, and frustrate the process for settlement of this suit which was agreed before the Court of Appeal on December 3rd 2007.

In the circumstances, the Court confirms and certifies that it is appropriate that the over-drawings of the First and Second Defendants shown in the relevant accounts prepared by Mr. Forde be brought into account and provide the basis for ascertaining the respective amounts due by them to the former partnership and consequently to the Plaintiff. As clearly contemplated by the Court of Appeal Order of December 3rd 2007, such accounts (including the partners' over-drawings) will also provide a basis on which judgment for the Plaintiff may be entered."

The judge then went on to state that judgment against the first defendant is entered in the amount of $441,576.00 and against the second in the amount of $661,541.00. At the end of 2002 the amount that was charged to Griffith was $1,224,784.18 and to Watson $1,316,566.83. For information the amount charged to me was $751,093.94, an amount long since repaid by the over $2,000,000 I injected into the firm, as my affidavits attest. This cumulative deficit with the overdrawn accounts was the nearly 4 million in deficits that I was faced with and for which I borrowed money to deal with. One of the greatest losses I have suffered is that it took 7 years after the partnership ended for a figure to be entered against my former partners which was much lower than the amount due from them at the beginning because various credits, primarily the amounts received from Kingsland in 2006, were taken into account.

What became evident during the 14 days of hearings, and this is clearly borne out in the transcripts of the evidence, is that the clear intention of the defendants was to attempt to reduce the amounts due from them by any means possible. The fees that were due to be credited to them were legitimate, but an argument arose over certain accounts that showed amounts due to clients that had not been on the books for in excess of twenty-five years. Many of these transactions stemmed from the bad Simmonds days and were left on the books at the time. It was clear over the years that as no one had ever come forward for these accounts that they were not in reality moneys due. Watson was the first to argue that these accounts had to be taken into account and written off as against the amounts due from the partners.

I lost my arguments with Carlisle Forde that this was a nonsensical argument. The over-drawings showed what each person had drawn and was charged to them; it was money actually received. How on earth could you now discount the amount due to be paid back by crediting some balances, many of which were on the books from long before I joined the firm? I found it particularly obnoxious that debit balances still in the accounts as attributable to the Simmons mess should now be used by Watson in particular, who used to call down every possible punishment for Simmons when he was bemoaning what he did to the firm, could now want to seek to utilize these amounts to reduce the deficits they owed. These had absolutely nothing to do with the money used by them as shown in their debit accounts. The effect of this is that it reduced the indebtedness that they were found liable for, and because I had paid money into the firm to cover the cash shortage. I eventually took the whole loss of in excess of $250,000. This matter which was already a nightmare was fast becoming as akin to the sword of Damocles over my neck.

It was to get worse. A line item of $78,000 approximately was disallowed on the basis that I could show no evidence that I had requested my former partners to incur these legal costs. This was one of the few fundamental disagreements I had with the judgment. Kingsland, of which I have written, continued to be embroiled in litigation and this time it was in Canada. I was forced to retain counsel to represent the interest of Cottle Catford, and it irked me that my former partners reaped the benefit of their share of the fee from Kingsland, but I alone had to foot the legal bill for defending on action brought as a result of that work.

The ludicrousness of what went on was that receipts prepared by Smith alleging that the money owed by Delvina Watson appeared on the official court file (unauthorised, as Crane Scott, the then Registrar, confirmed in writing) in settlement of her debt for 151/152 were added to the amount that they owed. Thus money that the Watsons spent, Joyce now found herself having to be responsible for. When this was happening I was chided by the judge for my outburst in court to Griffith: "You stupid woman can't you see what he is doing to you?" It is Carlisle Forde who best summed it up to me. He said: "Philip,

Watson played Joyce and got her to support him because whereas both of you felt she was an idiot, you told her so, but he courted her to his side." Nothing could be truer, as she never expected him to up and leave like he did.

Shortly before Justice Crane Scott gave her judgment, in anticipation of the court finding in my favour, Julie Harris painstakingly made an application for a prejudgment Mareva against the two defendants. It was heard before Justice Cornelius finally on September 9th 2009, who not only ruled that she would not hear it *ex parte*, but then subsequently refused to grant it on the ground she did not believe the defendants would dissipate their assets (see Appendices Seven and Eight).

I have since had to answer more than one query from attorneys as to why I never applied for one and there was general disbelief when I said I had. I have appeared before Justice Cornelius on more than one occasion since Watson absconded without payment and have taken the opportunity wherever possible to point out that he is no longer here, but as I was to find out, few people have genuinely understood far less believed that this man in effect was a closet thief, and thus while I did eventually get my Mareva in 2013 against him and Griffith, it was more a case of bolting the door after the horse had run.

Hardly had Justice Crane Scott finished delivering her judgment than Watson was on his feet delivering verbal notice of his intention to appeal to the Court of Appeal. My horror story continued with that institution.

The Death of a Friend

MONDAY OCTOBER 15th 2007 will be etched in my memory forever, like the date of 9/11 for much of the world, or that day in April of 1970 when men walked on the moon. Many Barbadians recall what they were doing when news of the passing while in office of three prime ministers broke. For me news of the totally unexpected death from natural causes of my great friend and confidante Stephen Alleyne on that October day stunned me and left me in my own private grief, as I was halfway around the world.

Anyone who lives to adulthood will with some frequency come face to face with death at some time. Most times it usually occurs when one has to say goodbye to others, be it their friends or relatives who have run the good course and lived a long life. Young colleagues such as Peaches, the young Jamaican law student in my class who lost her battle with epilepsy while we were at first year at NMLS in 1984, and Piano, a gifted young Jamaican student, made you question why them and not you. Piano met his death in a tragic vehicular accident shortly before he was due to be called to the bar, succumbing early to the fate that will befall us all. Their passing shocked me into the reality that life is precious and short. Both being colleagues about to embark on a career after years of toil, it made me stop and think about life and question whether it was indeed fair.

Before Stephen's death I had lost class colleagues like Reuben Bayley, Llewellyn Rock, another all-round sportsman and academic like Reuben who died tragically a few days after his first child was born in the early 90s, and for me the greatest personal loss before Stephen was on New Year's Day in 1994 when I lost the closest thing to a sister I ever had, my trusted friend Barenda Brewster, who lost her eight year battle after being diagnosed with lupus in 1986.

Stephen's death not only knocked the physical wind out of me, but as at the time he was the only person who knew the full extent of the problems I was facing at Cottle, my one impartial support system disappeared in one fell swoop. Being literally halfway around the world in Singapore attending a conference of the International Bar Association when I received a call at about 4 pm my time — which was 4 am Barbados time — I was left virtually on my own. As I understand the grieving process, persons tend to gather at the home or place the deceased used to frequent to remember them. I could not participate in this.

On that fateful day my wife called me, and on reflection her voice was strange, but I had no idea of the bombshell she would release. She asked where I was, and I stated that I was just about to attend the presentation being made Edmund Hinkson at the conference centre.

She requested that I sit and then told me that my friend Roland Holder had just called for me and she advised him that I was overseas. I thought this was very strange. Why would Roland be calling at 4 am? Then I thought, maybe his father Reverend Holder who was in ICU when I had left home had passed. Beverley then sighed said there was no other way to tell me this, but Roland was calling to say that my friend Stephen had died. She stressed friend, because my brother is also named Stephen. I asked her "what nonsense are you saying?" and she repeated: "Stephen has died. It is not a joke."

That was my first reaction, she said, as I was half asleep when

I answered the phone. But Roland said it was no joke and that she should call me, as he would not like me to hear it for the first time when it became public.

After Beverley hung up I thought about it and called her back to see if it was true, as for the second time I had not recognized her voice and was wondering if it was a prank, the first being when she called me after the birth of our first child Carissa when she sounded so spaced out. I later learnt it was from the epidural she had been given, that it took her sister coming on the phone to confirm the good news then. This time I was hoping for a hoax, but Beverley said no, it was true. After speaking to her I next called Orson Simpson, who subsequently told people that his wife was awakened and answered the phone and said Philip was on the line babbling something about Stephen Alleyne dying. He had not heard, but soon called me back to confirm it.

My next call was to Julie Harris. I have always had great fondness for Julie from the time she came to Cottle around the year 2001 to do her in-service training there. She had worked closely with Stephen on secondment from Cottle as in-house counsel to World Cup Barbados in the lead up to the hosting of Cricket World Cup successfully staged just months before.

She was at the time of his death at home, away from the office, having just given birth to her first child. Her mother answered the phone and after I told her the devastating news she asked what type of accident it was before calling Julie to the phone. Neither could comprehend that it was as a result of natural causes, for at 47 he was a relatively young man. Julie herself called me back on more than one occasion to confirm what I was saying, as it had not become public knowledge in Barbados until the news was broken just after 6 am.

In Singapore I informed Eddie's wife Beverley, who was travelling with him, of the news that I had just received and asked her not to tell Eddie until his presentation had finished so that he was not distracted, and then left the conference centre to walk about and clear my head.

I believe I walked the streets for two or three hours, by which time Beverley was frantically trying to reach any other Barbadians that she learnt were in Singapore to find me, as she could not reach me. I had turned my phone off and just walked and when I returned to my hotel Eddie and Beverley were waiting for me in the lobby. We chatted briefly. I told them I would be okay and retired to my room at about 8 pm local time. In my hand were two new cellphones that I did not recall buying, and which I took over two years before using.

That night for me was of course the day in Barbados I would never forget as my cell would not stop ringing. Not many people knew I was out of the island. Those who did contacted me at my hotel and the calls were many and constant. Many people called to find out how I was doing, which to be frank was not good, but as bad as I felt, it could be in no comparison to his family, especially his wife Yolanda, whom I had known since she came over to Harrison College in Sixth Form in the late 70s, and his young children. I received calls from all over the world, some expressing incredulity and some simply calling for confirmation of the bad news. An attorney from Jamaica who was intimately involved in the Cricket World Cup and as such worked closely with Stephen called me to say: "Philip I am hearing rumours of a disturbing nature and I have said to people that if one man will know it has to be you, and I am calling for you to give it to me straight." I said, "Sadly, it is true."

Among the calls was one from June King, one of Yolanda's close personal friends, who said Yolanda wished to speak to me and gave me a cell number to call her on. I believe my number had been passed on by Marguerite Knight Williams, who I had also called with news of Stephen's death.

When June called I told her I had not even bothered to try to call the house, as I could imagine what was going on. I shortly after called Yolanda. Truthfully, I can't recall much of what we talked about because we both were very upset, although my memory was that she was more composed than I. I did tell her that first thing the next morning I would be making arrangements to come home.

After a fitful few hours of sleep, I left the hotel early for the nearest British Airways office to make arrangements to return home as soon as possible. Though this was before the days when airlines delighted in charging you an arm and a length for the slightest change you made to your reservation, I was not looking forward to getting this done. Singapore is about a twelve hour flight from London and then you have another eight-hour journey.

On the flight out, after disembarking and making my way to immigration and customs, there was a constant message over the intercom for travelers arriving from London and who were transiting to Sydney Australia to make this turn. I was perplexed, wondering who in their right mind after such a journey would get back on another flight of not much shorter duration than the one I had just finished, but then remembered an occasion when chatting with Sir Gary Sobers, when he said he always liked to travel to Australia direct, no breaks, and I said "Boy you really were great."

I presented at the British Airways office in Singapore and explained why I had come, and was astounded to learn from them that their Barbados office had already sent a message that I most probably would be coming in to seek a change, and they should give me as much help as I needed. The magnitude of his death at home I had not appreciated, as I was not there, but I was to learn of it when I returned.

After confirming that I could leave that night, I went back to the hotel, called Eddie and told him I was leaving, and got things ready to leave. My flight to London was one of the most difficult I have ever endured. On arrival on board I was greeted with raised eyebrows, as it was the same crew who took me out and who were returning after their 48 hour rest period and were surprised I was going back so soon. I told them the reason and they did check in on me several times to see that I was okay. I could neither sleep nor pay attention to the movies.

I was booked straight through to Barbados, landing at Heathrow early enough to make the transfer by coach to Gatwick to get the daily flight to Barbados.

As I have told many people, after arriving in Heathrow I was shattered, as it had now been virtually two sleepless nights, and while I was making my way to the coach depot, I could hear Stephen saying to me: "Philip what is the matter with you? Where do you think you are going? There is nothing you can do. Try and go and get some rest." It was typical of Stephen; always thinking of someone else's welfare. Not for the first time, I listened to his sage advice and booked a room in the Gatwick Hilton, and after informing one of Stephen's brothers, Jeremey I think it was, that my return would be delayed by another 24 hours, I just crashed on the bed and let nature take its course.

I returned to Barbados on the 19th and only then fully appreciated what his death had meant. There were dozens of calls to my office and requests from CBC and the local newspapers for my comments on his death, but by then I think the initial shock had begun to wane and I did not think there was much purpose in me saying anything. By then I was aware that his family had asked me to say a few words at his funeral, which was fittingly to be held at Kensington which he had been so instrumental in redeveloping, and which he now would not see in all its splendor. I really would do a disservice now to try to change my immediate thoughts at the time, and so I am going to simply reproduce here my eulogy of the 22nd October 2007.

Before his funeral Stephen was brought to his home away from home at Bank Hall, the home ground of the great Empire Cricket Club with whom he had a lifelong relationship. That Monday afternoon hundreds, if not thousands, streamed through the gates of that hallowed ground to pay their respects—people from all walks of life. It was then on to Kensington the next day, and I was very nervous in addressing one of the largest gatherings ever for a funeral in Barbados. It certainly was only exceeded by the turnout for the former Prime

Minister David Thompson Q.C., and as I was able to tell his eulogist, another friend from campus, Brian Clarke Q.C., I fully appreciated the emotions he was going through in delivering a tribute to his dear friend. These were my thoughts. I know many of them would have embarrassed Stephen, but as I was delivering them I said to myself: "Sorry buddy, but you can't stop me now."

I was amazed in the days after the funeral at the number of persons who spoke to me about the eulogy. Several asked for copies, which I gladly provided, but by far the reaction I remember the most was one that I received in Atlanta a couple of weeks later when I answered the phone at a friend's house and the caller knew it was not the resident of the house, but recognized the Bajan accent and enquired who I was. When I gave my name he said "You are the guy who gave Alleyne's eulogy. I listened over the internet up here..." and he went on to compliment me on it.

By far however to me the best compliment I got was from a mutual friend, Richard Jeffers in Canada, who said "Philip if I had received such a sendoff I would have got up and shook your hand." His words sadly could never be acted on, but there were so many times in the ensuing eight years that I wished they could.

AN APPRECIATION FOR A GREAT INNINGS

As I sat here listening to Rawle speak so glowingly of my friend it is akin to waiting for one's turn to bat. I could hear my friend talking to me and saying: *"Philip you coming early today. The pace hot! You sure you can handle this? Look me down at the other end. Try and nudge one and I will take over."* It then dawned on me that I was merely dreaming, for I would never hear those reassuring utterances again. Yes, the pace hot, but after surviving this last week, Bird, I feel I could handle you and all at this time.

When I got the news that so shook Barbados it was 4:00 in the afternoon where I was and 4:00 am in Barbados. Cable & Wireless could probably attest to the fact that there was unusual usage of the telephone system at that hour of the morning. Roland Holder had called, but I was away and it was left to my wife to break the news. I missed her first call and was in the process of calling when she rang again. On reflection, her tone was strange, but it gave no foreboding of what was to come. She inquired about what I was doing and I replied that I was just getting ready to attend Eddie's presentation when she said Roland had called. I frowned because knowing that it was four in the morning, I thought, maybe, because of the 14 hour flight, I was not reachable when he had called at what would have been an expected time. Then I thought, maybe he was advising of a personal tragedy at that early hour of the morning. However, Beverley, clearly searching for words, sighed, took a deep breath and said to me with a sigh *"Philip, there is no other way to tell you this... but your friend... Stephen Alleyne... has died."*

It is an understatement to say I was stunned and for the second time in my adult life I was reduced to tears. The other time was when an equally dear friend, Barenda Brewster, died at an even tragically younger age. For me, and I suspect for many others here, it will be one of those moments indelibly etched in one's mind as to what you were doing at the time, forever akin to September 11th, or more pertinently for Barbadians, when one heard news of the passing of Tom Adams and Errol Barrow. Even now as I begin to put together my thoughts to write this tribute some 30,000 feet above the ocean on my way back to London, my eyes are again filled with tears as I relive some of the memories that Stephen and I shared during the course of our life-long friendship. In the words of Julius Caesar, *'he was my friend, faithful and just to me.'*

That friendship started at the Merrivale Preparatory School—Mrs. Carrington's School—of which Stephen is undoubtedly its most celebrated student, and continued without interruption until last week. That friendship and that bond strengthened over the last decade as I had a first mate's seat in the ship of life captained by Stephen. I would not want to refer to myself as the co-pilot, as that would somehow suggest we were equals in ability. That journey has taught me many lessons which I hope to be able to illustrate to you as I attempt the impossible in the few minutes allotted—to pay tribute to a scholar, a confidante, a gentleman, but above all a friend. To borrow a phrase, "a Proper Man", who touched all whom he came into contact with.

It is my hope that by the time I have finished we who are left can strive to take up the mantle that he bore so manfully and that I, in some small way even if it is only a passing grade, have conveyed to you the stature of Stephen Mark Clark Alleyne.

My first abiding memory of Stephen was trying to console him at primary school. He was in detention because, to put it in Bajan parlance, he had taken a big rock to

Andrew Sealy's head. Even then at that youthful stage of his life, Stephen was practicing the diplomatic skills he later became so famous for by trying to convince Andrew that there was "*...no need to go to teacher because there was only a little blood coming.*" Mind you, in today's AIDS conscious society, the flow would have created panic, but Stephen was not daunted at the thought of trying to convince Mrs. Carrington otherwise.

Andrew, however, was not buying it and went to teacher. I remember Mrs. Carrington's admonishment, and I can still feel the lashes from that much vaunted strap that many a recipient had to fetch before it was administered to them. As I look around I see several, including myself, here today who have tasted that strap and we would all probably testify that we are all the better for having done so. "*I would have thought better of you Stephen,*" he was told. What probably hurt him more, however, was what he was facing because all he said to me was, "*I still have to go home.*" Home to Charles and Hazel, and after her death, Austin, who all helped mould him into the man he was to become.

I mention this incident simply to illustrate that Stephen was a typical boy at school. Andrew, another great friend of ours, bore no ill will to him, although, given that it was completely out of character for Stephen and as a defense counsel, I would be searching for some act of provocation on Andrew's part. Only yesterday on Empire's pasture Andrew was proudly pointing to the impact zone. Legacy Stephen was starting to prepare already.

Stephen went on to Harrison College where he excelled

both in the classroom and on the field of play, winning in 1978 an Island Scholarship in Maths and English. Now, imagine that—Maths and English. What a combination! Most people who have a command of English cannot figure out Maths, and most people who can do Maths are lost in the quagmire that English may seem, but Stephen won a scholarship in them both.

Shortly after he entered Harrison's he lost his mother Hazel, which is my second earliest memory of him—attending her funeral some 37 years ago in the company of my mother who was trying to explain to a wide-eyed youngster what was going on. I suspect many mothers are here today doing similarly to their charges.

Stephen was the year ahead of me at school and, as all of us know, one tends to remain with one's year in those formative years and so, during school, while friends, we were not bosom buddies. That honour went to Richard Jeffers, whom I know is devastated by Stephen's early departure and pained by the fact that he has been unable to return from his outpost in Canada to be with us this afternoon.

Our friendship continued to grow throughout school because, as Stephen said while speaking at my wedding, we knew one another well because we played on the same cricket team, firstly that winning 1974 Ronald Tree Cup team captained by another of his early childhood friends, Curtis Cephas Campbell. It was, however, in opposition on the cricket field that Stephen taught me one of my early lessons in life.

We were opposing captains in a set match when he threw

the ball to another great friend of ours, Allan Smith, who has returned from London to be with us today. Now Allan was not known as a bowler, but had been barracking from the time I arrived at the wicket that he could get me out because I could not play a short ball. Barracking, known today as 'sledging', or an exercise in mental disintegration at the higher level today, but at that time it was just good-natured ribbing—among schoolboy friends.

Along came the short ball as predicted, and I gloved it and was caught. Allan was mockingly running down the wicket and something in me refused to walk, no doubt embarrassment that Allan had got me out in the manner he had been proclaiming he would to all and sundry. The umpire was some junior boy from the house of which I was captain, and so there was little likelihood of that dreaded finger coming up, so I stayed.

I can still picture and hear Allan saying *"Man, Philip Nicholls, you know you out. Leff bout here!"* I would not. Not my finest hour, I must admit. Stephen said not a word. Even when I tried to convince him (already starting to practice as a lawyer) that the hand was not holding the bat at the time the ball hit the glove and so I was not out, he was indifferent, disinterested in what I was saying. Not a word. Neither did he curse me as some of the others were already doing (Alan of course not stooping so low), and in fact insisted that the cursing stop. All he said was *"Leave him!"* Needless to say the rest of my time out on that field that afternoon was miserable and, as I was to discover, more than the embarrassment of falling to Allan.

The next day I sought Stephen out and apologized to

him and admitted that I was out. His reply was *"Just don't let it happen again. If it does you have not learnt anything! Your greater sin was not in not walking, but the incredible and unfair pressure that you put on that youngster who was umpiring. Because all you were concerned about were your selfish desires."* I am happy to report that it never happened again, but I can see him smiling now and saying, *"Mate that had nothing to do with me. You were never good enough to last long enough where you would have the opportunity of not walking."* Typically, he took no credit, for he was never one to take any credit for achievements that were rightfully all of his own doing.

Some 20 years after that incident I was umpiring a local game in which Stephen opened the batting for the club he loved so much, and where such devastation at his passing was so evident yesterday, but at the same time the abiding love and respect that all the members, young and old, had for him. From the first over the opposition were chirping, *"Well, no decisions for us today. They on the board together, they share a flat, so fellas, we got to hit the stumps and hope Lumpy doesn't call a no ball."*

Well, as fate would have it, an appeal was made against Stephen and I had to make the decision. I was genuinely not sure if he had hit it, and was about to say not out when I noticed that he had turned and departed. After the game I thanked Stephen for helping me out and all he said was, *"Remember how you felt when you did not walk all those years ago at school? Well, I would have felt the same way and to besides you are my friend and for me not to walk when I knew I was out would have exposed you to ridicule, because those fellas out there would never have believed that your decision was based on how you saw it, rather than friendship. Friends do not do it... Right! Payback time! Drinks on you! Barman, the umpire's fees for Mr. Nicholls he donating to the bar for the fellas! I doing his job, so at least I can get some benefit."*

That concern for his friends and loyalty to them I am sure many of us here this afternoon can attest to. His sense of loyalty was acute. In the immediate post short era of the BCA Board there was a phenomenon known as 'the early morning telephone call' that some of us were subjected to. I remember discussing these with Stephen and expressing my unease at the conversations. He simply said, *"Philip this is all you have to say: Cammie is the captain of this team and as long as I am on it I see my duty as being to support him especially in areas he may be weak and to help him, as we working for Barbados cricket. My calls dun long time ago,"* he said. *"Try it!"*

He was very much a believer in the team concept, as the Team Barbados that he so masterfully led into the World Cup is testimony to. It thus hurt him to hear criticisms from members of his own board that he was unilateral or stifled discussion. I can say without fear of contradiction that nothing was further from the truth. In fact, he used to drive me to frustration in his desire to hear the other man's point of view, even though it may have been arrant nonsense and, when I fumed, would always chide me that as a lawyer I should know better.

Few of us can recall Stephen being angry about anything. His two mottos were "Take it easy" and "If you fail to prepare, prepare to fail." I, along with about a dozen others, was witness to an angry outburst from him that has gone down in folklore... We were discussing the financing for the redevelopment of the Mitchie Hewitt Stand. The financial terms of the loan repayment were right up Stephen's area of expertise and, as various statements were being made, he took out his calculator and started making his own calculations. It was clear from the discussions that he was extremely skeptical about what was being presented. As the discussion became more animated, I am loathe to say, Stephen snapped but for the first and only time in my life that I am aware of at the board level. He angrily declared that his concerns which were backed by his actuarial training were being trivialised and he was not getting any answers to the legitimate questions he was putting on the table. There was stunned silence. The meeting ended.

What is not generally known is that after the meeting Stephen phoned me, clearly disturbed, not about the numbers that so alarmed him, but by his behaviour. He was tormented because he felt that he had disrespected the chair by raising his voice. All he said was, *"the Chair, the Chair, the Chair is paramount even above any views that others may have, correct as they may have been. I must apologise to the chair!"* My response was: *"Apologize? You are something else... The Chair want busing, if you ask me."*

This philosophy re the chair guided him during his time in the chair. Every person must be given the opportunity to speak, but the paramouncy of the chair must be respected. I can assure you that friendship played no part in his rulings. I left a meeting in a huff and puff because he asked me to withdraw a remark that I had made. I was not prepared to and frankly I thought he needed certifying. After stewing for about a week I raised it with him and he explained that he felt my remark, however much I was provoked, and believe me I was provoked, was disruptive and that if he had allowed it to stand the meeting would have degenerated. Stephen said to me, *"Philip this is not about friendship. It is about principle."* By the same token, even though I indicated to him that he not insist that an offensive remark made to me be withdrawn, he refused to stand down on his insistence that it be withdrawn and immediately adjourned the meeting when neither the remark nor the individual making the remark had left the meeting despite being asked so to do.

It is fair to say that the nearly six years while he was president and I secretary of the BCA can be regarded as some of the more turbulent times of the association. This worried him and sometimes he felt he had failed because nothing he did seemed to lessen the acrimony of meetings. In the end I said to him, *"Stephen there is nothing more that you can do that will make a difference."* For as others have often said, Stephen was a victim of what can be termed 'Generation Jealousy.'

On occasions he was tempted to give up the leadership, but he would always rise above the challenges he encountered and rededicate himself to the cause of Barbados cricket.

Stephen's resolve, however, was severely tested in the days leading up to the last BCA election that he contested in 2005. There was a sustained and vicious campaign amongst certain sections of the membership of the BCA, who should have known better, to have him replaced. He never publicly vocalized his feelings, but in comments he made to me over the last couple of months about the BCA, it was apparent that this period was one of the darkest in his life.

The Sunday before that last election was particularly difficult for him. We met all day in my office. In true form, he put everything on the table and methodically went through the pros and cons with respect to his position as BCA president and CEO of World Cup Barbados. Even in the face of the rancor and harsh criticism which he endured during his tenure as the head of the BCA, his gentlemanly qualities superseded personal hurt and disappointment. He never uttered a harsh word about his critics. I uttered several during that meeting, but all he would tell me is: "cool it."

He was not driven by self-interest or personal aggrandizement. He remained committed to his ideals in the interest of cricket, his club and his country Barbados, but like any human being, he was stung and hurt by those attacks not because they were being made against him, but because they had been made against his wife, the woman that he loved, in an attempt to pull him down. He just could not believe that she would be the subject of such attacks for simply practicing her profession.

Stephen then stunned me while in my office by leaning back in his chair and saying reflectively that if he was forced to choose between being CEO of World Cup Barbados and president of the BCA, he would give up being the CEO. For the second time I thought he wanted certifying, but he explained that there was a structure in place at World Cup Barbados and that he had an excellent team which he was confident could deliver, whether he was there as CEO or not. His concern was for West Indies cricket, and he could not serve on the West Indies Cricket Board unless he was on the BCA Board. He felt that he could make a greater contribution on the West Indies Cricket Board to the development of cricket throughout the region.

I never felt in our conversation that he was blowing his own trumpet, and as Dr. Ali Bacher has said in his tribute, he was the right man for the job. It was only us here that could not or would not see that the attendant confusion that has reigned in West Indies Cricket since his removal from the board shows what consequences the naked and selfish ambition of a few have caused this region. This drive for what was best for West Indies cricket characterized his approach to the staging of the World Cup, for he always argued that anything Barbados could come up with or develop for the hosting of the games that would benefit the other territories be shared with them as a matter of course.

The last email that I ever received from him was on the subject of West Indies cricket. Though short, it sums up the stature of this man tellingly.

It is a tragedy that, after all his hard work, fate would determine that the first time that this wonderful ground is brimming with people since the ICC Cricket World Cup Final is for his funeral. We talked long about what would happen to Kensington… about how it would be used. We are here today in this magnificent stadium and while one may not be able to refer to it as the house that Alleyne built, like how the Yankees refer to their stadium as the house that Babe Ruth built, it is no doubt that this building is here because of the untiring efforts of Stephen and we the members of the BCA owe it to his memory to ensure that, without further delay and acrimony, we settle all outstanding issues as to its future management so that he can rest in peace, as I know these past six months of uncertainty over the future management of Kensington have disappointed him.

As you know, my direct association with Kensington goes back longer than Stephen as a member of Pickwick. Having overseen the redevelopment of this ground which necessitated the removal of Pickwick, he was saddened at the hardships the club faced because of the non-payment of the compensation it was entitled to. He offered, on more than one occasion, to meet with the club members directly, but I indicated to him that our problems were not of his doing. In his own way he tried to ensure wherever possible as much support as could be given to the club from World Cup Barbados would be given, and typically did not reveal this when others blew their trumpet as having orchestrated it. As I told him more than once, Pickwick's history may judge me unkindly because of my reliance on his assurances when we were negotiating with respect to the club. In my defence all I would say is that at all times I was dealing with a gentleman, and thus did not feel it necessary to invoke the saying 'put it in writing'.

Many would have paid glowing tributes to my

honourable friend over the last week, and sometimes you might question whether he was *really* that close to being a perfect gentleman. Nearly all of us will agree that he displayed such gentlemanly and highly professional qualities at all times. That is something he learnt from his late father. The day after any BCA election Mr. Alleyne would be on the phone expressing regret at disturbing you so early (a welcome early morning phone call, I may add) but needing to express his gratitude for your support of Stephen. I have never met a man who was prouder of the achievements of all his children than Charles Alleyne, and the only comfort I can find in this sad occasion is that he predeceased him and is not here to bear this tragedy with us.

Stephen followed in his footsteps. He always prefaced the start of any telephone conversation initiated by him with one of these phrases. "Do you have a minute… or a moment for me…. or is it convenient?' As my colleague Ms. Julie Harris, whom I must thank for editing several drafts of this tribute, has said that during her six month stint at World Cup as the Finals drew near, everyone was up to their eyeballs in work, but Stephen's manner of approach meant that you always made time to entertain him. What impressed her most, however, was his willingness to listen to and respect the views of anyone, however young and junior they might be to him.

I would say the only ungentlemanly thing that Stephen has done in his life is in the manner in which he left us and as we all know that was beyond his control.

Stephen was a scholar, a man of outstanding intellect

and acumen, and one who was as at ease with royalty as with the common man. I would think that if he was in a room there was a more than even chance that he was the most brilliant individual in the room, but you would never know it from the way he interacted with people. On my return to the island on Saturday, I was met by that Dean of the Red Caps at the airport, Blackie, who simply bowed his head and said, "A proper man gone." He then proceeded to extol the virtues of Stephen to all who cared to listen, local and foreign.

It would still continue to amaze me in conversation with Stephen in public how all manner of people from all walks of life would try to catch his eye and get an acknowledgment and he would do so without fail, whether by a blink of an eye, the raise of his eyebrow, or a wave of his hand.

He was fully aware of his responsibilities as one of the generation of post-independence Barbadians who benefited from the toil of our forefathers that we needed to give back to our people. His love was cricket and through it he strived to give back to Barbados what it had given to him.

As a scholar he knew the history of our game and of our greats, and hence the concept to him or in today's marketing jargon, the brand of the Legends grew. It always mystified him why others seemed at the time to resent the position of the Legends in Barbados and indeed West Indies cricket. He felt these men had given to this great game as well as to this country for little, since there were no financial rewards when the majority of them had played. They had put this little nation on the map and, therefore, we who may be better equipped because of our training needed to ensure that they got recognition for what they had done.

I remember one day after a day's play in a test match at Kensington, he pulled me aside and said, "Philip look at that: Gary, Wes, Charlie, Seymour, Cammie, David, Prof, Desmond, Everton, Joel, Clyde, Clive, Gordon, Lance, Malcolm and Peter round a bar having a drink and we two fellas who not fit to lace their boots up here. And we don't even have to pay for the drinks! You know, men pay hundreds, sometimes thousands of pounds, to be in a room to hear these fellas speak and hope that they may pass them on the way out of the room and catch their eye and yet we spend time round a table arguing about whether Seymour attends enough practice games to pick a team!" He sucked his teeth, then he added: "Man, Seymour could watch a man put on his gloves and tell whether he could bat!" (Seymour had a special place in his heart. I think it stemmed from the fact that both of us were at primary school with his daughters and we used to report excitedly to the other if we had seen him when he dropped them to school.) And then with that mischievous look in his eye he gave this belly full of a laugh, looked at me and continued. "At least he gave you the benefit of the doubt because he let you face a ball in the nets at Kolij before calling out, next man, come quick!"

He appreciated the value of these men and I believe they likewise appreciated him. In fact, one of my proudest moments was when I was introduced to Sir Conrad Hunte for the first time by Stephen's father at that Barclays

Terrace House that is a font of and repository for much wisdom. Mr. Alleyne introduced me to Sir Conrad with these words: "Conrad, this is Philip Nicholls, a dear friend of Stephen's." Sir Conrad shook my hand and with that beaming and infectious smile we all know he said to me: "Any friend of Stephen's must be a friend of mine."

But I have spoken of Stephen primarily from a cricketing perspective. There was so much more as you have heard or will hear about this man. I venture to say that he is today one of the most recognizable Barbadians because of the staging of the World Cup in Barbados. This was an incredible achievement for one so young, for he was neither sporting star nor politician. But his guiding of Barbados to be awarded and then to stage the third biggest Sporting Spectacle in the World was not only a huge undertaking, but one that Stephen approached with his usual methodical and meticulous self. Conceptualise this: the finals have previously been held in London, Melbourne, Karachi, Bombay, Johannesburg. Those cities have districts bigger than Barbados. In fact we are so tiny that it is said that 'Barbados' was the venue, not 'Bridgetown'. We have this man to be grateful to for the pride this national achievement has brought to Barbados.

I had the honour of leading the legal team with respect to putting together Barbados' bid and then the subsequent matters following the awarding of the matches. I thought one day that I had headaches until I went to a meeting at World Cup headquarters some three years ago and it dawned on me that while I might be focused on one area and knew its problems inside out, Stephen had to have the macro view of the whole project and still have the intimate knowledge of every aspect of the preparation. I honestly do not know how he did it. The financial data that he had to sift through was in itself enough to make any sane person mad, yet Stephen was on top of it. But then he had a love affair with numbers… that was his profession. Law was not. But I say unreservedly and have said so more than once that I would have hated him to be my opponent in any legal jousting. On several occasions when dealing with legal problems unrelated to the World Cup I have run them by Stephen and have received more pertinent and constructive comments than from some of my colleagues at the bar.

About a month ago I attended a meeting with him and others at Kensington. In my company was a young research student who did not know Stephen, as she is not a Barbadian and not a follower of cricket. So she presents her research and Stephen begins to probe and follow up with questions which I have seen too often before. When we left, she said to me: "Mr. Nicholls you did not tell me that Mr. Alleyne was a lawyer too!" She too, though she only met him once, feels a sense of loss by his death.

He was never too busy for his friends. Even though he was extremely busy, he still found time to assist me with some personal challenges that I have had recently. As the hosting of World Cup drew nearer I would shy away from speaking to him about them only to get a call from him asking for a report and chiding me for not keeping to the plan of action that we had settled on.

Unlike many, I was also to know Stephen privately. He

loved his family dearly, and Ayanna was the apple of his eye. About three weeks ago he called me up to say he is taking Ayanna to the Drive-In and had told her she can bring three friends and she wanted Carissa, my eldest daughter, to come. There was silence on my part. He asked me what the problem was. I said, "I trying to conceptualise you, Stephen Alleyne. Can you manage three young girls in the Drive-In? I feel that at the last moment you going to remember a meeting and Yolanda will have to step in." He said, "Listen, the name of the picture is 'Daddy Day Care' and while I may be asleep within the first thirty minutes it is an important process of being with your children that you visit the Drive-In." He continued, "I am a man of many talents. So taking my daughter to the Drive-In should be possible. I am not sure about you, though. You need to try it." So Ayanna we have a date some time in the not too distant future. Carissa who is here is going to keep reminding me.

He then proceeded to talk about Ayanna, saying that the other day he had gone somewhere with her and was hailed as usual by several persons. He said Ayanna said to him "Daddy, you like you know everybody in Barbados." It was evident from his voice that this filled him with great pride. And so little Ayanna and your new sister Tyra, I say to you today that though your Daddy did not know everybody in Barbados, surely everybody in Barbados knew him.

We his friends and family will all now be there with you in what must seem a very lonely time. Ayanna you have a new sister and fate has decreed that she will not have the opportunity to learn at all from him as you have already begun learning. But we will have to in our own small way step up to the plate and fill in as best as we can. Stephen and Yolanda did me the honour of asking me to be your godfather and I want to say publicly there will always be a place in my home for you and your sister.

And so dear friend, the time has come for me to say goodbye. I don't know when I will see you again, but I am sure whenever that is, you will have made whatever preparations you have deemed necessary to accommodate me. I am taking notes of what has been said and by whom, because I know your first greeting to me will be: *'Report. What has been going on? You know I like notes, so let me see yours.'*

It was a short innings, but it was too sweet, akin to the 43 Sir Gary made against Australia on this very ground and that unforgettable 48 that was made here one Thursday afternoon way back in 1974 by Lawrence Yagga Rowe that so enthralled him and all who saw it at the time. Though numerically of that number the worth of his innings was like the triple century that both of those players were to make in their careers. It can only be that He who knows best has determined that Stephen's energy and talents are needed elsewhere and has called him home. And so as I bid farewell I would ask that when he takes his exit you accord him the traditional send-off that a returning player to the pavilion receives on these grounds and in doing so salute a true son of this soil.

To Yolanda, Auntie Austin, David, Jeremy and Lisa and to all his extended family, I extend from my family and indeed the family of Barbadians our deepest sympathy at what is not only your personal loss but the loss of a nation. Gone he may be, but his legacy will live forever!

May he rest in peace.

16

Final Resting Place

IN THE MIDDLE of 2004 it was necessary once again to uproot stumps and find another home. After extensive environmental tests there was enough evidence that the air quality in the building at Warrens were the firm had relocated to from High Street was having an effect on the female staff, and so I had to relocate. The move was to 2nd Avenue, Belleville, Alphonso House, and this turned out to be the final resting place of Cottle Catford. The death occurred on October 31st 2009, but the funeral still has not taken place because the burial has not yet taken place. The body is still missing in the form of about three million dollars due to its Client's Account, and until I recover this there will always be questions to be answered.

Whenever its funeral finally occurs it is unlikely that there will be any mourners because the stench created by what has happened over the last ten years has meant that all those who used to flock to the firm have gradually turned their backs. In a way this is reflective of human behavior—in times when everything is 'A-OK' everyone wants to be associated with you, but that crowd disappears when things are tough. All that will remain of one of the pillars of the legal community will be dusty files, deeds and wills that will interest only historians. As recently as August 2015 a client from the United States was contacting a former employee to tell her he had been reading things in the underground press regarding me that were disconcerting to him, but was reassured when she explained what I was facing.

The need for the move from Warrens came unexpectedly within 18 months after I had moved from High Street. It was an expense that I did not budget for, and as such put more financial strain on me in addition to distracting me from what should have been my main purpose: rebuilding my practice. This, when added to the fact that it was now nearly two years since the partnership had ended, meant that my initial finance was running out and I was becoming financially stretched. The creeping interest payments I was making were having an unrealized effect like the arthritis I was afflicted with while studying in England. By that time virtually all outstanding fee income due to Cottle other than the amounts due from Kingsland had been collected in 2005, leaving my day-to-day cash flow under severe strain.

One of my first priorities after the move to Belleville was to institute the suit against my two former partners in 2005, but still nearly ten years after I have recovered less than five hundred dollars. If in 2005 I was under strain, I do not think many people know far less realize the level of despair and torment I have undergone during these last ten years. A cricketing friend who lost a personal friend to suicide once said to me: "Philip, when I think of the financial problems you have gone through and have kept your strength and sense of humor you must be some sort of man when I think how …… killed himself. He had no troubles compared to what you are going through." I have heard it often, and even though it lifts my spirits temporarily, the lift soon disappears when I think of the many sleepless nights I endured because of not only the disgraceful delaying tactics of my former partners aided and abetted by attorneys such as Smith and his cohorts who have ashamedly used the defects in our justice system plus unethical measures to further delay me without a care in the world. I can only believe there is a hell waiting for all of them.

During my time at Belleville the storm clouds that had been building for nearly a decade eventually burst despite all my attempts to stop the deluge. In retrospect, if I was aware or ever thought for one moment that the battle I was in would last for ten years, I would probably have approached the incurring of certain expenditure when I took over the firm in a different way. I genuinely did not believe that my two partners would have reneged on the responsibilities that they admitted belonged to them, and I continue to be convinced that behind all that they did was this man Smith. The economic cost of their default to me can never be calculated, but the method used by the courts to award me interest on the judgments as they did means that these losses will in some respect be greater than they should have been.

This is because I will never recover some of the losses, not only because of the difficulty of establishing a causal connection to the losses, but because at the time I simply undertook some of them as the lesser of two evils and have not kept accurate records of all the expenses I incurred. One of these losses, for instance, has been the need to keep all the records of the firm — especially ledger accounts and cheques — for the duration of the litigation, as despite acknowledging for years that they owed me the money they put me to prove every dollar that they owed. It was not until after the judgment of Madam Justice Crane Scott in September of 2009 when I made the decision to close the firm that I determined at that time to dispose of much of these records.

Up until that time I had been keeping these records of the firm, paying rental for the space they were occupying. I well remember the current speaker of the House Michael Carrington coming to my office to collect some documents, and when I took him into my storage room for deeds, etc. he was amazed at the size and the number of deeds and books therein, commenting that the area was larger than many people's offices. Yes it was, and I was absorbing the rent for same.

I have continued for instance absorbing the cost of not only keeping but collating, and when necessary, searching for the hundreds of wills and thousands of deeds in my possession as the 'Last Man Standing' so to speak. As the only one then with knowledge of what had to be kept and what could be destroyed, I estimate over the years that I have spent hundreds of man hours sorting through the documents on my own to determine what should be kept or what could be destroyed.

It has thus amazed me how not only laypeople, but many lawyers, would want to quibble for the minor fee that I have charged when people despite being written since 2003, now show up to collect their deeds. While I will happily concede that the keeping of deeds was a practice that the old partners used to encourage as part of the overall design to ensure that when the person needed further legal services they would come back to the firm, times have changed. Often I was getting requests from persons and indeed other attorneys to check for deeds to send to them to complete work that their client wanted. I therefore took the view that having notified you since 2003 to come for your deeds, within a three-month period after which there would be a charge, that I was entirely within my rights to do so.

Unless it can be established that the deeds are in my possession for some legal reason and not simply because of being left for storage, I have charged before releasing them. Mr. Strang—the Canadian henchman who implemented the merger between Barclays and CIBC—has long left these shores, but his contemptuous attitude towards me and the firm in 2003 saw me a few years later having to write the then CEO of First Caribbean Oliver Jordan complaining of the unreasonable attitude of his staff in writing to continuously enquire of old files, etc. when the firm had to all intents and purposes been fired as being surplus to requirement, but are suddenly remembered when documents of bygone days can't be found. I have made it clear: "If you want me to look, send a retainer of $1500 or produce a court order mandating me to search."

Recently I had a call from someone at First Caribbean whom I had known through cricket connections asking for some help. From the conversation it was clear he knew nothing of the history. I said I would get back to him and I did when I sent him copies of previous correspondence. He was gracious enough to call back to say that he was sorry for troubling me.

Other than the few persons working with law firms similar to Cottle, I don't think the profession as a whole understands the magnitude of the task I have been facing with respect to old deeds and indeed wills. It has become too much, and now I am trying to list many of these documents to send to the Archives for storage, having taken the decision that anyone making a will prior to 1970 must be presumed to be dead. Similarly all deeds prior to 1970, as in many respects they are no longer the primary root of title. There will of course be the exception that proves the rule, but I can no longer continue with the storage. There has been a treasure trove of old plans which by and large have a sell-by date of twenty years, and I have turned most of these over to Gerry Phillips, a land surveyor who has always been quick to assist me when my clients needed surveying services.

During this time at Belleville there was a greater turnover of staff than before. Some of the professional staff like Doria Moore, Kynara Roett, Alex Jules, Juel Garner and George Bennett left because of opportunities elsewhere, and Anne Gayle retired after more than 25 years of service. In addition I lost my secretary of nearly ten years, Juel Holder, primarily because she was uncomfortable dealing with the myriad of Cottle's financial queries that increased with every passing week with clients asking about this payment or that.

In the non-professional staff I soon encountered a problem, as the two young ladies in the accounts department got offers that would lead to their career advancement elsewhere, and decided to leave. For a period I was without anyone to deal with the accounts. One day in exasperation I asked one of my pharmacists who I knew was studying accounts at Cave Hill whether she could not find somebody willing to help me. Her reply was that she was going on holiday, but would be back in two weeks and would come and help me out until the next term started.

Allison Brewster thus joined the staff of Cottle in 2007, supposedly on a temporary basis, but she remained in my employ until the end of 2012 when she moved on to First Caribbean. Along with Sharon Carter and Julie Harris, two young attorneys who have always helped me tremendously and been supportive in my troubles, I owe a debt of gratitude to all of them that I will never be able to repay. As the finances of the firm became under greater and greater stress, it was she who fielded many of the irate calls and pacified persons that I was doing my best to get their funds. On two occasions disgruntled clients made complaints to the police about her re delaying to pay funds. These complaints about her were unfair, as she was simply managing what was there. As the contact person in the firm for payments, inevitably rumours started about her involvement in the firm's difficulties, but I need to be absolutely clear that she never had control of any funds and contrary to the usual rumor-mongering by persons with nothing else to do, the money had long disappeared into the hands of my partners before she joined the office.

Sharon left Cottle before I closed the firm, but Julie and Allison had not, and they subsequently declined to make a claim from the NIS for severance as they were entitled to with all other employees at the time of closure when they realized that even though the NIS would pay, as Cottle had no money, ultimately a claim would be brought against me for the payment out of the fund. I owe a debt of gratitude to them both for the sort of gesture that was done by several persons who in one way or another assisted me throughout this ordeal.

As Vernon Smith continued with his single-minded effort that I bear the full responsibility for the sins of omission of my partners by all manner of delay, I was at my wit's end as to how to raise finance, as my funds were rapidly running out. I saw what I thought was an opportunity, but you have guessed it, Smith raised his ugly head. I was aware that Cottle was working for the purchaser in a matter in which

Joyce Griffith was working for the vendor. We held the balance of purchase price of about $160,000 and so when the matter was due to close I requested the attorney handling the matter, Sharon Goddard, to bring me the file to complete the matter.

When Joyce called for Sharon to complete the matter her call was transferred to me. I reminded her that up to that time in 2006 she still had not paid the over $500,000 that was due to me and she and Watson seem to be totally oblivious to what it was doing to me. I said to her that I was proposing that she pay the balance of money to her client that we were holding for the balance of purchase price, and I would deduct this amount from the amount she owes me.

Not surprisingly, the sale became delayed. Cottle's client kept calling to say that Ms. Griffith had informed the vendor, her client, that I was holding the money and not paying it over, so that the matter was being delayed by my actions. I simply said to him that I hold no money for Ms. Griffith, and that she knows that I am ready and willing to complete the matter.

Unknown to me, the vendor and purchaser were half-brothers, and so were in constant contact with one another and our client sent the vendor evidence that the money had been paid to me. On the face of it the money was clearly with Cottle, and he could not understand what I was saying about how I had no money for Griffith, which was quite understandable. In the meantime Griffith had gone to see Vernon Smith. As will become evident when I relate the happenings at the BCA involving Smith and me which was running alongside this saga, I have always felt that the choice of Smith to represent them both by Watson and Griffith was deliberate, as his clear antagonism towards me was well publicized by then.

Typical of Smith, he reported me to the fraud squad. I say 'typical' as I was to learn later in life that this is a regular tactic of his when he has a dispute with attorneys, which begs the question: Why? Why does he want to use this method to solve disagreements as his first option?

Why is he unable like other attorneys to look someone in the eye and find a resolution? What is it that he has to hide by seeking to give the impression that he is the guardian of what is proper and right in legal transactions? Why are the offices of the fraud squad his favorite port of call? Is it the case of the rooster guarding the hen house? I don't know, but maybe one day he will have to answer.

While this was going on I had to be admitted to the Queen Elizabeth Hospital for minor surgery, and was still hospitalized when the officers from the fraud squad called at the office. Pam Sutherland, my office manager at the time, made the decision that the best thing in the circumstances was to pay the money to Griffith. Honestly I could not have faulted her for so doing, but once again my efforts to collect some of the money due to me from Joyce were thwarted. Smith's actions are evidence of the tangled web that Smith was part of with respect to the Cottle Catford money. Amazingly, he later sued me or wrote alleging that I have libeled him by suggesting he is party to the money missing from Cottle (see Appendix Ten). Two things on this score: it is clear that he has been and continues to be an accessory after the fact with respect to the funds due from Watson and Griffith, not to mention Mrs. Watson, and secondly, you need a reputation before it can be lowered.

I was fortified in my view that his suit had little merit after consulting a silk in the UK who was a noted libel lawyer, who advised that my words would have been construed as mere vulgar abuse. Smith, for reasons that I could only speculate, was unable to have his suit heard by any judge — not sure if he tried hard — but a few years later he had Hal Gollop approach me with an offer to settle same if I wrote a letter of apology, in which I told him that I can find better uses for toilet paper than appending an apology to someone I have no intention of apologizing to (see Appendix Twelve).

In 2006 I obtained some financial relief when the fees due to Cottle Catford as a result of the Kingsland litigation were finally paid. As will be evident when I write about the Kingsland saga, the amount that was paid bore little in comparison to the years of unpaid work that several attorneys had undertaken for that company for over a decade. The company's very existence, as the Privy Council noted when delivering its judgment in what was the final appeal from Barbados before it withdrew to join the Caribbean Court of Justice, was made possible by the firm that had provided all the services necessary for the company to survive for a number of years. Nominally the amount to be received was 1.1 million, but when the deposit on the sale of the shares ostensibly held in Cottle's accounts was taken into consideration as well as other amounts due to be paid to Kingsland, the actual injection of money was in the vicinity of $750,000. It was to sadden and amaze me in later litigation with my former partners how this was to become an issue.

The stark reality, however, was that because of the deficit in the Client's Account from not only the amounts due from Delvina Watson, which I have alluded to before, but the failure of my former partners to repay the money they were due to meant that as the deficit was now going on for over five years, I was on the precipice of disaster. I did not realise that it was creeping up on me, although as I think back I recall a conversation with Stephen in which he outlined to me that my situation was much worse than appeared on the surface.

As he intimated to me, I had borrowed by that time in excess of a million dollars. My debt service required interest payments in excess of $100,000 a year and though I was paying back an amortized amount of close to $15,000 a month at that time, the reality was that the interest that had accrued over the five years since the end of the partnership meant that the amount that was available to settle the Client's Account was far removed from the actual amounts borrowed when you factored in the interest component.

I was caught between a rock and hard place — more borrowings meant increased interest payments; if I made no further borrowings I did not have the necessary injection of capital needed every six months or so to keep the firm going. Firstly, I refinanced the mortgage on the property that I owned jointly with Beverley when I changed the mortgage from First Caribbean to Bank of Nova Scotia. My relationship with First Caribbean had deteriorated gradually, and the $50,000 overdraft that I was surviving on for monthly payroll expenses was discontinued with less than twenty four hours' notice. Yet they still wanted me to look for deeds—steupse!

With the cancellation of the overdraft and the continued struggles I was facing, I applied to Globe Finance for temporary funding to support my monthly expenses and other expenses of the firm, especially to help fund the repayment needed to clients. It is not generally remembered that the money that was due came from the Client's Account, which has continued over the years to be short by this deficit due from my partners. The loan was originally treated as a bridging loan, whereby I paid monthly interest on the amount borrowed of approximately $4500 a month, but was later turned into a mortgage over land belonging to my parents which was to become the subject of much contention later. The dispersal of this loan in 2007 was the last significant funding that I was able to raise to deal with the deficit in the accounts. The subsequent litigation by Globe to try to evict my parents from their house, which was never part of the charge, is reflective of the mercenary attitudes that many lenders are adopting of late when trying to realise loans that have run into default.

I have never argued that the loan was not in default. How could it be otherwise with me not recovering the money from my partners which Globe knew was the reason for the loan together with the implosion of my practice? My issue with them was that the land that was provided to cover the security, which did not include my parents' house, would obviously be more attractive with the house. Their mercenary pursuit of this option has led me to believe that there is a degree of credibility in many of the complaints that I have heard and indeed have been consulted on with respect to their actions to recover cars where loans go sour.

During this time I was pulling out my hair as I tried to balance the finances at Cottle. I took a decision that was to have a significant bearing on later litigation against Sagicor several years later. According to a partnership agreement in existence when I was admitted to the partnership, retired partners were entitled to a monthly payment from the firm. At this time there were two retired partners, namely Mr. Hutchinson and Mr. Hinkson, and the monthly payments to them were becoming more and more challenging for me to meet because of the financial pressure I was under as a result primarily with Watson's and Griffith's refusal to clear their deficits. There was not a hope in hell that those two would help with any contribution either. As a result I had a meeting with both Mr. Hutchinson and Mr. Hinkson and their spouses and explained the situation, and both were very sympathetic.

Mr. Hutchinson was often on the verge of tears during his visits which had become fewer and more spaced when he popped into the office to ask how I was doing. It was clearly distressing him how the other two had abandoned their responsibilities, and as his health deteriorated I took the decision not to raise it with him and cause him undue stress. Until he died late in 2007 I had maintained an office there for him to come and use, but after his death I offered the desk to his family. It was only after his death and more particularly after I made the decision to close the firm that I brought myself to go through the hundreds of files and deeds still in the filing cabinets that he used throughout his career.

My affection for both of these gentlemen who had mentored me during various stages of my life was great, but now I felt helpless and guilty at this state of affairs as I could not continue to maintain their pensions. After much thought I came up with what I thought was the best solution—purchasing and annuity from Life of Barbados with the excess surplus in the pension plan—even though I knew by so doing it would ultimately have a financial impact on me, as I would be required sooner rather than later to start paying the premiums that the surplus the non-contributory pension plan was paying.

I approached Life of Barbados, one of the predecessors of Sagicor, with a proposal to purchase an annuity out of the surplus fund in the Pension Plan to pay for the two pensions for Hutchinson and Hinkson. The surplus in the plan had accrued over a number of years primarily because of the departure of a number of Cottle employees whose pension entitlement had accrued at the time of their departure, and which, other than any individual contributions made by them which were returned to them, was ploughed back into the plan, a non-contributory plan paid for by the partners since its establishment in 1963. This surplus was then used to pay the premiums of the non-contributory plan, thus relieving the partners from making the payments from the earnings of the firm. In my opinion it was not unreasonable to fund an annuity to pay the former partners' pension from the plan, especially as it would not affect the other members of the plan.

Life of Barbados agreed to my request, and I purchased annuities at a cost of just under $100,000 so that both men were to have pensions for two years, certainly in the case of Mr. Hutchinson, and three years in the case of Mr. Hinkson in accordance with the meeting that I had with them. Prior to this payment in 2008 I had also agreed to a payment being made to Joyce Griffith representing what could be calculated as the portion attributable to her as a result of being a partner when the surplus accrued. Correspondence from the company dated February 20th 2004 indicated what would have accrued to her, but stated and I quote: "Ms. Griffith is not entitled to this benefit unless your company discretionarily grants some or all of it to her."

This I did, and I have always found it not only sad but dishonest of her to suggest that I left her in the lurch. The fact that she was allowed this payment more than a year after the partnership ended when she still had reneged on her agreement to settle what was due from her to the firm, as well as being allowed to use the premises of High Street for seven months without paying a cent towards the cost, suggests otherwise.

Having Life of Barbados take responsibility for the payment of the pensions for the two former partners was one of the many creative ways that I had to try and adopt to reduce expenses, but try as I may there really was only one option that bore fruit, and that was for me to raise finance. As I had been at pains to point out before, during our partnership meetings at Cottle, savings could only do so much and did not provide you with the large capital finance to deal with the many claims. And the claims were coming faster on me and as I was told by former Attorney General now Sir Louis Tull during a chance meeting in a supermarket: "Philip hard as it may be, some people feel that your father will help you out as he does not want to see you go to jail for the sins of others." He did admit that it was unfair, and "that is life", but by then I was beginning to feel persecuted.

As time has gone on I have come to the realization that my attempts to ensure that clients faced as little dislocation as possible as a result of the partnership problems was used as an excuse by my former partners to do nothing. In this attitude they were directly assisted by one or two attorneys, but also by the indifference in the legal profession to my plight whereby persons would be generally sympathetic to me or when speaking about me, but were unwilling to do anything positive to ensure that the missing funds were repaid. Both Watson and Griffith were accepted and worked with by all the senior players who could have made life impossible for them if they insisted that they took active measures to see that the amounts owing were paid.

I have learnt to my cost, as others have said, that my brethren did not have such an altruistic bone in them, and it is one of the reasons I have become so cynical towards the profession.

The daily stress associated with making sure that the monthly amortized commitments were met as well as maintaining a practice soon took its toll. In early 2008 I was ordered to take a complete break from work unless I wanted to plan the next World Cup with my friend Stephen by continuing to come to work. That was in 2008, and some true friends marvel how I have continued.

My health was not helped by two matters that occurred at the end of 2007 and early in 2008. Due to my inability to recover the funds from my partners, newer clients were funding the requirements of earlier clients, as I just could not source any finance. I was pushing myself trying to secure that major client whose work would generate for me the fees that would substantially ease my cash flow, but that never materialized.

In late 2007 a client who was due money presented for his funds much earlier than anticipated, and the delay in sourcing them led to a very unpleasant time for me. I tried many avenues to raise the funds, but they were not forthcoming. A complaint was made to the police and eventually I had to have Sir Richard Cheltenham intercede on my behalf with the client to work out a compromise. My memory of him was not pleasant. He was very caustic, accusing me of letting down my race now that black people were in charge, causing problems he never experienced while Mr. Hutchinson worked for him. All I could do was to bite my lip. Eventually, as the matter was settled, Sir Richard explained to him the challenges I was facing and that I had not personally used his money. He did telephone me to apologise for his harsh words, but I just listened said thank you and hung up.

Years later I was to learn that his sudden need for his funds was that he was one of the people being targeted by CLICO agents to put funds into their investment portfolios which subsequently went south. Tragically he has died without recovering his money from them.

The other was the Connor matter which has had far reaching consequences for me. Neither of these matters would have arisen if the funds due had been repaid and the unpleasant fact for me is that I having settled some of the claims and am now seriously in debt.

Upon my return to work my first order of business was to get the long delayed action against my partners moving and when this finally came to an end in September 2009 I determined that it would be best to close the firm. One of the letters I wrote on closing was to Life of Barbados indicating that the firm was closing with effect from October 31st 2009, and at that date the pension plan for the firm would close.

Close it I did, but it still lingers on to haunt me.

Photo Plates

With my parents on my 40th birthday

Greeting Stephen Alleyne on my 40th birthday

With the girls at Alton Towers, UK in 2011

With my mother, Gregory Hazzard and Stephen on my 40th birthday

Stephen Alleyne being greeted by my father

Me making the rounds as head boy at Harrison College

Me playing cricket with my father

The Harrison College Cricket Team circa 1978

With Sir Everton Weekes, Stephen's godfather, and Jeremy Alleyne, his brother awaiting the arrival of his casket, Kensington Oval, Oct. 22nd, 2007

Backing the camera is Chetnam Singh from Guyana, next to me is Conde Riley, Clive Lloyd and Clyde Sobers, at Empire Cricket Club on Oct. 21st 2007 for the viewing of Stephen Alleyne's body

Fellow LLA student Peter Masoe (Uganda), Manchester, 1986

With Allan Smith in England in 1986

Edmund Hinkson, John Blackman. me, Frank Belgrave and Gary Peters at Bert's Bar, late 1980s

Left to right. Front Row: Richard Edwards, William 'Billy' Griffith, Kerry Cummins, Frank 'Friction' Belgrave; Second Row: Hugh McClean, Allan King, I-Man; Gary Peters, Kenneth Maynard; Third Row: Richard Deane, Mark Evelyn; Back Row: Elridge Thompson, The Great Phillip Nicholls, Vernon Andrew Sealy and Edmund Gregory Hinkson

Philip Nicholls and Associates

AFTER MAKING THE decision to close Cottle Catford at the end of October 2009 I spent the rest of the year preparing to resume my practice in 2010, and after much thought determined to open a practice under my name. The two months that intervened were full of finding new premises and creating a new identity. It was my hope that having established a separate persona, I would be able to continue and build a career away from the mess that was Cottle. Unlike my two former partners, who with the aid of certain attorneys have cynically turned their backs on their legal, but more pertinently their moral responsibilities with respect to the amounts due to the firm, it was never my intention to do this and I and my many friends and indeed many independent persons who know the true story have found it more than ironic that I have been the sole person facing the brunt of the fallout.

I was perhaps somewhat naïve in thinking that a change of name would make things easier. I never expected that Cottle would simply disappear—too many people were affected by it. But what took a while to slowly dawn on me was that by this time I was being seen as the lone face of Cottle, and it is fair to say that my success in stopping the impending implosion in 2002 was now becoming a potential death knell, especially as the attorneys representing Watson and Griffith continued to argue that the modern day problems that I was facing were not their responsibilities. Give me a break. You take out over three million dollars and you have no responsibility for the impending results? It's amazing, but I guess that is life.

As any second year Law student would know, the Tort of Negligence is replete with instances of the legal doctrine of causation, in that if your initial action precipitates the subsequent injury which is reasonably foreseeable, then you bear legal responsibility for same. It has made me despair how intelligent but clearly intellectually dishonest people, including two men who have been supposedly elevated to the inner bar, could continue to hammer me as if the events of the past had nothing to do with my current predicament. The warning of many that my name in this case was more recognizable than theirs and would show all roads leading to me could not be truer, so in some respects I became not so much a victim of my own success, but a victim of my public persona.

It was not my former partners or their apologists who first caused me trouble at Philip Nicholls & Associates, but one of my attorneys, Sharon Goddard. I do not think it was deliberate, but when a client contacted her about money that was due from Cottle, she simply told her that she believes that I now would be responsible for paying it from Philip Nicholls and Associates (PN&A). I could only despair, for if one of my own attorneys could not make the distinction between Cottle and PN&A, how can John Public make the distinction? Her statement was to cause the disgruntled person to institute legal action against PN&A, after going to the newspaper when I genuinely tried to show how I was trying to sort the Cottle problem. The result of this is that she has got my goat up, and I determined that if you are being an idiot about it, so be it. The inevitable suit has been defended on the ground that PN&A is being sued for something that occurred before it was formed.

I had opened office at Seaston House, Hastings, Christ Church, which ironically was on top of the Fertility Clinic that had been established to assist couples who had been having trouble with conceiving a baby. Ironically, as my practice began to struggle, I could only wonder if I was in the wrong profession as I watched the use of the clinic increase.

This new birth was always destined to be short-lived, as it was similar to someone born with a chronic illness, and as a result of this life was likely to be short and troublesome. Within a year there was an appreciable downward spiral of the income of the firm, and it became a struggle to maintain the monthly rent. By this time I was extremely careful to ensure that I did not mix the payment of business or personal expenses from funds that were due to clients, and despite all the insinuations, I am comfortable within myself that clients' money was spent on clients and not my personal or business endeavors. There were no debit accounts for the use of myself or my family as had been the forte of my previous partners.

In my opinion this was one of the underlying problems that Cottle faced, as the ease with which cash became available when profits from earnings were drying up camouflaged the need for urgent corrective action of the underlying problem which became akin to the honey trap that some attorneys have fallen into. Eventually the money has to be repaid, and no one is aware of that as much as I am, as I am still trying in January 2016—nearly thirteen years after the partnership ended—to recover this money from my former partners. As one has absconded overseas and the other has so convinced herself that everything was my fault for wanting to end the partnership, my task is not easy.

The problem with the types of borrowings that occurred at Cottle is that it becomes extremely hard to repay these sums simply from earnings unless you were to suddenly become the benefactor of great wealth. I was the only one who made capital borrowings that I paid back in the firm to settle the amounts charged to me because of losses that Cottle had made, but when their losses as well as the debit accounts that had racked up were not settled quickly, it meant that I was under tremendous strain with my prolonged debt servicing.

Thus, when I opened (PN&A), I was unable to continue borrowing to assist with the set up costs and inevitably my cash flow suffered, and when the income dwindled it spelt the death knell for me. This is the legacy of 151/152 and 1612/1613, cases going on for more than a decade in our court system.

In reality I was drowning in my own debt, and was caught in a vicious cycle, as I could not afford to attract experienced staff to boost my earnings, and the need to monitor constantly the junior staff eventually took its toll on me as I was exhausted. As a result inevitable mistakes were made that I had to bear the cost of correcting.

Two matters in particular during these last few years have troubled me with my practice at PN&A. One in particular has been the funds due now to the estate of Connor. Persons legitimately ask what has happened to them, but in spite of those who want to believe the worst, they have not gone into my pocket to support an extravagant lifestyle. I own no property; I have no trappings of success that the jackass of a DPP wants to seek a forfeiture order against for money laundering. Maybe he wants to extract and sell my daughter's braces or the defibrillator inserted in me to keep a regular heartbeat so that I do not have sudden cardiac arrest. Maybe he wants to sell the cricket book collection that I have donated to Cave Hill. But then again cricket is not his game; he is found on the golf links with his son, something I can't enjoy with my daughters if I wanted to.

Since I had been unable to borrow since 2007, borrowings that I was using to supplant the shortfall in the Client's Account at Cottle, this inability, when coupled with the fact that the deficit in the account due from Watson and Griffith had not been repaid meant that I was stretched amid constant calls for payments. By this time most of the original Cottle clients had been settled, and it was now mine that were having difficulty, as in effect Peter was paying for Paul. With the declining revenue due to the fact that there was a significant fall off in work, this became all the more drastic for me.

Hastings Attorneys had obtained a civil judgment for the estate of Connor against me for the amount of money that was due from Cottle. Not satisfied with the civil judgment that was obtained against me on behalf of the estate of Connor, a suit I did not defend which in retrospect was a mistake, Gale, spiteful bitch that he is, used this civil judgment as the basis to support his request of the police that I be arrested, not so much as implying but screaming from the rooftops that I had absconded with the money. I will not dignify Gale's statements as being the unkindest cut of all, because that would suggest we were friends when in truth and in fact he is little short of being a sanctimonious bitch for having harbored Watson for five years, benefitting from the fees he was generating, and now disowning any responsibility for the nearly million dollars he walked with while associated with Hastings. What else should I expect of this upstanding citizen?

Gale, through his subordinates at Hastings, continued his attack on me at a time when not only was he working in the same office as Watson, but the said Watson was being defended in the actions I brought against him for the recovery of the money due to Cottle (see chapter 14) by Gale's partner at the time Leslie Haynes in association with one of their employees Ivan Alert.

He had me examined as to my ability to repay the debt before the Master, even accusing my accountant at the firm, Allison Brewster, of lying when she indicated that the fee income of Philip Nicholls did not allow me to make a repayment of more than $3,500 a month, which was a stretch in any event. I was subsequently unable to maintain the monthly payments of $3,500, payments about which he threatened in writing that he would bring an application for me to be committed to prison for debt or for contempt of the order to pay. I told him "Barry be my guest... the truth will soon out" as he had earlier told me he did not give "one fuck" about the money Watson owed me.

It has always been my suspicion, though I have no written proof, that his action that triggered my arrest was not as a result of pressure from the client. Certainly the message given to my parents by a mutual family friend that they knew nothing of it suggests that it was simply driven by Gale. The client wants and is entitled to their money, but by destroying my practice and assisting with the harboring of a criminal, he is not making things easier for me. After all I do not have an alternative form of income, especially since the physical limp I have been carrying since 1990 prevents me from indulging in the cultivating of exotic agriculture that bears quick returns.

Prior to my arrest Gale engineered that the clients make a complaint before the disciplinary committee of the Bar. Of course, coward that he is, he did not have the gumption to represent the complainant at the hearing, and sent Alert to do so. It is fair to say that I was livid with this because here was Alert appearing before the committee to represent a former client of Cottle who was owed money, while at the same time he was on record in 1612/1613 as the attorney representing Allan Watson in association with Leslie Haynes, Gale's partner at Hastings, where the said Alert was employed.

If the fact of his representation alone was bad enough, when this was coupled with the fact that he Alert had deliberately disobeyed orders of the Court of Appeal in December 2007, the result of which led to a delay in my obtaining judgment against my former partners, I can be forgiven for thinking there was a witch hunt out there for me.

It was not only my opinion but my father's that it was preposterous that he could now seek to represent a client complaining that money was due from Cottle, while at the same time being responsible for putting road blocks in my way to recovering the money. But this showed the level of indifference that I was generally faced with in the profession. It was my problem alone and no one gave a rat's ass about how it was affecting me.

At the first hearing of the complaint my father represented me and stated these facts succinctly, but the Committee declined to prevent Alert representing, saying that the privilege was not mine, but Watson's, an incredible cop out. My father left the hearing in disgust, saying that he would advise that I bring a constitutional action that my rights have been infringed upon if they made a decision on this basis. So Alert could stand before the Committee with a straight face and allege that Cottle owed money to his client, while he on the other hand and at the same time, or his firm, was doing the utmost to stop me enforcing the judgment against Watson for more than was due the complainant.

The Committee also refused my requests that they summon as the Act provided, Watson and Griffith as material witnesses, saying I could call them if I wanted, to which I responded "If they have refused to honour their agreement since 2002, do you think they will attend a disciplinary hearing in 2010 at my request?"

When the hearing resumed my father at my request did not attend, for as he said privately to me they clearly could not understand the basic point he was making. I was of the view that he should not demean himself by attending before people, none of whom have reached the status he has, when they clearly were not prepared to entertain what he was saying. Instead I took with me as much as for a learning experience as anything an in-service student from Jamaica by the name of Taneisha Evans.

The committee was not sure how to deal with this, and asked whether I had no representation. I indicated that Ms. Evans was representing me, there was no requirement that I needed to have an attorney present, I had previously been represented by as eminent an attorney as possible, but they had dismissed his arguments in a manner that both he and I felt was to do violence to my rights, and that it was a waste of time for him to attend.

I indicated to them that only because I was a former chairman of this committee that I was here as a matter of respect, but as I was of the view that it was little more than a kangaroo court now, should any finding be made with Mr. Alert participating in these matters I would have to take the matter further.

Ms. Evans was asked rather condescendingly whether she had anything to say, and she indicated that she had worked with me over several summers and was *au fait* with the matters that I was facing and was appalled that I was being called to answer charges when it was clear where the money had gone, and none of those persons was here to answer. She was moved to tears as she described the lengths that I had gone to recover the money that was missing from the Client's Account, and that it was unfair what was being done to me. The committee was presented with evidence that the same account to which the purchase money re Connor was paid into was the same account that my former partners were found liable for money for, and that until this money was repaid I would always be playing catchup.

The upshot of the matter is that the Committee never made a finding, and subsequently became functus, as its life had expired. Gale by this time was president of the Bar and he wrote to the Disciplinary Committee demanding that action be taken against me. By this time Gale was clearly on the war path, as I had sued him along with all his partners, First Caribbean and Allan Watson for money belonging to a client by the name of H and G Limited that Watson had walked off with while he was attached to Hastings.

H and G Limited was a company that Cottle Catford had acted for since its inception. It was one of the legacies of Mr. Armstrong. When I told Watson in 2003 that I'd had enough and to leave, he was in the midst of a transaction to sell land at Blackman's, St. Andrew on behalf of the company. Watson had set up practice with Leslie Haynes at first, until Haynes entered a partnership with Gale and others at Hastings Attorneys. When he left, Mr. Challenor, the chief cook and bottle washer of H and G, had called me to request that I allow Watson to take the file pertaining to the sale with him. I told him I had no objection. I could not have Mr. Challenor assured that the other H and G work would remain with Cottle; not that I was too worried, as this was really mostly dealings with tenantry land and I did not think that anyone wanted the headache.

The land in question that was being sold by H and G was not part of a tenantry. In fact the purchase price was in excess of $300,000. For reasons that are in the main irrelevant to what has transpired, the completion of the sale first agreed in 2003 was protracted and did not finish until 2009. When the matter was due to be completed Mr. Challenor called me and stated quite innocently that Mr. Watson had informed him that he was unable to complete the matter because I was holding the deeds amongst Cottle papers and he could not retrieve them.

I stated that Mr. Watson had never asked me for the deeds, but could not ask me because any conversation with me would have seen me raise the matter of over two million dollars that he and his wife owed to Cottle Catford since 2002. There was silence, and I had to ask whether he was still on the line. When he had regained his composure I explained to Mr. Challenor what I had been undergoing for many years, to which he said he had no idea, but now understood over the years why he was never willing to call me and requested to get information usually from Ms. Goddard. I explained that the staff was under strict instructions that if either Griffith or Watson called regarding any matter, the call was to be referred to me. I stated to him that I would not send anything to Watson, but "as the deeds belong to you, if you request them, I will send to you" and this I did.

A few months after this conversation Mr. Challenor was to call and say to me sheepishly that I had warned him, but he now could not reach Mr. Watson despite several messages, and he had learnt with concern from the buyer that the sale had been completed some time ago. I indicated to him that I was due to see Mr. Watson in the Court of Appeal the following week, as he had appealed the judgment I had obtained, and I would hand deliver a letter to him indicating an urgent need to contact him. This was done by Julie Harris in December of 2009, and in January of 2010 Watson disappeared from the island. I was instructed by Mr. Challenor to contact Hastings Attorneys where Watson was working at the time of the transaction and make a claim.

Amazingly, Gale has defended the claim on the basis that Watson was in no way associated with Hastings for the last five years before he left, and was operating as an independent contractor, and neither he nor his partners are liable for his defalcation. So on the one hand he does not give a f__k about my problems with Watson and the money missing from Cottle, but when Watson does the same thing under his watch at Hastings he seeks to disassociate himself from it.

These actions by Gale led to an exchange of emails between he and I when he was seeking to be re-elected as president of the Bar in 2014, in which I told him in no uncertain manner that he was not fit for the office because he was trying to give the impression to all and sundry that he was an upstanding attorney of high moral standing, when in fact he was a two-timing bastard intent on stabbing people in the back so as to protect his dark secrets. These emails have been reproduced elsewhere in this book. Nothing gave me greater pleasure than when he was unseated from the presidency of the Bar, bucking a trend that the incumbent president is almost always returned for another term if he desires, with more than one attorney saying to me privately that they attended solely for the purpose of kicking him out when they read the emails that he had made public in which he admitted that he had written the police demanding my arrest.

I have no doubt that Gale's actions in urging my arrest were payback for me daring to sue him on behalf of a client for the recovery of money that Watson took while at Hastings. In that regard I place him and Smith in the same contemptuous column that I have for people who exude a public persona totally different from what they are in an attempt to fool john public.

Needless to say, with all this going on, I was under severe mental strain, not helped by the financial strain I was under. My main stream of income—the offshore sector—was taking a beating not only because of general economic climates around the world, but the cash flow was making it impossible for me to continue on the relentless grind of promoting myself overseas, and then my arrest was the final nail in the coffin. I have had no work from this sector, and my practice has virtually collapsed.

It was not a surprise to me that my frequent travels led to accusations that I was a globetrotter rather than staying at home to expand my practice. It is clear now that this was not the case with the drastic reduction in income that has occurred since I stopped. What I resented, however, was when these statements started coming from supposed colleagues who did not know the full facts and would sometimes surmise that my travel in business class was an unnecessary luxury. As a frequent traveler you earned perks, and for me this meant that I used my miles to upgrade to a higher category of travel where I was not only more comfortable than the cramped space of economy, but at less risk from developing a blood clot not unknown on long flights, and because of which I have been on blood thinners for more than a decade at the insistence of my goodly Dr. Massay.

During the Disciplinary Committee hearing, Alert made this allegation with respect to my travel and buttressed it by saying I was using client's money to maintain my lifestyle. I was incandescent with rage. "What lifestyle?" I asked. I was living month-to-month; now it is day by day. However, after I calmed down and reflected on what he said, I determined that unless I was able to show conclusively that every month I was earning enough to pay staff and myself in addition to the horrendous monthly repayment, that he may have a point. I therefore in 2011 took the decision that I should forgo payment of my mortgage amounts. In making this decision I genuinely believed that the challenges I was facing from my partners would be ended by then, but was I ever overtly optimistic? This decision has now come home to roost, so to speak, as the former matrimonial home has been foreclosed on and sold.

With all these matters going on it was a wonder that I was able to do any work. The financial predicament that I was facing despite this was still dire, and I was desperate to get an injection of capital. The only area where I could see this coming was from my entitlement under the Pension Fund. When I closed Cottle at the end of October 2009, I wrote to Life of Barbados advising them of the closure and requesting that they provide a statement of what the seven remaining members of the plan were entitled to, as the Plan was at an end. Life of Barbados accepted that it was at an end, but it took over a year to provide this information. Over the next two years much correspondence passed between Sagicor the successor, correspondence that Justice Reifer in her judgment in 2014 stated was becoming increasingly acrimonious over my instructions as to the manner in which I wanted my entitlement under the plan paid.

I made no secret in correspondence to Sagicor of the reason why I needed the funds. This was to help with the financing of the deficit at Cottle. The principal players at Sagicor at the time, Sandra Osbourne and Althea Hazard, were both lawyers who were well acquainted with my plight, but it soon became apparent that I was wasting my time.

Sagicor was insisting that I was not entitled under the plan to either a cash payment or to purchase, as I requested Government Bonds from the Central Bank. Their argument was that only at the retirement age of 65 was the cash option available. The alternative that they offered was that I needed to roll over my entitlement into another form of annuity which (surprise, surprise) Sagicor were the main providers of on the island.

My arguments all along were that as the plan had come to an end because of the closure of the firm, it triggered various rights under the plan which were not restricted to what they were offering as my entitlement. As Sagicor would not budge, I was left with no option but to file an urgent application for relief. Pat Cheltenham Q.C., in association with his junior Natasha Green, appeared on behalf of Sagicor when the matter first came before Justice Randall Worrell. At that initial hearing Cheltenham indicated to the court that he was confident that a settlement could be reached and proceeded to have conversations with my father to this end.

It soon became apparent that this was not going to happen, and to the great disappointment of my father, Cheltenham, after months of what I can only describe as dithering on the subject, finally admitted in court that his client was not willing to settle the matter and that it would have to go to trial. This necessarily meant a further delay. I know this admission by Cheltenham was a great disappointment to my father who had gained the impression during his talks with Cheltenham that he would have been in a position to opine to Sagicor that the matter be settled.

With no settlement on the horizon, the matter was set down for hearing with the sole issue for trial the interpretation of Section 6 of the contract which dealt with payment of benefits after the contract came to an end, which everyone agreed was October 30th 2009. The initial date of trial had to be vacated in 2013 because of my surgery. Wally Scott from Jamaica had been prepared to come to argue the matter for me, having provided many authorities with respect to Pension Plans in Jamaica. With the delay he was no longer available, so two of my contemporaries from NMLS stepped in.

Rudolph 'Cappy Greenidge' and Errol Niles, both contemporaries with me at NMLS, in association with Cappy's sister Eleanor Clarke and Charmaine Delice Hunte, were the ones who ultimately represented me and I have to pay tribute to them for getting to grips with over three years of arguments in a short space of time so as to have the matter heard early in 2014.

Justice Reifer delivered her decision on November 25th 2014, and found in my favour. In doing so the seminal Clause 6 of the original contract entered into in 1963 between the then partners of Cottle and Manufacturer's Life was construed to allow for my interpretation of the contract. Sagicor, through their counsel Cheltenham, had argued for a literal interpretation of the 1963 contract which had been enacted prior to legislation in Barbados with respect to pensions being enacted. This literal interpretation was rejected by Justice Reifer, who cited a recent Court of Appeal decision in Barbados that the contextual approach to interpretation of contracts to give them more commercial reality was better suited. In this connection, the words of Lord Diplock in 1985 were quoted as follows:

> "...if detailed semantic and syntactical analysis of words in a commercial contract is going to lead to a conclusion that flouts business commonsense, it must be made to yield to business commonsense."

As the learned trial judge found, in interpreting contracts it is necessary to apply a contextual approach to same rather than the literal approach, and thus the contract executed in 1963 has to be interpreted in today's realities.

One of the matters that swayed the judge's decision in my favour and to reject the literal interpretation that the contract must be read within its four corners only, was the fact that they had allowed payments outside the strict confines, such as to Griffith when I had given my consent that she be allowed a sum from the accumulated surplus, and because of Sagicor agreeing to allow the purchase of an annuity to provide for pensions for my two former partners Hutchinson and Hinkson from said surplus. It was clearly redundant to argue therefore that in interpreting Section 6 you had to apply the Literal Rule of

Interpretation to a 1963 contract. Listed below is part of the judge's decision.

1. That on a construction of Clause 6 of the Group Pension Plan, employees, inclusive of the Claimant has been provided with the following options:
   (1) To receive a cash refund of contributions plus interest; or if greater,
   (2) To receive the cash value of the paid up annuity;
   (3) To receive the amount of paid up annuity at normal retirement age (65); or
   (4) To purchase an individual deferred annuity on an annual premium basis (within 60 days of the termination of coverage) for the employee's then age.

   This is without reference to the Claimant's liability to tax under the Income Tax Act, Cap 73 of the Laws of Barbados.
2. In short, this Plan does allow disbursement of the Claimant's entitlements before the retirement age of 65.

Sagicor were granted a six week stay of execution on the judgment which expired on January 6th. Finally at the end of January the money was paid, but just as I was thinking that one nightmare was over, Sagicor started another. They retained 25% of the judgment, claiming it was withdrawal tax. Sometimes I think I am mad when I hear attorneys like Pat Cheltenham telling my attorneys, my father and I that they genuinely want to assist me in my plight. I must wonder, because having clearly lost the case, how can you come now to argue that there is a withholding tax because I am taking a withdrawal from the fund? The fund is at an end. It can't be a withdrawal that would be the subject to the 25% deduction that was applied if you made a withdrawal from the plan.

But this was not the only reason why the decision of Sagicor to make this withdrawal and pay it to the Inland Revenue, according to them, was vindictive in the extreme.

Firstly, I had since 2010 been asking to have the money to purchase government bonds, and had been allotted some bonds which, if you keep them for five years, do not attract tax. Having refused to honour this request which the court by saying I was entitled to the money outright impliedly ruled was incorrect if I suffer now from being assessed to tax, they themselves are liable to me for the loss for their negligence.

Secondly, this was not an express decision of the judge. Both parties went before her for her clarification on the point, and she stated she had not addressed the point. As such, for Sagicor to deduct 25% from a court order was a contemptuous disregard of the order. In the part payment Sagicor had included interest on the whole as per the court order. Is that interest now payable to Inland Revenue? Interestingly enough, Sagicor have refused to settle the costs awarded against them because they are insisting that they are only willing to pay costs on the 75% paid when the order from the court was costs on the 100%.

Thirdly, if the money was being taxed on a withdrawal basis, then that presupposes that I am no longer part of the plan. As the administrator of the plan at the time it ended, what of the other seven persons? If I am no longer a member of the plan, why have they not contacted the other members to inform them of their status in the plan as the judge's clear ruling suggests her decision is applicable to them?

Not satisfied with their action, I made an application for a Judgment Summons for them to show cause why they have done this, and amazingly, when my application came on towards the end of July, it was adjourned to 2018.

My father and I have always held to the view that the actions by Sagicor are because they have been overwhelmed managing the pension portfolio under their management, as this has grown all out of proportion with the folding of other insurance companies. Over the last decade they have expanded greatly the pension plans that they are responsible for, but the expertise in the department has not expanded likewise. It is clear that Sagicor are fearful that if the effect of this decision is made public, that there will be a significant run on their fund because they have been refusing to pay beneficiaries of plans that have vested before the Occupational Benefits Pension Act came into force, and prevented such payments as I was awarded.

I have always argued that if I am liable to tax, then it is for a determination with the BRA and it simply necessitates that Sagicor report the payment to me. Goodness knows I have significant losses to show in any tax filing. My pursuit of my entitlement under the fund is not to enjoy any extravagant lifestyle, but simply to assist with repaying the clients that the defalcations caused by my partners have made it impossible for me so to do, and so I must include Sagicor as an accessory after the fact in stopping this repayment, as well as lament the actions of another senior attorney. His failure or refusal to recognize the difference between a withdrawal under the plan and a payment to a beneficiary of the plan, it having come to an end, is inconceivable for an attorney of his stature and suggests other reasons are in play.

I have had little to do with Natasha Green, and have always felt that some of the positions adopted in the case are because of her total misunderstanding of the law, as some of the reasons that were subsequently advanced I found difficult to square with the knowledge expected of a leading Q.C. My father pointed this out to him in a letter of August 2015, bemoaning yet again the delay in completing the matter, which after all started in 2012 and now was adjourned to 2018, and urging him to have it sorted before he took exception.

My father subsequently received a letter from Leslie Haynes accusing him of slandering Pat, demanding an apology and $20,000 in damages, which he totally rejected. Still absolutely nothing has been done in the intervening four months, and I am left floundering.

The matter, like 151/152 and 1612/1613, must of necessity be considered subjudice and thus can't be touched by the CJ to ensure that it be ended, but by the same token more than one person desperate for me to be put into funds to allow me to settle debts are advised to report me to the Bar's disciplinary committee.

The Chief Justice has consented to bring forward the given date of hearing the judgement summons of 2018 to December of 2015. Any hope of Christmas charity was soon dashed when at the hearing on the 21st of December, counsel for Sagicor continued with his assertions that the question of the withholding tax was a legal issue to be heard by the court. The Chief Justice was understandably now sitting at first instance, having not had early insight into the case. The trial judge had determined that to make more efficient usage of judicial time, the best course of action was to send the matter back to the trial judge for determination, as despite the fact that Justice Reifer had delivered her judgment over a year ago, she would still be better able to come to grips with the matters at hand.

I think it is within my province to speak about the nonsense that has occurred in this matter in spite of the ire of Mr. Cheltenham—so much so that he would demand that my father retract a letter written to him on the subject of the role he is playing in causing me more anguish by delaying and delaying a final resolution. His counsel (Leslie Haynes Q.C.) suggested a payment of $20,000. Not surprisingly, my father dismissed the request as not worthy of the paper it was written on. The reality is that whatever manner Mr. Cheltenham seeks to paint this in, the facts are clear.

A judgment for $425,000 approximately was handed down against Sagicor in November of 2014. At no time during the preceding five years did Sagicor acknowledge or offer that I was entitled to a cash payment. They denied this, but now that the court has ordered the cash payment, they say it must be subject to the 25% withholding.

The judgment was not appealed against.

The matter is thus no longer subjudice, but despite seeking the clarification of the judge since February of 2015 and not getting it, they continue to procrastinate with the matter. Doesn't this behavior sound familiar? Yet they have arrogated to themselves that they are entitled to withhold 25% tax on the basis that it must be withheld when persons make a withdrawal from a pension plan. In other words, a court order is contemptuously disobeyed.

As the plan no longer exists, how is this payment a withdrawal subject to tax withholding tax? Such a tax only arises when you withdraw your pension entitlement before you were entitled to it, surely not when the plan has ended when any payment would be subject to Income Tax, not withholding tax. Is it not the entitlement under the plan that I had paid for over the years, which they now want to ascribe a 25% tax for? Surely if there is any tax, then it is income tax. But I guess I must continue to play the game. Hopefully when this saga finally ends all of the persons who have been misled by Sagicor over the years with respect to these payments can cause a run on the company.

18

Court of Appeal

WATSON AND GRIFFITH were granted a six-week stay of execution—a normal stay of execution following judgement which technically meant that as of the end of November 2009 I could have started proceedings to execute the judgement. During the hearing I found it baffling how Griffith appeared at times disinterested, and when asked by Justice Crane-Scott to state her position, she simply replied whatever Mr. Watson said his was... she was in agreement with whatever he said. At the expiry of the six weeks stay I wrote them both a letter demanding settlement, to which they replied in separate letters but in identical fashion, stating that as an appeal had been filed, they would request that I not do anything. Just when I thought that the end may be near for the near seven-year nightmare, I ran into another obstacle—the Court of Appeal.

Prior to my letter on October 2nd 2009, Leslie Haynes Q.C., who had not attended any of the 14 days of the hearing before Justice Crane Scott nor sent an excuse for his non-attendance, filed an application on behalf of both defendants for special leave to appeal against the order of Justice Crane Scott. It was scheduled to be heard on the 11th day of December 2009. Haynes listed 20 grounds of appeal. On November 25th 2009 Allan Watson filed an affidavit in support of the appeal in which he listed 25 grounds. Nothing was filed by Griffith, but the appeal proceeded as if both were appealing.

When the appeal came on for hearing, Chief Justice Simmonds recused himself on two grounds: that he was shortly leaving the bench, and that he had knowledge of the matter from outside the court system. During the long periods of delay as described above, my father had requested an audience with him to express his grave concerns at the effect that the delays, obviously perpetuated by the defendants, were having on my life and how the court system was being abused by Griffith, Watson and Smith in particular by the obvious methods of delay. CJ Simmonds had requested of Smith by letter to meet with him and my father to see if a form of settlement could be arrived at, but he flatly refused. This was no surprise because he had set out his stall from day one to delay, delay and delay with no intention to assist me with recovering these funds, but yet when in 2005 I suggested that he has acted in a manner to assist others in keeping clients' funds belonging to Cottle, he filed a law suit for libel, which to this day he has been unable to have heard (see Appendix Twelve).

It therefore fell to Justice of Appeal Peter Williams, who had sat previously on the 2007 appeal, to be president of the court. The court noted that the proposed appellants did not have to seek leave to appeal, and thus the application was wrong. It has always mystified me why the court simply did not dismiss it out of hand, because it would have clearly now been out of time. Instead, the appellants were ordered to file the proper appeal within a week with the respondent (me) filing any answer within three weeks. The learned judge commented at the time that from what he saw from the filings for the leave to appeal that this appeal could easily be disposed of by February of 2010. I guess that was the kiss of death, or as sports commentators on TV say the 'commentator's curse' — as soon as you say something positive about a player, the opposite happens. And it certainly did.

December 11th 2009 is however significant, as it represents the last time that I have set eyes on Watson. Just prior to the court hearing I had been contacted by a long-standing client indicating that he had been trying without success to reach Watson for several months with respect to a matter started by him at Cottle Catford, and which he had continued to work on when practicing with Leslie Haynes and subsequently when he was operating from the offices of Hastings Attorneys. The client reported that he understood that the matter had been closed since March of that year, but he was still awaiting receipt of the money from the sale which was in excess of three hundred thousand dollars. I indicated to him that I would have a letter delivered to Watson advising that he wanted to speak to him as a matter of urgency, and this was done and the letter hand delivered prior to the start of the appeal by Julie Harris. More than six years after the sale the client is still without his money and a report to the Fraud squad has gone nowhere, the same fraud squad that was quick to act on a statement by Barry Gale against me. But what is worse is that since April of 2015 an arrest warrant for Watson was issued by the High Court, and though his present address in the United States has been communicated by me to the authorities, nothing has been done to effect the warrant to the best of my knowledge

It is my belief that this is one of the geneses of the hatred for me that Barry Gale has displayed to me, as his statement to the police followed on my filing of a suit on behalf of H and G against Gale and his partners and First Caribbean, the bank that Watson had the account with from which the funds were directed for use other than to H and G for whom the funds were due. His hypocritical stance for years has been that I must bear the responsibility for what happened at Cottle Catford, but he has nothing to do with what I am now led to believe is the over one million dollars Watson has taken from clients while associated with Hastings. It would surprise no one to know that despite that action being filed in 2011, that it has become bogged down in the system with all manner of technicalities being argued by the defendants, three of whom are attorneys.

In compliance with the order of December 11th 2009, Leslie Haynes Q.C. filed a Notice of Appeal on December 18th, listing 20 grounds of appeal. As entitled, I filed a notice in response on January 8th 2010, indicating solely that when the appeal was heard I would be seeking to have the rate of interest varied. The rate awarded had been 4% from the date of filing the writ until judgement—August 2005—which meant that in the over four years that had elapsed since the filing and judgment I was losing 6% as the money I borrowed was attracting a rate of 10%. The rate of 8% awarded from the date of judgment until payment was also in my opinion too low. I was repaying the money borrowed at the rate of 10% money that I had borrowed to repay their debt.

My cross appeal also sought that the award of interest should run from a date earlier than the date of filing of the writs, and in addition that the interest should be awarded for a period of time on higher amounts than was the eventual judgment figure, in that substantially greater amounts were due from the appellants prior to the receipt of the Kingsland fee.

Bearing in mind the statements of Justice Williams that the matter should be easily disposed of by February, I soon became somewhat agitated that nothing was happening. As the appeal was on behalf of Watson and Griffith, it was up to them to prosecute the appeal, but it soon became apparent that they had no interest in pursuing the appeal. All entreaties to Haynes including letters from the Deputy Registrar of the Court of Appeal that he settle the record to allow for the appeal to commence, went a-begging.

I therefore started making attempts at enforcing the judgment on the ground that the stay had expired and there was nothing to prevent enforcement. These attempts came to nothing, as Watson's whereabouts were not known, while Griffith simply filed certificates of sickness over and over that she was unable to attend court, a clear abuse of the system. When I complained to Justice Kentish before whom Griffith had been summoned to be examined as to her ability to settle the costs, she simply raised her hands in frustration, indicating they were tied.

More than one date was set for settling the record, but nothing came of it. Later Leslie was to indicate to me that he had just facilitated Watson in filing the appeal, but he really had nothing to do with it. It was the type of cop-out that I was to hear from him and others with respect to their interest in the matter. The result was that the appeal went nowhere and my debts continued to spiral out of control. In addition, my parents and I were being hauled into court to seek execution against property that we had put up as security for the loans advanced to me to help keep Cottle Catford afloat.

At this time I was drowning in debt, and as I had no way to refinance, the banks made it clear that they were not prepared to lend any more as they did not believe that I would recover the amounts, and this debt could not be used in measuring the whether the loans should be granted. I lost count of the number of different avenues I explored, even to selling the judgments to a financial institution in return for immediate cash. Only one countenanced the idea, but the mark down made it ridiculous.

It was with this in mind that I felt a growing desperation to have the appeal heard. No funds were available, yet on paper judgments that would have significantly eased my cash flow predicament were due to me. Finally, on June 22nd 2011, Edmund Hinkson filed an application for the appeal to be dismissed for want of prosecution and the matter was scheduled to be heard on the 20th day of July 2011. Justice of Appeal Sherman Moore heard the application on the 20th. Leslie Haynes did not appear, nor did Watson, who had been out of the island for over a year now, but Griffith appeared in person and pleaded for time to settle outstanding matters for the appeal to be heard. Justice Moore exercised his discretion not to dismiss the appeal, because the record of appeal had been filed on June 17th 2011 by the said Leslie Haynes, now eighteen months after Williams had indicated it could have been settled. By this time, he too had retired from the bench.

Justice Moore set the date for the appeal to be heard on September 21st 2011. I was represented by Edmund Hinkson and Charmaine Delice Hunte. Julie Harris, who had represented me faithfully almost from the inception of this case, had moved on with my blessing to another job in corporate Barbados. Later Elliott Mottley Q.C. and Andrea Simon of his chambers would present arguments.

When the matter came on for hearing on the 21st, Mr. Amilcar Branche indicated to the court that he was holding papers for Mr. Haynes, who was out of the jurisdiction, and his instructions were that Mr. Haynes desired to withdraw from the matter. The court comprised the recently appointed Chief Justice Sir Marston Gibson, along with Justices of Appeal Sandra Mason and Andrew Burgess. The court, however, after giving Mr. Branche an uncomfortable time (to be fair to him he knew little of the matter), adjourned the matter for a week, indicating that they wished to hear from Mr. Haynes in person as to his reasons for withdrawal.

On September 28th Leslie Haynes advised the court when it resumed sitting that he had not seen nor been in contact with his client Allan Watson in over eighteen months, and as such did not have continued instructions to prosecute the appeal and was craving the court to grant him permission to withdraw. He referred also to the suit that I had filed on behalf of H and G to recover the funds taken by Watson, saying that he now personally was facing a suit because of his actions. At no time did he indicate he was acting for Griffith or that she had been in contact with him.

His request to withdraw was granted, at which point Joyce Griffith, who was seated at the bar table, though not robed, started wailing about what was she to do because she regarded Haynes as her attorney as well, and was now without representation to prosecute the appeal. I found this at the time and since then utterly amazing. Griffith was present on the 21st when Blanche made the request, and it was evident from Haynes' statement to the court that she had never been in contact with him, and yet she was crying foul. After all, it was nearly two years after the original decision had been handed down and the appeal filed.

The court indicated to her that the appeal would now be heard on November 11th 2011, and told her that her skeleton arguments must be filed by October 21st and that she would have to assist whoever she retained to come up to speed, which should not be too difficult as she was a practicing attorney. The court also dismissed the appeal by Watson for want of prosecution, noting that he had failed to appear on the two occasions and on July 20th when the application for dismissal was heard. By the admission of his counsel that he was out of the island and had been for some time and as he had not appeared, it must be deemed that he was uninterested in pursuing the appeal.

To say that this action (with respect to Griffith) dismayed me would be an understatement. Griffith had done absolutely nothing to advance the appeal now nearly two years since it was filed, and during this time the fact that I was suffering severe financial hardship was known to the court from the affidavits filed when I sought the dismissal of the appeal. To grant a further delay to the person who had done nothing to ensure that it was ready to hear was mind boggling. The subsequent criticisms of the CCJ that the Barbados Judiciary has to take some blame with respect to the delays in the system could not be truer.

On November 11th the matter was again called and a tearful, almost hysterical Griffith informed the court that she had been unable to retain counsel in the intervening six weeks, trotting out the same story that I had a hand in it, as no one seemed to want to assist her against me. It was amazing to behold that she was saying this and almost on every occasion that the matter came up, Michael Springer, Smith's cohort and one who was involved with her in an elaborate scheme to assist Mrs. Watson by preventing the enforcement of my judgment against her, was in the court observing proceedings, but yet could not assist. It was clearly another attempt at delay, a disease afflicting the Barbados court system which is hard to eradicate.

On November 11th Griffith was advised that December 14th was the date for the appeal, and in the words of the president of the court, the Chief Justice, "come hell or high water" the appeal must be heard, as the matter has a long history. At the time I felt that this was—as Bajans like to say—a 'lot of long talk blustering' because honestly it should have been dismissed out of hand. By this time I was becoming very agitated as I watched the proceedings from the gallery. I chose not to sit at the bar table, and I fixed my stare directly on the court, saying not a word, but my facial expression would have revealed all. It did elicit a comment from the CJ that I appeared to want to burst when granting what he said was the last adjournment.

On December 14th 2011 Eddie and I arrived at court and were approached by Amilcar Branche, informing that he had just been retained by Griffith, had not got all the relevant information, and would be seeking an adjournment. I asked him if he was aware of the issues at hand and the history of the matter and stated that it was my right not to agree to same. Amazingly, despite all the long talk of the previous occasion, the court granted him a two-month adjournment until February 13th 2012, when Murphy's Law dictated that my lead counsel Elliott Mottley would be out of the jurisdiction. As a result this adjournment turned out to be for three months, as the appeal was finally heard on March 5th 2012, more than two years after Justice Peter Williams had suggested the matter could have been disposed of.

On March 5th 2012, Branche painted an elaborate picture to suggest why the appeal should be upheld. He conceded that most of the grounds of appeal were untenable and concentrated on two alone. To be honest, it took me a while to figure out what he was saying or suggesting, especially as it appeared that he went out of his way not to offend me by suggesting on more than one occasion that I had done the correct and honorable thing by trying to ensure that the clients of Cottle Catford were repaid.

After addressing the court for about two hours, he finished and Elliott Mottley addressed for about thirty minutes, in which he adopted what was stated in our skeleton arguments (prepared by me of course), simply buttressing his arguments with some authorities that he had recently found. The justice retired to reach a decision after two and a half hours of argument.

What happened next was unbelievable, to be kind, and a disgrace, to be more charitable. It took nineteen months for the court to deliver its decision. I know that during the delay my counsel on more than one occasion enquired as to when the decision would be forthcoming, but to no avail. Finally the decision was handed down on October 4th 2013, and it is worth quoting from the judgement of Burgess J. in CV 22 of 2009, if only that it illustrates the dishonesty that was prevailing not only in my partners, but in the attorneys who manipulated the system so that it took the better part of ten years for a relatively simple issue to be determined.

Burgess J.A. The issues in this Appeal.

> In September of 2009, Ms. Griffith filed a notice of appeal against this order of Crane-Scott. J. In early December of 2009, this Court, at the hearing of that notice, determined that the notice was defective and granted leave for the filing of the proper notice. This was filed on 18 December 2009 and on 8 January 2010 Mr. Nicholls filed a respondent notice. After a number of adjournments the appeal was finally heard on 5th March 2012.
>
> The notice of appeal contained twenty grounds of appeal and the respondent notice a claim for variation of the rate of interest awarded by Crane-Scott J. Be that as it may, it has

emerged from the written and oral submissions to this Court by the appellant and respondent that the determination of this case really involves three principal issues. The first is whether Mr. Nicholls' action in the High Court (Civil Suit No. 1612 of 2005) in his own name against Ms. Griffith to recover the money's owing by her was properly brought. The second is whether Crane-Scott J. wrongly applied the law in settling the partnership accounts. The third is whether the rates of interest awarded by Crane-Scott J. should be varied in any way.

We will consider each of these issues seriatim.

First issue—Was Mr. Nicholls' action in his own name against Ms. Griffith for the moneys owing by her properly brought?

Mr. Branche for Ms. Griffith has with admirable courage and no little skill, attempted to craft a case for answering this question in the negative. His entire argumentative edifice was constructed on the elementary principle of partnership law, espoused in cases like Crawshay v Collins 2 Russ 325 at p. 347; West v Skipp 1 Ves. Sen at p. 242; Foster v Donald 1 Jac &W 252 per Lord Eldon; Richardson v The Bank of England(1838) 4 My & Cr 165 at pp. 172-174, that the relation between partners is not that of debtor and creditor, unless and until the partnership accounts have been finally taken after dissolution and a balance has been ascertained to be owing from one to another. Building on this basic rule, Mr. Branche argued that, at the time of filing of the action by Mr. Nicholls, it could not be said that Ms. Griffith was indebted either to him personally or the former partnership as the accounts had not been settled. This action, being not an action for a partnership account, was defective and could not therefore have been maintained and should have been dismissed by Cornelius J.

Mr. Branche's argument continued that the consent order

made by this court was made without prejudice to Ms. Griffith's foregoing defence and was not intended to, and did not cure the defect in the original proceedings. According to him, the consent order made by this court was to the effect that, upon settling of the accounts of the former partnership, that they be submitted to the High Court to be entered as judgments in respect of the appellant's liabilities to the partnership. Consequently there should have been an amendment to the cause of action initially filed in the High Court by Mr. Nicholls to bring an action for a partnership account.

Mr. Branche observed that, despite being granted leave to amend his statement of claim for the purpose of showing the increased amounts due from Ms. Griffith upon the settling of the accounts, Mr. Nicholls did not amend the cause of action initially filed. For this reason, Mr. Branche submitted that the action before Crane-Scott J. was not maintainable and that this Court should not uphold the reasoning of Crane-Scott J. as Mr. Nicholls' "claim is not adequately supported".

According to Mr. Branche, as a corollary to the foregoing, another fundamental partnership principle applied to prevent the respondent in the action as instituted by him. It is that a partner, like Mr. Nicholls has no right of action against another partner, like Ms. Griffith for the balance owing to him until after final settlement of accounts, and money lent to a partnership by a partner cannot be recovered in a common law claim for money lent: a partner is only entitled to be indemnified by the partnership out of its assets or by way of a contribution by his partners. So that where partners, like Ms. Griffith and Mr. Nicholls, are under a joint liability in respect of a particular transaction arising out of or connected with the partnership, and one of them is compelled to pay more than his share of such joint liability, as Mr. Nicholls admittedly had to do in this case, the court will not enforce his right of contribution in respect thereof against his co-partner, Ms. Griffith, except in an action for a general partnership account.

It is evident that this elaborate analytical structure erected by Mr. Branche is predicated on the applicability of the general principles of partnership law to this case. So, during the course of his oral submissions to this Court, the Court raised the question with him as to whether these general principles had supplanted common law freedom of contract principles and as such were not subject to any agreement between the partners. He answered, as he had to, that they had not. After all, section 21 of Cap. 313 provides generally as follows:

"The mutual rights and duties of partners, whether ascertained by agreement or defined by this Act, may be varied by the consent of all the partners, and such consent may be either expressed or inferred from a course of dealing."

And both section 26(1) (which sets out the rules as to the interests and duties of partners) and section 46 (which sets out the rules for distribution of assets on final settlement of accounts) of Cap. 313 are expressly stated to be "subject to any agreement" between partners. It is here that the difficulty in Mr. Branche's submission on the first issue lies.

It is palpably clear that the action filed by Mr. Nicholls against Ms. Griffith in the High Court in Civil Suit No 1612 of 2005 was based on an alleged breach of the dissolution agreement made on December 31st 2002 between himself and the other partner, Mr. Watson. Ms. Griffith, in her defence and counterclaim did not deny this agreement. In fact, as has been seen, she claimed to rely on clause 4 of this agreement for a defence to the action, namely, that it was a condition precedent to her liability to pay moneys due under the agreement that the indebtedness of each partner be ascertained by an audit of the firm's accounts as at the date of the agreement.

The conclusion, then that Mr. Nicholls and Ms. Griffith's dissolution rights and duties were the subject of the dissolution agreement is impatient of debate. Accordingly, Mr. Nicholls, as a party to that contract, was entitled to sue any other party to that contract, including Ms. Griffith, for breach of that contract. This is basic contract law and sections 26 and 46 of Cap. 313 are expressly declared to be subject to any contract between partners. The upshot of all this is that Mr. Nicholls was fully entitled, as he did, to bring the action in his own name in the High Court in Civil suit No. 1612 of 2005 against Ms. Griffith for breach of contract. There was no need for him to bring an action for a general partnership account under partnership law.

The case has always been treated, and we may add correctly, as a breach of contract action. It was so treated before Cornelius J. who made an order on this basis and in pursuance of Ms. Griffith's counterclaim for the accounts of the partnership to be audited and for specified accounts to be made and taken as a condition precedent to her liability under the dissolution contract. We pause here to stress that it was never contended by Ms. Griffith that the condition precedent here prevented the formation of the dissolution contract: her only contention was that the condition precedent had to be fulfilled for liability to arise under that contract. The subsequent consent order in this Court was made on the same basis of that of Cornelius J.

It is our judgment, then, that in the foregoing circumstances, Crane-Scott J. was correct to interpret the consent order of this Court as inferentially upholding the cause of action as originally filed by Mr. Nicholls. Ms. Griffith, having counterclaimed for a partnership account pursuant to the terms of the dissolution agreement, could not at the same time deny Mr. Nicholls' right to sue for breach of that contract. Accordingly, Mr. Branche's contention that Crane-Scott J. "wrongfully failed to determine as a matter of law the correct cause or causes of action in the Plaintiff's claim and the defendant's defences thereto" is misconceived. What was the correct cause of action was not in issue at any stage of the proceedings and there was certainly no reason for Crane-Scott J. to treat it as an issue for her determination. Her only task was to settle and confirm the accounts of the former partnership pursuant to this Court's consent order and she did just that.

Justice Burgess then went on to examine whether Justice Crane Scott had settled the accounts properly and held that she did, and then went into a lengthy exposition with respect to the interest rates awarded under Section 35 of the Supreme Court Act to rule that Justice Crane-Scott had properly awarded interest under the section and to deny my counterclaim for a variation of the interest rate.

The effect of this decision is that I will suffer even if I recover every cent from my former partners approximately a loss of as much as $1,500,000 dollars because of amounts that I have incurred in charges paid to the banks for amounts that two courts have found were the responsibility of my former partners, and for which they had signed an agreement more than ten years prior that they were responsible for.

I had reason to write to the Chief Justice after the judgment with respect to another aspect of this matter, and took the opportunity to point out to him that this decision has virtually driven me into the depths of bankruptcy, as have Watson and Griffith been given a free pass with respect to their liabilities, and have been allowed to profit by their actions of delay after delay. There has never been so much as an acknowledgment of receipt, nor of other letters talking of the abuse of process of the system by Smith et al while I try to enforce the judgments. While checking my records recently I have counted twenty letters over the last four years to the registrar of the Supreme Court seeking assistance with getting the road blocks being put up by Smith cleared, but these have fallen on deaf ears.

All things aside, it seems to me that the court had forgotten the equitable maxims that would allow the legal principle of "Restituto In Integrum" to be applied to this case. In other words the wronged party would have been allowed to be put back into the position he was in as if he had never been wronged, such as the position I would have been in if I had not been saddled with the debt of my former partners. It is a sentiment that my friend Wally Scott Q.C. in Jamaica has constantly surmised when opining that Burgess got this wrong, but then he would add he was never an equity lawyer. Equity lawyer or not, he was certainly well versed in the law of contract, and if this is a simple contract case and you have breached the contract then damages that follow from your actions must be for your account. As it is, all the losses have fallen on me.

It has always been my view that the preoccupation with the question of the partnership accounts is what led to this. As the court said, this was never a bar to my suing and even if it was, surely the court would have to look at not only the number of letters—100 plus were written to my partners over a period of about eight years—but the content therein on the subject of the accounts. About half a dozen of these letters not only demanded an audit of the accounts (which they outvoted me on), but indicated to them the stress that bearing the whole debacle was having on me. It has always infuriated me that much of the delay has been orchestrated by Smith, and yet he has walked away clean from the mess. It is for this reason that I feel that the maxim "if you start wrong you must end wrong" must be in play, for although the court stated that Justice Cornelius ruled it was a contract dispute, she entertained the nonsense of Smith about having to have the accounts of the partnership settled prior to a suit being instituted.

I will be the first to admit that this would be a prerequisite if it was an action for the partnership debt, or a share of the profits or a contribution to any losses in the partnership, but my actions were quite clearly predicated on the fact that I had paid funds to clients that they were liable for because they had been paid into the previous partnership and were not there when the clients came for them. Furthermore, at the time of the actions the accounts could not be settled, as there was a massive payment still due from Kingsland. As it turned out, because of the delay orchestrated by the defendants, by the time the matter came on for hearing the accounts could have been settled, so I find it hard to believe that the argument could be posited that I was supposed to bear this expense all along, and then having borne it, I was not to be not so much as compensated, but only refunded the interest that I had paid in borrowing the amounts that my partners were responsible for.

The upshot of the matter is that they have walked Scott-free from the interest charges I bore alone for two years before I instituted suit, and then have benefitted because of the delay in the system which saw this simple issue take nearly ten years to be litigated. Whatever one may say, it is not fair and I blame the actions of Smith who trotted out this nonsense from the beginning and the judiciary who have clearly missed the point as partly responsible for the financial morass I have found myself in by allowing this nonsense to be propagated in the courts.

To some that may appear bad enough, but now that I am attempting to execute the judgments, I still two years later have not received a cent—I lie: I got 64 cents from First Caribbean (which I sent back, pointing out that this was surely a joke which I took in very bad taste: postage costs 65c) and $400 plus from the Credit Union, both on behalf of Griffith. I have not received one cent from the Watsons, as Smith and his cohorts continually re-litigate the same nonsense in enforcement proceedings that I have brought as they did and were found wrong before. The sad thing is that they are doing it now while purportedly acting for Mrs. Watson, and have gone so far as to file applications in 1612/1613 on her behalf, a suit she was never a party to, and in a scandalous assertion wrote a 11-page letter to the CJ signed by Delvina Watson accusing the judge that granted me various *ex parte* orders in November 2013, as she was entitled in law to do, of judicial misconduct in handling my applications for enforcement.

Some of his actions have been unethical and others clearly contemptuous of the courts when he advised Mrs. Watson, as her affidavit would attest, that she did not have to abide by an injunction against sale of her property, property which she subsequently sold with his connivance and that of Griffith and Springer.

After the decision was handed down, the matter of costs became an issue and the matter was adjourned until January of 2014. By then not only had I undergone heart surgery, but I had been arrested for allegedly stealing money from a client of Cottle Catford. As that bastard Babb continues to say every time he comes to court seeking another adjournment as I try to recover the money from the Watsons, I am the only one he sees arrested. He repeated this taunt as recently as 20th July 2015 when he openly lied to the court with respect to the availability of his seniors to invoke the already criticized practice of getting an adjournment.

When he repeats these assertions, I can well sympathise with those who have similar or other grievances who resort to other methods of settling them, but all I will say of him is that he is a conceited, unethical parasite and one day he will be exposed for the true person he is.

When the court reconvened to consider the costs, there was the usual objection from Blanche, claiming uncertainty as to whether an award could be made for costs. Though not robed, I requested to speak, as Griffith had done several times. I stated that this whole issue had been turned into a circus by several attorneys, one of whom—Springer—was present in the court, and that I was not going back there again whether they awarded costs or not, because it had been 12 years since the partnership ended, and I had not received one cent, and the costs which I estimated at $100,000 would not make a dent in the interest I had to pay. I stated "...either award them or just don't waste my time about coming back." Surprisingly, they did.

This statement was made after Tariq Khan made an application to the court to withdraw my application for leave to appeal to the CCJ. I had been incensed by the dismissal of the interest claim, as I realized from long ago that I was suffering a tremendous loss. However, on the advice of Dr. Massay I withdrew the appeal, as he was of the view that the added or continued stress would likely be fatal to me. The goodly doctor was well meaning and I have always accepted his advice, but the stress that I have undergone since and as I am still here suggest that I should have not followed his advice and should have pursued the appeal. This has been my eternal regret, as it is evident that the CCJ knows how to deal with Smith, who has been allowed to run roughshod over the courts for years without his wings being clipped as the CCJ has had reason to do on at least two occasions recently.

It is positively amazing that having withdrawn from representing Griffith in the substantive matter, Smith now turns up representing Delvina Watson as I try to execute my judgment by seeking a charging order over property Allan Watson owns. Notice of my application has to be served on her when I seek the final order after getting the provisional charging order *ex parte*, and he now enters an appearance for her and seeks to argue that the original judgment was defective and so the charging order cannot be good. It is amazing that the courts would continue to allow him to further delay my enforcement of the judgments.

In one matter he attacks the judge as biased and appeals her decision, arguing that I am out of time seeking to enforce a judgment that he first argued had been satisfied. Now he argues that the substantive judgment is defective, having withdrawn from the original matter and not appeared when the appeal was heard in the Court of Appeal when such matters should have been heard. A decision on his arguments was adjourned in October 2014 and I am still awaiting the decision.

Life sometimes is not fair.

19

Still Married to Cottle

DESPITE THE DECREE absolute being pronounced sometime in 2013 declaring the marriage between Beverley and I over, as I write this story it is evident that I am still married, yoked to the Cottle partnership. No matter what I have done or the measures that I have put in place, that union that started on January 1st 1992 is still haunting me, and though provisionally severed at the end of December 2002, the decree absolute has not been pronounced.

My friend Eddie could not have put it better when, in the Court of Appeal during one of the frequent adjournments of the hearing, he described the woes that have befallen me as a result of this partnership as a relationship that was "worse than any marriage," because at least you can end a marriage, but the effects of a failed partnership may follow and have followed me around for the last decade. The old common law learning that one partner is liable for all the debts of his partner has never been truer in my case.

Readers other than legal scholars or those in historical or sociological spheres would probably be unaware of the times long ago in Victorian England when a man was liable for his wife's debts. During those bygone days when women did not have the presence they now do in the workforce and were certainly regarded as and treated as second class citizens, they were able to obtain credit for goods and services on the basis of being married and pledging their husband's name.

Payment for goods obtained in such circumstances became the responsibility of the husband on the basis of the pledge by the wife, and he was liable to be sued for the debt. That ends today's history lesson, but that was the norm prevailing in society at the time, so the requirement that partners be responsible for the debts of one another was not such a quantum leap away, as in a sense they were married to one another in a business venture.

Partners were ideally supposed to be individuals who knew one another well and trusted one another. Each ideally shared the same outlook in the endeavor that they were participating in. As the world of commerce has developed, this model has become unworkable and is much less used. Certainly legislation has now come into place that allows for persons in such a relationship to ring-fence their assets from seizure as a result of debts incurred by their partners, whether by dishonesty or negligence, under the Limited Partnership Act. Instead of partnerships, entities prefer to use the Society With Restricted Liability (SRL) as one of the preferred models for doing business if the harsh, stark commerciality of an incorporated company is not needed.

The legal profession, no doubt bowing to that old friend of ours—precedent, has been slow to react to the realities of today's world where a mistake of one could spell the ruin of the other, far less if there were activities that could be considered a breach of a partner's fiduciary duties, and unlike the accounting firms, the legal profession has been slow to embrace change. As a result, as archaic legislation had prevented groups of attorneys from practicing together as a body corporate, the partnership became the order of the day.

Fewer partnerships are being formed in the local landscape, and while they can be a very useful training ground for the young attorney, as the debt of the partnership can have catastrophic consequences for an individual who has not incurred the debt as a result of the actions of his partners, it is rightly no longer attractive in the more litigious society we are now living in. I know that many young attorneys have been warned of the perils of partnership with the words "see what it did to Nicholls."

Back at the end of 1991 when I was offered the chance to be admitted to the then existing partnership of Frederick Hutchinson Q.C., Allan Watson and Samuel Rudolph Hinkson along with Joyce Griffith, flashing hazard lights were nowhere on the horizon in my view. As I reflect and with the advantage of not only the failure of Cottle but the experience of life and a legal practice, there must have been a certain naiveté on my part in not considering whether there were any 'cons' to the obvious 'pros' at the invitation to join the partnership. I don't recall that I was offered time to think it over, but to be frank, even though Cottle had gone through the Simmons scandal at the turn of the eighties, it was a no-brainer that I would accept the invitation.

I have since heard from some distinguished and senior Queen's counsels, and been told by many persons that my father should never have allowed me to join the firm given what had happened in the past. I believe, however, that such sentiments are really being wise after the event, the 'Monday Morning Quarterback' or the 'armchair critic' who has much to say after or during the event, but never will participate in the event. No one at the time expressed to me or my family any reservation, and I can still vividly recall the many verbal and written congratulations at achieving such an elevation within five years of being admitted to practice at the bar. All I have heard as the true story of what happened comes out, is a feeling that one would never have imagined that Watson would have behave like he did.

It is my firm belief that what has befallen me is not only the result of the debt to the partnership that Watson and Griffith left, but as it was a debt that arose from a clear breach of their fiduciary duties to clients, I found myself in the position that I was morally and in some cases legally obliged to try and settle, which increasingly became impossible.

Looking back, I have divided what has occurred since the start of 1992 when I became a partner until the end of the High Street partnership at the end of 2002 into three distinct periods.

The first of these was the period until 1995 when Mr. Hutchinson suffered a stroke, and for all intents and purposes ceased being the *de jure* head of the firm. This was really the honeymoon period. Everything was going well. Under his watch the firm continued its traditional path. He ensured that every month the accounts of the firm were scrutinized. The income of the firm was closely monitored, as were the expenses. Obviously during this time the firm's income was decreasing, not only because of the general economic situation in the island—it was the time of the Stabilisation Tax of the Sandiford administration—but more critically the effect of Mr. Armstrong's initial illness which drastically reduced his level of output, and then his subsequent death, as he was virtually irreplaceable. The serious impact on the bottom line of the firm may not have been appreciated outside the firm, but even though as Jack Dear had once said he was not one to overcharge, the sheer scale of work and the type of work that he undertook meant that he earned more in fees in one month at times than some others did in a whole year.

I well recall at those early meetings Mr. Hutchinson stressing the need for us to monitor our expenses and not incur additional unnecessary expense, as with Mr. Armstrong's retirement, or to put it colloquially as he had gone home from the office, the fees from his work would soon disappear. The impact his death had really needs to be emphasized, for upwards of two years after he died work that he had started and left in train was being completed and fees were being earned. As such, I for one never begrudged the payment to his widow for the rest of 1994—he having died in February—the monthly amount that he was paid as a consultant up to the time of his death.

Ironically, given what is happening now as Barry Gale seems

determined to wreck my personal and professional life, he is the person that benefitted a lot from Mr. Armstrong's retirement. I have often said that contrary to the persona he tries to put out that he is this great legal luminary that has built a successful practice solely by his own efforts, he was hand delivered some of Cottle's major corporate clients by Mr. Armstrong. Many a morning after he retired from the partnership around 1990, Mr. Armstrong would have Gale meet him in his office early in the morning, and like any junior or secretary, Gale would be sat in that chair to his left while he gave him a précis of the file and no doubt advised him on how to proceed.

It is for this reason that I have been so livid with what Gale has done to me, for it has outstripped the requirements of someone fearlessly representing a client. Gale not only knows well the help he got from Cottle, even though I have never heard him acknowledge it, but as we never pitched marbles together I may have missed his acknowledgement.

Having learnt of the true problem at Cottle, he has been disingenuous in trying to portray me as the culprit. This has become clear as a result of the handing over of documents after my arrest, which included a letter from him to the Commissioner of Police in October of 2013 demanding that I be arrested for misuse of funds. Gale well knew that the funds had gone into the coffers of Cottle, but deliberately tried then and has continued to portray me as the villain of the piece. Can it be that he is seeking my destruction so as to divert attention from the fact that Watson, whom he gave shelter to for five years at Hastings Attorneys after I had thrown him out from Cottle, has walked with approximately another million dollars from clients while he was at Hastings, a fact that is not generally known?

The handover of work to Gale by Armstrong was a necessity forced by the lack of succession planning at Cottle that all the partners including Armstrong and Hutchinson have to be partly blamed for. They clearly did not envisage the drastic change in the profession whereby in the past generation after generation of families simply returned to Cottle or the firm that represented the family when they were in need of the services of an attorney. After all, some of these later generations were now becoming attorneys themselves, or had friends who were, as the ability to join the profession had widened from the few persons who went the traditional route of articled clerks, with the establishment of the Cave Hill Campus of the University of the West Indies. The result of this was a reduction of expected work for the firm as these clients went elsewhere.

   I took no offence at the time when he enlisted Gale. As I have often said about British Airways, however outstanding its young trainee pilot is, he starts at the bottom of the rung, not flying their flagship 747 or 777. I was not experienced enough at the time to undertake his corporate portfolio. Many times thereafter I had to journey to Gale's office in Gills Road pertaining to matters that started at Cottle. Many will recall the heated conversation I had with him in 2008, during which he called me a thief when I told him to "walk down the f....ing corridor from his office and knock on Watson's door" and when he got the cheque, give it to the client. He is nothing more than a hypocritical son-of-a-bitch, but I will let the reader be the judge from the emails that passed between us in 2014. The email to him was private, but he copied it to all on the Bar mailing list in an attempt to discredit me. I have reproduced them herein, but removed the names of all the members the mails were copied to. It gave me intense pleasure when I learnt that days later he had been kicked out of office as president of the Bar.

   From: Barbados Bar Association [mailto:bar@caribsurf.com]
   Sent: Wednesday, June 25, 2014 9:27 AM
   To: Barbados Bar Association
   Subject: FW: PRESIDENT'S MESSAGE TO MEMBERS RE: 2014 AGM

From: Barbados Bar Association [mailto:bar@caribsurf.com]
Sent: Wednesday, June 25, 2014 9:26 AM
Subject: PRESIDENT'S MESSAGE TO MEMBERS RE: 2014 AGM

Dear Members,

Please find the attached correspondence from the President for your attention.

>>On Jun 26, 2014, at 7:04 AM, "Phillip Nicholls" wrote:

It may mean little but as long as Gale is President of the Bar Association I will have little to do with it. He spouts and talks a lot of rhetoric about protecting the Interests of a Bar and its Members but has been complicit in fostering and protecting an Attorney at law who walked the same corridors as he did for five years and who has relieved others of Millions of dollars and with another precipitated my present situation and contemptuously resorts to all nefarious tactics and antics to try and disassociate himself from the individual while seeking to portray himself as a paradigm of virtue. None of us are without sin but as long as I am allowed to live I will ensure that the antics of a few Members who portray to John Public that they are men of virtue belonging to a class called the Q.C. thinking it means Queen's Counsel but in reality it means..... I will ensure the true story is told.

When he gets on TV and portrays that Attorneys are lacking in respect and ethics in not responding to colleagues, but thinks that he is above the law himself then that is the height of hypocrisy.

I have deliberately replied only to the person distributing his diatribe as President (no doubt under his instructions) of the Bar and copied him. Don't waste time responding asking for an apology and or alleging it is libelous. If it is in his opinion which counts for nothing in mine and among many others, file suit. I am sure he knows that truth is a defense to any allegation and I would welcome the opportunity to air the dirty secrets of the legal profession for if the President seeks to assert that this is an organization designed to protect Members but he on the other hand carries out by using his Position as President to try and carry out his own personal self-interest and attack on one of its Members in the guise of protecting a client , after benefitting by the handing over of substantial parts of his early practice from the Institution that has now been rendered asunder through the actions of two of its former Members, then he is not fit to be president.

He would do well to remember that one need not lie explicitly but there is something called lying by omission and when he exhorts people to attend a meeting and presumably vote for him because of all the "great" things he has done he forgets that while having turning a blind eye to one whom walked the same corridors as he did for 5 years from which he practiced law and which person was listed in telephone directory as either being an Associate or Consultant with Hastings Attorneys a man who every Attorney with more than ten years call knew what the real story with him and yet he continues despite the Court of Appeal Vindication of what was clear in relation to the Cottle Catford debacle (and this is what you should be dealing with the long time it takes to get Judgments on simple issues and the unethical practices of certain Attorneys in delaying and re litigating issues) he is trying to pin solely on me as your letter to the Commissioner of Police demanding my arrest evidences the fault for missing clients money. If that is not hypocrisy in light of your protestations in the virtual toilet paper missive you have distributed touting your run for re election then I don't know what is. But then again the clients who came to Hastings Attorneys and this gentleman relieved of them of money and now face road blocks at the Disciplinary Committee in part by his actions may think differently and he wants to be President. Stupes. As they say not only does the apple not fall far from the tree but things growing in your back yard tend to belong to the owner.

So Mr. Gale as I have told you before as you only understand Spanish.

NO Me CHINQUES, CALLATE,
! Chinga usted, carbon !.

Philip Nicholls

From: Barry Gale
Sent: Thursday, June 26, 2014 7:30 AM
To: Phillip Nicholls
Cc: Barbados Bar Association
Subject: Re: PRESIDENT'S MESSAGE TO MEMBERS

RE: 2014 AGM

Philip

What a pathetic small minded person you are and spineless as well! Stop blaming others and repay the hundreds of thousands of dollars you wrongly and admittedly appropriated from poor old people in a nursing home, one of whom died without even seeing a penny from the sale of his house thanks to you.

I only feel sorry for your family given what you have put them through. I would not dignify you with suing you for defamation. We all know who you are and what you have done ... Keep blaming Watson and Griffith.

By the way do you have a mirror in your house? If you do have a good long stare at it and see if you really like what you see! The Bar needs no assistance from you and perhaps soon your ability to practice as lawyer will be a thing of the past. Have a wonderful day

BG

Sent from my iPad

From: Phillip V. Nicholls
Sent: Thursday, June 26, 2014 10:49 AM
To: Barry Gale
Cc: Barbados Bar Association

Subject: Re: PRESIDENT'S MESSAGE TO MEMBERS RE: 2014 AGM

> Thank you Barry the only fucking idiot (and that's not Spanish) who has called me Spineless in my life us you. We will see but if I have paid two Million dollars into the firm verified by accountants pray tell how I am blaming others. You are a piece of shit who only has got where they are because of the perceived color of your skin. Fuck off and that's not in Spanish as well you have always spouted thus diatribe about me blaming others and have no fucking idea what I have done to keep a scandal at bay while cocksuckers like you pretend to be above board.
>
> You are not even fit to kiss my ass but you may lick it clean

---

From: Barry Gale
Sent: Thursday, June 26, 2014 4:19 PM
To: Philip Nicholls et al
Subject: FW: PRESIDENT'S MESSAGE TO MEMBERS RE: 2014 AGM

> Dear All
>
> This is the level where some members of our profession have reached ....judge for yourselves and be warned!
>
> BG
>
> >>On Jun 26, 2014 8:58 PM, "Phillip V. Nicholls" wrote:

That's where you are a bigoted liar and why I will go to my grave with my head held high I never appropriated any money but being the Jackass you are if two million dollars are gone from the account courtesy of my former Partners and I have not got it back as yet any 10 year old can tell you it's only a matter of time when I am unable to keep borrowing before the money runs out.

I am tired saying this to you but you are so bigoted in your beliefs that despite the letters Q.C. behind your name you cannot see. This is why when judgment day comes I have nothing to fear

Philip Nicholls

From: Barry Gale
Sent: Thursday, June 26, 2014 8:52 PM
To: Phillip V. Nicholls; et al
Subject: RE: PRESIDENT'S MESSAGE TO MEMBERS RE: 2014 AGM

I will with pleasure as well as your letter of admission and the default judgment for the money you appropriated.

BG

From: Phillip V. Nicholls
Sent: Thursday, June 26, 2014 4:21 PM

To: Barry Gale et al

Subject: Re: PRESIDENT'S MESSAGE TO MEMBERS RE: 2014 AGM

Maybe he can distribute all the correspondence now

From:
Sent: Thursday, June 26, 2014 9:21 PM
To: Phillip V. Nicholls
Cc:
Subject: Re: PRESIDENT'S MESSAGE TO MEMBERS RE: 2014 AGM

It is unfortunate that you would have sent this to the general members of the Bar.

Nicole C. Roachford
Attorney-at-Law

Sent: Thursday, June 26, 2014 9:50 PM
To: Phillip V. Nicholls
Subject: Re: PRESIDENT'S MESSAGE TO MEMBERS RE: 2014 AGM

I did not mean you

Nicole C. Roachford
Attorney-at-Law

>>On Jun 26, 2014 9:26 PM, "Phillip V. Nicholls" <pnicholls@nichollsandassociates.com> wrote:

If you read the trail it was Gale who sent it the Membership have no idea what Gale has been doing to me these last few years. I have had enough. Money has gone from Cottle and for ten years I have been trying to recover it while I have had the sole responsibility of repaying it. During that time he has given harbour to one of my Partners who took the money his Firm defended him and then he turned around and sued me for money Cottle could not pay while Watson was still at his Firm. Not satisfied he instituted disciplinary proceedings that came to nothing and now has orchestrated police charges while claiming to be a President for all Members.

Philip Nicholls

I was conscious of this failing whereby the firm was losing work because of poor succession planning, and would in all probability die if this leak was not stopped. As such, when I became a partner, I was determined to try to rectify this problem. During the years 1992 to 1995, I urged my other partners that it was necessary not only to ensure the survival of the firm in the future, but to compensate for the expected loss of income from the death of Mr. Armstrong to expand the firm by taking on young, vibrant attorneys so as to diversify what services the firm would offer.

During this time or shortly thereafter, Rosalind Smith-Millar, John Forde and Doria Moore joined the firm. Regrettably, it didn't have the effect that I had hoped. Rosalind, who had revived the firm's trademark practice, also developed a thriving family law practice before she left the firm, fed up around 2000 with the indecision of the partners, in particular Watson, to grasp the need to modernize the firm. Her departure was a loss, and true to the saying that one man's loss is another man's gain, she is now a partner with the biggest firm on the island, Clarke, Gittens and Farmer. In light of what has happened, she clearly made the correct decision.

I myself had been offered to leave in 1995 and join another attorney in his wide financial practice, but felt that as both Mr. Hutchinson and Mr. Armstrong had been very loyal and supportive of me that I should not jump ship. The portents at that time were not foreboding, but I know that as the problems intensified and I became more wrapped up in them, it was a source of some irritation to my wife Beverley when my temper was short due to the stress of work, as she constantly reminded me that I had the opportunity to leave earlier. This did nothing to endear her to me.

As recently as 2013, I was reminded by another close friend, Alan Smith, that during a visit to the UK in 1995, while walking along the bank of the Thames with two other friends—David Myers and Gary Peters—I was mulling over whether to leave and was at that time greatly concerned at the debit accounts that had started accumulating on the books. Ultimately, as Mr. Hutchinson was away sick at the time and Mr. Armstrong had recently died, I determined to stay and help with the revival of the firm.

John Forde and Doria Moore, who both joined the firm during this period, have both disappointed me for differing reasons. John, a very intense young man, some would say strange, really never lived up to expectations and to be frank was not earning anything like what was required to cover his salary and the expenses associated with maintaining his office. He was always at work, but come the end of the month one didn't see the results. I was the one on the principle that I had recommended his recruitment, charged with the responsibility around 1998 of informing him that the partners felt it best that we go our separate ways. He has never spoken to me since, and passes me like a full bus if our paths cross anywhere up to present times. He may think it is his way of insulting me, but maybe one day he will grow up.

Doria, on the other hand, has to my mind betrayed the trust I reposed in her. I fought for her to join the firm, as there had been two other associates employed shortly before her. After joining she became the contact person for the clients in the great Kingsland saga. She was the conduit between the firm, the clients, the Deane family whom we represented, and with the senior attorneys, particularly the late Sir Harold St. John, who worked closely on the matter. She continued working with me for two years after the High Street partnership ended before leaving to set up private practice.

I have no quarrel with people moving on and have encouraged others in the past like Julie Harris and Sharon Carter to explore other opportunities if they became available, and they have. Unlike the aforementioned two, both of whose weddings I attended, I now have no time for Doria, as it has become more and more apparent that she was plotting the moment to leave when it was most advantageous for her to do so. Leave she did, and the main client that the firm was representing, having not paid for the better part of ten years, went with her.

Both Julie and Sharon have criticized me for making it too easy for her to go with the work. As the Privy Council said in its judgment in the last case that was heard from Barbados, the firm had provided services over and above what was expected of a firm of attorneys, and it was only for this reason that the company had survived that long. Truthfully, I was sick of Kingsland at that time. It was a nightmare taking up professional time with no fees, and in my view there was little to be gained from not allowing access to our records, as out fees would only be forthcoming when the matter was complete. Doria left at the end of 2004 and the fees were not paid until 2006, fees that I have always maintained were a gross undervalue of the years of service that the firm had given, and it is something I have not forgotten, and I will find it hard to forgive her role now acting for the new owners of the company who had purchased the shares from the clients for whom we acted for many years.

It is clear to me that Doria planned what she was doing. She took with her copies of many records to assist her going forward. As she was fond of pointing out, her numbers with respect to writing up fees could not be judged without taking into account the fact that the work she was doing for Kingsland was not being paid for. The fees for Kingsland were not paid for nearly a decade after the work started, and she was well aware of this, yet within weeks of leaving she was pressuring the clients to have me use money ostensibly held by Cottle to pay her a retainer. But by far what has saddened me is her arguing against the amounts that were due to the firm for the years of service that were not paid, despite internal memos from her indicating that the firm's fees were substantially more than what was eventually paid. I will never forgive her for her deceitfulness.

Sometime in 1995 Mr. Hutchinson had a stroke, and the *de facto* running of the firm turned over to Allan Watson. Mr. Hutchinson remained the head of the firm until he retired in 1997, and Mr. Watson became not only the *de facto* but *de jure* head of the firm. At the last partners' meeting that he attended, Mr. Hutchinson warned that the partners needed to watch and monitor the over-drawings of the partners, which he indicated then were beginning to cause him alarm.

At this time I was on the board of the Barbados Cricket Association, as well as holding a senior position at Pickwick Cricket Club. Yearly the accounts of the two institutions—in particular those of the BCA—came in for scrutiny, but I paid them a cursory glance. I will readily admit that accounts bored me. It was a trait from Law School, the only course that I hated, and as it was examined not in exam conditions but by assignments, I, like all my colleagues, got much assistance from fellow students who were reading the subject. In my case my assistance was right at home from my cousin Nickie, Auntie Marina's daughter.

Regrettably, I never paid attention to the details and did not pick up early enough on the warning signs. Many on the board of the BCA at the time would not recall, but during one meeting Stephen had chided me for my obvious lack of interest as we went over the numbers to prepare the annual report with the statement that I needed to pay more attention, as it would help me in unraveling the mess I was in professionally with the firm's accounts. It was not said so explicitly, but I got the drift and started teaching myself, and can now peruse many a balance sheet and look for the warning signs. It has proven a salutary lesson to me as I constantly impress on young attorneys the need to pay attention to their accounts, tedious as they may be, as they can quickly get away from you.

But it may well be asked how in the case of Cottle, as its accounts were audited every year, that the signs were not picked up earlier. They were. As I indicated, Mr. Hutchinson expressed concern prior to falling ill, and despite all the clap trap spewn by Smith in his posturing after I filed suit against my former partners in 2004 that I needed to file audited accounts as his client at the time (Joyce Griffith) could not and did not know whether what I was alleging she owed was correct, the situation was well known to each of the partners and every monthly meeting started with a careful examination of the accounts and more particularly the monthly expenses.

Smith's argument was not only a ridiculous argument, but a dishonest one, as each partner had an idea from the monthly internal figures what the financial position of the firm was, and certainly knew by how much they were overdrawn. Whereas each partner knew the overall picture of the firm, only the senior partner knew every detail, as he received accounts for all attorneys including the other partners, but the other partners didn't receive his. This in itself was a flaw that he took advantage of to hide what he was doing.

My lack of attention to the accounts meant that I did not pick up early enough that he was vastly overdrawing himself. After all, it was the system I found which the senior partner was responsible for, and I believed like Armstrong and Hutchinson before that he was playing by the rules. He was not, and I am paying the price now for that.

During this early three-year period of the partnership, I believed that one of the ways to increase our income portfolio was not only by getting more hands to the plough, but by diversifying and getting into the lucrative offshore sector. As such I joined many of the promotions held overseas, and our income in that sector started to increase. It has pained me now that after all those leg hours my standing and indeed my involvement in the sector has disintegrated as a result of the ridiculous money laundering charge that I have the DPP Charles Leacock to thank for.

My delving into the sector has taught me another lesson about partnership. Partners are your bedfellows, and just like any marriage or relationship, you should know exactly who you are getting in bed with. 'Know your client' is the refrain of the Anti-Money Laundering Authority, and for me it should have been 'know your partner'.

The system that I found at Cottle really didn't foster that before you became a partner. Though they were white Barbadians, I had far more in common with Armstrong and Hutchinson than I did with either Watson or Griffith. Like me both of them had strong club affiliations, not to mention sporting affiliations, something that Hinkson also had with Spartan, but the other two did not. Joyce Griffith is a female, but more and more females are not only involved in clubs, but other social organizations. She was involved in neither, and I suggested to her more than once that it would help improve her name recognition if she were to join the Kiwanis or the Lions, for instance. She was always too lazy to make the effort.

Watson was a completely different animal, as I was to learn to my cost. I doubt he knows where Kensington Oval is, and while some may scoff at the importance I place on that, I doubt he knows either where to find the National Stadium or the Gymnasium or the Garrison. It was too late by the time I realized this and had become bedfellows with them. This was important because unless everyone is singing from the same hymn sheet there is not much chance of moving forward or out of any adversity that is being faced by the partnership.

I am not the perfect person — just ask Beverley — but it was clear that my desire to take the firm forward into the 21st Century was not shared by the others, who were content for it to stay as it was and just receive the annual handouts. That was fine, but when the handouts became a poisoned chalice, gangrene set in.

I started to get an indication early on after the beginning of our partnership as to Joyce's attitude. She was very insistent to the staff members that her name must appear before mine on everything, something that didn't faze me one way or another, but which I was surprised was important to her. After all, she was already getting more than I was from the partnership. But it was in the area of travel that I sensed some form of jealousy. Many persons, not her alone, viewed this as luxurious living, but all of us who have spent time on the circuit will tell you differently. Even when travelling you still have to ensure that work at home is being taken care of, and in those early days the instantaneous communication with smart phones was not yet a feature.

I found travel to Europe the most challenging. Very often before leaving for your day's meeting or seminar you would have to ensure that work was done before the office opened at home, and then after a day's work there, you would come back to your hotel to find that follow up questions needed to be answered, as it was just after lunchtime at home. By the time home finished work, your day would be a fourteen hour day. Not glamorous at all, but on one of my early trips to Mexico to attend a Caribbean conference, Joyce insisted she wanted to go. To this day I doubt she has ever read the manual, but the purpose was really the in-transit stop in Miami, because that was when I got my introduction to the mad scramble of the shopaholic.

Travel was a necessity if you wanted to expand your portfolio in the offshore sector, but it could be exhausting. I recall on one occasion travelling to Edmonton in the winter on the same flight as then Minister for International Business Reginald Farley. Edmonton was snowed out and so we had to land in Calgary and were bused through the night to Edmonton. From an arrival initially at 8:00 pm the night before, we actually arrived at the hotel at about 4:00 am to find our reservations cancelled, as they thought we were no shows. The meeting we were attending was scheduled to start at 8:00 am, addressed by him, and as Minister Farley said to me as he was taking his leave "at least you can rest after." He had a flight out of Calgary at 2:00 pm that afternoon to get into Toronto in time for the flight the next morning back to Barbados, to attend a cabinet meeting later the following afternoon. My schedule was in no way as taxing as his, but it was not all fun and games as some thought.

On the one occasion that I decided to take an extra day just to relax, I found myself ejected from my room for a couple of hours because the now Justices Cornelius and Richards needed to change for their midnight flight, having checked out at midday to go shopping, and on return to the hotel that the conference was at, being told that I was still checked in. Maybe that is why Mrs. Watson was to later allege that she was biased towards me.

It was clear to me that Joyce and Watson did not share the same vision of what was needed—the long hours of work etc. I recall calling her home at 8:00 pm from the office one night to sort a matter out, and her young daughter answering the phone and asking her who in their right mind could be in Cottle at that hour. I laughed, as in the 15 years that her mother and I worked together, I never saw her in the office after 5:00 or on weekends. Yes, she had other responsibilities, but I have worked with other mothers who have managed that. One instance I vividly recall. I was working on a matter with an attorney in Australia. It was morning here, so clearly it was night there, and every time I sent off the email thinking it was the last time, a reply would come, the last of which by my calculation was at 11:00 pm her time.

Seeking some humour, I said to her "Is it not time to go home lest your husband put you out?" after which the next email that came was from her husband, who said he was with her in the office, but "Thank you for your attempts to get her home", because he had failed in his attempts.

As I look back, the seeds for the plunge of the partnership into serious problems were there, but I did not read the tea leaves. Like any marriage the consequences can be disastrous if either party is not true to it. The honeymoon was over, and as we approached the end of the 20th Century, something had to change. In this marriage, however, I went above and beyond the call of duty, and as Justice Cornelius once said to Vernon Smith in proceedings in court: "Why are you interjecting yourself into the affairs of Cottle and not sticking strictly to legal matters, for if you did maybe they will sort it out?"

I have no doubt that because of the animal that he is, he is chuffed with himself at what misery he has caused me.

20

Trying to Recover the Money Yet Again

IN 2012 I was really struggling financially. Borrowing from the banks were not an option, the Court of Appeal had not delivered its decision, my attempts to use my pension entitlement from Sagicor were stalled and heading for litigation, so I decided I had to make an effort to get the remaining 68% of the judgment never paid as awarded in suit 151/152 of 2004. This had become all the more important, as I had learnt through a colleague that Mrs. Watson was attempting to sell her property which could be used to satisfy the judgment.

I thus made an application to the court *ex parte* as the law allows for a Charging Order to be effected over her property. The law had changed since the judgment in 2004 and a Charging Order was needed before the judgment ranked in priority over land owned by the debtor. The application was heard by Justice Chandler. He quite correctly pointed out that he was unable to grant the Charging Order because Notice of Intention to proceed in the suit had to be served on the defendant. No legal proceedings in the suit had been undertaken in the previous 12 months prior to the application and thus the need for notice to the defendants.

To do so, I stated, would make my application redundant, as if she was attempting to sell, she would simply speed the process up. The only route was for me to make an application for an injunction prohibiting the sale of the property in question, pending the hearing of the application for a Charging Order.

This I did, and the application was heard by Madam Justice Richards on July 5th 2012, who granted the injunction *ex parte*. I therefore had notice of the injunction served on her attorney on record, Vernon Smith, who returned the documents the next day under cover of a letter saying he no longer worked for Delvina Watson. Anticipating this obstructionist behavior, I had obtained from the court at the time an alternative order for substituted service via the newspaper, as all efforts to locate Mrs. Watson at her residence in St. Philip had drawn a blank. Notice of the injunction was published in the *Sunday Nation* of July 16th 2012.

From that date I made attempt after attempt to have the matter of the Charging Order heard, but to no avail. By an application dated October 5th 2012 filed by Alwyn Babb, Mrs Watson made an application for the injunction to be lifted. An affidavit in support of her application was filed not only by her, but by Vernon Smith, who had previously indicated he no longer worked for her. From a misdirected fax received by my office it was clear that he was instructing Babb. The basis for seeking the discharge of the injunction was that the full debt was repaid and both her affidavit and that of Smith listed in support the 32% paid to me along with the receipts from her husband Allan and Joyce Griffith, evidencing the payment of the other 68%.

Both my application for the Charging Order and this application to lift the injunction seemed to fall into abeyance for one reason or another, and it was not until October of 2013 that the application for discharge came on before Justice Reifer. I disputed at the hearing that the debt had been paid and Justice Reifer indicated that she was not minded to lift the injunction, as the judge who had granted it was still available and advised the applicant Watson through her attorney that the matter should be taken back before the issuing judge.

I have been the subject of some dishonest attempts to prevent me from recovering the funds due to me in this whole Cottle saga, but the circumstances of 151/152 following from the granting of that injunction show the seedy side of the practice of the law by some attorneys, and I make no bone for saying that this practice is completely unethical.

The filing of the application for the discharge of the injunction makes one thing clear—both Delvina Watson and Vernon Smith all had actual knowledge of the injunction granted in July of 2012 prohibiting the sale of property belonging to Delvina Watson. The subsequent sale of the property in December 2012 was a clear breach, and an even clearer contempt of court. Not only was Watson in contempt, but clearly Smith was and her subsequent affidavit that she did so on his advice that the injunction was bad would be no defense to a contempt charge.

Besides the two of these, Springer and possibly Griffith, who had to sign the release of the mortgage they purportedly held over the property to allow for the sale to be completed in December of 2012, may well have been liable under the principle that they knowingly assisted someone in breaching an injunction.

Smith was the attorney preparing the release of the mortgage, and he witnessed the execution of same by the alleged mortgagors Griffith and Springer. However, the attorney acting for Watson in the sale in December 12 was Keith Mayers, and he later swore an affidavit that he was unaware of the injunction. At the time of the sale occurred in December 2012 I was unaware of it, only learning of it in December of 2013. I have always felt that this was a plan orchestrated by Smith so that knowledge of the injunction would not come to the purchasers. This has been supported by the fact that Mrs. Watson was later to say under oath that she has had only two attorneys all her life, namely her husband and Vernon Smith. I doubt Mayers knew, and so would not have been constrained when replying to requisitions that he knew of no reason why the property could not be sold.

Both Delvina Watson and Smith knew at the time that Babb had appeared in court in 2013 to apply for the lifting of the injunction against the sale of the property that had already been sold in December of 2012. Babb was later to swear that he did not know this at the time he made the application, but as I was to tell him later he had such a conceited and inflated opinion of his ability that he believed all along that Mrs. Watson had approached him to help her get out of my clutches, spinning him a yarn about how I am taking things out on her because I could not reach her husband. The truth was that when, in keeping with her Lady Macbeth character, she was assisted by Smith in keeping the loot that she and her husband had raped from the coffers of Cottle. While one should at all times seek to follow instructions, surely her instructions could not have made him deliver the verbal foul-mouthed assault on me when we left court in October 2013 that I was seeking to rob an old lady. Is he that foolish that he had no idea of what was going on?

Shortly after this episode in October 2013 I was arrested, which brought home to many the problems I was facing with this ongoing debacle, as at the time of my arrest the partnership had ended for nearly twelve years, but I had received not one cent from the partners found liable by the courts for the money due to the clients of Cottle.

One of the calls that I received the night after I was arrested and had returned home from my stay at Hotel Coleridge Street was from the Prime Minister, who called to express his concern at what had transpired, as he was aware of the battle I was facing. He informed me that as soon as he had heard the news he had called the CJ to enquire whether the long outstanding matter with my partners had been dealt with, and was informed that the decision had been delivered earlier that month.

I indicated to him that yes, it had been delivered, but as it was merely four weeks after the decision there was precious little that I could have done to enforce it. In addition, my attempt to enforce the remainder of the judgment outstanding against Delvina Watson was bogged down in the system. Unofficially I was advised (not by the Prime Minister, I hasten to add) that I should make application to the court for various orders to try to seek enforcement, and so on November 19th I made urgent applications, *ex parte* as any student of equity will tell you is the standard procedure, for various freezing orders against the defendants in 151/152 and 1612/1613. These were granted on November 21st.

While doing due diligence with respect to the applications, it came to my attention that Delvina Watson had sold part of the property, as alluded to above, that was the subject of the injunction. The Injunction granted on July 5th 2012 was still in place on December 4th 2012 when the sale took place.

After the granting of the various freezing orders by Justice Richards on November 21st 2013 under a certificate of urgency, Babb's application for the injunction of July 5th 2012 to be lifted came before Justice Richards on November 23rd for hearing. Mrs. Watson and Babb were served with the orders granted *ex parte* on the 21st outside the court before the matter was called. I had the day before served the several banks and other financial institutions in Barbados with the freezing orders granted.

When court started, Babb rose before Justice Richards and began to make his application for the injunction of July 5th 2012 to be lifted. At that time he was stopped in his tracks and informed by the judge that from what was presented before her on the 21st the question at hand could not be whether the injunction should be lifted, but whether there had been an act which could be considered a contempt of court.

The look of bewilderment on Babb's face was one of the enduring moments of this whole saga that I will remember with somewhat of a smile. His appearance and subsequent mutterings would suggest he had no idea or perhaps on reflection I would say he did not understand what was being done. He then asked for a short adjournment to consult with his client and upon the matter coming back on for hearing. The matter was adjourned to another date. I was being represented at this time by Tariq Khan, who was later to go on to replace Gale as the president of the Bar.

It was clear to me what was happening. Watson and I would hazard a guess that Smith had a part in this. Babb had been instructed to have the injunction lifted and I suspect he was simply told the debt had been repaid and thus the injunction should not have been granted, which any lawyer worth his salt would know is not a reason to flout it. At the same time Mrs. Watson, who was later under oath to say that she only had two attorneys work for her in her life, namely her husband and Vernon Smith, had been represented by another attorney, Keith Mayers Q.C., when she sold property in December of 2012. I was to later conclude that this was all an elaborate structure to continue the perpetuation of the fraud on Cottle and indirectly me, so that I could not get hands on the assets in the Watsons' possession from which I could seek to enforce my judgments. Both Babb and Mayers have denied knowledge of the injunction and the fact that the sale in 2002 was done in a manner to evade my judgments. The smell test would probably suggest differently.

As I dug further into the transaction with respect to the sale of the property that was the subject of the injunction, I discovered that the property was bought by a purchaser for whom Fiona Hinds of Carrington and Sealy acted. The property was bought with the assistance of a mortgage from Sagicor, and Stephen Farmer of Clarke, Gittens and Farmer acted on behalf of the lender.

As a result I spoke to Stephen on the phone and expressed my extreme disappointment that he, knowing the challenges I was facing, could act in a transaction where Mrs. Watson, who he well knew was the wife of my former partner, was getting funds and could not have thought of alerting me. On several occasions in the past he had commiserated with me on my predicament and yet now was taking a back seat. He pleaded as an excuse the fact that as there were no charging orders in place, he did not think that my judgment against her of which he was aware would prevent her passing title. I was not impressed, and told him so.

My next port of call was to Carrington and Sealy to speak to Fiona Hinds, but she was out of the island. I was really not looking forward to the conversation, as she was one of Beverley's closest friends and we have hardly been on speaking terms since the breakup of my marriage to Beverley. This I could understand, but at the time I marveled at how when news of my arrest spread she had been in such a panic as to the welfare of the children and their whereabouts as she knew Beverley was out of the island, and had either contacted her or my father to ascertain that they were alright, yet did not feel any compunction towards me by raising a red flag. After all, her concern for my children should make her realise that the problems affecting me could conceivably affect their well-being.

I thus spoke to the senior partner Adrian Cummings. Again after my arrest Adrian was one of the people who called me to express his horror at what was happening. He perhaps at the time of that conversation had not connected the dots, but during our conversation when I called on him he admitted that when the transaction with the sale by Mrs. Watson was going through they had had extensive discussions as to whether she could pass title though there was a judgment, but where there was no Charging Order. They had come to the conclusion with Stephen Farmer that she could.

I knew both Adrian and Stephen well. Adrian was part of that Harrison College 6th Form from which 6 attorneys had emerged, while Stephen, a former Barbados all-rounder, had served on the board of the BCA with me. Ironically Stephen had cut his teeth at Cottle Catford and was articled to Joseph Armstrong.

I expressed to them both my extreme disappointment that they would have acted in the matter knowing well who Delvina Watson was, and that she and her husband were indebted to Cottle. I was not expecting any breach of client confidentiality, but as other attorneys have told me and have illustrated, there was a convention going back years whereby someone would have called and said "Look I know so and so owes you money… she is coming into some soon… you take the information and run from there."

If such a call had been made, I would have drawn to their attention the existence of an injunction which it was not unreasonable to believe they were unaware of. With the scheme concocted by Smith, no doubt Mayers would not have known as well. How would that have assisted me you may ask? I am sure given that both have admitted that the judgment was discussed, they would have insisted on the lifting of the injunction prior to completion, which I would only have consented on if my judgment was settled out of the purchase price of $600,000.

I explained to them that for reasons I know not, the application for the Charging Order has never been heard, but I disagreed with their contention that in its absence clear title could pass, because having knowledge of the judgment meant their clients could not be considered bona fide purchasers for value without notice.

As unbelievable as it may sound, I have until the end of October of 2015 been unable to get a date for the granting of the Charging Order. I have lost count of the number of letters to the Chief Justice and/or the Registrar of the Supreme Court, and the verbal discussions with senior staff in the registry about why this application filed since June 2012 has not been listed for hearing, or if it had been listed, not been heard.

More than one reason for this state of affairs was given to me: the file could not be found, then the matter inadvertently did not appear on the list for the day originally given for hearing, or that it was adjourned because the Chief Justice was said to have stated that all matters involving Cottle were to be heard by one judge (something I had requested in a letter to him). My checks with the clerk of that judge revealed no knowledge of this directive. The feeling I was left with is that I was pursuing a problem that no one really wanted to deal with.

I felt terribly let down by what was done. As I have said I have never expected handouts in assistance, but the failure of them both to do something that was not legally required, perhaps not even ethically necessary, but which would have been morally right, is what has bedeviled much of the dealings I have faced in the profession. Few have lifted a finger to directly help me.

The substantive matter adjourned on November 23rd 2013 came back on for hearing on the January 10th 2014 and (surprise, surprise) Vernon Smith now turned up and entered an appearance, along with Michael Springer, as senior counsel for Delvina Watson instructed by Alwyn Babb. Babb was clearly out of his depth. I had developed an intense dislike of him from the time of his first attack on me outside the court over a year ago. He was called to the bar just before Cottle Catford was closed, and cannot know anything about the firm or in particular the history of the matter which had been tainted by the antics of Smith.

His claim to others—including on social occasions when he sought to portray me as a predator trying to feast on a defenseless woman for whom he was a knight in shining armor rushing to her assistance in forestalling all that I was doing, had drawn my ire. His only knowledge of the matter was based solely on instructions from Delvina Watson, hardly a person with an objective state of mind, and to take her stance on matters is fine, but to treat the opposing side and a fellow attorney with the contempt he displayed is a sign of the immature idiot he is despite his advanced age.

That said, when the matter resumed in court I made it clear to the judge that as the central issue surrounded the repayment of the judgment debt, I would be exercising my right to examine under oath both Delvina Watson and Vernon Smith, who had sworn affidavits that the money had been repaid. It had always been my argument that the money was never repaid and that the position of Smith that it had been was at best the fabrication of a fertile mind or at worst the work of a psychotic liar. Smith countered that he would wish to cross examine me, to which I responded that I have nothing to hide.

Smith was subsequently sworn and cut a sorry figure trying not to commit an act of perjury. He insisted that his payment of the portion of the judgment debt to Allan Watson and Joyce Griffith was in accordance with the law because as partners at the time the debt arose, they were entitled to receive it whenever it was repaid.

When it was pointed out that the judgment was for clients' money and was not for any profit of the firm that the partners were entitled to, he responded in his typical irascible manner that the Client's Accounts were owned by the partners, a position he continued to hold even when Justice Richards said to him surely that can't be correct as the partners hold the accounts on trust for the clients. One may from this answer speculate as to how he views his own Client's Account.

He was questioned as to the method of payment of the amounts allegedly received by Watson and Griffith, and responded that the receipts indicated that the money was received. I insisted that he produce the cancelled cheque evidencing payment similar to the one he had been brandishing as evidence of payment to me. His response was that he did not keep those records at Smith and Smith, nor could his bank provide them. In response, the judge stated that surely they possessed ledger records in the firm suggestive of the payment which could be produced. He stated that he did not keep the financial records of Smith and Smith and could not produce them, giving the impression this was a minor matter that he could not be expected to know about. When asked whether someone in the firm could produce the records, he said no one was available. By this time he was not appearing to be a credible, far less honest witness.

Smith then stated he now recalled that he would not have had records of the payment to Griffith and Watson because these payments did not come through Smith and Smith Client Account, unlike the payment to me. He intimated that this payment to me in 2007 was an advance by him for which he was only repaid from the sale in December of 2012. Is not the date ironic? The logical question therefore was where the other payments to Joyce and Mr. Watson emanated from.

At some point during my examination of him, as I looked at him directly in the eye, I said with as much contempt in my voice as I could muster that: "I am sorry I that I ever used the epithet to you of 'Uncle' in the past which was suggestive of a mark of respect because I now have absolutely no respect for you as a man, especially as you try to justify reasons for a payment that you know is false." But I added "… who am I to expect any bona fides from you, for if you will do things inimical to the interest of your own flesh and blood, what should I expect?" (See the last chapter of this book.) I was asked by the judge not to go down that line, so I said no more. Both he and Watson were questioned on the same date, April 23rd 2014, to avoid any coaching of her.

Delvina Watson was then questioned under oath and stated that she had used two attorneys in her life, her husband Allan Watson, and Vernon Smith who was her attorney for everything. She indicated that at no time had Mr. Smith ever informed her that he was no longer acting for her, and was unaware that he had sent a letter to that effect to me. She further stated that the question of settling the judgment debt was in the hands of Mr. Smith. She left everything with him and he informed her that all moneys due were settled. She had no reason to doubt him.

In response to questions about the mortgage in favour of Griffith and Springer in 2007, she said she did not recall getting the money from the mortgage. Justice Richards questioned this, saying she found it difficult to comprehend that someone would not remember receiving in excess of $300,000. At that point she said — to the objection of Smith, which was overruled by the judge who said she wanted to hear what she was saying—that the mortgage really didn't concern her, she did it as a favour for her husband as he received the money.

So the question for all to consider is if what she is saying is true, namely that the money was not received by her and that this is the money that Smith is intimating was used to pay my 32% and then to repay Allan Watson and Joyce Griffith the other 68%, was this in effect borrowed by Allan Watson who then repaid himself from the money he borrowed? As I have always maintained, this scenario was concocted by Smith who has lied and been party to an attempted deception of the court, an offence that should see him sanctioned by the Disciplinary Committee.

My cross examination by Smith was lengthy and was basically him trying to get me to sanction or agree with his belief that Cottle Catford never existed after 2002, because "you can't have a one-man partnership." As I said to him, he had paid and received cheques from Cottle Catford between 2002 and 2007, but probably because of advancing senility, he did not remember. Further in 2004 when he had not defended the original claim he had not raised this point that I lacked capacity to sue, but was now raising it as I attempted to enforce the judgment.

My cross examination of May 7th 2014 was due to resume on June 10th. On the 10th Vernon Smith informed the court that he, in the interest of time, was finished with his cross examination of me because he wanted to make an *in limine* point. Justice Richards confirmed more than once with him that he was finished with his cross examination and he said yes.

I responded to his request by stating that you cannot take an in limine point in the middle of proceedings. Arguments between the parties ensued, during which time Smith said that no matter what was decided he was going to appeal any decision, at which point he was asked by Justice Richards what was the point of her presence if he had already determined that whatever decision she makes he would appeal.

It was clear to any objective person that what was being attempted as an explanation was a tale of no merit. Mrs. Watson, when shown the cheques that had been cashed by her and her husband from the account—the same account that Smith was saying he was entitled to part of the judgment because he owned it—claimed she could not read as she did not have her glasses. As I was to point out to the court, she had been sitting in the back texting away and was well able to see the smaller keyboard of the phone. As his fanciful and elaborate tale was falling apart, Smith now launched another tactic, as is par for the course with him.

Justice Richards advised him she was not prepared to hear argument on his point now that I was out of time in my efforts to enforce the judgment without notice being given to the other side, and adjourned the matter July 21st 2014, giving him two weeks to file and serve his arguments and two weeks for me to respond.

This is where the matter started to go askew. As the proceedings were being recorded, Smith was well aware that a transcript would show the duplicitous nature of his arguments which had been contradicted by Mrs. Watson, as she was not cunning enough to continue the façade created by him, or simply was not party to it from the beginning. The only reasonable conclusion that can be gained from an examination of the evidence—even if one is to feel that I am biased—is that the whole thing was a concoction of lies and that the full amount of the judgment has never been paid.

His decision to change course midstream from arguing that the money was repaid to now argue that I was out of time in trying to enforce the payment of the money is typical of Smith. He has and always seeks to practice law by ambush. He is never interested in obtaining justice, just his way, and is not averse to sharp practice in so doing. The CCJ, as stated before, has commented on this.

Arguments were served on me as ordered. However, as there was no application as to what he was seeking, simply arguments as to why my application to enforce and presumably all the injunctive relief before be discharged, I was unsure about what he was claiming, so I determined to be safe and cover all bases by responding by affidavit to his claims.

When the matter came back on for hearing on July 21st 2014, Elliott Mottley Q.C. represented me. Smith argued that I had failed to comply with the court order re filing of arguments and that he needed time to respond to my affidavit and requested an adjournment. This, after all, has been what this matter has always been about. If he had taken the time to read the affidavit he would have seen that all his arguments were responded to therein. After all, a rose by any other name is a rose, so because it is not headed 'Arguments' doesn't mean they are not there. But then the collective wisdom of those three would not realize that.

Elliott Mottley informed the court that this was a storm in a tea cup, that he did not have need of my affidavit to respond to what was filed on behalf of the defendant and would show that the case he was relying on to state that my action was precluded by the limitation did not say that. The judge invited him to proceed and he made his arguments. Smith was invited to respond, but stated he stood by what he had filed and the judge adjourned the matter for her decision.

On November 14th 2014 Justice Richards gave an oral decision dismissing the application by Smith and ordering that the matter as to whether the money was ever paid be concluded by her issuing subpoenas for Joyce Griffith and Allan Watson to attend on February 24th 2015 to testify. Not surprisingly, Smith has appealed her decision to the Court of Appeal, which is where we are at.

His modus operandi continues… spin and spin matters out. Having not opposed a default judgment in 2004 for moneys paid by Watson to himself and his wife, as well as to all manner of persons on behalf of the Watson family, he is now ten years later appealing to the Court of Appeal to determine whether I am too late in trying to enforce the judgment after arguing for years that the whole judgment had been paid, when it was clearly not.

But if one thought that was bad enough, at the end of October 2014 a letter signed by Delvina Watson, 11 pages in length, purportedly under her hand, and citing much of the legal issues at hand with usual legalistic jargon, was written to the Chief Justice demanding that action be taken against Justice Richards for grave judicial misconduct. I say 'purportedly' because for an individual who to my knowledge at best has a school leaving certificate, this letter would put many senior attorneys to shame. A clearly contemptuous action. I leave the last word on this from my father who by now has become incensed as to this travesty that I am facing and determined that a letter to the Chief Justice was in order.

It was clear that the intent now was to have Justice Richards recuse herself from the matter and thus force me to start all over again. I know she contemplated this, but decided against it, so for once his despicable acts have failed. The whole sordid mess prompted my father to write this letter to the CJ in early November of 2014.

> Dear Sir Marston:
>
> My son, Philip Nicholls, has shared with me a letter addressed to you by ...... who had copied it to him as an interested party along with a copy of a letter from Mrs. Delvina Watson, accusing her of judicial misconduct.
>
> I have been a member of the Legal Profession in Barbados for nearly fifty-five (55) years. During this time neither I, nor any of my colleagues with whom I have discussed it, have ever heard of a litigant writing to the Chief Justice to

complain about the manner in which a Judge has exercised her discretion and demanding his or her removal from office for judicial misconduct.

It has always been my understanding that if a litigant is so dissatisfied with the manner in which a presiding Judge is conducting the trial, then either an application can be made in open court to the Judge to recuse himself/herself from the case or an appeal can be made against a Judge's decision after the conclusion of the case. However, if a Judge were to recuse himself/herself from a case on the basis of such a letter, a bad precedent would be set which could have the potential to disrupt the judicial system.

It should be noted that Mrs. Delvina Watson is the wife of Mr. Alan Watson, one of Philip's former Partners at Cottle Catford against whom he obtained judgment for the payment of the sum of approximately $650,000 which with interest and costs to date the amount owing is in excess of one Million. Although this judgment as you will recall was confirmed by the Court of Appeal by dismissal of his appeal for want of prosecution in September, 2011.

Mr. Watson has not only contemptuously refused to comply with the judgment but he has actually left the jurisdiction and has been traced to an address in the States by my son at cost to himself. It is hard to believe that Mrs. Watson or her Attorneys in Barbados do not know where he is. In fact Mrs. Watson has filed an Affidavit stating that her husband has severed the joint tenancy of property that she owns with him which property Philip is trying to levy for satisfaction of his judgment. Mrs. Watson herself now seeks to complain about a judgment against her that she did not defend and which remains unsatisfied to this day.

In my opinion Mrs. Watson's letter was designed to prevent the Judge in this case (Dr. Richards) from hearing an application for contempt scheduled for November 21st against her and her several Attorneys arising out of her selling property in breach of an Injunction granted by Dr. Richards against the sale of the property in July of 2012 and which was never discharged.

In my opinion Mrs. Watson's letter can therefore be regarded as such an interference with the Court's powers as to constitute a contempt of court or even a criminal offence. In this regard I am taking the liberty of referring you to the Fourth Edition of Halsbury's Laws of England at page 21 paragraph 27 and the heading of Scandalising the Court. Reference is made thereunder to the Privy Council case arising from Trinidad in 1936 of Ambard and the A.G of Trinidad and Tobago and I draw reference to the judgment of Lord Atkin who cites a judgment of Lord Russell of Killoween in R.V Gray in 1900 as follows:

> "Any act done or writing published calculated to bring a Court or a Judge of the Court into contempt, or to lower his authority, is a contempt of court .That is one class of contempt. Further any act done or writing published or calculated to obstruct or interfere with the due course of justice or the lawful process of the Courts is a contempt of court. The former class belongs to the category which Lord Hardwicke LC characterized "as scandalising a court or a Judge." That description of that class of contempt

is to be taken subject to one important qualification. Judges and courts alike are open to criticism, and if reasonable argument or expostulation is offered against any judicial act as contrary to law or public good, no court could or would treat that as contempt of court."

But even if Mrs. Watson's letter is not considered to be a contempt of Court or in breach of criminal law, Mrs. Watson and her Attorneys would have achieved their objective of further delaying and frustrating the enforcement by Philip of his judgment against her if ..... were to recuse herself from the case. This attempt when taken with the disappearance of her husband and the difficulty of enforcement against him as a result has meant that as both judgments were for moneys used by them from Cottle's clients' accounts which Philip has had to replace, the problem that he has faced since 2002 is not only apparent but quite frankly it has crippled him both professionally and personally.

As if these actions are not enough Philip has uncovered further evidence of continued attempts by Mrs. Watson and her Attorneys to delay the enforcement of the judgment against her husband for whom they continue to state in Court they do not represent. Documents purporting to be on behalf of Mrs. Watson who is not a party to the suit have been in filed in the Registrar's office and served on him and I believe he will be writing you about this.

Sir Marston, Philip has been attempting for over a decade now to recover funds owed to the client's accounts of the former Law Firm known as Cottle Catford. This is well known within legal circles in Barbados and in fact in Jamaica and Trinidad where many of his contemporaries are now practising. They remain astonished at what a few members of the profession bent on his destruction have engineered.

That the firm is no longer in existence is not a surprise and though he has borrowed over two million dollars and challenged most into the firm in a failed attempt to keep it going the staggering debt service that he has had to undergo, which in no way will be compensated even if the entire Judgment awarded to him is recovered, because it has been outstanding for so long has impacted negatively on his present practice which itself is on the verge of collapse because of the length of time that has elapsed since the end of the Partnership and the knock on effect this debt has had on him.

As I write Philip has outstanding loans in excess of two million dollars .These loans are now in default and the lending institutions are pressing for recovery. My son informs me that at the height of his debt service repayments he was paying almost $25,000 a month in amortised payments and it is thus no surprise that default has occurred and indeed his health has suffered. His present practice does not on average over the last year bring in more than $5000 a month.

My wife and I in 2003 though both of us were by then retired had permitted our property to be charged as security for the repayment of the loans to Philip as no one would have envisaged that his former Partners would have reneged on a written agreement to pay their indebtedness to. It was also never envisaged that the litigation that he had to pursue would have taken as long as it did to get through the Court system both because of the inherent problems which you are tackling so diligently and the questionable antics by his former Partners and of Attorneys acting for them.

In a meeting with your predecessor as Chief Justice sometime in 2006 Sir David expressed to me that it was incomprehensible that two Senior Attorney's such as Philip's former Partners could renege so easily and wash their hands of their responsibility to the deficit at Cottle Catford . To my mind this delay by them has been facilitated if not directly encouraged by a particular group lead by Vernon Smith Q.C. for reasons I can only speculate at.

I must point out that as far back as December 2007 an appeal to the Court of Appeal by Smith against an order in the substantive matter by Justice Cornelius was disposed of by a consent order yet it took more than 15 months for this order to be perfected namely that the accounts of the Partnership be settled between the parties and judgment entered for Philip. With nothing happening Philip made an urgent application to the Courts in 2009 and Sir David assigned a specific Judge to hear the matter leading to Judgment in September of 2009. It is surely not coincidental that Smith withdrew from the case in 2009 has not been a party to it since even in the Court of Appeal but seeks now in 2014 seeks to reenter it in the guise of acting for Mrs. Watson who was never a party to the suit in documents served on Philip recently.

I have watched saddened and with a sense of helplessness over these last three years in particular as my son has struggled daily with making ends meet and simply trying to find funds to meet claims of creditors and indeed some clients. The

> tool on his health, on his family life has been immeasurable and he now no longer has a practice of any merit while others continue to be unconcerned by his plight and are even reveling in it. Further he has been unable because of the restrictions put on him as a result of the criminal charge to easily leave the island to get the follow up care he needs for recent heart surgery.
>
> As a concerned parent and as one who has bene associated with the law for in excess of Fifty years I believe I have earned the right and am entitled to express a reasoned opinion as to whether what is going on is equitable or not. It clearly is not and in the circumstances I am requesting to be granted an urgent audience with you so that I may be assured that all is being done to put an end to what is clearly sharp practice by persons sworn to be members of an Honourable institution but who appear contrary to all the traditions of this Honourable profession to have an agenda for my son's destruction.
>
> Yours Sincerely
> Neville Nicholls

It took over three months for the CJ to respond to this letter, in which he said he did not feel he could accede to a meeting on a matter that was subjudice, and that if my father wished to he could lay a complaint against Smith with the Bar's Disciplinary Committee. It is now November 2015, and this subjudice matter has not been heard. Often persons say the Law is an 'Ass'. I really cannot find a suitable phrase to describe what this whole situation is and the actions of the CJ who allows the misuse of the system by Smith to continue.

I have no doubt I will eventually have to get the matter to the CCJ, but my energy is being drained; my ability to earn a living severely compromised. This has been the familiar tactics of Smith in all his practice and yet despite the condemnation by the CCJ, the Court of Appeal headed by the CJ seems impotent to put an end to this nonsense.

21

Annus Horribilis 2014

THE YEAR 2014 has been a horrible year, an *annus horribilis*, to quote the phrase once used by Queen Elizabeth in referring to a year of personal turmoil for her and her family.

The year has in effect stretched back for fifteen months from the time of my arrest in October of 2013. In the immediate aftermath of my arrest I was not made aware of any fallout or loss of face, but I knew from experience that it would follow. Clients did not immediately walk, but their affairs went elsewhere and my earnings from the offshore sector, which were already in decline due to the state of the world economy, plunged to nothing. With the exception of one company, I was no longer sought after for advice or to sit on their boards, while I took the decisions to remove myself from others so as to avoid them having to make the tricky decision.

I was doing what I always thought best: placing myself in the other person's shoes so as to look at things from their perspective. I have often felt that many persons are incapable of doing this, but if you do not, not only may you not find an ability to reach a compromise, but you may not have an understanding of all the issues at stake.

In my present case the failure of a law firm has been well documented. It plunged into the abyss for a variety of reasons. The main one — not the only one—was that its continued existence was made impossible by the refusal of two of the partners, one of whom had enjoyed seasons of plenty, to repay what they were not entitled to.

The failure of the firm was well known to all concerned in the legal profession, and to many in the business society as well. I feel that somehow I am being stigmatized for having tried to save it; for not running and jumping ship at the first sign of trouble. I am now being told "well, you should not have stayed," and have heard it whispered that my ego wanted me to be seen as heading a large firm. These comments by supposed friends, along with comments about how or where the missing money from Cottle went, have been some of the unkindest cuts. There was a clear ignorance as to what actually occurred, as it was not akin to a bank robbery where the loot disappeared in one fell swoop, but more akin to the creeping cancer that was surely eating away at the fabric of the firm.

The number of persons who have put their hands up to help me, not by handouts but simply trying to recover the money I had borrowed to keep the firm afloat, can be counted on one hand. There is no senior attorney with whom I have not held discussions, sought advice, or pleaded with for help over the last decade. It distresses me to say that I have received little, and in this case the mention of those who have helped can be taken as a sign as to who has not. I have been left with the feeling that persons feel that 'there but for the grace of God go I, and therefore I am not getting involved' and I know I have heard from more than one senior person in the profession that there was a feeling that my father would bail me out. Contact was often only made to me when there was a need for some help that necessitated the delving into the records of Cottle, and after a while I simply declined many of these requests.

During 2014 I have had to face the expected fallout from my arrest. After all, I can understand persons worried about the potentially bad publicity. I can understand people worried about trusting me. I can understand people who knew not of the circumstances, deciding it was better to go elsewhere. What I detest, however, is those who know what the facts are, and have tried and indeed succeeded by casting aspersions on my character to cause me much harm. Lying by omission is as deadly in some cases as outright lying, and simply stating to all "he has problems..." as if I have the plague is unforgivable, but is not surprising in the dog-eat-dog world that the legal profession has become.

Unfortunately, human behavior has made me realize that many would seek to take advantage of my downfall by spreading rumours behind my back in order to get work that was coming my way, or to suggest that I was delaying matters because it was to my advantage to keep things going on and on, or as I have heard, because I have too much animosity for my former partners that no one can speak to me. Last I checked, there are about 100 letters written to them pleading with them to come to the table and suggest a resolution. Only three replies, and other than Griffith suggesting she would pay back a debt at that time of about $600,000 by $1,000 a month, there has been no offer. And she has the gall to suggest that was a serious offer, or her present attorney to suggest that she has tried to find a resolution, but when asked directly by the judge whether she is prepared to mediate for a solution, resort to the well-known refrain: "I have no instructions." Give me a break—what instructions need you have when your client has been found liable for now nearly $900,000?

The result of this fallout was that my practice has imploded further. I could not even maintain the $2,000 a month that a client was asking me to pay to share their rental accommodation, so that went asunder, so that since the end of September 2014 I once again have no office, doing what work I can from my residence. From once employing about 30 persons, I have found it impossible to meet the monthly payments for two staff members. I have had to turn my car back in—in reality it was repossessed, but without the embarrassment that would follow in public for a second time, so that for the first time since 1988 I do not own a car and during the week of Christmas had no transport available to me.

While the impact on my personal life has been great, the stress associated with this has been increased by the helplessness I have felt with respect to my parents' situation and the hounding they have faced by creditors for a default that was not their doing. In my mother's case, illness has meant that she has not been able to fully absorb the magnitude of the problems that I have been facing, nor has she had knowledge of the fact that the house she has been living in since 1976 was scheduled to be auctioned (illegally in my opinion as a result of which I had no option but to obtain an order prohibiting the sale from the High Court) on December 4th 2014 by Globe Finance, one of whose major shareholders is Sagicor, the same Sagicor against whom I was awarded a judgment in November of 2014 and contemptuously only settled 75% of same up to the end of November 2015.

I have written about what I have viewed is the hands-off attitude with some attorneys to my plight. I am not the only one to complain of this feeling, but at this stage I must now indicate the total outrage I have felt about the treatment meted out to me and by extension my parents by Clarke, Gittens and Farmer, one of the biggest firms if not the biggest.

I earlier mentioned my annoyance with how they had by their decision allowed Lady Macbeth to walk off, further with her loot. Now another arm was trying relentlessly to kick my parents out of their home because of my inability to repay. Yes, the loan is in deficit, but how can I repay? Other avenues for settling the debt were proposed, but for over a year they appeared hell-bent on carrying out the wishes of Globe to foreclose on my parents' property which there was clear evidence was never intended to be part of the security. My parents had mortgaged land outside where their house stood valued at more than the loan granted, yet they were insistent on taking their house with a value of more than three times the loan, all because it appeared in the same deed but had a spate designation to the land charged. It has been a nightmare.

Through it all I have tried to put on a brave face, but the extent of my financial predicament meant that I often had to juggle paying some bill so as to leave cash for the purchase of necessities, in particular the feeding of my children. I owe a debt of gratitude to a few close personal friends who have readily assisted me in my times of need, and must acknowledge that without my father I would have been reduced to a virtual beggar on the street.

I have never been an overly religious person. Some would say I was more cynical, but during this time both Dean Frank Marshall and Reverend Jeffrey Gibson, who has recently been appointed Dean Marshall's successor and who played cricket at Pickwick, offered me spiritual guidance with the assurance that the Lord must have a purpose for what is happening to me. Daily persons such as Julie Harris-Hill, Jacqui Caesar, Shernell Cole, Rowenia Warner, Tanesha Evans, Shatara Ramsey, Lauren Cundari—a very dear and supportive client who adopted my girls as nieces of hers—Roland Holder and my Aunt Janice Bradshaw, offered words of advice and encouragement for which I will be eternally grateful, even if at the time I didn't appear receptive as I saw no end in sight for my troubles. Others who are too numerous to mention have assisted me through these dark periods, either by words of comfort or affirmation that they and right thinking people knew that I was not corrupt.

In August of 2013 I returned to Barbados after my heart surgery in the US. This surgery was recommended for nearly a year by Dr. Massay, but was delayed because (surprise, surprise) Sagicor, my health care provider, wanted it performed in Barbados. The difference in cost of course played no part in their opposition. Dr. Massay insisted that it be done overseas because he was of the opinion that while it could be done in Barbados, because of my size I was not a routine patient, and in the event of an emergency he wanted the resources, both physical and manpower, that were not available at the Queen Elizabeth Hospital.

The surgeon who operated on me was Dr. Trevor Greene, a Barbadian who was a couple of years ahead of me at Harrison College. The operation lasted less than an hour and when he visited me that afternoon he said everything went well, but I had to call Jeff and tell him he had made a good call that it be done in the States, as I was a tricky patient. Dr. Greene had implanted a device to monitor my heartbeat and regulate it within a certain beat pattern. As events have unfolded since early 2014 I have had no health insurance, as my insurance was cancelled by Sagicor for nonpayment of the premiums. I simply could not afford it, and though the courts have ruled that at the time Sagicor owed me the small matter of $425,000 from my pension plan, it looks as though I will be forced to file another action to have it reinstated, as all entreaties to them through their attorney for it to be reinstated have come to nothing.

Dr. Massy had previously discovered that my heartbeat was irregular, and that I was prone to a massive and possibly fatal heart attack. The stress I had been under this last decade had not helped, and it was virtually on his instructions that I abandoned my appeal of the Court of Appeal decision not to vary the interest rate awarded to me on the amounts I had won against my partners to be more in line with the interest I had to pay the banks I had borrowed money from. His warning was that he could not guarantee that I would survive the stress of the appeal, given the emotions that accompanied it. I made sure that this was brought to the attention of the Court of Appeal in January of 2014 as the reason why I was not appealing their ridiculous decision on the question of the amount of interest awarded.

Just after two months after I had returned from surgery, within the three-month period that he had prescribed before I resumed my full activities, I was arrested. As a result of that and the issues surrounding it, I have not travelled because in the first instance my passport had to be handed over, and then because quite frankly not only was my cash flow critical, but I felt uneasy travelling when still owing money to persons, including staff, so the follow up visit to the hospital has never been done.

With all the stress that I had been under this past year, during 2014 my godson's mother Rowenia Warner had been urging me to come to New York for Christmas to spend the time with her family and take my mind off things. I was ambivalent about travelling, especially as I was still experiencing challenges with paying my staff and other debts. In addition, with Sagicor deliberately refusing to settle the amounts awarded to me on November 25th 2014 after a four year battle until it seemed the final day they had to pay which was January 6, 2015, I had little spare cash.

However, Rowenia was insistent and so just to be on the safe side, I applied to Magistrate Douglas Frederick like a common criminal for permission to leave the island, since I was on bail. My sureties, Andrew Sealy and Suleiman Nana, advised the magistrate they did not have any objection to my travelling. As a precaution I obtained a letter from the court that I was granted permission to travel. I checked online for flights using the miles that I had accumulated over the years, and was able to secure a seat to New York via Miami leaving at 7:45 am Christmas morning.

I arrived at the airport to check in, and encountered a delay because the agent could not get my boarding pass to print, so the agent went to into the office behind the counter to reissue the ticket. After about ten minutes he reemerged and advised me that his attempts to reissue my ticket were met with a message that my visa had been cancelled and that I had to visit the United States Embassy to sort it out.

I guess I am now perceived as a dangerous terrorist or a mastermind criminal, as the agent said I must have done something for them to do this. Surely the US government, who can't even track all the subversives — both US citizens and foreign — in their own country have all the resources to monitor and track people who have been accused of activities that cannot be considered a security threat to them and take actions based on such an accusation. As I am not a citizen, I presume it will be argued that I am not entitled to the presumption of innocence that is the norm of civilized legal systems, and which they have been at pains to point out must be upheld when dealing with the fallout from the recent deaths of black men caused by questionable police action.

On reflection, I sit here thinking about how a country who always preaches the need to follow due process to others can revoke a visa without the courtesy of informing the holder. Why the secrecy? As far as I know I have committed no offences in the US. Of course any country has a right to deny entry to anyone they deem a *persona non grata*, but I have a sneaky feeling I have not heard the end of this, nor for that matter will John Public from me, but only when the time is right, as again I smell the proverbial rat.

Could their action to cancel my visa be a result of my expressing an opinion that the actions of the US to force the rest of world to accept their FACTA legislation are an arrogant imposition by a country of what they believe is in their best interests because they have the financial might to cripple you if you don't comply? I doubt that very much. The requirement for the world to comply with FACTA requirements under US law is nothing short of a requirement that domestic US legislation on tax matters be given worldwide enforcement. In short form, the law requires all foreign institutions who hold accounts or transact monetary transactions on behalf of US citizens to report the names of these persons to the IRS. The premise of the law is that US citizens are evading their tax responsibilities in the US by stashing money overseas.

Any third year student of law would attest that countries do not enforce the tax laws of another country, but the US has insisted in this case that if other countries do not comply they will face penal sanctions from the US. They have deemed the taking advantage of low tax jurisdictions by American citizens to be tax evasion, rather than the acceptable tax avoidance that many offshore centres encourage persons with wealth to invest in, thereby lowering their tax liability that would be applicable in their place of residence or as US citizens in the US.

It is inconceivable that my privately expressed views to one or two could be the basis for this action, and so I am left to surmise that if it is a result of the ludicrous charges I am facing, it must be that someone has somehow made the US authorities feel either that I would seek to abscond in their country or that I am a threat to national security. My clear following of the rules to travel give a lie to that, and as I have never so much as held a gun in my life, I guess I have a secret persona I know nothing of. Now I have Charles Leacock to thank for this one, for his money laundering charge under a piece of legislation that deals with the fight to stop assistance to terrorist funding by the laundering of money, and this was like waving a red flag to a bull(y).

Having had my charges dismissed, I will now be in a position to ask about the reasons for the decision, but I suspect that if a reason is given at all it will simply be that that's their position. The US has appointed itself for years to be the equivalent of the World Police Order. Nothing makes that more evident than the FIFA indictments which ironically given the pressure they place on jurisdictions like Barbados to 'clean up their financial system to stop money laundering', is as a result of the illegal use of the financial system in the US which went undetected for ten years.

A horrible year was coming to the most ignominious of ends which saw me spending Christmas day eating biscuits and the cheese I was taking for my friend, along with the Christmas cake. One should be grateful for small mercies, but even though my father requested my brother to come for me—the rental car I was using for the last six weeks was returned—to eat dinner with them, I begged off, as I was not in the frame of mind to be company for anyone.

The continued 'licks' that the West Indies were receiving on the field of play in South Africa also made for painful viewing, making this a very depressing Christmas for me. Other than one or two, I have told no one what has happened, as I really need to get to the bottom of this. It has reminded me of the continued assertion of my former classmate from Jamaica who has been a tower of strength, Wally Scott Q.C., that when I find out who is behind the pulling of the strings, my nightmare will quickly end. I really hope and pray that 2015 is that time.

As 2014 ended I tried to stay as positive as possible in 2015. I attempted to learn without much success why my visa was cancelled. In light of what has transpired and a message from the local embassy that it was cancelled because information had come to the attention of the State Department not known when it was issued, and that if I wanted to reestablish my eligibility I need to reapply.

I have taken the decision that I don't need to be subject to the humiliation of it being rejected and have chosen not to reapply until this whole sordid mess is at an end. I have visited the States many times and it is just inconvenience not being able to go. If and when I learn the actual reason, then I will reapply. The one thing that I was concerned about was my inability to travel to Jacksonville to visit Dr. Greene for a checkup on how the implanted device was working. Dr. Greene came into Barbados in October 2015 and gave me and other patients he has here a checkup. I must say the results were mind-boggling, as he was able to show me on the print-out—like that of an EKG—that on February 21st at 3:18 am my heart had stopped during sleep. The device was working, as it did what it was supposed to do—restart it.

The debt of gratitude I have for Dr. Massay for recommending that I undergo the surgery and fighting with Sagicor that I have it overseas, and for Dr. Greene who performed the surgery can know no bounds, as without it I would not be here to finish my tale. I must also extend sincere gratitude to Dr. Livy Forde and Dr. Collette George, who over the last fifteen years have managed my diabetes.

Coping With Stress and Disappointments

A CHANCE ENCOUNTER with a former school colleague who I'd spent countless hours playing cricket with has prompted the writing of this chapter. Through his mother he has connections with Cottle Catford, and thus has more than a passing interest in my predicament, and during our conversation he urged me to write something on how I have coped with stress over these last few years.

I don't pretend to be an expert on the subject, but it is an accepted fact that modern day life in itself leads to all manner of stress. An internet search reveals this following definition of stress:

> "A state of mental tension and worry caused by problems in your personal life work, something that causes strong feelings, worries or anxiety, physical force or pressure."

I can relate to that definition, as I am sure many can, and though many times hyperbole may define what you are feeling as stress when it is something else, I firmly believe that I have lived in a virtual pressure cooker for the last dozen years, and many, not least myself, have wondered how I have not exploded to date. I am sure that my children will disagree profoundly with that statement and their mother would probably say she could write a treatise on the subject. As with many other aspects of life, events that are stressful to one person are not to the other; the proverbial maxim that one person's terrorist is another's freedom fighter is an apt description. As I look back at what I have faced this last decade I laugh at the stress of writing exams which at the time seemed so terrifying, akin to the end of the world, especially if one was unsuccessful.

As I have intimated above at times, usage of a word can be contextually wrong. I think particularly of the words 'hero' and 'pressure', used in the sporting context, for example to describe excellent sporting endeavor or an extreme situation facing a participant.

The colorful illustration by the great Australian cricket all-rounder of the 1950s, Keith Miller, whose exploits were the bar for the tag of 'greatest cricketer' until our incomparable Sir Garfield came along, rings in my mind. He was being asked about the pressures of battle on the cricket field and simply said that pressure is "when you have a Messerschmitt up your arse," not when you are playing cricket. Miller had seen combat in World War 2 as a fighter pilot, and was basically conveying that we at times get carried away with too much hyperbole when describing situations which are in no way life-threatening or perhaps have no potentially life-changing consequences.

The death of Nelson Mandela in late 2013 spawned an outpouring of grief and admiration for his life from all over the world. As I followed the unfolding events I was able to reflect on his life and what he faced and compare his troubles with the obstacles that are currently in front of me. I came to the conclusion that there is absolutely no comparison between the two. In fact, other than the fact that we were both born male to African descendants and studied law, there is absolutely no comparison between the two of us and in particular what we faced.

As I reflected on how he rose to overcome his obstacles to walk out of prison after more than twenty-five years of unjust incarceration with the ability to bestow forgiveness on his harshest adversaries, it touched me and taught me some valuable lessons. The hardest of these lessons has been that of dealing with your enemies, and to some extent it is the part that I have not been successful at. As Mandela has said often, harboring resentment and hatred eats from within and prevents you from being truly free.

I could only think at the time that however harrowing were the events that I was facing, it was nothing compared to what this man went through when he was unjustly locked away during the prime of his life and in a manner that was the most inhumane, namely the denying him of intimate contact with his immediate family. Reflecting on those events, with his liberty having been taken away for so long, and then comparing it to my situation where my liberty was taken away for one day, could I say really say that the events in my life were so stressful as to have a profound change in me or create a reaction out of all comparison with what his was?

The phrase that 'one man's terrorist is another's freedom fighter' rings hollow or true depending on who proclaims it, and as I thought of this I reflected on how stress or the effects of stress affect people differently. But though it does, it does not mean that the events for them were any less traumatic. The events facing me have clearly had a life-changing impact on my way of life, some changes for the better and some for worse, but at its darkest hours I have never been driven to such a state of despair that I would consider making the ultimate gesture that many have resorted to. Having not done that, does it mean that I too have not undergone significant stress? The simple answer is no, and as I try to determine in my mind why persons have such widely different reactions to the stresses that they face, I have come to the conclusion that this is because we are human and not robotic.

I have come to realise that my thinking it could be worse was one of the mechanisms that I have come to use, not intentionally, but more as a reflex action, to deal with my problems. As difficult as my situation appeared, at times the contemplation of Mandela's life situations at the time of his death, and looking in amazement at the reports of the barbarity around the world that was being inflicted on people whose faith is different from that which ISIS has determined is the prescribed way of life for all men, I tried to put my plight in perspective.

The stressful situation that I have faced in one sense has made me a better person, as it has made me more conscious of the resilience of human beings to extraordinary plights. It has also reminded me that these difficulties I have endured, especially within the last two years, are sometimes not even comparable to what the daily lives of some persons around the world face, such as the migrants seeking a better life in Europe and facing the real prospect of death, and then virtual incarceration if they don't die.

These people are the true heroes, not our sporting icons. I do not think that I am in any way similar to them either from the perspective of what I faced, what was done to me or my reactions to it, because many times the stoic nature of what these heroes have faced in true adversity has deserted me, as a more Pavlovian response of wanting to strike out at your perceived enemies had taken over my being.

With that warning in mind, I am still willing to put my head on the proverbial block (in spite of the threat of ISIS who may want volunteers to practice on) and say that what I have encountered over the last two decades can only be deemed a highly stressful situation.

The Cottle Catford meltdown was the catalyst for all kinds of stress in my life. I faced work stress in the initial five years as I drove myself, often working as long as 12 to 14 hours which led in turn to relationship stress which was not helped as inevitably I became the sole person with the burden of Cottle Catford. Financial stress as the firm floundered and I tried unsuccessfully in the end to keep it afloat was inevitable. The mental stress that I have undergone has been the most significant. I have virtually lived for the last dozen years fearing for any phone call as portending some further problem, or some other fire that needs quelling. This has led to an inability to adequately rest, which in itself leads to some irrational decisions and thoughts at times. Often I am so tired that I can't sleep and have to put myself in front the TV to shut off mentally so that I may fall asleep.

Life at the top or when you are the sole owner can be very lonely, and having lost my main confidante midway through with the untimely death of Stephen, it was no surprise that the stress I was under affected not only my personality, but my health.

These events make me, in my view, as qualified as any layman to make my two cents worth of comments on this phenomenon of stress, what effect it has on you, and how to attempt to cope with it. I do so not as an expert, but as one who has had to learn to live with it so as to avoid the fate that Dr. Massy—who has been treating me for all the time that these events have been ongoing—said was awaiting me: that of an early journey to the hereafter, as he put it, to plan the next World Cup with my then recently departed friend unless I relieved some of the stress in my life.

When he uttered this stark warning to me early in 2008, I was in a mess. I was unable to sleep, was irritable, edgy, all these the symptoms then of six years of fighting to recover from my former partners what they had agreed to settle. His dictate to me was that unless I first took a complete rest and after that learnt mechanisms to reduce stress, I would not be around to care for my young family. Seven years later the situation is still the same in that I have been unable to recover what is due, and my personal situation from 2008 has deteriorated further, so how then am I still around? Has the stress been alleviated or has it increased in any way?

Dr. Massay and any reputable practitioner will tell you that whereas the death certificate may say 'stroke' or 'heart attack' (in layman's language), the precipitating factor would be some form of stress. A recent discussion with him made me aware of something that the medical profession calls 'broken heart syndrome', a layman's expression for a condition that causes death because of stress. His warning at the time was stark, especially the reference to Stephen, as one of my haunting memories of Stephen is his words to me less than two years previous when we met in my office to chart a way through the problems I was facing: "Philip you have a young family. Whatever you do you can't let this thing kill you."

His comment then and his subsequent early death have haunted me and still haunt me to this day. A day seldom passes where I don't try to draw on his wisdom.

The only thing that has come close to those haunting words was an ironic statement to me by our former Prime Minister the late David Thompson. During the 2008 election campaign, which he eventually won, he had been critical of the enormous cost that the government had incurred with the refurbishment of Kensington, and had made an off-the-cuff statement, I believe in a debate somewhere, that all Barbados had to show for the BLP's squander-mania regarding Kensington, as it was becoming a White elephant (I think that's how he put it), was a final (the World Cup Final), and a funeral (Stephen's).

We met somewhere by chance shortly thereafter and he was quick to say to me "Philip I was not criticizing your friend Stephen [who had been CEO of World Cup Barbados] that had undertaken the transformation of Kensington." As he put it, the chance to "put a lash in Owen [Arthur]" was too tempting. Attending his funeral at the same Kensington in 2010, these comments came flooding back to me and I would not be human for not thinking we must not tempt the Gods by what we say.

As the situation at Cottle deteriorated, I found myself floundering over what to do. In a peculiar sense I found myself unable to fully trust anyone in the profession with the extent of my problems because there was always that gnawing feeling in the back of my mind that a close friend had told me, and which I know from frequent reminders as I grew into adolescence from my mother, that many people would only be too happy to see me fail. As such I internalized much of the pressure, and the only outlet would be occasional outbursts on family, friends and staff.

I recall vividly one day how Carissa, then about 6 or 7, kept coming into my study with question after question and request after request to do this or that. I was beginning to boil, as I had some deadline to meet occasioned by my problems, when it suddenly dawned on me that she was just being a child. She had no clue about what problems I was facing, and frankly these were irrelevant to her, and I at the time felt much remorse as I realized I was shortchanging her, so I stopped what I was doing and played whatever game she wanted. But many times I probably failed, and one of my greatest regrets is that this whole affair sapped my energy and time and thus ability to be a more hands-on dad with my children.

But you may well ask what this stress was. As I look back I am convinced that a lot of the stress that I went through developed because of the upbringing that I had, whereby it was instilled in me to try and do things the correct way, and try wherever possible not to cause persons to suffer because of your actions. Well, Cottle Catford was thus a disaster waiting to happen. For the last few years of the 20th century and the first two of the 21st, it was clear that Cottle was sinking.

I genuinely believed that my two partners were sincere in their promises to do their utmost to get us out of the mess, a belief that led to strong words with my brother Stephen, as I felt he had allowed his knowledge of our problems at Cottle to influence his decision while working at the then LOB not to grant a request by Griffith for a loan. Certainly she felt slighted, and I was very strong in my criticism of him, a criticism as events have shown was unjustified and for which I now publicly apologise.

When it was clear that the firm could not go on, I felt that I had a responsibility towards the clients and indeed the staff there at the time to try and continue it and ride through the rough waters. Those rough seas have become dangerous swells, and with hindsight I should have bailed or simply let the chips fall. That was not my make-up, and even though the waters became choppier, I pressed on because deep inside I felt I was part of the problem and therefore needed to get it rectified even at a personal loss.

I have been ever critical of the actions or lack thereof of my former partners, not to mention the abuse of the judicial system by lawyers acting on their behalf, who have used the failings within the administration of the judicial system that has allowed this abuse to continue for over a decade. I have never been shy of saying that as a partner of the firm I must bear some responsibility for what transpired, but I feel tremendous anger that unscrupulous lawyers have been able to make my life a misery these last ten years with such impunity, especially when the Court of Appeal states that this matter was really a simple issue.

That responsibility would follow naturally from the fact of being a partner in the firm and as such in law responsible for the debts of the firm. By correlation, one would be entitled to any benefits accruing from the partnership. Unfortunately for me there were few benefits since my admission to partnership in 1992, as within three years the storm clouds were gathering and the sad fact is that I have faced the debt burden on my own whilst funds used by my former partners on their families continue to be outstanding.

On reflection I should have jumped ship when I had the chance, but that has never been my makeup, a decision that has virtually cost me my professional life and will in all probability cause me my personal life as I go down with the sinking ship, but with my head held high and not hiding as a fugitive in another country.

I can honestly say that there has been little time in the last twenty years when the problems in the firm have not just been at the back of my mind, but in the forefront, and I know that the constant worry about finding finance for another claim or to make a delayed payment has not only worn me down, but it has changed my personality and caused me to suffer severe health challenges.

An off-the-cuff comment by not only a friend but my long term pharmacist Allison Hutson-Daniel a few years back has of late resonated with me more and more. Allison has always been someone who expressed a genuine interest in the challenges I was facing, and as she is married to an attorney, was able from discussions with him to understand better some of the legal challenges and obstacles I was facing from supposed colleagues somewhat better than others. She commented a few years ago that this burden has affected my personality over the years. In her words, I had transformed from a jovial individual into a grumpy old man within a period of ten years.

Her assessment was correct, and while I did not feel any sense of anger towards her, I felt renewed anger towards my former partners and to my profession for being the root cause of this change, a change that my family and my ex-wife will no doubt be the first to say they were the main victims of, but I think in particular of my children, Carissa especially, who suffered throughout.

This has been one of the major disappointments, in that I have not had the energy to participate in the growing up things that they would have liked. Being blessed with only girls, my escapism to cricket didn't appeal to them, and as this was one of my major escape valves, it was not something that I could enjoy with them. My eldest Carissa has berated me more than once on this question by saying I never took the time to teach them about it; time, the elusive measure of our existence which we are slaves to.

The first time I heard the maxim that 'busy people always find time to do things' was when it was said to me by the former president of the West Indies Cricket Board Pat Rousseau, himself an eminent attorney in Jamaica. The occasion was the funeral of Sir Conrad Hunte in December of 1999, and while we were making our way from the ceremony he said to me as the newly elected secretary of the Barbados

Cricket Association that all of us would have to rally around Stephen, to whom the reigns of leadership had fallen within two months of Sir Conrad's election as president.

My response to him was that Stephen now had so much on his plate (at the time the uncertainty of what was going to become of Life of Barbados was consuming him) and he simply said "busy people never say 'no'. They find time to do things that idle people don't have the time for." In Stephen's case this was apt, but it may have well have been one of the factors that impacted on his untimely death.

Since then I have often tried not to use lack of time as an excuse for not doing anything and to be frank have accepted requests that on reflection I should have rejected. But then all of us do, as was evident in a brief conversation I had with former Prime Minister Owen Arthur at Stephen's grave site when he said that Stephen never said 'no' to any request and reflected maybe we all requested too much of him.

Stress associated with expectation is what we all face at some times. Expectation that you will get the job done as quickly and as best as you can. What I found, however, was another form of stress associated with the expectation that I could always assist persons with their personal problems. Very few people knew what I was going through and I faced much anger from persons when I turned down requests for loans (in reality gifts) saying I just didn't have the money. On several occasions I was accused of lying and I would just sigh.

My major disappointment, however, has been how my time has been eroded, not only by the incessant filings of court documents to get a decision that money was owed by my former partners, but by the delays that existed while doing so, and then despite the finding, the inevitable appeal to further delay matters which when dismissed were now transferred to attempts to stop execution of the judgment. As I have said over and over, if this was a business deal gone sour I would have washed my hands of it, licked my losses and started again. This has not been the situation. Money due others was not available for them. To continually fight to evade the responsibility of replacing same was, while understandable because of human nature, wrong from every moral and ethical point of view. For attorneys to assist others in so doing is in my mind a breach of the ethical canons of the profession.

For the last couple of years my life I have tried to reduce the stress that I have been under by my adoption of an attitude that I have tried my best and that there really is nothing I can do about my present predicament as long as I am unable to recover the funds that I have judgment for. This has hung like the sword of Damecoleges over my head. The time between my arrest and the eventual dismissal of the charges against me has not helped, but I have had to learn to make do if only as an act of self-preservation.

It has not been easy, and will never be because of my personality. I do not have a cold heart, and despite many times being bitter at what has been done to me by others that should know better or for whom I have shown much affection in more ways than one, I have found it in my heart difficult to be retributive. This has meant that I will always feel some form of stress, as I feel partly responsible for the problems that many have faced and continue to face because of the meltdown in my practice. Those attorneys who have contributed to this delay in a resolution of the matter and in particular those involved in the Sagicor litigation have no idea of the enormous mental stress they have put me under.

Despite this I have had to learn to live with the ignominy that comes where I can no longer afford basic items. It is always a trade-off between what I want and what I need. Many a time, similar to many parents, I have gone hungry so that my children can eat. That I should face this in my sixth decade of life has been all the more humbling, but not as much as the loss of reputation or perception in the eyes of some as to the individual that I am. I was recently met by Mr. Joseph Maynard, who taught me at Harrison College, where he remained until last year as he has moved on to be principal of St. Leonard's, a deserved promotion for more than 35 years of service at Harrison College.

He was urging me to remain strong for my family. He said many persons were shocked at my arrest, but most of them did not know the facts I was facing, something he knew from our conversations. It is persons like him and countless others that I cannot name who have striven to let those who don't know what the real truth is and have made my life partially more bearable in the face of opposition from others who should know better.

The change of a mental approach has been the best way I have known how to cope with this adversity. In addition, these times I found relaxation in simple domestic chores for my children, and by watching on YouTube a lot of comedy by our Caribbean comics. But by far the most cathartic exercise has been writing this story, as it has given me an insight into human nature and in many respects shown me that the best virtue that one may have is to be humble. It has comforted me that many people have not judged or shunned me because of the charges that I have faced. Some others who do not know all the facts may have, and I have learnt that there is nothing I can do about that. All I can do is set the record straight and hopefully this tale has done that.

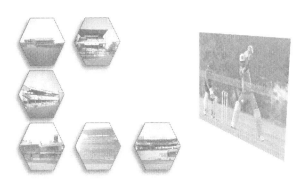

23

Pickwick Cricket Club

THERE IS AN early picture of me around the age of two playing cricket with my father. I am told by my mother that my father was in the habit of coming home at lunch time to bowl to me when I was a toddler at our residence in the Garrison barracks. Our residence was but a stone's throw away from his chambers, which were located then at government headquarters on Bay Street. Our flat was directly opposite the power grid of the Barbados Light and Power Company if you exited from the back door and on the opposite side were the offices of the Barbados Statistical Service. It is now part of the complex that is home to the Barbados Defence Force. My father's early introduction of me to the game of cricket is probably the only thing he has failed at, if one considers the little prowess I made on the field of play, but it would be unkind of me to lay blame on him for this. He certainly gave me all the encouragement that he could and frequently came to watch my junior games at school.

My early introduction to the game certainly fired my love for it and my dream, as many young boys similarly had, was that one day I would wear the maroon cap of the West Indies. It is a dream that I am sure my younger brother Stephen did not share, because typical sibling rivalry meant that he has had no interest in the game, as anything

I liked, he hated. I doubt that this story is apocryphal, but when he attended the Leeds University in the United Kingdom in 1980, he was named to his Hall of Residence cricket team based solely on the fact that he was from Barbados. He subsequently had a difficult time trying to convince them that he'd never played the game and in fact loathed it, and cared not for the exploits of Roberts, Holding, Marshall and company, not to mention Lloyd, Richards, Greenidge, Haynes, and Dujon, whom he would have been stretched to name as part of the team that toured England that summer during the halcyon days of West Indies cricket.

My youngest brother Christopher did develop my love for cricket and the duties of backyard bowler to him had passed to me from my father by the time he started to play. Given my seven year advantage in age, and as at these games once you were dismissed you had to bowl, this prevailed in my favour for several years until Christopher developed his game and I begged off, using the excuse of studies at the Faculty of Law. I found it more and more difficult to dismiss him in these backyard games.

Just as my father's career in law inspired me into that discipline, certainly his introduction of me to cricket fuelled my love for the game. Not only do I recall those early practice sessions, but I also remember my trips with him to Kensington Oval to see regional games. Stephen was never one to come to those games, and Daddy was later to tell me that my presence was most welcome, as he had the perfect excuse to make his way home at the end of play. He was not a big drinker, something that he has passed on to me, and there was always a crowd of men whose composition has only changed by the changing faces of time who readily looked forward to close of play to discuss the day's events or the topics of the day around the bar.

I also recall at that time the annual match between doctors and lawyers which used to be played at the Maple ground in St. James with such noted personages besides my father as Oliver Brown (who many knowledgeable experts were to later tell me lost his opportunity to represent Barbados when he went overseas to study) and Michael Simmons among the lawyers, with Oscar Jordan and James Williams among the doctors on show, while the late Justice Colin Williams who regularly umpired local Division One Cricket was one of the officials. Being around these adults in a cricket setting was a big thrill, as was attending games with Daddy on Saturdays. I well remember attending the local derby between Spartan and Empire at Bank Hall, and having difficulty seeing because the crowd was so thick. How times have changed now as those crowds have long gone.

My early dreams of that West Indies place were however brought crashing down to stark reality by my performances on the field whereby my greatest accomplishment was being the dominant partner in that ninth wicket partnership with Mark Sealy against Lodge in 1974 that played such a crucial part in the Harrison College Under 15 team under Curtis Cephas Campbell going on to win the Ronald Tree Cup. Memory recalls that Mark, who subsequently went on to represent Barbados in three disciplines—cricket, squash and hockey— contributed nothing in a fifty-run partnership other than his presence at the crease. Still it was a pivotal partnership that led to us winning the cup with victory over our arch rivals Lodge, a game that a local cricket commentator Wayne Holder reminded me about recently at a domestic game, as he was watching his older brother Ian Holder play for Lodge. The media coverage of youth cricket then was certainly not what it is now, so much so that my only recollection of the coverage was when it appeared in 1999 in the 25 year 'Looking Back' section of the *Barbados Advocate*.

By the late 70s, when my friends and contemporaries Stephen Alleyne, Curtis Campbell, Richard Jeffers, and Allan Smith had all moved on to national trials with the Barbados Youth Team, leaving me behind, it was clear that my career on the field had ended before it even started. The latter three did go on to represent Barbados at youth level. Curtis was captain and advanced to National Senior Trials before he migrated to the US, while Stephen, as it is not generally known, played First Class Cricket for Scotland while studying there and gaining valuable work experience.

After I left school in 1980 I joined the Pickwick Cricket Club, whose home ground was Kensington Oval. I was thus back in the ranks, as for the last three years I was first the captain of the Schools' Second Team before taking over from Stephen as captain of the First Team and started by playing days as a member of the Second Team. My actual membership of the club dates back to 1977 when I was introduced by Hallam Gill, who was a colleague of my father at the Caribbean Development Bank. I learned a lot, not so much on the cricket field as I was never good enough to be in the First Team where contemporaries from school like Adrian Grant, Clinton St. Hill, Hendy Wallace, the Reifer twins George and Elvis (recently deceased), Odwin Gilkes and Raymond Denny were starting out on their association with the club, but from being in the dressing room with men who had succeeded in virtually every aspect of life. The stories were varied and hilarious and I recall on more than one occasion being disappointed it was my turn to bat because it meant missing out on the tales of yore.

The junior teams of the Pickwick Club were very sociable entities whereby at the end of nearly every day's play there was a night of entertainment, mainly food and lots of drink, at the house of the person living nearest to where the game was being played. As a student at UWI at the time I was exempt from hosting these parties, but I was always reminded that my turn would come and true enough it came when I entered the world of work. In the dressing rooms of those teams were seasoned members of the clubs, many of them players who had previously represented the club's first team, but now were playing for fun, and as some would say to get away from home for some peace and quiet on a Saturday. Many of these individuals, men like Ken Marshall, his cousin Steve Marshall, Valance Connell, Richard

Matthews, David Jones, 'Tottie' Warren, Desmond Marshall, Trevor Mayers and Orson Simpson, were experienced and successful men in their line of business, and their views on all aspects of life and society were an eye-opener for a youngster like me.

Pickwick was certainly in transition when I joined. It had been for a while. I was witness to a Barbadian who had been away for over twenty years coming back to the ground to watch a game and nearly fell off his chair when he suddenly realized that the Pickwick team was in the field and no whites were in the team. Like Wanderers, the doors to membership for all previously restricted by race were opened in the 70s. I can honestly say that I never encountered any resentment or what I would consider discriminatory treatment during my time in the club, but do recall a hilarious circumstance that occurred during a Second Division game. I believe it was in the early 80s at Eden Lodge.

The first two batsmen, yours truly and Ronald Toppin (who went on to be MP for the area and still represents the area) who were listed together in the order were all black. We happened to be the youngest by far in the team, and Ipswich who we were playing had the feared Paddy Hall, a quick in that division in their lineup. The rest of the team was all white. Some wag passed, had a look in the scorebook, and then went off saying at the top of his voice: "...these people keeping the segregation going so much that they have to bat with one another." No one in the team had thought of it and it brought fits of laughter to us that afternoon.

When I returned to the island from studying in 1987 I was elected as honorary secretary of the club, and this was the start of my tenure in the leadership of the club that was to continue until I demitted office as president of the club in 2009 after nearly a decade there. By that time Pickwick were on their way to establishing a new ground in St. Philip, which has subsequently come to be known as the Four Square Oval, having had to move from Kensington in 2005 to allow for its redevelopment into the fine modern facility it now is in time for the hosting of the 2007 Cricket World Cup.

My initial sponsor to the Committee of Management of the club as secretary was Ken Marshall. I have always remained grateful to him for helping me find my way in running the club. At the time that I became secretary, Arthur Bethell was president and Hampton King was first vice president. He was followed in the post of president by Carl Rayside, Steve Marshall, and then me.

Ken gave me my grounding in the responsibility for running the club. Never having been on the committee before I became secretary, I used to check with him before making any decision pertaining to the club until he told me one day: "Philip you are secretary. Make the call. If they don't like what you do they will vote you out next year." At that time Pickwick ran Kensington outside the four- or five-month clearly defined West Indies first class season when the BCA took over responsibility for the ground.

The position of secretary meant that I interacted with all persons who wanted to use the ground during this time and it certainly kept me busy. The club was the centre of a lot of activity and it was possible to find some activity around the club every single day of the week. As a test ground, virtually every touring team to visit Barbados wanted to play there, and this put such a strain on the club to put out teams that many times we would have to invite others from other clubs to help out. As Sports Tourism took off in some years we had two games a week to attend to.

Around this time the treasurer of the club was Orson Simpson, whose friendship with me developed over the years and has continued through him succeeding me as president. The two of us virtually ran the club at this time, as the older members drifted away from its day to day running. Part of the problem that Pickwick and several other clubs have faced in Barbados of late is that, just as Orson and I have now drifted away as tends to happen as you get less active on the playing side and business and family commitments become more demanding, the next generation of youngsters have not stepped forward to take our place.

The sociologists will give you the reasons, but it is clear that club life in Barbados has changed dramatically from when I knew it, and even then from the generation before when, as Arthur Bethell's wife June has always said, her three children were raised at Pickwick partly by Dick (Prescott), the barman who ensured they did their homework, for if Arthur was not playing cricket, she was playing hockey. Sadly, Dick was to pass earlier this year (2015) after living the last ten years of his life with failing eyesight. I was honoured that his son asked me to say a few words on his behalf for the club he served for in excess of fifty years. A loyal servant to the club, though he was much older than me, he always referred to me as 'Mr. Nic' and despite my urgings not to he just would not change. Dick was the man of business for the club, the barman, groundsman, watchman, the first there to open it and the last to leave when he locked it up. His kind will never be seen again.

Many tales could be told about the social aspect of life at Pickwick, but one particular episode stands out in my mind with respect to the old pavilion: the hilarious night when the effects of hours around the bar and the witnessing of one of the early Run Barbados races saw a race being held in the pavilion which ended with one participant at the casualty for two broken hands as a result of not being able to stop in time before crashing into the wall. While awaiting treatment for his injuries, he was asked by an orderly what cologne he was wearing. His reply was: "Some ESAF White Rum…" no doubt foretelling the club's later sponsor.

There were many humorous incidents that occurred on and off the field of play. The motto was: enjoy yourself to the fullest. The host of one of the after-game parties had felt it was time that his guests leave, so he went and changed into his pajamas as a hint, only to find himself seized upon and thrown into his duck pond so that he could just as promptly change back out of them. When it was my turn to host one such event I had to gently retrieve an individual who, having partaken of the drinks on offer, was found in serious argument with a tree, the subject being that it was not there when he arrived so it had moved to block his progress.

Playing in the lower divisions meant that one always made sure that you took along someone who could act as umpire, as the Barbados Cricket Umpires Association at the time did not have enough registered umpires to go around. Failure to do so could mean you played at your peril. In our games Tootie Warren always picked up our umpire who lived near to him for the journey into St. Lucy, I think it was. The umpire was pressed into duty and as fate would have it was called to make a decision against Tootie. He gave him out and Tootie returned to the pavilion muttering. He said nothing to our umpire and at the end of play left with him on the return journey.

Half an hour later another player driving home passed the umpire walking and stopped for him and said: "Where is Tootie?" He said "Me and Mr. Warren got in a quarrel and he put me out. I was apologizing to him for having to give him out when he said: *You mean you not satisfied with teifing me out, but get in my car and insist that I was out? Get out.*" All was well that ended well, as Tootie belied his reputation which the great Sir Everton Weekes would testify to of having the umpire in your pocket by picking him up the next week when he was bowling. Sir Everton always recounts that playing against Tootie in the days he was at Carlton, when there were vociferous appeals for a decision, he would calmly say "man umpire these fellas don't know what they doing, he can't be out." Of course when Sir Everton was facing and the ball would clearly be missing his stumps, Tootie would be bellowing at the highest "I got him now ump!" The perils of being a great batsman.

Pickwick was indirectly responsible for the change in a category of phone rates by the telephone company. The club's phone line in the pavilion was in constant use in the days before the cell phone.

That 426-3151 number is etched in the memory of many Pickwick members and indeed Barbadian and West Indian cricketers, as it was their contact with the outside world when playing at the Oval. I can distinctly recall a West Indian player who shall remain nameless other than to say he was from Antigua, after being left out of the final XI on the morning of a test match, being on the phone at the bar when it was indicated to him that there was a need for a sub to carry something onto the field. Clearly not amused by his non-selection, he did not move, and when pressed said: "They have lot of men in Barbados with white clothes who can oblige if need be… I am busy."

The phone at Pickwick was classified as 'residential', paying the low residential rate charged to residential customers. That was always the rate from time that I became involved in its administration. The phone was clearly not a residential phone, just as clearly as it was not a commercial phone, as no commercial activity was being carried on there.

After more than 25 years of paying the rate charged to a residential customer, a notice turned up one day saying that with effect from the next billing cycle, the club's rate would be increased to the commercial rate, as the domestic category that the club was listed under was done in error. I wrote a response objecting to the attempt to change over 25 years of usage with a two-week notice and stated that the club would not be paying the increase without proper notice. I suggested that six months, in my view, was reasonable especially as the notice had stated the error was not the fault of the club, but a misclassification on the part of the company.

The club continued to pay the usual rate, and eventually the phone was disconnected for arrears. I saw red. I made an urgent application *ex parte* before Justice Frederick Waterman, as he then was, and he granted an order directing the company to turn the service back on. Armed with my order, I proceeded up to the telephone company to visit the head, Trevor Clarke. While I knew he would not deal with such a minor thing as restoring service, which would be the province of some technician in the exchange, he could not be expected to restore the service without orders from above. I was met by one of Mr. Clarke's secretaries who advised that he was in a meeting, was busy, and I could not see him without a prior appointment.

I explained to her the nature of my visit and that "I have taken your name as the person who received service of the Court Order and that unless the club's phone is turned back on within 48 hours the court would be looking for you to answer a contempt charge." Mr. Clarke was promptly made available.

Arising out of the episode, the club met with officials of the company, including its then secretary Vernon Williams who I would later serve with on the board of the BCA, and it was agreed that a new category with special rates for clubs like Pickwick, other social clubs and even churches who were clearly not residential but also not commercial, needed to be established and this was soon put into place by the company.

As the folks at Kensington Oval Management Inc. (KOMI), now responsible for running Kensington after the World Cup Development are currently finding out, the running of Kensington, even excluding the cost associated with maintaining the several grand stands, is a high and time-consuming exercise, as great care needs to be taken of the actual playing area and its surrounds.

I do not believe that Pickwick Cricket Club has ever truly received the credit and recognition it should have for the tireless job it did in maintaining the playing area and surrounds at Kensington over the long time it was in residence there so that it did not become the cabbage patch that it easily could have and has become, embarrassingly for the BCA, at the end of 2014. To do this meant expense. Many clubs only had one permanent member on their ground staff. Pickwick had four: legendary figures like Boo Medford, Tall Boy, Dick the Barman, Ranny the tractor driver and Finny Boo's loyal assistant who though never officially on staff was given a little berry for helping out. These men were to be followed later by the modern day crew of Hendy Black Dick and Corn Man, men who together all saw to the maintenance of the ground during their time.

There has never been adequate recognition of the stalwart service of men like Arthur Bethell and Hampton King, who often themselves drove the tractors to cut the wide expanse of the field, not to mention Robert Williams, Winston Kelly and Toni Moore who single-handedly ensured that the field was in top notch shape for the annual hockey festival that saw the club as its primary host before the Hockey Federation got its own home.

The income from the thriving bar at the club, a feature that has long since disappeared, existed primarily through the great patronage of the playing members of the club, who by the time I became involved were more enthused with the social side of cricket than with the actual playing of it. The club's ability to pay its weekly wage bill was ensured largely because of the turnover in the bar. Not only those mentioned before in this regard, but honourable mention should be made of Desmond Marshall, Jackie Warren and Richard Matthews, the grandfather of the teenage sensation of West Indies women cricket Hayley, for their direct contribution to the finances of the club.

These funds, however, were not enough and it was necessary to have annual fundraisers to cover the additional running costs of the Oval. First there was the annual party at the residence of Carl and Betty Rayside in St. George, and after that the club was fortunate to strike a deal with Spectacular Promotions from Trinidad, who brought their Calypso Tent show to the island for a number of years for which Kensington was the venue.

The loss of this income has been a source of the club's financial demise. It was never overflowing with cash, but it was never cashed strapped as it is today. It's survival to date has really been as a result of several benefactors and the willingness of all those who have been president to pull their pocket when it was needed. To this end the current president Desmond Marshall will probably be afforded a statute, but I am sure he would much prefer a dedicated seat at the bar with an unchecked tab to use if and when he pleases.

Clubs today are very dependent on their sponsors for survival, and we have been lucky in that the club's sponsor for in excess of a decade now has been E.S.A. Fields. Not only has Sir David Seale provided sponsorship through his company, but he has donated the lands that the club now has its facility on to the club free from cost. Clubs nowadays are finding it very hard to make ends meet. Players coming out of youth systems and age group cricket where all the gear they use was given to them in exchange for advertising the sponsor are not inclined to the view that they need to pay to play. It is frustrating for those who have to balance club books, as there is little income coming in from members. An example will suffice. A few years back at the request of players I had caps for the club made in the UK with the club crest. They all disappeared, and when I asked where the payment was for them as I had to pay the supplier, they wondered what I meant, feeling the club had provided them.

With the move to St. Philip the opportunity that Kensington presented to stage functions that earned revenue similar to our partnership with Spectacular would obviously be no more. This particular venture had ended years before the time of the move because of what I have to say were spiteful actions by Tony Marshall when he was president of the BCA for the first time back in 1998/1999. Marshall, for no cogent reason, frustrated the club's attempt to host the show, which by then was an annual affair, by refusing to hand the ground back over to Pickwick after the end of the international season. The convention had been for many decades prior was that the grounds were handed back the day after the last international game had ended, just as it was turned back over to the BCA by Pickwick the day after the local domestic season ended.

Based on this precedent the club negotiated the date for the show when the ground would be expected to be turned back over to Pickwick, only to find that Marshall was refusing to hand back over the ground, citing a variety of reasons, with the result that the Spectacular organisers took the show to the stadium, never to come back. He certainly killed the goose that laid the golden egg for the club, and must be a proud man now to see the club financially struggle as a result of a debt incurred in building its premises at Foursquare.

When the West Indies were awarded the right to host the 2007 Cricket World Cup, it was realized that either Kensington would have to be substantially redeveloped or a new stadium would have to be built elsewhere to conform to the requirements for the hosting of the final and other games that Barbados had been awarded. Eventually a decision was made that Kensington was to be redeveloped, and at the end of the 2005 season Pickwick played its final game there.

At the time that the decision to renovate the ground and facilities was made I was secretary of the BCA and it became obvious to me that this position might conflict with my duties to the club as president, as the club would have to vacate the premises for at least two years. Many meetings were held between the BCA and the club meetings, at which I made it clear I was representing the club.

After much thought and bearing in mind that the new facility would require year round expenditure that Pickwick could not ever undertake, the club gave its agreement to the proposal that the ground be redeveloped and that it would move. Discussions eventually settled on the fact that the club would move and that it would be paid compensation for giving up its right to stay at Kensington, which was enshrined in a 99 year lease, the destruction of the Pickwick Pavilion which belonged to it, and for the years of upkeep of the ground which had been done gratis. This compensation was to be paid to allow the club to find another area to remove to and develop the field and a pavilion.

It is fair to say that many of the older members of the club were initially opposed to the idea of moving. This was understandable, as the club had celebrated its 100th year anniversary at the ground in 1982. In my heart I knew it was time to leave and was eventually able to convince the skeptics that it was clear that the window that the club was getting to call Kensington its home was narrowing every year from the clear seven-month window when I was first secretary from April to December. It seemed that weekly there were requests from the BCA to use the grounds to accommodate a variety of games at times when the ground was in the hands of the club, as more and more teams from overseas visited the island, not to mention the increasing regional and international competitions that were played outside the traditional First Class season under the auspices of the West Indies Cricket Board.

In light of what transpired with Marshall later on, the question of payment of compensation to Pickwick, I have always felt it was a blessing in disguise that I had declared my interest up front in negotiations between the BCA and Pickwick for the terms of Pickwick leaving. It was clear to me there was a conflict of interest, and it should be declared, but as I was to learn in my years on the BCA board, some people either did not understand the concept of conflict of interest, or felt it could be ignored when it was inconvenient to them.

As such I had requested that the former president of the club Arthur Bethell and my later successor Orson Simpson join me in these talks with the then president of the BCA, Stephen Alleyne. Arising out of these talks, it was agreed that compensation would be paid to Pickwick not only for giving up a 99-year lease of the ground by leaving early, but also for its contribution to the up-keep over the years of the ground, not to mention that its pavilion which was once used as the dressing room for players would be demolished. Under the terms of the agreement an approach would be made to government for part of the compensation to be paid from the funds being sourced to redevelop the Oval.

What subsequently transpired with the paying of this compensation despite the agreement being reached between the BCA and Pickwick was nothing short of a scandal! After the 2005 BCA election at which a slate of candidates headed by Stephen and me lost to Tony Marshall, an experienced former banker with Barclays and one who was well versed in the history of Kensington from his previous service on the board, he, now as president, immediately reneged on the agreement, saying it was a friend's deal between Stephen and me. Nothing could be further from the truth.

All the evidence that existed showed clearly that the deal was above board, and in fact part of the compensation to be paid to Pickwick was to come from the government of Barbados, who had a vested interest in seeing that the country was able to host its share of World Cup Games, and to do so Pickwick needed to go to redevelop the ground. The rest of the compensation was to come from the BCA, which Marshall now refused to honour, and I know this fact caused Stephen great distress. He offered on more than one occasion to come to the club's AGM's after we left the ground and were still awaiting the share of the compensation to come from the BCA, to speak to the members about what actually went on as the club had left its home and had no ability to develop another ground. It did not have enough finance and understandably I was being blamed. I said to him that my back was broad, 'thanks but no thanks' and it will all work out.

Part of the compensation payable to Pickwick was received long before the amount due from the BCA was finally paid, due to the efforts of the then Minister of Sport Rudolph 'Cappy' Greenidge. I have never heard it suggested that my friendship with him going back to our days at the Norman Manley Law School played a part. Yet here was Marshall posturing, and by so doing he delayed the ability of the club to finance the building of its new home.

It has always saddened me to note that Marshall, by his bigoted attitude towards Stephen and me, driven I believe by that Cabal he appeared to be a member of along with his agent provocateur Vernon

Smith in dealings with the BCA when Marshall was not at the helm, created such hardship for the club. He clearly was not satisfied with his previous actions that led to the loss of one of the major fundraisers for the club, the annual Spectacular Calypso show that was held at Kensington. I have often asked myself why individuals behave this way. What are they hoping to achieve? As I would later in other aspects of my life find out, it is part of human nature.

In an attempt to get a resolution, I removed myself from the negotiations with the Marshall-led BCA and enlisted the help of Deighton Smith, a long-standing member of the club, but more importantly one who had worked with Marshall at Barclays for some time in an effort at resolution, but to little avail. It was not until Joel Garner became president of the BCA in 2007, some three years after Pickwick left the Oval, that the club finally got the funds to allow it to start the building of its long overdue pavilion on its home ground, donated free of cost by Sir David Seale, at what is now known as the Four Square Oval.

It was not only Marshall's actions that did serious damage to the club's finances that seemed to satisfy him. I am convinced he tried to engineer the closure of the club. After the club left Kensington, it was accommodated by the University of the West Indies by allowing the club to use its facilities at Cave Hill for the First Division team to play its home matches. The other two divisions of the club became virtually nomadic teams during the 2006 local cricket season.

The use of the ground at UWI was always meant to be temporary until the club developed its new facility, which was now on hold, hampered by a lack of finance as described above. After its initial season at the venue, Marshall, despite assuring the club at a meeting that I attended in 2007 that the rumours that UWI would be having a First Division Team for the 2007 season were unfounded, subsequently within a matter of weeks of that meeting and with less than a month to go before the season was due to begin, announced that UWI had been promoted to the First Division. This meant that the continued use of the ground by the club was not possible. Clearly an agreement had been reached between Marshall and Sir Hilary Beckles, the principal of the Cave Hill Campus, whose aggressive determination to develop at Cave Hill a sporting program was second to none, and while admirable, was having an effect on the club.

The deal reached, however, was so secret or to use modern jargon, not transparent, that the Bristol club, perceived by many in the cricket community as the next in line for promotion before the University of the West Indies, obtained an injunction against the start of the 2007 season pending their promotion to the top level. To avoid a lengthy legal battle which would have seen no cricket being played, the BCA admitted them into the First Division as well.

The inevitable delay that occurred while these matters were sorted allowed the Pickwick club some time to seek an alternative venue to play its games, and reached agreement with the First Caribbean Sports and Social Club in its hour of need to use its grounds in Wildey which used to be the base for their vibrant Barclays team of the 70s and 80s, a team that boasted of players like Conde Riley, Pearson Bovell and Jeffrey Wiggins. Though not ideal, the club was grateful for their help at this time, but as it was now three years without a fixed abode of its own which the dwindling membership expected, this was having an effect on attracting players to the club. The efforts of Rondell Yearwood (the club captain at the time), in keeping the club going were tireless and the club owes him an enormous debt of gratitude.

I have two regrets about moving. The first is that contrary to the agreement, there has been no permanent plaque or other structure put in place at Kensington to recognize the pivotal role played by the club in the history of Kensington. It was to be one of the losses occasioned by Stephen's untimely death, as he was actively in negotiation with members of the club as to what type of memoriam should be established and where in the new ground it would be placed.

The second regret was that I was unable to see the building of our new facility at Foursquare through to completion. It was completed under the watch of Orson as president, but much work was done by Deighton Smith who chaired the committee dealing with the construction of the building. In the end the actual cost of the building ended up being far in excess of the amount of compensation, which was not only less than what was agreed in the end, but the delay in receiving it meant that the actual cost of same inevitably rose. By this time I was fatigued. The burden of Cottle was dragging me down and I had virtually been involved in one form of cricket administration or another for more than twenty years. I was waking up on mornings and saying "not another meeting to go to" and I just knew it was time to get out, so I informed Orson who had been my vice president for many years that I would not be seeking re-election at the 2009 AGM, and he succeeded me as president. It was nevertheless a proud day for all concerned when the late Prime Minister David Thompson opened the club's new pavilion.

Sadly, Pickwick has suffered the indignity of finishing last in the 2015 season and being demoted from the Elite Division where it has played for over 130 years. Many reasons can be found for this happening, which is no reflection of the current President Desmond Marshall whose tireless work has ensured that there still existed a club to be demoted. I am sure it will rise again from this disappointment.

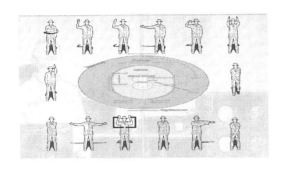

A Cricket Umpire

AT THE START of the domestic 1987 cricket season I had every intention of playing now that I was back home. It was already proving difficult to arrive early enough from work to get any meaningful practice, as I often had to sort out club matters first when I arrived as the secretary of the club. With four employees there was always something going on. Just prior to the start of the season I had attended the annual training session of the Barbados Cricket Umpire's Association to qualify as a local umpire. This involved studying the laws of the game, which was right up my street.

I passed the required examination quite easily, and later went on to pass the practical exams of the West Indies Cricket Umpires Association, which resulted in my qualification to stand as an umpire in Regional First Class games. With the encouragement of local senior umpires like Lloyd Barker, Stanton Parris and Nigel Harrison, I decided I would give it a try and thus informed the club that for the moment I would no longer be playing. It would later transpire that this would be the end of my fairly modest career on the field of play. The last game I played was the annual match between lawyers and the legal clerks.

Between 1987 and 1995 I stood mainly on weekends in local games until my work schedule made this impractical. After the birth of Carissa in 1997 it became even clearer to me that finding the time to stand was unrealistic. I do have some fond memories from my short sojourn with the white coat. I found that it was much easier for me to interact with the players, many of whom I knew from my active days on the field. I think it was helped by the fact that as I was a member of the Board of Management—some players were wary of showing dissent at decisions because of the likely repercussions of a report. If that was so, well, I benefitted, but like all human beings we make mistakes in whatever we do.

I recall in one game at Maple that there was a shout for LBW that the batsman was clearly out, dead to the world, and I shook my head. There was utter disbelief by the players on the field. At the end of the over, which was bowled by the former Barbados fast bowler Emmerson Jordan, he came up to me and said: "Nic, tell me what happened there… the guy was dead." I said: "Emmerson you had overstepped by a long way… a clear no ball. As you don't usually bowl them, it caught me by surprise, and I just could not get the call out and as fate would have it you struck him plumb. Thankfully for me he wasn't bowled, so I just didn't give him out as I should have made the call." "Okay," he said. "I accept that." Emmerson was around this time making his way into the Barbados team very late in cricketing life. Many will recall he had a smooth flowing run up and while I was liaison officer for the Jamaica team in the 1988 tournament Michael Holding, next to whom I was standing, said to me "I would have liked to get my hands on him ten years ago."

In another game at Empire my great friend Stephen was batting. At that time we were flat mates and I was dreading making a mistake one way or the other. The players on the opposing team to Empire for whom Stephen played were aware of our friendship, the fact that we were on the board together, and as the game started and Stephen came out to open the batting I could hear: "…well fellas, nothing in this for us today, you can't expect Lumpy to give him out." As fate would decree, Stephen got a feint touch to a ball behind. I wasn't sure at the time, so in accordance with the rule that the batsman should be given the benefit of the doubt, I was clearly undecided. There was a lot of hysterical screaming at me for the catch and some verbals started flying, whereupon I said: "Don't you see the batsman had given himself out? There is no need for a decision."

After the game I tackled Stephen. I said "I genuinely was not sure and would have given you Not Out. Why did you go?" He said: "Philip I am your friend and your job out there if I had stayed would have been intolerable. I knew I hit, so I left." That's what friends do.

But by far the most interesting encounter on a cricket field for me was during a Regional Under-19 Game between Trinidad and Guyana and it involved a certain Mr. Didinath Ramnarine, who was to subsequently leave his mark on West Indies cricketing politics over the years in his battle with the West Indies Board on behalf of the West Indies Players Association.

On the second day of the game there were frequent interruptions for rain which favoured Trinidad, who had been dismissed cheaply on the first day. After another lengthy break, myself and Mervyn Jones, my colleague in the game who was at the time a First Class umpire, determined that play should resume and we took to the field. We were followed by the Trinidad team led by Ramnarine, who approached us and said "Ump I don't agree with us playing." Mervyn's response was in the order of "Skipper, we feel that play is possible, and play it shall be…" Ramnarine was clearly not impressed and advised us that he was warning us that if any of his players are injured in the damp conditions he would be suing us.

After being somewhat taken aback that a youngster—after all he was under 19 at the time—would have the gumption to act as he did, I responded to him by saying that he was free to do as he pleased, but should he serve my colleague or I with any writ, that I would simply have no choice but to defend the matter. He looked at me quizzically and queried whether I was a lawyer. I replied in the affirmative, to which his response was: "What you doing down here?" I just laughed at his reaction, but the cricket played peaceably without a peep from him after that. His reaction to a lawyer umpiring I had seen before. I had been at pains to ask local commentators of the games not to stress the fact that I was an attorney, lest I received a complaint that I was getting unfair advertisement.

I recall a few instances of hilarity on the field of play. Two occurred at St. Catherine Sports Club. On arrival one day for a game, as I took the field, there was the usual banter among rival supporters. One was clearly not a fan of mine and shouted "…that man Nicholls don't like Spartan. All he going to do is tief the men out…" whereupon a St. Catherine supporter countered by saying "Man you got to be an idiot. He is a big time lawyer. You feel he going leff he office where he can tief more people money to come up here and tief out your team for $50?"

Now given what has happened with my firm, does not the disturbing characterization of lawyers by members of the public provide us in the profession with a salutary lesson? Nothing has disturbed me more in my troubles with Cottle Catford than the effect it has had on innocent people who have had their expectations shattered. It has caused me many sleepless nights, but while I am not blowing my trumpet, I have often been told: "you may have them, but the others certainly don't."

The other incident surrounded a St. Catherine player, a young guy who misfielded a ball struck off the former West Indies fast bowler Milton Small by allowing it to pass through his legs and end up in the boundary. As fate would have it the youngster had to retrieve it and return it to Small, who simply stared, saying nothing to the youngster's words of apology, and appeared to be going back to his mark and resume bowling when he said: "Youngster I don't blame you… I don't blame you at all. It is your mother I blame. She should have kept hers closed 20 years ago." Crude, I know, but the game stopped for about 5 minutes while people recovered and the poor boy got his composure back.

While umpiring a game in St. John at the St. John's Sports Club vs BET, the great former West Indies bowler Joel Garner was playing. He had stopped playing cricket at the highest level by then, and advised he was only there to play as a batsman. The St. John batsmen had got stuck and so his team mates begged him to bowl a few. As he was unprepared, not having his bowling boots, he was tentative and went for a few runs, much to the delight of the home supporters.

When the time came for their second turn at the wicket, Garner was seen going to the boot of his car and bringing out his bowling boots. A miserable man at the best of times on a cricket field, he set off, saying "you laughing now…" and put down a spell of fast bowling that drove the fear of God into the batsmen's lives. These were the pre-helmet days in local cricket, and though he had quit the test arena about two years previously, Garner was out of their class and such was the mayhem that he created that some of the batsmen waiting their turn went on to the main road outside the ground and hijacked passing motorcyclists to relieve them of their helmets, stating they had more pressing need. All this time Joel was saying: "…you laughing now."

Fast bowlers have always whetted the appetites of Bajans. In another game I stood in at Bank Hall, Patterson Thompson, who briefly played for the West Indies and is now the head of the Leeward Islands Pilots Association, was in the midst of a hostile spell to a young school batsman who continually tried to hook his bouncers and was palpably too late. He was not wearing a helmet, and after the fourth occasion in a few overs when the ball whistled past his head, Thompson went down the pitch and simply said with a lot of feeling: "Youngster, I would suggest you cut out that shot for your own safety."

Standing in a trial match at Kensington, Vaspert Drakes was bowling like the wind before he suffered a back injury that caused him to lose his express pace. He had already uprooted the stumps of Sherwin Campbell when Roland Holder came in, and he completely beat him for pace, the second ball striking him plump in front, and Vaspert screamed at me in appeal. I was reflecting on whether there was any doubt. After all, Roland was my friend and I didn't want to disappoint him and myself by a wrong decision. I will swear to this day—but Roland denies this—that before I had raised my finger Roland was passing me on the way back to the pavilion, asking me why I was taking so long.

Those trial games at the time were fiercely competitive. Michael Matthews seemed to draw the ire of Ezra Moseley every time they played, and in one game when he was batting without a helmet, Moseley bowled him a bouncer and he turned white as he took evasive action. The ball parted his hair and went smack bang on to the sight screen. Quick it was, but thankfully it missed him, otherwise there would be no Hayley Matthews to speak about, and even I, standing at the other end, let out a gasp.

None of the players at the time would forget that character of umpiring, Stanton Parris, whose greatest claim to fame was standing in the match at Port of Spain between Combined Islands and Trinidad and Tobago, made famous by Paul Keens Douglas as the Tanti Merle match in his skit. Stanton was a character always willing not so much to engage you in a discussion or argument of cricket as to espouse his views at the top of his voice with a beer in his hand.

There was no topic on which he was not willing to offer his opinion, whether it had been asked for or not, and I can still see a picture of him holding court during a test match in Manchester in 1988, as the West Indies decimated England, shouting at the top of his voice at the bar that he could pick eleven West Indians watching the game in the stands who would give the West Indies team a better run for their money than the English team could. Not diplomatic, but at the time not incorrect either. What he would make of the current state of West

Indies cricket would make for interesting listening.

I was standing with him in one of those Barbados trial games when there was an appeal against a batsman for a low catch in the slips, when he wandered over towards where I was standing at square leg in an apparent show of consultation. When he reached me I said to him that I myself was not sure, whereupon he pulled out a notepad he had in his pocket checked it and muttered to me "he is not in my team for next week, so he is out." The entire episode looked comical, except if you were the batsmen whose innings was ended.

Soon it became impossible for me to devote an entire weekend to standing in these games with all the other things I was doing, and with a young family now to boot. I therefore suggested to the BCUA (Barbados Cricket Umpires Association) that I would be prepared to be on call to stand in for an umpire who had an emergency at short notice and could not stand in a game. I indicated I would only do this in the First Division, as the chances of it happening among the ten matches were much reduced than among the 50 other games played around the country. I also felt that it would then avoid having to disrupt lower games by pulling one of those officials to do the affected game with the consequent domino effect that the removal of that official would cause.

To me this appeared logical. I certainly wasn't suggesting it for any particular benefit, but some of the BCUA members felt I was picking and choosing my games and objected. I was told that basically fellas in the lower division looked forward to these situations, as they got the chance to move up amongst the big boys where the pay for umpires was greater. That consideration of the pay had never entered my mind, as I lost every time I umpired, given what I could have earned (not stolen) by putting in extra work, but I guess I was not appreciative of how others think. I just stopped and have not umpired in nearly 20 years.

I saw umpiring as just a part of the game you got involved in because of your love of the game. The receipt of a stipend for standing in the game to me was merely a by-product. I have not had much involvement with the BCUA since I stopped standing, but I sometimes receive a call from them for assistance when they have a legal problem. Of late on more than one occasion this question of entitlement to pay for standing has arisen with more than one person seeking the assistance of attorneys to argue that there is a quasi-contractual relationship between the BCUA and the umpires that would entitle them to be paid in circumstances where they have not stood because of injury occurring during a game, or because they were not appointed to stand because of a dispute with the committee of the BCUA.

The BCUA is an unincorporated body made up of persons who pay an annual membership fee to their association. To stand in games you need to be a member and the match day fee for standing is received by the BCUA from the BCA who has passed responsibility for the appointment of officials for the playing of games under the auspices of the BCA to the BCUA. It surely must be the time we live in that a member could now think he has the status of an employee with his association and as such is entitled to be paid for whatever reason he does not stand in a game. What next, may I ask?

25

The Barbados Cricket Association

MY PARENTS GAVE me a twelfth birthday present in 1972 of membership of the Barbados Cricket Association (BCA). My love for cricket was very apparent by then, and like any budding youngster I had dreams of playing for the West Indies. By the time I had completed my 'A' levels it had long been clear that this would never happen, and thus when the opportunity presented itself in 1988 to join the board of management I readily agreed. Other than for a period of a few months, I served as a member of the board until 1998 and thereafter as secretary from 1999 to 2005.

I had been a frequent attendee at the association's Annual General Meetings held at that time at the Dover Convention Centre, and watched as the Annual General Meetings events unfolded. I was too young to even dare make a contribution from the floor, but listened as many eminent personages in Barbados society debated the ills of the association. The president all this time was Captain Peter Short and it was he who approached me to ascertain my interest in joining the board in 1988. I have no doubt that he had previously consulted Mr. Armstrong as to my suitability, which was also enhanced by my recent election at the time to the post of secretary of Pickwick Cricket Club.

I readily consented and in those days the nod given you by Short and the other members of the executive guaranteed your election.

At the time I was one of the youngest, if not the youngest to be elected to the board. That distinction has now been passed on to Kamal Springer, and he probably feels as I did then the wide-eyed wonderment as I began rubbing shoulders with some of the icons of West Indies cricket. I had to pinch myself, as immortals from my childhood days like Sir Gary, Sir Wes, Sir Clyde, Sir Everton, Charlie Griffith, Cammie Smith, Seymour Nurse, David Holford and Peter Lashley referred to me by my first name or the more familiar 'Nic'.

In my 17-year association on the board I have witnessed what I would describe as the complete transformation of the association from the early equivalent of a genteel country club administering the yearly competitions of the BCA, to a more robust and commercial organization that had to deal with the realities of what was a pastime for many becoming a demanding professional endeavor. The advent of the Instant Money Game championed by Peter Lashley had, with the finances it brought over the previous decade prior to my joining the board, allowing the board under the guidance of Captain Short et al to firstly upgrade the infrastructure at Kensington with the building of then modern stands, and then to gradually expand the Secretariat from a pure voluntary one into a paid Secretariat.

During this time the concept of voluntarism took a back seat, as more and more persons demanded some form of compensation for lending their assistance to the BCA. This in part went hand in hand with the changing nature of cricket when it clearly moved from being a recreational sport to that of a business.

Not surprisingly, elections of persons to the Board, which over the years were by and large a rubber stamp of what the Short administration preferred, became at times bitter contests which sometimes produced surprising results. One such result was that Duncan Carter (now deceased) lost his seat on the Board at an annual meeting during a time when he was a sitting Member of Parliament in Barbados. It sounds amazing, but it happened and I don't think Duncan, a good man, ever understood what hit him.

I have never run for political office, and have no intention of doing so. I don't mean to trivialise those who do run and indeed serve in our parliament, but if what I saw at play during my stint as secretary of the association when election time came around is considered even a microcosm of what to expect on the national scheme, then I want no part of it—character assassination, deliberate untruths, misleading statements and even anonymous messages on my voicemail that if I continued running then the Cottle Catford mess would be exposed to the public in 2005.

That and the dealings with what I might describe as certain unfortunate behavior of some members in my time on the Board exposed me to another aspect of human behavior that I was at the time not too familiar with. Backstabbing is not too strong a word. Again my persona that you do what is right and not necessarily what is most beneficial to you seemed, as I spent longer and longer on the board, not to be the main agenda of some who attained office. After all, you are offering yourself for a voluntary position, and why then should you expect personal gain?

In addition, as the BCA is a corporate entity enacted by parliament, one of the last few around, why would you think that the common law rules applicable to directors of companies do not apply to you as a board member (director) of it? It was with amazement that I watched how certain prominent people in society would claim a right to do as they pleased when representing the Board, and by extension the wider membership of the association by voting as they desired and not as mandated by the Board.

During a disciplinary hearing arising out of a complaint laid by the England Cricket Team during their tour of the West Indies in 1990 for an on-field incident against Gordon Greenidge, an exclamation by

Greenidge illustrates my point about how the old vanguard of service was the watchword for the members elected to serve.

These were the days before the all-important match referee, and I was part of the committee that heard the matter when a comment was made to Greenidge about the makeup of the panel being all volunteers, as were all members of the Board. His response was interesting. He said "you mean Mr. Keith Walcott all these years running around behind us never got a cent?" This was confirmed as correct, to which he expressed astonishment.

Keith Walcott was one of the persons who took me under his wing when I joined the board and showed me the ropes. He was an excellent administrator and a true gentleman. He had a wealth of experience, and he and Captain Short were Barbados representatives on the WICB for years, but his mantra was one of service to the game he loved and he never received a cent for all his work. Someone may talk to me about per diems or refunds of expenses or indirect benefits, but trust me, when you think of the number of meetings that one attended and the volume of work that was involved, no benefit or honorarium could ever truly compensate for what was a labour of love. Keith was a traditionalist and many stories abound of his consternation as times changed and he could be heard muttering then: "What is going on? This is just not cricket." What he would have made of today's world is anyone's guess, but he gave long and dedicated service to the game. Keith was not unique at the time or since; there have been several Keith's here and in the other territories who provided the backbone for the organization of cricket long before secretariats and paid functionaries came into place.

When I joined the board, Captain Peter Short was president, with Cammie Smith as first vice-president. Cammie had previously been the longest serving honorary treasurer of the BCA in the days before the all-empowering computer with its accounting programs which made the task of preparing the annual accounts that much easier.

Still he never missed a deadline in producing the annual accounts. Nowadays, doing two things at once is called multitasking, something that many of the early board members who had day time jobs could do.

During my early time on the Board, Cammie was a loyal lieutenant to Captain Short—not a 'yes boy', something that was later to be used against him by those who should have known better when pushing an agenda for the election of Tony Marshall to the presidency instead of him. In this respect I can empathize with him, because many times when I was secretary with Stephen as president many persons felt that I simply rubber stamped what he said. Nothing can be further from the truth; we had our disagreements, but one could disagree without being enemies.

I was never as incensed as when one day, prior to Stephen arriving at a board meeting, there was a discussion about the news that the Barbados Mutual wished to have directors on the board of Life of Barbados. At the time Stephen was president of the latter and I was asked what I thought of the idea. Before I could respond, someone who worked at the Mutual said that I would only agree with whatever Stephen's position was. At the time I had not known what his was, but was very caustic in saying that it was a ridiculous suggestion, as the two companies were competitors and if the Mutual wanted LOB so badly, why did it not take over the f...ing thing? Well, as they say, the rest is history, not that my utterances had anything to do with it.

Short, because of his military upbringing, ran the Board with the style of an army major, especially with respect to time keeping. He never, however, could be described as dictatorial, and while he kept a very close circle of confidants with whom he discussed everything, often reaching a decision by round robin of his inner circle on what course he would prefer to follow before it came to the Board, a fact that caused much disquiet to those of us left out of this circle, most notably Charlie Griffith and Joel Garner.

How 'the Robin' worked is that if something needed to be decided between meetings, to avoid the necessity of summoning a meeting, the then executive secretary Basil Matthews would telephone around (no email at the time) to sound out the opinion of the board as to how members wished to vote on a question. We all know that depending on how a question is put your answer may be given. Basil would many times first call the most senior of the Board, many of whom supported Short, and after he got a majority of the Board in favour of the position that was being put forward, would stop calling.

The result of this was that on many occasions persons like Charlie and Joel would only hear about the decision when it was conveyed at the subsequent meetings, and howls of protests would emanate that contrary views were being stifled. My suspicion was this was not necessarily of Short's doing. He may well have realized what Basil was doing, as Basil was a skilled manipulator, but it eventually led to the decision that 'the robin' is dead. It provoked many outbursts, and I can remember many short meetings thereafter to simply make such a decision, as the robin could no longer fly. Still one of the abiding memories from that time was that once a decision was made, that was it: a board decision accepted by all.

As I am writing this I have learned with sadness of the passing of Captain Short, and as I reflect on his tenure of leading the board, I would have to conclude that his greatest trait was that of his diplomacy. This was none the more evident than the role he played this time as president of the WICB in persuading Brian Lara during the 1995 tour of the UK not to abandon the tour and return to the fold. Nearly twenty years later his actions in going to meet with the players were contrasted sharply with the decision of the present president of the West Indies Cricket Board not to go and meet with the disgruntled players in India. The consequences of the players' early pull out from that tour are still being felt within West Indies cricket.

Both Charlie and Joel befriended me on the Board. Charlie was always suspicious of us 'Kolij boys', often telling us young educated upstarts that he had a degree in common sense, if not numbers, and we could not get things past him without him knowing. He used to tease me unmercifully in an attempt to get me to lose weight by insisting I was on a 'see-food' diet—see it, and eat it—but all for a good cause as he always said he could keep up with any of us youngsters.

I learnt a lot of the machinations that went on in the annals of West Indian cricket when he was a player, and it was clear that he carried a chip on his shoulder for what he considered with some justification was his unfair treatment by the administrators of the day that in his view had not done enough to prevent him being hounded by the English cricket press over the chucking controversy that dogged his career. Given Short's close connection with the English game, he was suspicious that while he may not have been in collaboration, it was his view that he did not stand up forcefully enough for him.

I leave that feeling to others to determine. It was before my time, but it led to many interesting meetings, as at times I often felt that Charlie was opposing a Short proposal for opposing's sake just to air his view. I was always told by others that Charlie was a fierce competitor on the field, but I always found him to be a gentle and caring giant and even in his opposition, once he had made his point, that was that.

Short was president for an unprecedented 20 years in succession, and was the face of the organization from the time I knew it. In the last quarter of his presidency, growing opposition to him appeared to be centered on the fact that he was white rather than on his competence, for after all at the time the BCA was the envy not only in Barbados but throughout the West Indies as a well-run association. Smith was not willing to challenge him as he repeatedly said on this basis, and it was thus no surprise that after becoming president after Short took up the presidency of the WICB that he was subject to a challenge just after two years.

Cammie's jovial personality meant that meetings under his

chairmanship tended to be more relaxed. In some respects this was his downfall, as he was not suspicious of the motives of others in the meetings. His abiding view was that when a matter is put to a vote and a decision made, you win some and you lose some, move on. It is a mantra that I found served me well later on, and one that I wished I could have displayed in blazing lights at every meeting, as several times at meetings after vigorous debates those who had not won the day in the boardroom tried later if not to have the decision overturned, then to disassociate themselves from the meeting, especially when john public became critical.

After all, board members were as akin to directors of a company, owing a duty of care to the company, and should seek to do what was in the best interest of the association, not them. It was a phenomenon not related to the BCA, as many persons have made it their life's work to get information with respect to organizations they are not a member of. Part of "we culture", to quote Gabby, but a breach of all concepts of corporate governance.

After two years as president, Smith was challenged by Tony Marshall and lost a tight election by about half a dozen votes in 1996. That was the official result, but there was uncontroverted evidence that some of Marshall's known supporters—prominent professionals and business men in society—voted twice, taking advantage of the relatively slack voting procedure then in place for BCA elections, as these were generally non-contentious up to that time.

Both Stephen and I became aware during the voting that something was amiss and urged Cammie to put a halt to it. Though pressed, he refused to do so, taking the attitude that if the membership of the association who turned out were so desperate to replace him, so be it. Smith refused to challenge the result even when, to quote Macbeth 'liquor loosens tongues', many loose tongues at the bar after in the Old Dover Convention indicated what had gone down, living by his well-known mantra 'You win some and you lose some… get on with it' and in his case he moved on to become one of the early pioneers of today's International Match Referees.

Cammie's stance and demeanor was one that I always respected, and to this day I have held him in the highest regard. My admiration for him has only grown this last year as he has personally assisted me with a place to live at a time when I had lost my home to foreclosure and my practice had been contracting greatly with the result that my ability to meet the monthly expenses of a home were severely compromised. The depth of gratitude I have towards him I doubt I will ever be able to repay.

I always tried to be guided by his simple philosophy with respect to decisions taken. One in particular I remember when I was outvoted 11-1 with respect to a matter that I knew was heading for the courts because of who the protagonists were. I was totally opposed to the situation which saw the Board deciding to try and seek mediation with attorney's who had written the board concerning, ironically, some disputed elections which were being challenged. I was of the view that no matter what we tried, the attorneys in question would put the matter in court because that was their trademark, so we might as well wait until they filed their challenge. So said, so done, but the Board having made a decision, I as secretary had to report on it. One of the most satisfying moments for me was being called by Owen Estwick after he heard an interview with me on the radio to congratulate me and express mild astonishment at how I was now in public so vigorously defending the Board's decision which I had in private spoken against and condemned as ill-conceived and illogical.

My response to Nobby was that it was a collective decision, I was a member of the Board, and that was that. I certainly don't want to give the impression that all members were guilty of divulging decisions or that I was the only one who observed the collective responsibility expected of board members. I can think of Charlie Griffith, who was pilloried in the press and by a player from his own club who had been controversially left out of the Barbados team when he was chairman of selectors.

The omission also created discussion prior to a board meeting. Charlie said nothing to the criticism, neither tried to justify it nor to say the selectors got it wrong, as results in the final Barbados was playing would suggest. After Charlie left the meeting, one of the other selectors who was on the board at the time said "Guys… give Charlie a break. You know he was outvoted 4-1." He wanted the guy to play and even though it turned out he should have he never threw the rest of us under the bus. He never let on even in the face of abuse from the player who left Empire in disgust at what he perceived was unfair treatment that he disagreed with his committee. Unfortunately, in my latter years on the Board, and from my observations since leaving the Board, this is something that is not followed. Current media reports where one member of the West Indies selection panel bemoaned a decision that they lost 2-3 would suggest that he would do well to speak to Charlie.

Moving on from a board that was run by Short and then Smith was difficult. I never became enamored with Marshall for the simple reason that I was of the view that his real interest was becoming president of the West Indies Cricket Board. Whatever and whoever could assist him in this desire became close to him, and unlike Short he tended to surround himself with advisors not on the Board who seemed to have as much if not more influence on decisions than the average board member. I always felt that when Smith was president, as a board member Marshall never gave Smith his full support and often tried to undermine him. It was clear that he was the ultimate beneficiary of the dissatisfaction with the handling of the Haynes affair and it is also clear that long after the event all the facts of the matter were not in the public domain and Smith received unfair opprobrium for his stance.

The Desmond Haynes affair, which led to the end of his stellar career as an outstanding opening batsman for the West Indies, arose because of the breach by Haynes of the then eligibility rule of the West Indies Board. The fallout from the affair was the catalyst that led to the unseating of Cammie as president, a decision that his now deceased wife Phyllis exhibited more bitterness about than he did. She was always quick to remind persons who were in the vanguard of removing Cammie what she thought of them and I have heard Desmond say more than once that he has received some fiery lectures from her and often got out of her path when he saw her in the distance.

The incident also highlighted the problems inherent in the system that obtained when the same persons who are directors of the West Indies Board are also directors of their local associations. In the Haynes matter, Cammie Smith found himself in this tight rope situation from a legal perspective as the president of the BCA, and as one of its directors he owed a duty of care to the BCA, whereas as a director of the WICB he owed a duty of care to the WICB and not to the BCA who had put him there, akin to representing a shareholder on the Board of Directors. While you may feel beholden to who put you there, when the chips are down the law requires you to act in the best interest of the company of which you are a director, in this case the WICB. This can clearly be a problem when there is the inevitable conflict between two institutions with the same representatives as directors.

As the 1995 regional season was approaching, Desmond Haynes was in South Africa playing cricket professionally. Basil Matthews, the then executive secretary of the BCA, on the instructions of the president Cammie Smith, had sent a fax to Haynes who was playing in South Africa enquiring about the date of his return to Barbados with a view to selection to the team. When no word was received, the Chairman of Selectors Charlie Griffith also tried to make contact with him by phone, and when he also failed to speak to him the Barbados team was selected and no reason was given for Haynes' non-selection.

Shortly after the start of the tournament or after the squad for the first game was selected, Haynes returned to Barbados and stated he was available for selection and to play for the West Indies, and sought a dispensation from the rule that in order to be eligible for selection he had to play in all games for Barbados unless he was injured or was unavailable for any other legitimate reason. When the request was discussed by the West Indies Board, Smith advised the Board of the attempts by the BCA to contact Haynes and, having not received a response from Haynes, he was not selected. He further said that in the circumstances he could not as a director of the WICB refuse to uphold its requirements which were well known to all the players and was part of the decision to rule Haynes ineligible for the series.

As Smith was to say, many senior players in the past had been excused for reasons that many would have thought were questionable, and had Haynes contacted the BCA, a similar excuse could have been made for him. He was clearly of the view that the problem was one of Haynes's own making.

The decision of the West Indies Board led to a public outcry in Barbados and the BCA held an emergency board meeting at which a resolution was passed requesting the WICB to change its decision. Cammie disagreed with the resolution, but was mandated as the rep to the meeting to put it into the meeting. Cammie has always said he felt strongly about the matter that Haynes knew of the rule and deliberately flouted it. He made it clear that he could not support the resolution put forward which now meant he was conflicted by his duties to the BCA and his duties to the WICB.

Along came the master diplomat Short, and sensing the predicament that his loyal lieutenant and friend for all these years was facing, engineered that when the matter was discussed at the meeting of the WICB, called in response to the resolution submitted by the BCA, a vote on the resolution was never taken because the meeting determined that the resolution contained nothing that had not been previously discussed that would warrant them reopening the matter and voting thereon.

The fallout surrounding this episode in West Indies cricket was not limited to simply Haynes' non-selection. Within the Barbados Cricket Association it led to great upheaval, as the then treasurer of the board Vernon Williams, a member with Haynes of the same club—Carlton—which club has subsequently renamed its playing facility the Desmond Haynes Oval, resigned from the board in apparent protest at the way that Smith had conducted himself with respect to the matter. Though there was never a vote at the WICB on the matter, he could have been accused of not following the mandates of his board if he had voted, as he made no secret of his intention to in a manner contrary to the dictates of the Board; he would have probably faced demands for his resignation. As it was, his goose was cooked and Marshall replaced him as the West Indies Board rep at the 96th AGM the year before eventually toppling him, an unprecedented happening, as the president had always been a rep, and the following year he defeated Smith. I have always found it more than ironic that Cammie was pilloried though he never voted against a mandate, while other members have deliberately flouted mandates for apparent personal gain without the same opprobrium being heaped on them, and their actions have led to changes at the helm of the West Indies Board.

Cammie is an honest man, one whom I have stated previously I have much time for, but I believe he misjudged the mood of the membership and paid the ultimate price, whatever the margin of the vote, as his principled stand was to become the catalyst for his controversial defeat by Tony Marshall in 1997.

By the time Marshall became president I was not enamored with him. I had seen firsthand at meetings how he tried to undermine Cammie, often trying to share with those who wished papers he had gained from the West Indies Board which in his mind indicated that Cammie had not been forceful enough in putting the position of the BCA. I have never understood the rabid desire of persons not on a particular board to seek obtained papers from the other board. I for one was never interested in seeing them and told him so. Many would find it hard to believe because of the close relationship between Stephen and I, but I never sought or obtained from him papers with respect to the West Indies Board other than those distributed to board members of the BCA as part of the information the territorial boards needed to know.

There were two exceptions to this. The first was when Stephen wished a legal opinion on some matter and the second was when at the last minute I had to deputize for him at a meeting in Antigua when business commitments prevented him travelling at the last minute. I subsequently watched with consternation and bemusement as at the meeting the then President Rousseau try to chair the meeting and take minutes at the same time, and after a few minutes I said: "Mr. Chair please forward your pad to me and I will take the minutes." He did so much to his relief, as I continued that it was nonsense to expect someone to chair the meeting and keep a record of what was being said. But despite all of that I am still to be refunded for paying for my flight down to Antigua out of my own pocket, so late was the decision made for me to attend.

Marshall made no secret of his desire to become more of a player in West Indies cricket and it soon manifested itself with an unbelievable turn of events. In the early part of 1996 the West Indies Board, as was done at the time, circulated to territories for nominations for manager of the team for the upcoming 1996 tour of the West Indies by New Zealand. Joel Garner indicated his desire and Marshall was instructed by the Board that Barbados was nominating Garner for the position. What happened next is akin to a story of fiction.

After the election of the manager I was telephoned by Stephen who tracked the number of the hotel I was staying at from my father. I believe I was at an International Tax Seminar in the Netherlands when late one night the phone rang. Stephen was on the other end and the tone in his voice suggested there was some breaking news. After the usual perfunctory questions about whether I was cold up there, it being winter, he asked of my recollection of the nominee by the BCA for manager of the West Indies team. I said we put up Bird. He then said: "Who you think is manager?" I said "Not Bird?" "No" was the response.

I must have spent the better part of ten minutes guessing every name from Barbados and the other territories that could in my mind fit the bill as a manager until Stephen, with amusement in his voice, said "you running up my bill. Let me tell you… it is Marshall." I said "Malcolm? I thought he was interested in being the coach." He said "No… Tony." Silence. He said "You still there?" I said "What happen to Bird?" and was told that Bird didn't even make the ballot. All I could do was say "signs and wonders" and that the upcoming meeting of the BCA Board would be interesting.

As usual, Marshall arrived late at the meeting, but the meeting had determined that whenever he came the issue under discussion would be deferred so that the Board could receive a report into what transpired at the West Indies Board Meeting. Bird was in attendance at the meeting wearing dark glasses with the permission of the chair, Cammie, as he said to him he intended to take a dim view of events. Imagine this. Big Bird seated, towering over everybody else in some dark glasses. You would strain to find a cricket picture of him wearing shades on the field of play. It was comical to say the least, as he sat there not uttering a word, just peering from behind these dark glasses with his face contorted in derision from Marshall's explanation.

Marshall was given the floor and asked to explain how he came back from a meeting as a manager when we had instructed him to put forward Bird's name for the post he was now holding. His explanation was that in the chit chat around the bar the night before the meeting (a regular occurrence and a sort of feeling out session to get support for your man that is a feature of all West Indian Board Meetings) it became apparent to him that there would be no seconder for Garner and when someone asked if he was interested he stated yes. By the way, he had never said this to the Board when we discussed putting up a nomination.

He continued that as he was told by one of the other delegates, he never said who, that he would be nominated for the position. He did the 'honorable thing' and withdrew from the meeting when the matter was came up for discussion. A lot of cross talk ensued before Stephen asked for the floor, addressed Marshall and asked if he was outside the meeting when the appointment of a manager was discussed, then who represented Bird in the meeting. Who put forward our wishes? That particular meeting was being attended by one rep rather than the usual two and Marshall was the rep.

The question could not be answered. Stephen continued with words to the effect that his responsibility was to nominate Bird whether he had a seconder or not, and let the nomination fail, "but we listening to you pat yourself on the back for doing according to you the honourable thing and withdrawing from the meeting to allow a free discussion of your candidacy. Who may I ask was representing Mr. Garner's interest or that of the BCA? The honourable thing would have been not to accept the nomination, attend the meeting and fight tooth and nail for Bird in seeking a seconder to your nomination."

Even now, nearly twenty years later, I find these events amazing. True to form, Marshall by his actions displayed that the nickname by which he was known (which I will not repeat here) was apt. West Indies Board meetings over the years always involved horse trading, after all, countries started with a maximum of two votes out of 14 at a meeting and needed to get allies. I have always felt that there was more in the mortar than in the pestle, and the time subsequently came when Marshall actually, but Barbados in name, had to repay the favour for support he received at that time, and it is not idle speculation as to who Barbados supported in 1998 when the captaincy of the West

Indies team passed from Courtney Walsh to Brian Lara.

Despite all of this, when Marshall was president I was never one to adopt an attitude of non-support for him, even if I did not agree with his methods, and can say without fear of any contradiction by anyone that while he was president and I was on the Board I gave him my full support in tending to the affairs of the association. After a while I gradually grew more disaffected, as unlike under Short and Smith I felt that whenever something was introduced by him you had to look out for the 'collateral damage' or the hidden agenda.

When I reached the stage where I felt I could no longer continue offering my unstinting support I decided not to seek re-election to the Board, a decision that had also been reached by Stephen Alleyne. I will admit that Stephen's decision not to run made mine easier, but I had basically made up my mind because of what I felt was a wicked decision by Marshall involving one of my clients.

For a number of years I had been representing Vaspert Drakes in his challenge against the rule that a player must represent his territory in all games to qualify for selection to the West Indies team. There was no doubt that at the time in 1998 that he would have walked into the team without this rule. Vaspert was a professional and at the time he could earn more playing in South Africa as a per diem than in a match in the regional competition. It was a no-brainer for a professional cricketer at a time when only persons actually in the West Indies team made anywhere near a decent living from the game.

I had been in general correspondence with the West Indies Board at the time, but it was getting nowhere. I did not think that court action was the best option, but as the 1998 season approached and the West Indies Board appeared not to want to deal with the matter, I decided a new approach was needed. As such I wrote a letter to Marshall in his capacity as president of the BCA setting out the issues and listing the points that could be made in support of a relaxation of the rule in Vaspert's favour. My intent was simply to ask Marshall that he raise it at an upcoming meeting of the WICB (in 1998) which he was attending as one of the representatives of the BCA before the regional season began.

To my horror, Marshall simply photocopied my letter and sent it to the WICB despite my indicating to him that it was a private matter. I was mortified and angered by the betrayal, and let him know that if I had wanted the letter forwarded to the WICB I knew their address, and would simply have copied it to them, but now his actions had taken away any chance of possible court action on Vasbert's part, as the proposed defendant would have seen all of his case. The laws of libel prevent me from speculating as to his motives in so doing, but having seen how he was strongly of the view that the BCA when Smith was president had a duty to support Haynes in his dispute with the WICB, it appeared to me more than ironic that he did not see it that way now.

I determined that I had had enough and was out of there. For me it was impossible to stay and serve with a man for whom I by then for a number of reasons had such a low opinion of and so the only alternative absent to challenging him was to shut up and get out.

It has always amazed me how subsequently certain members of the Board who have had areas of disagreement with the president or Board would prefer to stay on the Board and create mischief by undermining the work of the Board often in public. What is worse, some have even gone so far as to place the BCA in court while on the Board. I recognize the right of anyone to seek the court's protection, but if you feel so strongly about the issue that you want to have it be determined in court, then be man enough to resign rather than stay on the Board.

I have already spoken about the absence of collective responsibility by some members of the boards I served with. Another practice that was particularly otiose was informing players who had voted for or against them on a matter such as the appointment of a captain. The hypocrisy came to a height once when the Board, having made a decision, decided before the end of the meeting to reverse it. One person present when the original decision had been made had left, and thus was unaware of the change. The next morning Barry Wilkinson broadcast what he perceived to be a scoop of the original decision, not knowing it had been changed, and as such it was vehemently denied. The culprit who had leaked the decision was self-evident, yet when the offending member was taken to task he denied he had been the leak, which was true to form for the individual.

After Stephen and I declined to be nominated for the Board for 1998 to 1999, we soon started hearing that the Board would run better now because the two trouble makers were no longer there. This made the two of us laugh, because we had been called many things, but troublemakers? It was not long, however, before the Board started to descend in disarray and Marshall, whatever he says, must face up to the fact that his driving ambition to become president of the WICB rubbed some people the wrong way.

The vice presidency on the West Indies Board opened and as usual the Board discussed a nominee. As no consensus could be reached, a vote was held on the two names discussed, the president Marshall and Joel Garner. When the vote was held Garner was not at the meeting, as he was away managing the West Indies 'A' team. The vote was 6-6. A second ballot was held and the result remained the same. At this point Marshall intimated that as chair he was going to exercise the right in the event of a tie to exercise a casting vote. This led to howls of protest on the ground that after two rounds the vote was tied. It had to be presumed that Marshall had voted for himself. Garner was absent and thus did not vote, but it can be presumed that he would have voted for himself. For the chair in these circumstances to use a casting vote in his favour was not right, but he did. The upshot of it was that three members of the Board vowed never to attend a meeting again, including two who had replaced Alleyne and I, and the Board struggled at times to raise a quorum.

Eventually in all the confusion the Board did not summon the AGM in time for the constitutionally mandated time of the end of July, and eventually had to make an application to the court for directions as to what to do. It is worth noting that there was no hasty rush from any members to put the matter in court. The court ruled that the general body was the supreme body, and could set a date outside the constitutionally required date and eventually an AGM was held either in late September or early October, at which the heaviest turnout of members at an AGM election that was followed closely in the press and in general in Barbados, elected Sir Conrad Hunte as president over Marshall.

It turned out to be a blessing in disguise for me when I decided not to run in July of 1998, as being off the Board allowed me to meet in early 1999 with Sir Conrad Hunte who was asked to make himself available to be nominated as president. I was introduced to him by the late Charles Alleyne, Stephen's father. Stephen was approached to run as his first vice-president and I as Secretary. We were successful when the delayed election was contested, but sadly Sir Conrad died while on a trip to Australia later that year a few months after being elected. It has always been my view that his untimely death robbed Barbados and indeed the West Indies of a person who would have offered much more to cricket, this time in an administrative capacity, than he had already done in his distinguished playing career and his philanthropic work.

Sir Conrad was known to me, as would anyone my age with a fleeting interest in cricket, as one of our iconic players. There is still etched in my mind that iconic photograph of him appealing when the stumps were struck during the closing moments of the tied test in Australia in 1960. However, I did not know the man, but in the six to nine months that I was to work with him I learnt a lot about human behavior and dealing with one's 'critics, not enemies', he would say. He made one statement to me that has always lived with me and is something that has sustained me throughout my ten years of horror.

A story was run in the paper highly critical of him or of some position that he took. When we read it we were all mortified and engaged him in making an urgent rebuttal when he simply said: "Guys I have nothing to say. Anyone who knows me will know the story cannot be true and if they don't know me and read it and believe it then it's probably a good thing." I have often thought of this saying when I have been at my lowest. His death later that year was part of a terrible six-week time for Barbados cricket, as Malcolm Marshall had predeceased him by a month, and Sylvester Clarke died just over a week later.

After Sir Conrad's death Stephen performed the duties of president as first vice-president. He never styled himself as acting president, but true to form, Vernon Smith, backed by his usual crowd, went to court.

These constant court challenges were however to mark the next six years when time after time challenges were made, all in an attempt to destabilize the Alleyne administration. When the history of the association is written, it will become clear who or what was behind these challenges. I do not accept that it was because of any maladministration at the time, for far worse has transpired after, but the membership has chosen not to air their dirty linen in public.

In 2005, in the lead up to the staging of the World Cup, another challenge was made by Tony Marshall for the presidency and he prevailed in a close election over Stephen. I lost my post as secretary, for which I was not sorry as I had no intention of working with Marshall again. Out of respect for Stephen I will not delve into the reasons for his loss or of the circumstances surrounding it, except to say that when persons misrepresent what occurred at a meeting summoned by the then Prime Minister Owen Arthur with all parties involved in the election because he was concerned that the bickering would have an effect on Barbados' preparation for hosting Cricket World Cup 2007 in order to gain any sort of advantage, it is a sad day.

The experience of serving on the Board has not only taught me a lot, but given me the opportunity to meet persons both locally, regionally and internationally that I would not otherwise have met. While I may have highlighted some of the more disturbing times, I have fond memories of the camaraderie of many board members and the stories that were swapped around the bar at the end of meetings. It is my understanding that meetings now regularly run until after midnight, so I doubt there remains that opportunity to socialize.

One of the most enthralling meetings and conversations that I had during my time on the board was with the former Prime Minister of England John Major, along with Andrew Sealy and Allan Smith, while at a Test Match at the Oval in London. After our talk we were overheard discussing amongst ourselves how amazing it was that he just struck up a conversation with us at the lunch table, assuming that we were there to support the West Indies and must be involved in administration back home and that he appeared a regular guy without all the trappings of office. One of his security details told us that if he had his way none of the three of them would be there. I am grateful for that memory and the many friendships I have forged, if for no other reason, for my time on the Board.

26

Cricket and the Law

THROUGHOUT THIS BOOK I have traced my growing disenchantment with my chosen profession; how the mores as I understand them and was taught to practice them have been hijacked by one or two interested in their own self-aggrandizement in an attempt to not only discredit me but at the same time protect others who have abandoned all of their moral and legal responsibility for the partnership they were part of. This early enthusiasm has been blunted and destroyed by the manipulation of a system by a few and the failure of one in particular charged with the responsibility of ensuring that the cogs of the system are well oiled and working properly, with the result that I now despise not only my profession but share the view of many (some of whom may well place me in that bracket) that if you want justice, stay clear of lawyers and more importantly the court system.

My early fascination with the law was only matched by an earlier obsession with cricket, and it may well be axiomatic that as the two have met within me I have seen how use of the law has turned what was always regarded as a gentleman's game upside down. I recognize that times have changed and that in today's world the courtesies of the past are no longer extended. In cricket, players are now berated for upholding the traditions of old whereby you accept the word and integrity of your opponent, for instance that a catch has been taken.

I still vividly recall an incident about fifteen years ago when I was speaking with the Barbados team after a practice session at Queens Park about the nuances of the code of conduct under which they were playing, when a then recently retired great West Indian player berated one of the then current West Indies players in the Barbados team for 'walking on a recent tour of New Zealand'. His view was that times had changed and that after what had happened on a contentious West Indies tour to New Zealand with umpiring in the early 80s it was nearly akin to a treasonable offence for any West Indian to 'walk' in that country.

I have over the years ruminated about how the traditions in the game have slowly disappeared, and that has brought me back to how the legal professions has significantly changed over the near thirty years that I have been associated with it. This change has in the main not been for the better. It is a 'dog eats dog' profession, and if you can get one up on your fellow practitioner, good for you. No longer are the simple courtesies in the profession extended amongst members, and I for now would accept the word of a few that they intend or commit to doing something. Put it in writing.

When I think of cricket and the law there has been a significant change in its juxtaposition and in my view this change is perhaps as great as the on-field changes in recent times with the explosion of twenty/twenty cricket. I, like many old stooges, marvel at the ingenuity of players in this form of the game, but in the end I am of the belief that it is a spectacle, not true cricket, and more in keeping with today's instantaneous world.

My indifference to this form of the game and the lessening appeal that the game has for me is in many respects the result of the interaction I have seen between the law and cricket in my nearly two decades on the board of the Barbados Cricket Association. During this time the often quoted dictum that if the head is bad how can the body be any good came to mind. If the administrators and or the members of an organization were always locked in some legal battle trying to gain one on their opponents, how can you expect any difference from the players? Adults—and I can't excuse myself in this regard—are often not aware of how their actions are seen and interpreted by children.

To illustrate this I will relate a story that was told to me shortly after I joined the board of the BCA in 1987 re the happenings at a Disciplinary Committee hearing. A young captain of one of the school teams was charged with time wasting (he later went into politics in Barbados) and he said with all honesty at his hearing that he had seen a former Trinidad captain and West Indies player as a youngster watching the game employ the same tactics that he was charged with using contrary to the spirit of the game in a regional game. He stated emphatically that nothing happened to him, so he didn't understand why he was before the committee. He won his case.

My first taste of the interaction between law and cricket came in what has become the celebrated BCA case of Griffith and Reifer suing on behalf of their respective sports clubs—Police and St. Catherine—over the events that transpired in a cricket match at St. Catherine which had a bearing on the outcome of the cricket season in 1986 described earlier in this book.

Though not a deliberate parody, the heading of this chapter is the title of an actual book in publication by David Fraser, and it has on its cover the picture of an umpire raising that dreaded finger ('the hand of God', as one umpire on the local season used to refer to it). This title is an apt illustration of the changing face of cricket and indeed sport in general, as resort to the law courts to settle issues on the field of play became all too frequent. As I write I can see much symbolism in the cricket umpire, the football referee and the legal judge.

Until recently their decisions were final and not appealable, in some respects one may argue more of finality than a judge whose decisions were always appealable, but the common thread was that their rulings at the time were binding and final. With the advent of TV replays, the home audience often saw their decisions held up to scrutiny and indeed ridicule by commentators. Though the referral system for contentious decisions was not yet in place, a cartoon appeared in a cricket magazine in the 1990s of a lawyer representing a disgruntled batsmen with the two umpires in the dock under the caption saying: "My Lord this TV replay will show that my client's bat was nowhere near the ball at the time he was given out caught behind." It was extremely funny at the time, but prophetic in terms of how decisions on the field would soon lose the aura of the umpire's decision being final.

In my view the change to accept the review system in cricket along with the use in other sports of electronic technology to aid the making of decisions has in my belief arisen partly because of the willingness of society to not limit legal challenges to areas outside of sports, and there has been an explosion of textbooks and indeed magazines on legal issues of a sporting nature.

My good friend Richard Jeffers was given out in a Ronald Tree Under-15 game, and clearly disliked the decision. His dislike was so intense that at the interval he erased the manner of dismissal in the scorebook and wrote "Thief Out."

Later that evening his father turned up at the ground while we were in the field and went to check the scorebook for our innings to see how Richard had got on. He clearly was not impressed with the notation he saw next to Richard's name in the scorebook, and while taking Richard home at the end of the day he gave him a clip around the ears, informing him that there was no such dismissal in cricket, that the umpire's decision was final and must be respected even if wrong. Richard was chastised more I think by the mirth emitting from his teammates than at the annoyance of his father to his indiscretion, though to be fair to him anyone who has ever played the game has had similar annoyance as he did.

Casual research will reveal that as an organization the BCA, because of the fact that cricket is (was may be more accurate) a virtual religion in the island, receives an inordinate amount of publicity for its affairs. I am constantly amazed at the recognition I still receive from total strangers both in Barbados and elsewhere because of my association with cricket despite never having held public office and even though I have not been on the Board for ten years now.

Like in many other spheres of activity this publicity can be a double-edged sword. The column inches that anything surrounding the BCA generates has served as an attraction to some to feed on their insatiable appetite for free publicity by the institution of a legal challenge involving the BCA. Smith did not miss this trick in this regard.

For every conceivable issue that he disagreed with, he filed court action after court action—interestingly enough the majority of this took place during the tenure of Stephen Alleyne as president and I as honorary secretary. The argument has been made that we were the common denominator in these challenges, and as such 'where there is smoke there must be fire' on our part. With respect I would have to disagree that our actions could have been the basis for these constant challenges. It has become clear to me over the years that nothing would have prevented these challenges by Smith because this was his makeup.

The death in December 1999 of Sir Conrad Hunte shortly after he took office as president of the BCA was a case in point. Stephen was elected as Sir Conrad's first vice president and I was elected the honorary secretary on October 12th 1999. Sir Conrad had led a team that defeated the Tony Marshall administration that had become dysfunctional after dissatisfaction with his style of leadership.

Stephen and I, after serving for a year under Marshall after he had defeated Cammie Smith, had not sought re-election at the 1998 AGM, and were not part of the board, which for the first time in history had failed to summon the annual general meeting in time. One would have thought, given his track record, that Smith would have been the trumpeter against these wrongs, but there was not a peep out of him against the Marshall-led board when an application was made to court for the meeting to be held out of time, and so the meeting due at the end of July was held on October 12th.

That in itself meant that because of Sir Conrad's death he had merely had two meetings prior to same, and really was unable to leave a meaningful stamp on the association, but for those of faith we must presume it was the Lord's will. After Sir Conrad's death, and in Barbadian parlance with him still not cold, Smith led a challenge against the BCA for not holding a meeting to elect a new president.

At that time the press often referred to Stephen as being the acting president, something he never described himself as. We all considered him to be the first vice president, performing the function of the president who was absent albeit permanently. Smith and Edward Walcott, along with twenty others, requisitioned the holding of an extraordinary general meeting for the purpose of filling the vacancy for the unexpired term of Sir Conrad's two year term. This meeting was held on March 23rd 2000, and the resolution was rejected after those present were informed of a decision of the board to defer the election to fill the vacancy for the remainder of the term of the president until the next AGM. This had been stated time after time, but Smith was insistent a meeting had to be held to conduct the election prior to this.

The AGM was held on July 20th 2000, and Stephen defeated Owen 'Nobby' Estwick by a large margin for the post of president. Amazingly, on July 27th 2000, Smith and the said Walcott made an application to court for his election and that of other persons, namely David Holford to the office of first vice president, and Clinton St. Hill as a board member to be declared null and void. Justice Carlisle Payne denied the application on the ground that as the relief sought was discretionary, he did not think it was a case to grant injunctions and declarations, and in any event the office holders against whom the relief was sought were interested parties and had no opportunity to be heard.

But Smith did not accept that and appealed to the Court of Appeal where the matter was heard on April 4th 2001. The Court of Appeal on May 10th 2001 dismissed his appeal, ruling that contrary to the nonsense that Smith was spouting, the election to replace Sir Conrad could have been done in the manner that it was done, namely at an AGM and not necessarily a special general meeting as Smith wanted. As the Court of Appeal said, the election was done at an AGM which is the highest authority of the association. For over a year Smith wasted the association's time and energy, and amazingly the Court of Appeal allowed him to walk free of costs in the matter. This was all the more galling when I would hear him boast of a watch he had bought out of costs awarded when he took the BCA to court preemptively, but still was awarded costs. As the saying goes, the law is an ass..

The resort to litigation for every triviality was a cause of much regret both to Stephen and me. Not only was it a distraction that took valuable time and resources away from the main purpose, that of administering Barbados cricket, but there was an actual cost. As I have been reminded over and over, I found myself giving much uncompensated legal time in matters pertaining to the BCA in which others reaped handsome fees. But my far greatest disappointment was the fact that more than one person was comfortable with instituting legal action against the board that they were a member of because of a decision of the Board that they did not agree with. None of these individuals had the intestinal fortitude to follow up their actions by resigning from the board after instituting such action against the board. What is the saying—having your cake and eating it?

I am reminded at this time of the mantra of the former president of the board, Cammie Smith, who used to say of decisions made by the board: "you win some, and you lose some, get on with what you were supposed to do." No one had greater reason to challenge anything within the BCA than he did when he was cheated out of the election as president of the association to Tony Marshall, which on the face of it he lost by six votes. He refused to countenance a legal challenge to the result, though many persons including myself were prepared to swear that they had witnessed irregularities in the voting where persons, many of them known to be prominent supporters of Marshall, were seen voting more than once.

Cammie took the view that the association would be the poorer for the airing of its dirty linen, and accepted the result with much grace, an act that all of those who participated in the many challenges to decisions made would do well to reflect on.

In my time on the board it was clear to me that if the Cammie Smith mantra was accepted then there would not have been the resort to litigation that there was. I am fully supportive of a person's right to litigate where he believes his rights have been infringed, but to do so in the name of achieving cheap political points is of little credit to one's association, especially for decisions that you have been a party to, but don't agree with the final result. Man up and accept it. But then again to do so means one has to be a team player.

The litigation brought by Alexandra School was what many of us on the board at the time found the most disturbing, as basically it was brought at the behest of the then principal of the school Jeff Broomes, who at the time of both incidents remained a member of the board of the BCA. As subsequent events have shown in Barbados, Broomes has had an interesting history at Alexandra, and true to form, attempted on more than one occasion to try to assert his 'my way or the highway' policy with respect to any issue he was interested in when it came before the board.

In one of the cases that ended up in court, despite seeking the board's clarification prior to the game in question being played as to the eligibility of a particular individual to play for the school in the game, and being told emphatically by the board that the person in question was not eligible to play, he allowed the individual to play. When the board made the inevitable decision that Alexandra had forfeited the game, he proceeded to have the school institute an action on the grounds that the school had not been given a formal hearing to answer to the charge that they played an ineligible player.

I have always disagreed with the decision of Justice Inniss in this matter that, as he put it, the player was clearly ineligible, but because the board had not given Alexandra a hearing on the question, the decision to forfeit the game was quashed. This was completely different from the St. Catherine/Police game. Not only was Broomes present at the board meetings, but had on behalf of the school not once but twice made it clear he was representing the school when he spoke. How then could the school later claim they had not been given the right to a hearing? As in any other sport, fielding an ineligible player is a simple question of fact; your motives in doing so are completely irrelevant.

The antics of Broomes in this matter paled in comparison with what transpired in another dispute involving Alexander. The facts after all these years are hazy, but the dispute arose out of the fact that Alexandra was not in the final of a school tournament. On the morning of the final, Broomes obtained an injunction against playing the game. It has never been played since.

What irked me was the fact that a judge would grant a stay on a Saturday morning as if the matter was so urgent that the plaintiff did not have time to serve the defendants prior to the hearing. This same plaintiff though, could within half an hour of the order being obtained find the principals of the BCA, namely Alleyne and Nicholls, to serve notice of the order. Of course they had absolutely no idea during the week that the game was being played the Saturday. The headmaster of the school, Mr. Broomes, the third vice president of the association, had no idea how to find the president Alleyne or the secretary Nicholls before he went to court. It was a point that I made vociferously when I called the judge in question at home after he had issued the order. Though it was sometime before he later died, it was the last time that I spoke to him and I ended my conversation by saying that I should go now lest I said anything that I might be cited for contempt for in spite of my sarcastic reference to 'Uncle' on the phone.

Not only in cricket, but in other matters outside of sport, the use of *ex parte* applications, now known as 'Without Notice' applications, was done as a tactic to cause maximum disruption to the other side. In this case the school boys who had earned their way into a final were denied by the selfish nature of adults from enjoying their moment in time. Practice of law by ambush; sounds familiar. Birds of a feather really do flock together.

There was one other matter that ended up in court and that was as a result of the events surrounding the election at the Special Meeting of Members in August 2004. The special meetings were in effect the meetings to elect members to the Board and at that meeting four members were due for election. The chairman of the Elections Committee of the Association at the time and hence the person who chaired that meeting was Hensley Robinson. Hensley has served Barbados cricket in a variety of capacities as a domestic player and then as a long running secretary of the Barbados Cricket Umpires Association, as a standing umpire, as a match referee for domestic games, and as one of the behind-the-scene persons who ensure that Regional First Class Games and Test Matches come off without hitch. But perhaps more importantly he was a former Supervisor of Elections in Barbados.

The events of that August meeting in 2004 were to lead to more litigation launched by Vernon Smith and others on behalf of Vernon Williams and Calvin Hope, who alleged that there were irregularities with respect to the election of two members, namely Conde Riley and

Clinton St. Hill. The point of contention was whether their election could stand, as they were not financial at the time of nomination for election to the board and the subsequent election.

It was later to be confirmed that both Riley and St. Hill were indeed not financial. A dispute arose as to when this information was known and what effect it had on the elections. As it turned out, when St. Hill was informed that he was not financial he withdrew his name from the election, as he felt it was the honorable thing to do even though it was an honest mistake why his subs were not paid.

The differing treatment of the two men has always been to my mind one of the mysteries of the BCA. Both he and Riley were in the exact same boat, but it was clear that while St. Hill was the target of those seeking to have his election declared null and void, the default of Riley only came to light when the records of payment of subs with respect to all candidates were later checked. Having decided to withdraw and not make an issue of the matter, St. Hill disappeared from around the BCA, whereas Riley has gone from strength to strength. Again it was my view that the subsequent litigation launched by Smith and others on behalf of Williams and Hope was but an attempt to embarrass the Alleyne administration. An examination of the BCA's annual report for 2005 will reveal that both Hope and Williams were board members for the year 2004-2005 along with Riley, so with the withdrawal from the election of St. Hill, there was really no need for any litigation.

What was clear was that no one in the executive of the BCA at the time knew prior to arriving at the venue for the meeting that day that questions had arisen over the financial status of two candidates, although it is now clear that persons in the office and one of the subsequent litigants did know of the status before of the arrears of subpayments. Again an ambush. It was therefore not unreasonable that the board, on being presented with these facts, indicated that it would take advice on the effect of same before coming to a conclusion as to the status of the candidates to contest the election. Again the board was never given the chance to complete its investigations before unnecessary and costly litigation was launched, which ultimately the BCA had to pay for because it was clear that there had been a foul up in its offices with respect to the record keeping of the financial status of persons running for office.

Like the litigation over the election of a president after the death of Sir Conrad, this was unnecessary, just as was the fact that having been awarded costs in the settlement, Smith tried to take out proceedings behind the back of the BCA to garnish one of its deposit accounts at Cave Shepherd to have his costs paid. Smith had never demanded payment of the costs awarded so the BCA had the opportunity to settle same. I learnt of his scheme and appeared in court before the magistrate Christopher Birch with his cheque for his costs, which he still refused to accept on the ground that I had no right to be there. He eventually retrieved it from where I had thrown it to the floor at his feet after he refused to accept it from me, claiming I was not entitled to be in the hearing. This the goodly magistrate did not agree with, and told him that as payment had been tendered, he would not be granting the sequestration order he sought against the assets of the BCA.

As we left court I let Smith know what sort of individual I thought he was, and even though that was in 2005, my opinion of him has just got worse and worse. It was clear that the grand design was to have Marshall returned to the presidency of the association, which subsequently happened for a further two year period. It has amazed me over the years how certain experienced and sensible people in Barbados have felt the need at all costs to have Marshall elected to the helm of the BCA.

A few days before the 2005 BCA elections, the then Prime Minister Owen Arthur had summoned the opposing parties — the Alleyne Camp and the Marshall Camp — involved in the election to a meeting at Government Headquarters, as the PM was concerned that the turmoil with the elections might have an impact on Barbados' preparations for the holding of World Cup 2007. Arising out of that meeting, certain misinformation was leaked as to the reasons for it being held, and it was put about that the PM did not want Stephen to be heading both the BCA and World Cup Barbados. As someone who attended the meeting I can state that this is categorically not true.

Stephen lost a close election to Marshall and expectedly with him losing I was defeated for the position of secretary by Vernon Williams, and (surprise surprise) all the litigation stopped. The damage was done. At least Stephen lived long enough to see that the persons who championed Marshall's cause turned on him in 2007 and withdrew their support for him as president, at which point Joel Garner became president.

I have been off the board for a decade now, but still remain as a chair of a complaints panel which, according to the rules, has to be an attorney. Often I reflect with sadness how clubs often run into the boardroom to overturn a decision on the field of play on some technicality. The approach I take to these matters is to try where best to allow the decision on the field to stand, and if one party has been a victim of a serious infringement of the rules, then where possible, to have the game replayed. After all, it is a game, the outcome of which should wherever possible be settled on the field of play. I well recall how in one hearing that I was chairing an attorney objected, saying that the evidence infringed against the hearsay rules. I said to him "… listen, we are trying to find out what happened on the field. This is not a court of law and in particular not a criminal court, so I decline to follow the rules that we are constrained with at the other place." Regrettably, many of these hearings have now become adversarial over the last few years.

Stephen was however now free—not only of the BCA but of Life of Barbados, it having been taken over by the Mutual—to turn his full attention to the hosting of Cricket World Cup 2007. He was chairman of the Local Organizing Committee (LOC) and I was honored when he asked me to chair the Legal Advisory Committee that was part of the team that worked to put together the ultimately successful bid to host the Final of the ICC CWC 2007.

My work on that committee and after the award of the right to host games including the Final on the committee that oversaw the implementation of all legal deliverables required of the host venue is an experience that I will never forget. The host agreement that each LOC had to sign prior to hosting the games contained requirements of passing of certain Sunset Legislation and indeed various assurances that could only come from government, and as such the government of the day had to be a party to it.

The agreement between the CWC headquartered in Jamaica and the ICC for the hosting of the games was one of the most closely guarded secrets, and its contents, in the words of the then Attorney General Mia Mottley Q.C., represented a level of intrusion into the sovereignty of the island that she had not come across in all her public life in Barbados.

Two areas of the agreement impacted on what some would regard as the non-Caribbean atmosphere in the grounds. Musical instruments of any kind were banned, and all efforts at having this relaxed fell on deaf airs. It goes without saying that when West Indians saw later world cups embracing such instruments, there was a rightful feel of indignation, but I can assure that it was not for want of trying.

This tournament opened my eyes to the power of commercial sponsorship, as the sponsors were insistent that their products were the only ones in the ground. Hence from early, in Barbados it was pointed out that the local mix of Rum and Coke could not be advertised, as Pepsi was the sponsor. All efforts at persuasion that this nomenclature was not a discrimination against Pepsi failed to satisfy the rights holders and thus drinks were advertised as Rum and Mix.

One area of practicality, however, had to be accepted and that was the exclusion zone around the ground perimeter in which no advertisement of a non-sponsor of the event could be in place. It was pointed out that this two mile exclusion zone affected not only private residences, but went some way out to sea and on to some hotel chains, as the site of Kensington Oval was a Lara six-hit away from the ocean. The reluctant agreement to limit the prohibition to the ground and the precincts of the ground was eventually hammered out.

During this time I became the face of the presentation of what Ambush Marketing was. To be honest, I learnt a lot from studying what went on in other world games with respect to this practice whereby a company who had not paid the substantial rights to be a sponsor would seek to gain mileage from the event. It is recognized the world over and even expected that if there is a title sponsor, then its competitors will ambush on the principal that these games might be yours, but when it is mine you will seek to return the favour. This has led to some very creative ads as to what is and what is not ambushing, and it is really developed into an art.

It was drilled into us that this was an area that was of prime concern, and if there were significant breaches, could well see the claw back provisions in the agreement whereby payments were cut or withheld for breaches coming into force.

I myself was by this time becoming exasperated at what I considered trivial requests for offending brand names within the exclusion zone to be covered up. One case in point led to a hysterical outcome, in that in the warm up games at the UWI Campus, it was pointed out that the air conditioners in the playing pavilion were manufactured by a rival company to one of the Indian sponsors, and the sponsor was demanding that tape be placed over the name of the maker, as taking them out was impractical. I could not believe what I was hearing, and argued that when I or any reasonable person went into a room we did not look to see who the maker of the air conditioner was, and that by putting tape over same we would be drawing attention to what you wanted to hide, as a curious person would want to know what was covered up.

I lost my argument, so the evening before the first game we had all the units taped over where the name of the maker was. The next morning when the cleaners were checking that all was well, one determined that this clearly was not adding to the aesthetic appeal and removed all the strips. The LOC was cited, but we could do nothing but laugh. It was, if nothing else, an enjoyable but exhausting experience.

The World Cup Final was played in April 2007, and one of my eternal regrets is that Stephen, after all his hard work, died within six months before he was able to realise or rather see the full benefits of his hard work with the transformation of Kensington from the ramshackle ground (as an Indian journalist described it around 1997 to much anger amongst Barbadians) to the fine stadium it is today. Hopefully one day due recognition will be given for the role he played in making this possible.

With the end of the World Cup and my day-to-day involvement with the BCA at an end, my direct involvement with cricket administration was soon to come to an end when I gave up the office as president of Pickwick in 2009. Quite frankly I was exhausted after over two decades of constant meetings etc. I took a break from it all, but when Joel Garner took over as president of the BCA I found myself asked to get involved in the Complaints Committee which I have spoken of before.

It was however late last year that I found myself responding to a situation that in my wildest dreams I would never have believed. Pickwick Cricket Club received a letter from an insurance company written by their in-house legal counsel demanding a response within a certain time, otherwise legal action would be instituted. The ire of the insurance company was raised because they had to replace the windscreen in one of their insured's cars that was parked at the ground, as a result of it being broken by a ball so negligently hit by a Pickwick batsman.

I telephoned the writer of the letter, identified myself as an attorney, and said to her "...forgive me but I am getting on and don't know all recent graduates. Are you an attorney?" She identified herself as one and stated she had been practicing for at least six years. I then asked whether she wished me to really respond to her letter and she insisted I did, as I thought it was a practical joke. My response is attached. I have removed the name of the attorney so as to avoid further embarrassment. Not surprisingly, I have never heard from her up until today, but at least I can say the law was not a jackass that day, but was attempted to be made a jackass.

September 15th 2014
Co-Operators General Insurance Company

Dear Sirs:

Your letter of September 5th 2014 to Pickwick Cricket Club has been passed to the undersigned for reply. My response is made more in my capacity as a Member of the Club since 1977 including being a Past President from 2000-2009 than as a practicing attorney-at-law. In addition, during my service of 18 years on the Board of the Barbados Cricket Association (BCA), the last six of which were as Honorary Secretary, during that time I had occasion to deal with many instances where claims were made either of the BCA or advice was sought from the BCA by clubs as to their liability where damage had been caused by a cricket ball.

You will no doubt recall our telephone conversation of the 11th instant and let me apologize at the outset if any offence was taken by the incredulity in my voice when I asked whether you wished a reply to your letter. No offence was meant, but as in all the years that I have been involved in legal aspects of organized Sport in Barbados going back to the start of my practice in 1987, I have yet to see a claim made where a batsman is accused of being negligent because he maximized his skill by hitting a six. It is therefore somewhat ironic that the word 'maximum' is now in accepted parlance by persons interested in the game to describe the thrill of seeing a batsman launch a ball out of the playing area which after all carries the greatest runs scored by a single stroke in the game.

As I am unsure whether you are au fait with the game of cricket, I will simply state that the object of the batsman is to score runs and the object of the bowler is to prevent this, preferably by dismissing him, at which point he retires from participating in the game or by restricting his ability to score 'maximums'. Over the last ten years a phenomenon has developed around the world known as T-20 cricket which is a game of cricket with the basic objectives stated above, but which ends within three hours as opposed to the traditional seven hour game for which the World Cup is being contested in Australia early next year or the even more stately four day or five day games that traditionalists like me prefer, called Test Matches. As such, though the concept is the same, namely a team tries to score more runs than that of their opponents, in the T-20 game a premium is placed on scoring these runs quickly. The top T-20 players are handsomely rewarded making more in a six-week span than you or I do in years of slog with our practice.

It follows that the ability to hit maximums earns these players contracts into this big league. In this case the player who hits the six is an up and coming player aspiring to get into the big leagues, and therefore it was ironic to the extreme that you seek to ascribe what he did as an act of negligence, in my opinion. As many cricket officialdoms with whom I have shared the allegation in your letter that the batsman was negligent have asked, why did you not seek to hold the bowler liable for negligently bowling the ball that allowed the batsman the chance to hit the ball out of the ground, as this was his duty, as it was the duty of the Pickwick batsman to launch his deliveries out of the ground.

Please find attached pages 554-564 of the Fourth Edition of a Book named Sports Law by five authors, the last of whom is a lady by the name of Urvasi Naidoo, whom I believe is one of the attorneys on the staff of the International Cricket Council, the governing body for cricket worldwide. The West Indies Cricket Board (WICB) is affiliated to this body and in turn the (BCA) is affiliated to the WICB.

The BCA, which was established by an Act of Parliament in Barbados in 1933 is the authority under whose auspices the game in question was played and both Wanderers and Pickwick are members of the Association. For your information, the rules of the BCA charge the home club, in this case Wanderers, with the responsibility for all aspects of the game: preparation of pitch, crowd control, etc. and as such if any act of negligence occurred during the playing of the game which is denied it would be the responsibility of the home club to address, not the visitors.

You will note that the discussion within the pages sent to you surrounds damage caused by a ball that for all intents and purposes is equated with a projectile that escapes from its confines by some external force, which in this case was the willow of the cricket bat meeting the leather of the cricket ball and in this case the latter came of second best and was ejected from the ground.

The issue of liability for a ball exiting the playing area of a cricket ground has been decided by the courts in England since the 1950s, and I would draw to your attention to the well-known cases to students of Tort Law of Bolton and Stone and Miller and Jackson. There are some West Indian cases on point, but I do not have my notes at hand to accurately list them, but will refer you to Professor Kodilyne's compilation of Tort cases for this information which may be of assistance to you if these facts come before you again.

The basic tenet of these cases is that it is the ground authority, in this case Wanderers Cricket Club, which might be held liable for any resultant damage as a result of injury or damage caused as a result of the ejection of a projectile, to wit a cricket ball, from within the compounds of their property which is hosting the game. Any liability, however, is not as a result of the batsman hitting the ball, as after all this is what he is to do, not to be confused however with Gabby's *Hit It*, and in T-20, the more the merrier.

On this question I refer you to the dictum of Lord Denning MR in Miller and Jackson reported at page 561 of the pages sent, where he says "…..nor was the batsman negligent when he hit the ball for six." Lord Denning was considering a request for an injunction to prohibit the playing of cricket by a neighboring household because the balls kept landing in their yard. His discourse is worth reading. Suffice it to say that he was of the opinion that as especially in the case before him that the homeowner had built his house after the cricket ground was in use for over 70 years that the injunction should be denied, the Public Interest of Playing cricket overriding the Private Rights of enjoyment of their property.

A review of the cases that I have cited would illustrate however that the negligence, if there is any, is as a result of the failure of the ground authority to adequately prohibit the ball from leaving the ground. In those cases questions of nuisance were also discussed, but on the question of negligence, not only was the question of the measures taken to prevent the escape of the ball looked at in determining the question of liability, but equally as important was whether the ground authority would be aware of the likelihood of an escaping ball causing injury or damage, our old friend the test of reasonable foreseeability.

In the instant case it was clearly foreseeable by the ground authority that balls escaping from the Wanderers playing area would cause damage. Anyone with a passing knowledge of the Wanderers ground would know this. However, in this case it was not a question of the ball being struck over the perimeter wall which again is not special at Wanderers and by chance striking a passing vehicle which is itself not unusual. In this case the damage occurred to a vehicle that was parked within the compounds of the ground.

In such a case the ground authority would be well within their rights to plead *volenti non fit injuria* as the actions of your insured who parked his car within the compound must be looked at. He is currently the coach of the team and has been a former player with the Wanderers Club. His association with the club is over 30 years during which time he must have spent in day terms conservatively two years at the ground, perhaps more, and would be well aware of the potential for damage to vehicles at the ground, as it is not an infrequent occurrence.

The undersigned has been a visitor to the club since 1975 and is well aware that when you leave your vehicle there you assume some risk. Coincidentally, I was there at the time of the incident and had parked my car in a place where I reckoned there was the least likelihood of it being hit, but knew the risk. Mr. Clarke, your insured, surely knew this.

In other words the doctrines of *volenti non fit injuria* must apply, making a claim against the Ground Authority highly unlikely. Worth of consideration is the fact that Mr. Clarke, when parking his car, was aware of the risk and he tried to minimize it by parking with the back of the car, a smaller target area, to the field. Nothing more need be said.

In my time with the BCA, we encouraged clubs to accept the responsibility for paying, which is different from accepting the legal liability, for any damage occasioned by escaping cricket balls where the damage was caused to vehicles of persons who had to be at the ground such as players, match officials, etc. We also encouraged clubs where the property of neighbors was damaged to replace broken windows, or if a car was damaged while passing on the road nearby by such a hit, to repair the damage.

However, where the damage occurred to a vehicle parked, especially one parked in "cow corner" by someone who was a spectator at the ground, their claim was denied. In this case, as Mr. Clarke had to be at the ground, he should have requested his club as the ground authority to repair the damage. I do not know the reason this was not done, and why he made a claim on his personal insurance, but that is a matter for your insured.

In summary, I totally reject your claim of Pickwick, as it has no basis either in law or common sense, and would be deemed in a court to be frivolous and vexatious. I have replied on my personal letterhead rather than my professional one as a matter of courtesy so as not to burden my club with legal charges. Should you insist, however, on making a futile legal claim, please note that it will be resisted with all the force at my disposal. I have determined that to date my time thus far including researching the law to send to you equates to about $2,500 which while I am not seeking to recover at this time I will if you file action. I trust that this matter is now at rest, but will offer to you my services if you need them in the future on matters of this sort. Unfortunately, this would have to be on a professional basis.

Yours,
Cc Pickwick Cricket Club; Wanderers Cricket Club
Barbados Cricket Association;
Barbados Cricket Umpires Association.

Cricket and the Law... what can I say?

Banks and Other Financial Institutions

WHEN I JOINED Cottle in 1987 its major client was Barclays Bank, which over the years has metamorphosed into what it is today, namely CIBC First Caribbean. As a junior attorney my main dealings with the bank were with respect to simple chattel mortgages, which were documents turned out in the hundreds that allowed the average Barbadian house owner to secure a loan or a form of credit over the chattel house that they owned.

The chattel mortgage was a creature of necessity invented to deal with the particular social needs of the Barbadian community whereby the prevalence of chattel house structures for residences did not technically meet the general rules of securities for a mortgage loan on residential property, in that the owner in many cases did not own the land on which the house was erected.

In my youthful naiveté I believed that my fees for such transactions were being paid by the bank, as it was to them that the firm's invoice for its work was submitted and from them that payment was received. It was not until I received a call from Adriel Brathwaite, the current attorney general, who is fond of telling persons that I was his cricket captain at school, requesting that I inform the bank that I was prepared to waive my fee, a concession that attorneys make to one another, because although the loan was over his mother's house, in reality it was he who was getting the loan.

I readily consented to his request, as this convention among attorneys was one that I tried at all times to uphold where I was involved in a matter. Years later I was to benefit myself from such concessions as many in the profession have, although, as in all aspects of life, one will meet some colleagues who are not so minded.

After the call from Adriel I approached Anne Gayle for confirmation on exactly who was paying our fees, and it was she who explained to me that though the fees came in from the bank, the bank collected same from the borrower, and so in effect it was the borrower who was paying us and not the bank.

As I mulled over this fact I recall coming to the conclusion that this was massively unfair of the banks, and even though in the particular case of chattel mortgages there was little need for the borrower to have a separate attorney to represent their interests, as it was just a formality, in cases where the more conventional mortgage was being granted this was not the case. In these transactions the reality was that the borrower was paying two legal fees: his own lawyer and the bank's lawyer. On a loan of about $100,000 an amount of up to $5,000 not to mention government stamp duty on the documents being recorded would be the responsibility of the borrower, and often would have to be funded out of their own pocket.

Nowadays I listen and chuckle when I hear ads from several banks and other lending agencies enticing would-be home owners to come over to them and that they would be responsible for your legal costs up to a certain limit. Time and circumstances have changed attitudes as the economy has constricted over these last few years, making banks look at these expenses that potential borrowers have to pay.

I was of the view then and still hold the view now that his attitude of the banks in penalizing borrowers who had already paid negotiation fees to the banks and possibly other fees if the loan was not disbursed in a certain time, was nothing short of mercenary in this action. I held this view because with the level of interest chargeable over the course of the loan, banks recovered as much as twice the amount that was originally lent, so insistence on the borrower paying their legal expenses was in my view quite unconscionable.

Over the years another practice has developed with respect to banks enticing customers. Some loan officers have been suggesting to the unsuspecting customer that if they were to use the bank's attorney the matter would be quicker and cheaper. Quicker it may be in some circumstances, but cheaper hardly ever, as the attorney is still entitled to charge a separate fee. While the transaction may in some instances lead to a speedier conclusion, the downside of this is if the supposedly routine transaction goes sour, then the attorney often has to withdraw from representing one of the clients. There are no prizes for guessing which one is jettisoned. As the bank is inevitably the bigger client and the one that likely guarantees repeat business, this is not a surprise. Clearly the loan officers in the banks cannot alone be the ones to blame with respect to this practice, and I remember when I was involved in the Bar council over twenty years ago that these practices of some attorneys who basically were trying to ensure that they had an increased market share of the work was causing concern. Who knows? One day the Fair Trading Commission may get involved.

The possible conflict of interest that may arise in these circumstances where both the lender and buyer is represented by the same attorney is a salutary reminder to attorneys who would be minded to represent more than one person in a transaction that it is not wise, however non-contentious it may appear to be at the beginning. I have lost count of the number of times this practice of representing in this case buyer and the seller has come back to haunt me as I try to clear up the mess of Cottle.

In this case the well-intentioned practice of working both for plantation owner and qualified tenant in the purchase of tenantry land (often because as the fee was legislated at $10, few others would work for the tenant who was purchasing) has thrown up years later some problems because of mistakes made which would have been picked up had there been a second set of eyes. Some of these problems have landed on my doorstep with the melt down of Cottle, and it has become not only a cost that I have had to bear alone in time spent rectifying a problem that the client cannot be charged for, but a source of much irritation as I personally had nothing to do with the majority of the problems that have surfaced.

As I became more and more involved in corporate work with Mr. Armstrong, my sense of outrage with the banks grew as I saw on more than one occasion that where persons were obtaining large loans, and I am talking about loans in the millions of dollars, such persons refused in many cases to pay not only the bank's legal fees, but the ubiquitous negotiation fee that the Banks charged on the applications for loans. These persons argued on the basis, as I indicated before, that as the banks stood to recoup twice as much by the time the loan was repaid, they should underwrite these costs themselves. Naturally, as the bank wanted to book the loan, they agreed. So from early I was of the view that banks were a necessary evil, and a law unto themselves.

This view I have not changed. At present the only thing the banks don't charge you for is breathing the air on their premises. It is ridiculous. You are charged for depositing money, taking it out, requesting information on same, and then with the freeing up of the market by the Central Bank they don't pay you anything for your money that they have borrowed for you. Regrettably the Central Bank appears to turn a blind eye to some of these practices that affect the average banking customer every day.

As I mentioned earlier, Barclays were the major client of Cottle during my early years, but they were also the firm's bankers. They had played a major role in ensuring the firm's survival as a result of the Simmons affair. That was around 1980, and for years after I joined the firm the name 'Simmons' was a bad word. He, to be fair, caused havoc to the finances of the firm, and in the words of Mr. Armstrong, had delayed his eventual retirement from the firm by at least five years.

While I never worked as an attorney with Michael Simmons, my recollection of him from my time as a clerk was that he was always immaculately dressed and always busy and in a rush. His shenanigans with the use of clients' funds earmarked for the purchase of land on which the Central Bank now stands virtually drove the firm out of business when it was revealed by the then prime minister Tom Adams during a budget debate that the money was missing because, as he put in, the brother for the honourable member for St. James South at the time had 'thieved' the money from a leading law firm in Bridgetown.

It did not require Einstein to identify the culprit and the firm, and legend has it that both Mr. Armstrong and Mr. Hutchinson went home in shock at the impending fallout. This could not have been for long, as there was a run on Cottle Catford by clients anxious to secure their money, and this was only withstood because of the backing of Barclays Bank. The result was that Simmons was jettisoned from the partnership. He went into private practice before having to leave the island at very short notice to avoid arrest, because of—you guessed it—missing clients' funds. To this day he is still abroad some 30 years later, so there is a long road ahead for Allan Watson, who has now similarly disappeared.

Many theories have been put forward as to why Barclays stepped in to assist Cottle. Those who perceived an agenda based on race posited that it was done to spare the blushes of two prominent white professionals by their brethren, backing them up, although to my mind whether or not that was a consideration, Barclays were more concerned with protecting their interest, which would have taken a hammering if the firm went under. After my experiences over the years with respect to a similar situation and seeing how I was treated when I approached First Caribbean for help, I am not so sure whether my assessment that race did not play a part is entirely correct.

The fallout from the Simmons debacle was seen by the fact that nearly twelve years after it had occurred, by which time I had become a partner in the firm, there was a line item on the agenda for partners' meetings called 'H.M. Simmons Affairs', and though he had by then retired from the partnership, Mr. Armstrong usually attended to give an update on the efforts to recover the funds due the partnership and offer a way forward. I certainly suffered indirectly from his defalcations when the partners were assessed to additional income, as all the losses occasioned by the need to settle debts he had incurred were not allowed to be claimed by the revenue authorities.

I was to fully understand later his catastrophic actions and what it did to the then partners, as I was embroiled in my troubles with my former partners. Every conceivable effort was made to collect from him the debt due to reduce the deficit that the then partners were faced with. The following was but an illustration of what efforts were made. I was closing a sale, and as I was working for the purchaser, I requisitioned a cheque from our accounts department to pay the purchase price to Simmons, who was working for the vendor. When the cheque was not forthcoming, I enquired why and I was referred to Mr. Armstrong. I entered his office explaining why I wanted the cheque, and he simply said to me that the firm did not on any account pay money to Michael Simmons, and I would do well to understand that.

I was naturally bewildered as to what to do, as my client wanted to buy the property from Simmons' client. To my relief, Mr. Armstrong said he would sort it out, picked up the phone and called Simmonds' office. He announced himself to his secretary as "Armstrong from Cottle Catford calling for Mr. Simmons", and when he came on the phone he simply said to him: "Michael, young Nicholls here has some money for you. Before I release it [it was for $30,000+] I want some cash from you towards your debt. No cheque, cash. $25,000 sounds nice." End of story. Years later I tried the same tactic with one of my former partners to reduce their indebtedness, but without much success, I must admit, thanks in part to the antics of one Vernon Smith.

The support that Barclays gave to Cottle at the time of the Simmons affair was in stark contrast to the lack of support that I received when managing the fallout from the breakup of the Watson partnership in 2002. I had several meetings with them in the company of my father trying not only to negotiate loans to assist with the severe deficit in the Client's Account of Cottle that had been left to me to manage, but more importantly continued support by utilizing the firm as one of their attorneys. It would have been impossible to sustain the level of borrowings that I needed without a constant stream of income, something which, as one later judge was to remark, was self-evident. It was not forthcoming, and I have always come to the conclusion that my ability to contain the problems I was facing was exacerbated when the bank yanked away the $50,000 overdraft I was surviving on to run the firm with twenty four hours' notice. It was being repaid then; it is ten years on and it is tied up in a legal dispute re repayment, so from their end they must have been right.

It reached a stage where despite my father arranging with the then head of the Bank Mansoor to provide me with emergency finance, this was frustrated by persons at a lower level with the usual bureaucratic requirements to disburse the loan, so much so that when I witnessed junior officers aggressively questioning my father as to the reasons for the loan, I told him to forget it. I was not expecting a gift, but just the type of assistance that a court of appeal judge was to later comment that if it had been forthcoming the problems may have been solved.

It gave me great pleasure later, if only symbolically, when after years of participating as a judge in their Unsung Hero Competition, Daddy advised First Caribbean when they requested his continued participation that in light of their continued refusal to assist his son in his predicament, he could no longer lend his name to their promotion.

The change in the relationship between Cottle and Barclays had been some time in coming. In the late 90s Barclays decided that it was pulling out of Barbados, and eventually signed an agreement with CIBC that the businesses would be 'merged'. I have always stated that it was a buyout, and as over the years the Barclays staff and the manner of doing things were eventually replaced, this became apparent.

As rumours spread about this change, I remember contacting Allan Watson, then the senior partner of Cottle Catford, while on holiday in Jamaica, to ask him how long he was going to sit on his backside and allow major changes to our biggest client to occur without his knowledge and with apparent indifference about what to do. I demanded of him that as senior partner he needed to show some leadership and find out what was going on. I stated to him that though I was out of the island I had been able to contact business persons I knew from my membership of the Canada-Barbados Business Association (CBBA) in Barbados to get inkling about what was going on that was supposed to be top secret.

It was a call from one of my CBBA colleagues that alerted me to the fact that there was going to be a major announcement about a merger between Barclays and CIBC, or as I always maintained, a takeover by CIBC of Barclays. Despite my urgings to Watson to investigate, he took the position that it was a *fait accompli*, and he could not do anything about it. From then Cottle was frozen out with respect to being one of the new attorneys-at law.

In retrospect, I did not read the tea leaves regarding Watson as I should have, as he rarely ventured into social or sporting gatherings where legend has it many commercial transactions were discussed. From my dealings with Corporate Barbados I was aware that the golf course, horse racing or test matches at Kensington sometimes were the scenes for much business activity or to solidify deals started in actual offices. Watson and Griffith didn't move in these circles, and I found that after the Armstrong and Hutchinson era, the firm began to contract because it was very slow to expand its area of practice. There was only so much I could do.

The deal with respect to the buyout of Barclays was so secretive that the agreement with respect to the transfer of business was seen by few. I certainly never saw it, and I always felt that whatever your plans for going forward with respect to a new vision for your organization, if you felt that your present attorneys did not fit the bill, fair enough. Unlike the nonsense some idiot from Canada named Mark Strang said to me, I did not feel that Cottle had a god-given right to be Barclays' or anybody's attorneys (see Appendix Eleven).

To treat your attorneys for over 100 years in the contemptuous manner in which Cottle was treated after the so-called merger was not right. Cottle had some legitimate concerns going forward with respect to work that straddled the merger. Strang's continued refusal to allow sight of the agreement to some of the attorneys expected to continue working for the bank was a legitimate source of concern for us at the time, and was the height of arrogance which typified Strang. This he didn't seem to have the capacity to understand. In the course of such work preparing documents asserting that all statutory requirements of the new entity were in place was impossible to do without sight of the agreement which continued to be so top secret that the firm had to be provided with a letter of opinion from an attorney who had sight of it to allay our legitimate concerns about the new entity.

With the end of the Watson partnership I was faced as I continued on my own with a situation whereby one of the major planks of the firm's income was drying up. As less and less work came from the bank, I became more annoyed with First Caribbean, as its officers continued to call seeking information on matters of the past which took time for employees to answer because of the need to search records, which time was not being paid for either directly or indirectly because we were no longer retained by the bank as we had been for over 25 years, nor were we receiving any significant work from them.

After I took over the sole responsibility for running Cottle, I had switched the firm's main bankers to Royal Bank, as I wanted to put a distance between the accounts of the Watson partnership at Cottle and my then practice at Cottle. This lasted for about four years. I never really had a long relationship with Royal Bank, and as my practice constricted more and more and my cash flow situation deteriorated, it was only a matter of time before the relationship would end as the basic fact was the shortfall of money that I had to run a business made me a credit risk. As I had no long term relationship with the bank, I did not expect that I would receive finance from them to restructure my practice.

In 2006 the long due fees for the Kingsland litigation were finally paid to the firm. I was forced to go back to using First Caribbean as my major bankers, as the payment of the fees were all transacted at that bank. As such, my sojourn with RBC came to an end. First Caribbean for a time supported me in meeting day-to-day commitments by the granting of a $50,000 overdraft facility, but after that was cancelled with less than twenty-four hours' notice sometime in 2008/2009, it was clear to me that my time with them was up.

Barclays Bank/First Caribbean, Royal Bank were my bankers for my professional career with Cottle, while at the same time the Bank of Nova Scotia was my personal banker. Like most individuals, I had been introduced to them by my father, and regrettably now both of us have now reviewed our relationship with them, fed up with how we have been treated.

When I launched out on my own with Cottle in 2003, I needed immediate financing to deal with the immediate claims being made on the firm. This was provided by Bank of Nova Scotia on the security of one of my parents' properties. This was later to be further extended by the refinancing of the mortgage over my matrimonial home, which loan was initially with Barclays. So by this time in 2008 they were my principal lenders. At that time in 2003 I also incorporated a company by the name of Libra Management Inc. which would have been responsible for payment of expenses such as rent, telephone, etc. on behalf of the firm.

In retrospect, an early incident involving Scotiabank should have alerted me to their practices which were later to lead to the break-up. A client was refunding me some money that I had paid personally on their behalf—I believe it was about $100, a minor amount—by endorsing a cheque payable to them. The client had simply endorsed the cheque by just signing it and giving it to me. The endorsement, as it was simply by signature, turned the cheque into a bearer instrument like cash, meaning the risk was mine in that if it was lost, any finder could have cashed it.

Having recently at law school read banking law, and as at the time of the incident in 1988 I was teaching a commercial law course to students doing the CMA, I was intimately aware of the provisions of the Banking Act that such a cheque was payable to bearer. I attended at my bank BNS, not to cash the cheque, but simply to deposit the cheque to my account. This simple request was refused on the grounds that the endorsement on the cheque did not say pay to me. I was stunned at the apparent ignorance of the teller.

At that time in 1988 money laundering considerations were not yet bedeviling the financial system and even if they were, as the transaction was only for $100, such a consideration would have been ridiculous. I could not fathom the reason for refusal, especially in light of the fact that I was depositing the cheque, not attempting to cash it.

I indicated to the teller that the endorsement would be considered as a simple endorsement, requiring that the bank pay the bearer of the cheque, and there could be no reason not to accept it. As modern jargon says, my arguments were 'above her pay grade' and she summoned her supervisor, who informed me in what was to my mind a very contemptuous manner that this was bank policy and that was that. I was indignant.

With my ire up I returned to my office, got a copy of the Laws of

Barbados with the Banking Act in it, returned to the bank, slammed it on the counter and stated that their policy could not override the laws of the land which clearly stated a cheque endorsed as the one I had was meant pay to bearer. My point was substantiated by Asquith Phillips Q.C., who was in the bank at the time and the cheque was subsequently deposited on the instruction of the manager. The supervisor in question never spoke to me again in over ten years, as one of her colleagues indicated to me that she felt I embarrassed her by returning with a law book for her. That was not my intention, but bureaucratic nonsense I cannot stand.

On a somewhat similar note with respect to non-compliance with the provisions of the Banking Act, the banks routinely reject cheques and return them with a stamp that the words and figures don't match. The Act is clear that in such circumstances, you pay the words. I recall an incident whereby the same BNS, after selling me foreign currency to travel overseas on a Sunday morning, called later that evening to state the figures and words on my cheque did not match and could I come Monday and change it. I explained that I was travelling Sunday, and could not oblige. They had two options: return it as was the norm, or deposit it crediting the amount as stated in the words. As the cheque was payable to BNS for money that I had used to buy my foreign currency, it was no surprise as to what was done.

I am afraid that most of the banks in the island are like this, from complaints I have heard from clients, and even though my experiences are mainly with the two banks mentioned, I have no reason to believe that these banks were unique. It is my belief that because of the financial predicament I have been put in by my former partners' defalcations, I have been deemed *persona non grata* by most of the banks when it comes to extending even the simplest of excuses, and I have lost count of the number of times that items were returned when cash was in the account, but according to them, not cleared.

My credit worthiness has not been helped by the actions of Bank of

Nova Scotia, actions not befitting any reputable person far less a bank of that standing and indeed wide international repute. As my financial situation deteriorated as did the relationship with Beverley, the former matrimonial home was abandoned and returned to the bank, who got an order from the court. The bank advertised same for sale, but did not get any serious offers.

Sometime in 2014 the bank contacted both myself and Beverley with an offer to the effect that they were prepared to discharge all indebtedness secured by the mortgage over the property if we agreed to them selling it at whatever price they could achieve. With this agreement in place, the bank was freed of the legal requirement to try and ensure that they got a price as near as possible to the market value, so as not to prejudice the mortgagors.

After querying the amount that the bank stated was due under the mortgage which according to them was in excess of a million dollars, I determined that it made no difference if I agreed with the amount, as I would be getting a full release. The bank was insistent that I got legal advice as to their offer, which I told them I was quite capable of determining without legal advice. BNS required that I submit a letter that I had waived advice. All this was done and on September 1st 2014 I signed my agreement.

At the time BNS intimated that they required both the mortgagors to sign, so told them that Beverley and I were divorced, so they would have to deal with her. I had previously advised her I saw no reason not to sign. The house was empty and deteriorating, and I left it at that.

In February of 2015 it came to my attention that the property had been sold in December 2014 for significantly lower than the market value. I contacted the bank and indicated that I had not received from them the discharge of indebtedness as agreed. Their response was that it could not be given because Beverley had not signed. I was incredulous. I had lost patience with some of the nonsense Beverley had been doing of up to then, but that apart, I said to the bank: "…if you required both of us to sign to allow you to sell and you subsequently sold without both signatures, then the lack of one is irrelevant."

Thus I am faced with filing another lawsuit to protect my rights, as the outstanding amount as stated by the bank still turns up on all credit checks made of me. The action by the bank, however, is symptomatic of the complaint by many mortgagors as to the actions by banks when repossessing houses. In my instant case the bank, as I told them, had recouped more than the amount originally lent. What they were losing was interest, and I am sure they had written it off to taxes.

It is my belief that their refusal was related to another issue, and this surrounds part of my parents' property which had been used as security originally when I obtained my first loan to deal with the Cottle debacle, and which like many things has gone sour because of my inability to recover the amounts due from my former partners, and because of the incident I relate below.

I never once during my troubles with my partners hid from the banks that I was having severe financial difficulties in dealing with day to day operations. The need to settle debts due to clients and other organizations from personal funds was becoming more and more challenging as time went on, as this ability began to be severely hampered by reducing income from my practice.

The banks have many ways of indicating to you that they would prefer that the relationship with you as a customer ended, and BNS certainly set about theirs in a way that I am certain would justify my taking court action. I didn't, because I was simply tired of all the litigation I was involved in, and just decided to move on. The bank cancelled a corporate account I had which was ostensibly used to pay for rent and other such business expenses mentioned previously, which was opened since 2003. The closure was made without advising me.

What was more disconcerting was the way in which I found out. Having received a request for the renewal of my car insurance through the post, I had replied by enclosing a cheque for payment. I visited the bank the next day to place the funds on the account, which by this time was seeing on average maybe a transaction every two months, down from the twenty or so per month. I was stunned to be advised by the teller that no such account was in existence, to which I replied "you must be joking." I next swiped the account card that customers were given to access the account and the teller confirmed the account had been closed.

I immediately called the bank manager and let him have it, when he explained that as the account had been carrying an overdraft balance for some months they had decided to close it, as they had been unable from notes on the account to contact me. I said to him "you must be joking" as I advised him that in addition to myself the two other signatories on the account were my father who had a relationship with the bank for almost forty years, and my accountant who had a personal mortgage with the bank. I told him that was not a credible excuse, to which his response was that they had absorbed all the fees and written off the overdrawn account which was less than $100. I said to him: "I have written a cheque; you have now refused to take the money for the account, and if it is returned I will have an actionable claim." It was returned marked 'Account Closed', which is far worse than refer to drawer, as it would suggest a deliberate action to deceive. I still have time to institute a suit for defamation, but there comes a time when it is just better to tell the story for John Public to read than fight a legal battle in our courts that will last probably a decade.

It was clear to me that the bank did not want me as a customer anymore, so I have moved on. There really was nothing else to do, but someday I may have time to get my own back.

I am firmly of the belief that the banks carry on sharp practices, or if not sharp practices that are clearly designed to buttress their overall numbers. From around 2010 I found myself back in the clutches of RBC, they having acquired RBTT with whom I had an account. I can recall that on several occasions I would be called demanding that

I clear the deficit in the account by ten o'clock, as it had gone into debit, a cheque having been presented. Often these debits were as a result of monthly fees charged by them, which would not have been taken into account by me when writing the cheque, so there may be an argument that this was my fault. When I was called one day on my cell phone with respect to an overdrawn balance of $1.20, I had had enough. I will not repeat what I told the caller, but I subsequently purchased a draft for $1.20 at a cost of $10.10 from another bank, and sent it to them with instructions to close the account and a comment about their ludicrousness. The purpose of the cheque was to draw attention to it, as I am sure whoever processed it at both banks must have wondered why.

Another irksome stance of all the banks is requiring bankers' cheques from another bank to be deposited and go through the clearing system before being credited—a three-day wait. Bankers' cheques should be treated as cash, after all, these cheques are only issued once cash is paid and in this day and age where one can't simply walk around with more than $10,000 without triggering the interest of the money laundering authorities, it is nothing short of criminal that banks continue with this practice.

As if this is not bad enough, I recently presented a manager's cheque with relevant ID. I used to be a customer of the bank, and the teller referred to me by name and asked whether I still had an account there because if I did not it could not be cashed, as that was their policy for cheques over $6,000.

I thought back to some twenty-five years earlier when I heard this policy argument when trying to deposit a generally endorsed cheque and steam was beginning to come out of my ears when I stopped and thought: *she is only doing as instructed*. As such I informed her that I wished to see the manager to discuss this, and while he/she is coming could he/she bring the directive from the Central Bank and/or the laws of Barbados that state the reason why he/she couldn't cash the cheque. I was not interested in their policy manual, which must be subject to the laws of Barbados. She returned a couple of minutes later and simply asked "how do you want the cash?" No problem for me, but I am sure many others have been told that nonsense.

To the argument by the banks that it is for their protection, I say protection from what? Surely with only six banks on the island, the number of persons authorized to sign cheques on behalf of the bank cannot take more than 15 minutes to verify. How many times have you stood in a line in a bank while they count out the 25c or $1 coins from slot machines being deposited, but feel it is too cumbersome to check on the veracity of signatures from other banks? If, as some contend, this is because sophisticated forgery of instruments has escalated, then I don't know how an instrument issued here could be deemed valid quicker in the USA than here in Barbados.

I still remember with some incredulity what happened to me with Bank of Nova Scotia a few years back with respect to clearance of cheques denominated in US dollars. I had two such cheques in my name paid for fees for serving as a director. Both cheques were issued by First Caribbean Barbados bank from their US account here. I presented them to my bank BNS to cash, and was told in the first instance by the teller that it would take six weeks to clear, as it was a foreign cheque. My protest saw the waiting period first reduced to 21 days and then to 10 days I believe, both of which time spans I determined were unacceptable.

I indicated to the bank that these were manager's cheques drawn on a US dollar account held with a local bank. What possible reason could there be for holding them? In fact in my opinion they could have been cashed immediately. As I happened to be travelling to the US the next day, I decided to deposit one to the account and took the other with me and deposited it to a bank the next day via an ATM at Miami Airport, and it was cleared the next day. The upshot of this ludicrous situation which I drew not only to their attention but to that of the Central Bank, was that a cheque drawn on a local bank in Barbados was cleared in the US prior to a similar cheque that was deposited to a local account in Barbados. As I told the manager of the bank, if you were so minded you could have driven to the issuing bank and confirmed the authenticity of the cheque and returned in a time shorter than it took for me to fly to Miami. Why then the bureaucratic nonsense?

I have always contrasted this practice and indeed attitude to those of banks I have encountered overseas. An illustration would suffice. One day after arrival in Toronto I ventured out to buy some necessities. When I travel I usually take two wallets—one with Barbados cash for when I return to the island, and the other with foreign currency. By mistake I picked up the wrong wallet and at the checkout counter of a drug store found myself embarrassingly with only Bajan dollars. The lady serving me told me there was a bank next door who she was sure would change it, as I was sighing at the thought of the walk to and from the hotel in the cold.

I went into the bank, produced a few 'Grantleys', and was pleasantly surprised to see them pull out a book that appeared to have not replicas, but imprints of all currencies around the world, verified its features and cashed it, of course at a loss to me. I challenge any bank in Barbados to state if they would be willing to do so for someone turning up with Russian roubles or Indian lachs.

This is not a personal pet peeve, because at the time of writing I heard the pain of a small businesswoman expressed over the airwaves complaining about the 21 days it takes to clear a foreign draft. I have seen cases in today's electronic age where a cheque has been cleared by the paying bank, but the money has still not been credited by the bank that it was deposited to because of the three day rule. The banks are fond of returning cheques on the slightest whim, and I have had cheques wrongly returned in the past for issues such as the account having been in debit for charges wrongly applied, or that they themselves had credited the incoming wire to the account. And now they are charging the depositor a fee for depositing a cheque that is returned. Now I ask you: if you took a cheque that you had to the paying bank to ask if it was good before depositing, you would be immediately told they can't disclose customer information. So you deposit it and then are charged a fee if it is returned.

In the case of BNS this was particularly annoying. I would receive copies of payment advice from the clients overseas, and allowing for a couple of days for the money to be credited to my account, would write cheques only to have them returned for lack of funds, and when I enquired to find out that there was a mistake in the crediting to my correct account made in Trinidad. As I often said to them when I get on a plane in New York for Barbados that is where the compass is set, so when someone wires money to Barbados how on earth it ends up in Trinidad is beyond me. A wire is meant to be instantaneous, but often the norm with them was the same three-day rule.

The answer to that I think I learnt more than twenty-five years prior in Jamaica as a student. Habitually, Errol Niles, Rudolph Greenidge, Herbie Arthur and I were complaining about the time it took for wires of money sent from Barbados to clear. Our complaints were regularly defended by the banks on the ground that it was not them but the Bank of Jamaica who had the hold on the release of funds. Upon notification of a wire to me by my father sent through the Caribbean Development Bank, when I checked with the bank two days later it still had not arrived. I asked my father to check on his end, and it was discovered that the delays were routine, all linked at the time to the chronic foreign exchange shortage in the island. In that case the delayed processing was as a result of a simple balancing act, but I have always been of the view that the banks benefit individually from use of money for at least a day on each transaction without having to credit and presumably pay interest to the recipient. To the individual it is an irritant, but consider the wider picture from the point of view of profits to the bank.

Some Banks are now holding pension cheques issued by the government for three days. How much more unconscionable can you get? But then it is all about maximizing profits... is it not?

I have been consulted on more than one occasion for the antics of some finance companies when it comes to seeking to repossess vehicles for arrears. To this end it is my view that the hire purchase legislation needs to be urgently amended to deal with the amount of loans lent for such transactions, as the amounts where cars are concerned usually exceed the typical hire purchase transaction, and thus the protection afforded against seizure where you have paid more than two thirds of the purchase price is not there.

No prizes for guessing who is one of the main culprits. Banks and other financial institutions are a necessary evil.

28

Kingsland Estates

AFTER JOINING COTTLE Catford in 1987 I soon became aware of a company called Kingsland Estates Limited (KEL). I had no idea of and could not have at the time the profound impact this company would have on my life. In some respects the outward demise of Cottle has run parallel to the legal issues that bedeviled the company in the late 80s, throughout the 90s and into the 21st century. Now in 2015, though the firm ceased working for the company in 2005, its shadow is still looming large over me as I try to settle the debacle that Cottle has become.

Mr. Armstrong, as senior partner, was the principal attorney who handled matters on behalf of the company. Occasionally he would request me to handle some small matter that the company needed advice on. I recall matters such as a tree falling on the neighbor's property and causing damage and the need to work out severance pay for dismissed employees.

However, it was the litigation that originated amongst the shareholders of KEL in 1998 in which I found myself named as a defendant as one of the directors of the company that was to bedevil me for years. I was appointed to the board of directors of the company in December 1996. By this time Mr. Armstrong had passed and I have often reflected what the situation would have been if he had been around. My agreeing to serve on the board was to be the start of nineteen years of misery.

Two persons, Erie Deane, now deceased and Allan Watson, now absconded, were the individuals who came into my office and suggested that I could be of great assistance to the company by agreeing to serve on the board. At that time I did not have any reasons to doubt either of them, and their reasoning was that with the impending negotiations for the sale of the shares by the shareholders, some of whom were directors, would be greatly assisted by having an independent mind on the board. This sounded reasonable. The subsequent litigation between the shareholders of the company with respect to the sale of the shares in the company to Classic Investments, which eventually went all the way to the Privy Council and which I was a party to because of being a director, suggests that this was the second grave error I made at Cottle Catford. The Privy Council decision in 2005 was the last case decided on appeal from Barbados before that body before the Caribbean Court of Justice (CCJ) became this country's final Appellate Court, so if for nothing else, there is some history surrounding the matter.

After my election to the board of KEL, I came into regular contact with its chairman Erie Deane. My recollection of him is that of a small, very distinguished, extremely polite and almost deferential man who, before I was associated with him, I would often see coming in and out of Mr. Armstrong's office. The same would occur with Mr. Watson when he took over the handling of the affairs of Kingsland after the retirement of Mr. Armstrong.

While much of the blame for the financial woes that Cottle later endured were self-inflicted, be it from poor succession planning or lack of proper financial controls both with respect to expenditure, much of the problem existed because the firm was lax in charging fees, or in the case of Kingsland, did not charge fees for more than a decade of working for the company. That this work was done at a time which coexisted with the firm's decreasing income meant this was an accommodation that really should not only never have been made, but was one that the firm, in all its generosity, could not make. I have recently come across correspondence from me to my other two partners of September 30th 2001 urging that billing be done (see Appendix Eight). That letter was my resignation letter from the partnership, because of the stalled talks re merging the firm. It was not until June 2003 that a bill was ever submitted.

My memory is clear that I resigned from the Board in the first half of 2003, but for some reason the Notice of Change of Directors was not filed until sometime in 2004. I am not sure why this was done, but it has raised suspicions in other quarters, as unless there was an appointment to replace me, the Board did not have enough numbers to meet. Not for the first time, however, my hands were tied by something done at Cottle, as the firm was still acting for the company at this time even though I was not the actual attorney handling the matter.

I had seen Erie Deane before coming to work at Cottle, but could not quite place where until one day while he was in my office, my secretary at the time, a middle-aged woman called Ms. Grace Maynard, walked into the room and he almost jumped out of his seat to get to his feet. She herself was somewhat surprised, as she was just bringing me the file for the matter that we were dealing with and had previously shown him into my office. His reaction, however, jogged my memory.

A few years prior to this meeting which was in the late 80s, I was playing a game at Windward cricket club for my club Pickwick while home on vacation from the NMLS. During the game a friend brought one of our colleagues from NMLS who was visiting the island to the game. When she entered the pavilion all the Windward members who were watching the game jumped to their feet while we Pickwick men in the pavilion, as we were batting, initially remained seated until embarrassment made us rise.

Windward cricket club is in my opinion one of the few thriving cricket clubs still left in the island, and has improved its facilities by dint of the dedication and selfish work of its members, particularly the Thornton, Marshall and Bryant clan, so much so that the ground has achieved first class status for the hosting of regional cricket games and would have hosted many more if not for the requirement that wherever possible all regional games be played at the Test facility at Kensington. Its ground in the eastern part of the island in the parish of St. Philip is a picturesque ground, is an outstanding achievement for a club that does not compete at the highest level of our local cricket, but is testimony to the fact that one reaps what one sows.

I am not sure if Mr. Deane was a member of the club—the Deanes were and still are in the main a horse racing family—but he was one of the men who stood to attention that day and I learnt at the time that it was a club rule that whenever a young lady over the age of 12 entered the pavilion all men seated in the pavilion must stand until she was seated. That episode is one of my abiding memories of the persona of Erie Deane that I thought I knew, and which played a large part in my attitude towards the legal saga of Kingsland Estates, as my initial impression of him was that he was a simple, honest, straightforward man trying his best to do what he thought was in the best interests of KEL. I still remember my pleasant surprise at the receipt from him, on behalf of the board of directors, of a congratulatory card and flowers on the birth of my first daughter Carissa in Manchester early in 1997 just weeks after I joined the board.

I have over the years of the KEL saga come to realize that this persona was perhaps cultivated to extract the maximum amount of sympathy for his position, and as far as I was concerned I genuinely believed that he was fighting a battle with other family members who were being assisted by deep pockets from overseas so as to take control of KEL. While I am cognizant of the mantra that one should not speak ill of the dead, it is not surprising to me that as I learnt more and more of the machinations involving the Deane family dynamics with respect to KEL, that my perspective of the events viewed primarily through the glasses of Erie Deane as outlined to me at the time, has changed. I have digested the continuing fight over these last ten years since the Privy Council decision by Madge Knox, one of the last original shareholders and certainly the largest still remaining as owner of their shares and the now *de facto* owner of the majority of the majority of shares in KEL, Richard Cox.

My subsequent education—elucidation might be a better word—has led me to believe that there was a certain ruthless streak in Erie Deane which on reflection he did express at meetings of the board on more than one occasion. At the time I put this down to his frustration borne out of the protracted litigation that seemed in my view to be the result of the unreasonable antics of the Knox clan, but now I am not so certain. It is clear now to me that he was determined to prevail in his view as to what was best for KEL, or dare I say what was best for him over anyone who had an opposing view to his. This undoubtedly contributed to the KEL saga with respect to the sale of the shares of the company taking up more legal time in terms of litigation before the courts—and I say this without fear of contradiction—than any other matter in the history of Barbados civil litigation.

First impressions in any aspect of life are crucial, and my impression of Mr. Deane went a long way in contributing to the financial mess that I am now in, as I was of the genuine belief that he was sincere in what he was doing and that the dispute would soon end. While I would never seek to question the sincerity of his belief, I have concluded that his vision as to how the sale of the shares in the company should progress ultimately fueled much of the litigation.

I continued to serve on the board of KEL for over six years without any payment to either me or Cottle, and with every passing month the prospect of imminent payment to Cottle receding, as the litigation appeared never ending. This failure of the firm that started under the watch of Armstrong not to insist on charging even a nominal monthly amount to cover out-of-pocket expenses incurred in doing the work for KEL contributed in no small way to the eventual financial predicament the firm found it in.

The basis for this relationship with KEL which was also extended to other clients was sown before I became a partner of the firm. At that time the revenue of Cottle could easily allow for work to be done for a client without payment at the time of the work. After I became a partner it was evident to me that the firm could not survive much longer on this basis, with the retirement of Armstrong and the handing over of work to Barry Gale, unless different practices were engaged and the firm brought in new blood to diversify the services that it was offering.

I pushed for more associates to be recruited and Doria Moore was one of these. It is a decision that I now thoroughly regret, and one that has operated to my detriment as the Kingsland saga unfolded.

I now no longer think that Madge Knox, to use today's jargon, a lone wolf fighting a battle to protect her rights, was the character she was originally portrayed to me as. It is clear to me now that several others saw the company as ripe for a takeover, and eventually achieved same by paying a fraction of the price that the company was really worth. In many respects I have come to see much in her fight to achieve what was right for her as comparable to the fight I have faced with my former partners with respect to Cottle Catford, and now do not see her as the nuisance she was portrayed as, but as someone who was fighting against what was a hostile takeover of the family china.

It is fair to say that after all these years I have some very strong feelings towards KEL. As the Privy Council pointed out in delivering its judgment, the administrative support provided by the firm of Cottle allowed the company to continue functioning while technically bankrupt and suffering from the severe infighting amongst the shareholders, thus preventing it operating in a normal sense. This was a cost to the firm which went uncompensated. But then my anger should not be directed solely at KEL, because several times when I asked Watson to render bills etc. he would not, and even after the SBG agreement, an earlier agreement with respect to the sale of the shares in the company collapsed and the significant deposit forfeited, he chose to pay out all to the clients without charging a fee for over two years work at the time. I will go to my grave believing that he and Erie Deane had an under-the-counter arrangement regarding this.

I never held that view because the maths simply did not add up that the fees due from the work for KEL was the panacea for all the woes at Cottle. It therefore came as a surprise when during my court battle with my former partners to establish what they owed that the question of what was received from KEL became so contentious. At the time I was seething with anger for having banged my head for several years at partners' meetings to urge billing of KEL, and here now were Watson and Griffith challenging the amount that was eventually paid.

In my meetings with Erie Deane after 2003, every time I raised the fact that Cottle had for more than a decade been working without pay, he always responded that Joey Armstrong had said that the firm's fees would be paid when the matter was ended. Yes, Mr. Armstrong did say that, but that was in or around 1988, and I don't think in his wildest dreams he felt that this battle would still be raging after 18 years. Certainly it has turned into my nightmare.

KEL was a sugar producer in the island growing sugar on the vast acres of land that it owned. When the bottom fell out of the sugar market the company was left with large swatches of land under cultivation that had now become unprofitable. Despite the best efforts at reducing the expense of production, there was always going to be a significant cost to the same, especially in an industry that was at the time far more labour-intensive than it is today. When this was combined with the fact that unlike oil, the price you were paid on the open market was given to you and not what you set by the level of production, KEL and several other similar plantation owners became indebted primarily to government.

Government support was not going to be never-ending, and so the company began looking at ways at maximizing its resources. It was still owner of a lot of very fertile land that had begun to come out of sugar production, and indeed many of its lands have gone on to be developed into residential areas. One need only mention the word Kingsland and anyone familiar with the island knows that this is a large housing area.

With the construction of the ABC Highway bordering on tracts of its lands, this had the effect of causing its value to increase tremendously. There was a clear division of thought within the company as to the way forward, and a divide arose between the two camps within the company. The Erie Deane camp favoured sale of the company, whereas the Madge Knox camp, already suspicious of the Erie Deane camp, was opposed to what they saw as the selling of the family heirloom.

Depending on who you speak to, there is disagreement as to whether the company needed to be sold to survive or whether it needed an injection of capital and expertise to develop its assets for the benefit of the shareholders. I do not think there was ever any doubt that resources from outside the family structure had to be tapped to ensure that the company remained viable in the 21st Century. It was clear that its former main purpose as a sugar producer was not an option anymore, and therefore, going forward, the company had to channel its sights elsewhere. To develop the potential that its large tracts of now commercially viable land needed was, in the view of Erie Deane, beyond the capacity of the current shareholders, who were aging and some of whom had died and passed on the ownership to the next generation, many of whom had other careers outside the family business.

This is where the dispute arose after the first agreement for the sale of the shares in the company with an organization known as SBG Limited, a company with strong political connections across the political divide, collapsed. Despite all those connections and the obtaining of permissions for development of land in areas that raised eyebrows, their ability to finance the purchase fell through and the deal collapsed.

After the collapse of the deal, the board of the company, and by then I was a member of the board, recommended that the shareholders accept an offer from Classic Investment Ltd. to purchase all the issued shares at a price of $30 per share. The $30 a share purchase price has been hotly debated since then as to whether it was a fair market value, and I cannot remember much of what was discussed then and how it was discussed to arrive at the recommendation.

As a director of the company I was sued in a suit that had nine defendants. It was recognized in all courts that I had no personal interest in the matter, and that my purpose on the board was simply to offer guidance and advice when any matter of a legal nature was discussed. Still I became embroiled in the fight.

As I look back on my time on the board, which lasted until I resigned early in 2003 when I took over the running of Cottle, I believe that I acted in the best interest of the company from the facts presented to me. As I was to later discover, those facts were often skewed in a manner that made the decisions that I was part of seem to me to be perfectly legitimate, and I for one formed the view that the Knox family were just objecting for objecting's sake, or as Erie Deane often said, were a "bunch of troublemakers".

I was not one of the attorneys involved in the litigation, as it was handled by Doria Moore for Cottle Catford in association with Leslie Haynes Q.C., and the late former Prime Minister Sir Harold St. John Q.C. for the shareholders, the company and the directors.

However, while my decisions at board meetings were made by me honestly from what was presented to me, they were based on information provided to the board, especially by its chairman, and with the perception that I held of him I did not at the time have any reason to suspect that the information was anything but genuine. I have since come to the conclusion that whilst the information may not have been wrong, it was certainly presented in a light that favoured the interpretation that the chair wished to put on it. In assessing what was presented to make a decision as to whether the offer should be accepted, I genuinely believed at the time that if the majority of the shareholders were in favour of selling at that price, then it was the best deal to accept rather than one from Knox, whose backers were portrayed as persons who did not have the best interest of the company at heart.

My own assessment now years after the event is that while it was clear that several persons wanted to get their grubby hands on the assets of the company at a below-market price, I had unintentionally been party to the blacklisting of the wrong people. It is clear from the present accounts of the company that the value of the company's shares has increased tremendously without any apparent acquisition of new assets, and that the price actually paid was much lower than the true market value, something that I had begun to suspect in the early years that I was handling the affairs of Cottle and had more face-to-face contact with Deane on the question of the dues to Cottle.

In 2003, as soon as the High Street partnership ended, I met with Erie Deane and indicated that because of the parlous state of the accounts of the partnership I would have to press for some form of payment for the work done over the years. I realized that doing so would have been incompatible with my position as a director of the company, and as such I resigned in at the end of June 2003. At that time I submitted the first billing that the company received from Cottle.

During the preceding six months I had become increasingly more disenchanted with Erie Deane, as every time the question of the outstanding fees arose he continuously asserted what the late Mr.

Armstrong had said with respect to payment, and then added "you know Philip, a bill from the firm has never been submitted." Cottle was floundering, and as neither of my partners was—according to them at the time—able to inject finance, or as I now believe, were not prepared to make the hard personal sacrifice to do so; these constant excuses for not making any payments were beginning to run thin. As I was to discover later I had every reason to feel that I was being taken for a fool.

The final nail in the coffin with respect to my suspicions about the apparent arm's length transaction with Classic for the sale of the majority of shares was confirmed in my mind during a meeting with Deane which occurred shortly before the hearing at the Privy Council in 2005. He had visited me at my office and during our conversation I said to him that it was clear to me then that whether the value agreed for the sale of the shares nearly ten years prior was an accurate one or not, to maintain the agreement now at the same the sale price would result in a tremendous disadvantage to the shareholders. In my opinion the best thing for everyone was if the company lost the case in the Privy Council and then the shareholders would have been free to renegotiate the price for the sale of the shares.

My view, I indicated to him, was supported by what I had learnt when I had taken the opportunity while on a trip to the UK earlier in the year 2005 to visit the solicitors acting for the defendants in the suit in the Privy Council, namely Glovers, and that they had indicated that in their view attempts should be made to arrive at a settlement between all the parties, as a victory would still be a hollow one. It was clear to all that by that time the value of the shares was now significantly more than the contract price.

Glovers indicated to me during the meeting that the word 'compromise', even if exchanged for the word 'settle', still appeared to be a poisoned chalice. This view was confirmed in my conversation with Deane when he indicated that he hoped that this was not the case (losing), because he was a man of his word, and once given even if a better deal came up he felt bound by his word to honor the old one. I remember thinking this was strange, and his response has always puzzled me, but it was not until years later after his death when I repeated what he said to his nephew that I was made aware of certain of his foibles that would appear to confirm my suspicions—that there was some hold that the purchasers had over his uncle that drove him, as we would say 'gaga', to ensure that the agreement was completed under the terms signed.

Doria Moore, who handled all the litigation work on behalf of Cottle for the over 7 years involving KEL, resigned from the firm at the end of 2004 to set up her own practice. Initially I did not have a problem with it, as my attitude that everyone was entitled to leave was well known. I did not expect others to stay with the growing uncertainty surrounding the firm, and had often said that if you received a better offer or felt it was in your better interest, then do not feel constrained to stay. In so doing I was speaking from my heart, as by then I had realized that ten years earlier I had made the same mistake by not leaving because of misplaced loyalty.

I do not think that the use of the word treachery is too strong to describe how I viewed the totality of her actions after leaving Cottle, not only in relation to KEL and what was due to Cottle, but also with respect to what I viewed as a clear cherry picking of which clients she wished to take with her.

Shortly after she left I started getting requests from her for the transfer of minor amounts held by the firm on behalf of clients to her. She followed the established practice and submitted letters from clients that they wished for her to continue acting for them. Again this was not a problem, but I soon discerned from the persons that were indicating a desire to leave that one thing was common: Cottle held funds for them, whereas none of the clients that owed the firm money desired to leave and go with her. It may be coincidental, but just as with my former partners, I was now finding myself having to fund these payments from my own pocket.

This was mildly annoying for me. At the time there was technically no money in the accounts of Cottle, which she well knew. I had to find the actual cash and this irritated me, as she clearly knew my predicament. I now realise that I was slow to catch on to what was clearly her plan, even though both Julie Harris and Sharon Carter, both associates with me at the time felt was clear, but which I didn't see.

Shortly after Doria left, Erie Deane approached me saying that Doria was now on her own and KEL needed money to pay her a retainer. He was requesting that I make payment to her from money that was in account under his personal name. I lost it. What follows is a polite recreation of what I said to him. I said "…for the last fifteen years not a cent has been paid to Cottle for fees… you know it… Doria knows I have paid her a monthly salary since she joined the firm just under ten years ago and now you want me to pay her as soon as she has left from money that is under your name?"

The words were choice and harsh and I accused him of colluding with Watson in the whole sordid mess, and I let him know that I am sure he and Watson had arranged when the money from the first sale was forfeited that some went back to him and Watson. For the life of me I could not understand how Cottle took no fee from the forfeited funds, having at that time been working unpaid for almost five years, but paid all the forfeited money out to the shareholders.

Erie Deane naturally denied all my allegations and said he thought better of me because he knew my father and he would never have used the language I did to him. This I agreed with, but I did not really care at the time what he thought of me. He asked if I would formally transfer the work for the company to Doria and I said "…with pleasure as I am sick of Kingsland now." Words cannot express how frustrated I felt by Kingsland. However, it probably was one of my worst decisions.

A client can demand to change attorneys at any time, but an attorney has a right to hold on to the client's papers as a lien until he is paid. Though it was impractical to exercise such a lien in this case, as the long running matter had to be completed so that Cottle fees outstanding for over 15 years could be paid. I never thought or dreamed at the time that Doria would later double cross me when after years of working for the firm on Kingsland's behalf she would later argue against the amount of fees due to Cottle. My trusting nature once again, and all I can say is someday the truth will out.

As the date for the hearing in the Privy Council drew near the fees of the solicitors and barristers in the UK had to be paid. At the time I was convinced it was a plan hatched by Turney, attorney for Classic, the purported purchaser and the one who I was later to learn was really controlling things and Doria to request that I arrange to pay 87,000 pounds in fees out of the deposit that was notionally in Cottle for the sale of the shares to settle the amounts due the UK lawyers.

I was livid with this request. My situation was well known, but sanity prevailed especially when, acting on the advice of a senior attorney, I indicated to them that I was only prepared to pay the one third that I would have been charged as a partner with Watson and Griffith, as the money was paid to the old partnership. My condition for payment of this amount was that I would only do so if a request was made to the other two to fork up the remainder. It never happened, and while at the time I didn't think much of it, I am now convinced that Deane would never have made the request to Watson. I will go to my grave thinking that there was an under-the-table deal between the two. Interestingly, the fees were paid from elsewhere and I have since learnt they were paid by the proposed buyers of the shares. To my mind I was getting it from all around and my life was becoming a greater nightmare.

For some time I was acutely aware that whatever fee was eventually paid to Cottle for its work would not settle the indebtedness of the partners to Cottle. I had been making this point for several years before the end of the partnership in 2002 when urging my two partners that they needed to raise their own finance to assist with the settling of their dues. This they never did, saying they were waiting on the pay-off from Kingsland. So for nearly four years after the partnership ended in 2002 until payment in 2006, I alone carried the burden of the deficit in the accounts, something that I have never been compensated for and which to my great disappointment the Court of Appeal failed to address when the matter came before it. I knew that the greater the fee from Kingsland, the less the shortfall in the debt it would be, and thus I tried desperately to receive a fee commensurate with the work done and that is why I am of the opinion that Doria's actions in arguing against the amount were nothing short of treachery.

By the time the fees were paid I had filed suit against my former partners, for after more than two years of pleading and begging them to do right, other than a one-off payment of $35,000 from Watson towards his debt of in excess of one million dollars, there had been no payment by either of them towards their indebtedness. I was fighting a lonely battle by myself to keep the Cottle ship afloat, but with no funds from either of them or from Kingsland. I was getting desperate, a fact that Turney was to play on.

After the Privy Council gave its decision in 2005 when I felt that the end was nigh, it took almost another year of argument with the company, now controlled by the new majority shareholder Classic, before the fees due were paid. Turney, who was always its main counsel, was now joined by Doria, ostensibly now acting for Kingsland in quibbling about the fee to be paid. To achieve settlement with respect to the quantum of Cottle fees I left much of the negotiation to my father Sir Neville and my close friend Yvette Lemonias-Seale. All manner of requests were made to break down what was done over fifteen years of work into fees for the company, fees for the shareholders, and then fees in relation to the litigation. I was of the opinion that it was an impossible task, but now I am glad that I attempted it, as it clearly shows now how the firm was robbed.

A request that was insisted on was that what work was done on behalf of the shareholders be billed separately from work done on behalf of the company in the litigation. In my innocence I could not fathom what difference it made, especially because at the time, now that the services were performed, no one was making any distinction as to who the firm was working for. But Turney, on behalf of Richard Cox, the major shareholder of Classic, the purchaser, insisted.

It was at this time of negotiation that the extent of the treachery of Doria shone through. She had worked tirelessly, I may say, on behalf of KEL when employed by Cottle, but now pitched up working for KEL, its new owners, and argued against my claim for fees, often seeking a lower fee than her internal memos suggested was appropriate.

After constant badgering for months by me Watson, while still attached to the firm as a consultant in the first half of 2003 because he had been prime conduit with Kingsland over the years, produced a detailed bill for submission to the company for work done in relation to the sale of the shares which involved various aspects of the litigation. It had been like pulling teeth to get him to do this and he eventually did one for the work done on the share acquisition and this bill in the amount of a $1,000,000 was submitted in June of 2003 along with my resignation as a director of the company, but was never settled.

The sum of $730,000 was the amount that was eventually paid for the work in relation to the sale of the shares in 2006 after an initial offer of $500,000 from Doria Moore sometime in January 2005, I think. It was an insulting offer, but as I was later to suspect, the more she was able to skim off the amount paid to Cottle, the greater the amount to her. The accompanying correspondence makes for interesting reading. Doria would have been consulted by Watson in preparing the bill, and to later argue against it was as great a conflict of interest that I could imagine.

Back and forth the arguments went until finally, in desperate need of the funds, I settled in addition to the amount of $730,000 down from the million billed, the amount of $420,000, being the amount paid for litigation. Cottle's work in litigation that was ongoing for over 15 years or 180 months thus boiled down to about $2,500 per month or $125 per day when this was broken down, then not enough to cover the salary of a junior secretary at the firm. Though fees paid in the UK are higher, it is instructive that $300,000 was paid for about two years of work to the attorneys there.

Years later, information came into my possession that suggested that during the negotiations vital information was being kept away from the people negotiating for me, leaving me with the feeling that despite all the protestations from Turney that he empathized with my plight, he has been a principal behind the scenes in denying me my just entitlements.

Indirectly the shareholders were getting an increased value for their shares, and because this was never reflected on the share transfers, not only was the Cottle fee calculated on a wrong value, but the taxes due to the government on the transfers were low as well.

At the time that the fees were paid in 2006, I released various files and deeds in particular with the compulsory acquisition of land owned by the company by the government. The land was situate at Kendal. Prior to handing over the files I had Clyde Turney sign an undertaking to settle the fees due to Cottle as a result of payment received for the acquisition of the land. This was in April of 2006. The Notice of Compulsory Acquisition of the land was issued sometime in 1990 when Cottle was working for the company. The firm was thereafter involved in the negotiations with respect to the price to be paid with respect of the acquisition until 2006 when I handed over the files. During this time no fees were paid, which was not unusual, as these would have been paid when the government would have settled the compensation.

Sometime in 2014, the government indicated it did not have the money to pay for the amount requested for the land in 2006 of six million and returned the land to the company by withdrawing the respective Notices of Acquisition under the relevant legislation. The company subsequently sold the land at a price of $20,000,000 under private treaty. My estimate that the fee entitled to be charged by the Attorney acting for the Company with under the scale of costs for Attorneys was a minimum of $200,000.

Between the years 2006 and 2013, every time I raised with Turney whether the money for the acquisition was received he said no, so no fees had been received either. He, however, was silent on the question of the return of the land which I learnt of from a parliamentary debate. Of course I asked about our fee, and not surprisingly, he said none was due as technically there was no acquisition.

By his argument, which is classic Turney, Cottle did work for years with no payment; I released the deeds as far back as 2006 so the matter could be completed at an asking amount of 6 million which in all likelihood would be less. The property is returned to his client's control and they arrange a sale for 20 million, the legal fee on which was $200,000, and despite a letter of undertaking signed by him in 2006, he bold-facedly said that no fee is due to Cottle and has refused to settle any fees due to Cottle.

The result that I now have to tax the costs on the basis of the fact that Cottle is entitled to a fee based on the work that it has not been paid for. His attitude and that of other attorneys in other matters has added to my distress. There is no one in the legal profession over fifteen year's call which includes virtually every Q.C. on the rolls who is unaware of the predicament that I have been faced with, and yet obstacle after obstacle causing delay after delay is put in my path when I try to recover funds to settle debts due to clients not for me to build or live in a fancy house. I now despise my profession.

In light of what I was learning now in 2014 about what went on when the negotiations for Cottle fee were being carried on, it was clear that details that would have influenced those acting for me as to whether the matter should be settled were deliberately withheld from them. It was evident that he was the man behind the scene pulling the strings, for if as was to appear now that his client the original purchaser was underwriting the fees of the vendors for whom Cottle acted, then not only had our fee for the sale been calculated on a clearly lesser value for the sale, but it was clearly in his client's interest to have the fees paid to Cottle reduced as much as possible.

Yet when I cried foul at his antics he had the gall to tell me that I was behaving unethically in discussing matters with interested parties. Give me a break, Turney. My behavior is unethical, but yours passes the smell test ...and by the way where is he consultant now? Clarke Gittens and Farmer, who are also acting for the estate of Sir Harold St. John in collecting the fees due to his estate, and yet I am conflicted—*stupseeeeee*.

This behavior, allied to the behavior of seeking to claim from Madge Knox the taxed costs due to Cottle Catford, assigned at the time of payment of the fees in 2006 which add up to about nearly a million dollars when the company only paid out $420,000, is the height of hypocrisy.

To think that two brethren participated in this against me knowing what I was facing was the most hurtful part. The paper trail is there for all to see, but I am now firmly convinced that Madge Knox was robbed as she always alleged. The same shares which were sold at a value of $30 are now estimated by the company to have a value of over $100, as that is the dividend declared, which means a dividend payment of in excess of a million dollars to Madge Knox. But that is not the end, because the company now says she owed costs—the Cottle costs—it wants to pay the money into court pending an order that it be used to settle the costs that Cottle has assigned. Yet Turney accuses me of being unethical when I talk to the Knox clan to find out the truth of what has gone on. Please spare me your moralistic tone.

However, silly me thinking this was an end, because despite being paid in 2006, along came a spider in or around 2008 by the name of Donald Best, and instituted suit in Canada against the company, everyone who was a director, a former prime minister, a current one at the time and a future one, judges including the then Chief Justice Sir David Simmonds, and a host of government functionaries like the chief town planner and every single professional who had anything to do with Kingsland.

I was named in two capacities—as a director, and as a partner of Cottle. If nothing else I was in good company. By the time of the litigation I was on my own at Cottle and had to enter a defense, or to be more accurate, have an attorney in Canada argue that the suit brought in Toronto was in the wrong forum. Failure to do so, as I was constantly reminded by other defendants, would be catastrophic. It cost me nearly $80,000 in legal fees. Directors, as is the norm, are supposed to be indemnified by the company for any legal expenses incurred for actions they did as directors, but this has never been done to me, and when subsequently Justice Crane Scott in the one part of her ruling I disagreed with ruled that I could not seek a contribution from Watson and Griffith because I had not established that I requested their permission to pay for defending the suit, I could only ask what chance was there ever that they would pay, but now what difference it make?

I trust I have explained adequately enough why I wanted so much to be rid of Kingsland, as it was millstone around my neck. But what is worse is that Kingsland, now controlled by Turney's client, has failed to indemnify me for these costs because I was sued in my capacity as a director and the articles of the company stipulate this should happen. My battle has never only been against my former partners, but some charlatans as well.

No one can blame me for hating the name 'Kingsland'.

29

I Did What Was Right

APPROACHING THE 13th anniversary of the end of the partnership, there is much to reflect on. I am certainly in a far worse position than I was then, not only from a personal and professional perspective but also from a material perspective as my current debt is something I doubt very much I will clear in this lifetime. But my conscience is clear, as I did what was right.

I know that may well mean little to persons who are still without their money, a fact that causes me more angst and loss of sleep than anything else. There is seldom a waking hour that goes by without my thinking about some aspect of what has happened, leading me to wonder if there was anything different I could have done. I yearn for the end, as my life in my opinion is not worth living at present where day by day I am just trying to find money to meet expenses that were once routinely paid in the past. It has been humbling and somewhat demeaning, but if that is my lot in life, to quote the English singer Shirley Bassey:

> *Funny how a lonely day*
> *can make a person say*
> *what good is my life but...*

This is my life.

I can relate to those words and many others in her song, but at the end of the day despite help from many friends, it is my life and my problem that I have to solve. It has allowed me to see life from the perspective of many others who daily are faced with making a decision as to what to pay and what not to pay. I find it challenging to meet the monthly prescription medical expenses that I have now that I have lost my health insurance. That insurance was cancelled by Sagicor for non-payment of premiums—I just did not have the money—at a time when I was locked in battle with them over my pension payments, which I won. Have they reinstated the coverage? No, they have not, which I don't find surprising, but I am disappointed that when I seek to have it reinstated that technical arguments are again raised by attorneys on the other side.

Lest it be forgotten, Sagicor cancelled my insurance early in 2014 for me owing them $1,500, and they were later found to owe me $425,000. Yet when I try to have it reinstated, all manner of technical arguments why the application can't be heard are raised by the same attorney who wants $20,000 in damages from my father because he wrote that he was disappointed in his actions—*steupseeeee*.

My ability through all of this to remain sane has been due in no small measure to the fact that in my opinion and in the opinion of those who I either care for or value, I did what was right. Only one person, and I use that noun loosely, has ever thrown in my face the fact that I am facing criminal charges over this affair. That is because most right thinking people think it is grossly unfair, a travesty of justice, which had it not happened, I would not have been moved to write this story.

I have been uplifted throughout this ordeal by a close few friends, especially of late, who have stood with me and who have encouraged me not to give up and to stand with me. I have spoken of many of these before and will inevitably leave out a few people, but in these last few months of writing I have been encouraged a lot by Jacqueline Caesar, a human resource specialist by training who runs a camp every holiday for children from 5-16, and has assisted me greatly not only with the children who attend, but to think outside the box in finding solutions to my predicament.

Special mention must be made of one of my most loyal employees, Maxine Babb. She joined Cottle almost fifteen years ago and is the only member of staff from the High Street Office who is still with me. Maxine has come through the ranks and has given me loyal service. I know at times she feels that I have not appreciated her efforts. She is the first to admit that she is not the quickest typist, and often prefers to check and recheck everything she does with me rather than simply do it, which at times has driven me to distraction.

Maxine has more patience than Job, especially when dealing with the many tenantry clients that we had to deal with at Cottle Catford and still currently deal with. Her patience in dealing with these and other clients has often amazed me. I owe her a huge debt for sustaining the little practice that I presently have, as she has been able to explain to others why their matters have been delayed.

Maxine and Shatara Ramsey, who left early in 2015 with my blessing as I could no longer afford to keep her, have been of yeoman service in sorting the documentary mess that Cottle Catford has become. I still have in excess of four hundred wills in my possession, the majority of which belong to persons long since deceased, but which are still in need of cataloguing. These, together with deeds for in excess of five hundred persons, have become a nightmare to sort. Sort it I must, often personally. Thankfully the Archives Department has agreed to take these documents. For these last thirteen years I have had to store them and catalogue them at a cost which will never be recovered by me. It is part of the loss I will suffer from this debacle, and I have often wondered if persons have ever thought of the logistical nightmare that would have been caused had the firm gone under in 2003.

I must also express thanks to the numerous clients who have stuck with me while I have tried to sort their matters out because of the delays occasioned by the morass I have been in. Hopefully when they read the full extent of this story, they will have a better understanding of the problems I faced. Four in particular I need to add: H and G Limited, George Sahely and Co., Live Exchange Barbados Limited, and Miasha Layne, who have not only continued to seek my legal counsel but who have gone beyond the call of duty in enquiring as to my well-being. Not only clients, especially the few I have named, but I would like to mention three individuals in particular who have assisted me with reducing my monthly living expenses, a gesture that I have deeply appreciated, and I speak of Martin Moses (a former schoolmate), John Huggins and Cammie Smith.

I never considered taking the easy road and running to foreign pastures to leave a phalanx of accomplices to protect me with every unethical scheme they could think of. I did not throw my hands up in the air and say 'what can I do?' and pretend that the physical afflictions that I am suffering from were all because of the pressure put on me by 'that man who knows I had no money but is still hounding me'. I did not bury my head in the sand and hope it would go away. I tried my best to see what could be done, and this is the result that I am faced with—debt, a myriad of old title deeds and files, and a destroyed and reputation.

For every person that knows the story of what has occurred there are many that don't, as I was reminded by a former senior official at Sagicor who was associated with me at Pickwick and told me less than a year ago he thought I had gone rogue. If he can while resident here in Barbados, what of the foreign individual who when they are researching lawyers in Barbados see that I have been charged with theft and money laundering?

Would I have done things differently? Of course I would have with hindsight, but who among us would not? The 'Monday Morning

Quarter Back' or the 'Armchair Selector' has not only the benefit of hindsight, but the additional time to make decisions that fast moving events at the time did not allow and which may have been improved with the availability of such time or hindsight. My decision at the time to try to salvage the wreck of Cottle Catford that I was faced with in October 2002 (and I remember well thinking of the enormous challenge ahead of me) was based on the fact that I felt there were approximately 30 people in my employ who I was responsible for, and hundreds of clients who were unsuspecting of what had transpired, and would be severely disadvantaged by a meltdown. It had nothing to do with my desire to be head of the firm. Like it or not, I was the virtual head for the last two years at High Street, as Watson was hardly ever there and Joyce was as proven: totally useless.

Have I succeeded? Definitely not, but this was not for want of trying. In my mind the following factors played a significant or pivotal part in my failure. I do not think what I set out to accomplish was an impossible task, but in all my calculations I never took into account the human factor and those intangibles of jealousy, deceitfulness, greed and indifference of persons, many of whom I knew and some of whom should have seen themselves in a *loco parentis* relationship to me, but either preferred not to or could not be bothered to help.

Let me make it clear that whereas quite a few persons have offered me help, be it financial or by any other means, I am grateful to all who are too numerous to mention. I have tried in many respects to acknowledge those who have assisted, but many would not want public acknowledgement, and to set about naming them all publicly will inevitably mean that I have forgotten some because of the lengthy time of my struggle. Many of the problems that I have faced have been exacerbated by the need to cut through red tape to move my matters forward, which in several cases could have been advanced by the willingness to use the goodwill of these persons to use their office to assist me as I tried to do what was right. Any disappointment that I may have felt has been felt even more by my father, as quite a few of these individuals have not only professed to be his friend, but many have sought his help when in need themselves.

Specifically, I will pinpoint the following and by doing so I am not trying to create a list of excuses, but suggest what the obstacles have been over the years:

1. I never anticipated the deceitfulness of my former partners, who clearly had no intention of honoring the agreement they freely signed. It is amazing to think that if they had committed to pay $5,000 per month they would have repaid the principal due already. The minute book of partners' meetings has been conveniently lost by Watson. It will show the promises that were made to settle their debt. In retrospect, I was as John Knox has intimated to me with respect to the Kingsland saga, naïve in my belief—a naiveness that I began to realise when I discovered months after the partnership ended that Watson had procured a loan at the end of 2002 and had not paid any of it towards his debt, but simply kept it for him and Lady Macbeth to use.

2. I never expected the unethical behavior of a few lawyers led by Vernon Smith who appears to have been driven by an irrational hatred of me. The only cogent reason I have heard advanced by one of his sisters-in-law with whom he is also locked in legal battle was that he felt belittled by what Stephen and I did to him at AGM of the BCA. Truthfully, give me a break. From the time I took on the affairs of Cottle he was not only openly telling persons that a man cannot be a sole partner under the Partnership Act, but seeking to use this fact and the Act as the basis for challenging my right to attempt to recover the money from the Watsons and Griffith. A blind

man on a trotting horse with a rudimentary knowledge of accounts could conclude that they owed the money and had used it for personal benefits, and yet here he was trotting out this bilge.

What did it have to do with him? Madam Justice Cornelius may not recall these words, but when he was pontificating about the state of Cottle Catford back in 2005 before the courts, he was asked during proceedings why he felt it necessary to poke his nose into Cottle's affairs, having not disputed at the time that Delvina Watson was indebted to the firm. The state of affairs of Cottle in 2003, which only grew worse, dictated that I would never have wished to invite even my worst enemy to be a partner, and as the firm had been known as a partnership for decades, why change its designation? But this is the sort of technicality that Smith has become famous in trying to exploit so as to avoid the issue at the hand. I repeat the saying "When the facts are against you, you cite the law."

The reasons for his actions I will never understand, and must conclude that, as my mother was always wont to tell me from the time I was a teenager, some people will always be jealous of you because of who you are. He has boasted to friends of his who are acquainted with me that he has outsmarted me in this battle, so if that is his genuine feeling, kudos to him. He has viewed it as battle. I viewed it as trying to do what was right. I know where my moral compass was; maybe he should look in the mirror when he tries to find his.

This possibility of jealousy was again repeated to me shortly after I started my long journey by a Jamaican colleague at the local bar when I wondered why I was getting little assistance in trying to get Watson and Griffith honour the contract that they signed. I was told pointedly that persons, many of whom I might have thought to be friends, wanted me to fail.

While the worst criminal is entitled to the assistance of an attorney at law who is to work for him fearlessly—and recognizing such, I hold and held no brief for anyone who worked for my ex-partners and even now for institutions on the other side of the table from me—I feel however that there comes a time when you are abusing your oath when you continually assert positions that you know to be untrue and/or untenable, with the sole purpose of delaying the matter or to cause grief to the other party. It has become an modus operandi of Smith in many of his litigation battles, as the CCJ has had occasion to point out.

3. To this I must add the disappointing stance of the majority of the legal profession who to my face express commiserations, but who have adopted an attitude of 'let me stand clear because there but for the grace of God go I'. I have evidence of some deliberately letting potential clients know there was trouble at Cottle Catford, so it would be best to avoid them. 'Trouble at Cottle Catford' was what was said, never the refrain that I was trying to rebuild the firm. It always amazed me how attorneys could glibly look me in the face and commiserate at what was done by my former partners and wonder how I managing with all the stress I must be facing, and then work on a transaction where my former partners received large fees and say subsequently when I discovered same, simply: "You felt the only thing you could do was to try and morally persuade him to honour his debt?"

If one would scour the list of attorneys on the roll over the last ten years and determine those you would deem as seniors, whether by dint of the accolade Q.C. which I have already said I hold in no particular esteem, or by years of service, I have spoken with these either in the course of work or meeting on social occasions to at least 90% of my problem, but received little assistance. I have always felt, but was told it was unrealistic, that less than 5% who controlled many of the lucrative practices could have ended this by simply informing Watson and Griffith that they were not prepared to work with them while this matter was outstanding. They would not have lost.

This stance was taken not because of any vendetta against me, but simply out of indifference or a chance to get a bigger share of the pie. Only recently this same mantra was used to cause a client with whom I had worked for nearly a decade to take their work elsewhere on the ground that I was unsafe to work with. But to this day nothing has caused me as much loss as well as the ability to have the regular income to enable my practice to keep going pulled when comments were made about my suitability to handle the legal affairs of a bank that had been bought over by a Trinidadian entity for whom I was working. The original attorneys feared losing their pick, so to speak, and the rest is history. You simply need connect the dots and their identity is revealed all too easily.

4. The dysfunctional legal system. My dispute was described by the Court of Appeal as a simple issue, yet attorneys representing Watson and Griffith were allowed to exploit the weakness in the administration of justice in delaying a simple issue that it took eight years to be completed. Their intentions were clear, and despite this nearly two years after the dismissal of the appeal by the Court of Appeal, the same two years while I am facing criminal charges for the money that they owe me, the system that it is the responsibility of the CJ to manage and for which he was touted as having garnered lengthy experience while in the United States, has again been

found wanting.

As I write all my efforts at enforcement of the judgment which had taken eight years to be settled are stalled by appeals against the enforcement or the refiling of in limine points that have stalled the matter. It has been drawn to the attention of the CJ that the system is being abused, and his only response to date has been 'if there is an issue with the behavior of Smith et al then make a report to the Disciplinary Committee'. David Thompson's place in the annals of Barbados' history is guaranteed, but his role in setting in place the chain of events that led to the current CJ being appointed cannot be considered his finest hour by any stretch.

5. I never anticipated the innate conservatism and to some extent the racial discrimination of our financial institutions. I have never been one to play the race card, but I find it hard to believe when I see how loans have been disbursed in the past and faltering ones written off, the reasons why I have had so little assistance in managing my deficit. Justice Peter Williams opined when the matter first came before him that the problem could easily have been solved by an injection of capital, as long as the lenders were prepared to assist with a portfolio of work. It was clear years ago that the debt I was facing was becoming unsustainable, yet none of the banks were willing despite being asked to take all my debt, thereby reducing my amortization costs rather than each hold a separate piece.

As it would have been impossible for me to continue to sustain such loans without being able to reduce the principals by recovery of any of the funds, it would have been in the interest of all parties to see that I was able to manage my portfolio by regular work. The opposite has occurred, in that I have not worked for any major institution since the middle of the first decade of the 21st century, despite working for half a dozen in prior years, and quite clearly do not have the ability to pay them off without recovery from my partners. Thus I am facing action by them while unable to recover what is due to me.

What then have I learnt from this sordid mess? 'Trust no one' would be too easy to say. I certainly don't believe that everyone has your interest at heart, but I am also not of the view that everyone is your enemy, although I have lost all respect for many of my so-called brethren in the profession. I must draw a line, however, and state that this view does not apply to anyone (with one notable exception) who has joined the profession in the last decade. In many respects I pity them for what they are now entering.

My view of the profession has changed over the years. No longer being the wide-eyed youngster in the presence of such giants as Jack Dear, Joey Armstrong, Sir Harold St. John and Sir Henry Forde to name a few, whose every word you hung onto and who would take you under their wings and showed you the ropes, I have seen the profession change to one now that is virtually a cut-throat industry where you would do all possible to upstage your rival. Back then your word was your bond. If you said something it was as good as an executed contract; not now, especially when persons are trying to find any technicality get out of their obligations. This has led to a far more impersonal bar and a lack of pride in one's profession, and I no longer feel the same sense of pride that I did when I entered the profession.

Young entrants to any profession have to be guided by their older colleagues. I was fortunate to be able to learn from many giants in my infant days, and so regarded it as my duty to try to help as many young entrants to the profession as I could, often opening my practice to two students every summer. I saw this as a challenge, much like teaching, as they explored the wonderful area that the law is. However, not only has my ability to do so now been hampered by the virtual folding of my practice, but I have realized that my anger at what has happened has so coloured my respect for my profession that I may well not be of assistance to them by the negativity surrounding me. It is one of my regrets, but hopefully the pitfalls that I have described will warn others as to what to behold.

Still I take silent pleasure in seeing some of my former mentees blossom and take up their place in the profession, and in some cases seek to draw attention to my case without my prompting. Only last year Taneisha Evans, now back home in Jamaica, saw it fit—when part of a delegation from Jamaica to a conference in Vancouver, Canada that the CJ was at—to raise with him what she saw as the scandalous abuse of my rights by the failure of the judicial system in Barbados at a forum where the said CJ was touting how efficient the system was. Her report of her talk with him to me was that he beat a hasty retreat, claiming the matter was subjudice. Sounds familiar does it not? He trotted out the same nonsense to my father in reply to a letter asking when he was going to put an end to an abuse of the system by those seeking to protect Griffith and Watson. As nothing is happening in the courts, how worthy is it to trot out this excuse? But then again he may be too busy elsewhere to notice the crumbling system that he was recruited to correct.

I certainly now believe that I waited too long to try to enforce the agreement with my former partners. As I reflect on the end of the partnership, I remember a feeling of relief that I was shed of the physical presence of those two, because my feeling was that they were not prepared to embrace the change needed to arrest the situation. What I didn't realize or understand was that they were comfortable in their current situations where ready access was had to funds to keep their day to day needs going. Human beings instinctively look to protect 'number one' first, or to do things in a manner that number one would suffer the least pain. Having overseen the decline for a number of years, there must be some pain before you could get out of the woods.

I was brought up to look out for your fellow man and wherever possible to put your needs last with respect to others in whom you were *loco parentis*. My belief was ruthlessly exposed, and while I would not say that it was a lesson learnt, as I strongly believe my way was best, it has been a rude awakening. I am often told that few think like me, and while I am not extolling myself as any saint or without sin, it has been one of the sobering lessons I have learnt: that many people, while empathizing in the plight that others may face, are seldom willing to assist. Those who do are your true friends.

An example of my value system compared to that of my partners can be gleaned from the following. Shortly after the partnership ended, a claim was presented for a loan that had been granted to one of the firm's long serving messengers known as Davis. Davis was well known in and around Bridgetown during his long association with Cottle. His office as was a simple desk outside the vault area of the firm, and often he held court there with many ordinary men and women he had met while traversing the streets of Bridgetown with Cottle mail over the years. By the time I joined the firm he was long past his sell-by date, but just as I later felt with Mr. Hutchinson, the partners allowed him to come in whenever he felt like as it gave him something to get up for every day, and this he continued until illness took its tool.

As the young kid on the block growing a practice, Davis used to frog-march people off the street into my office for help when they expressed a need for an attorney, making them feel they were now in the hands of an expert. Many of these persons used to turn up at our High Street office asking for 'Solicitor Davis', thinking from the way he spoke he had to be a solicitor, but he would bring them up to your office with a twinkle in his eye and say "Mr. Nic, this one is above what I can handle." Long after his death, a claim was made that a loan to him had not been repaid. As usual, I was the person contacted.

The loan was secured over the house he had lived in. After his death his estate had been done by Joyce Griffith and this debt was overlooked when the funds were paid out to the beneficiaries. The lender now was calling for his money, and Cottle Catford received a letter. I wrote to my two former partners stating that as the loan had been disbursed during the partnership and had not been repaid at his death, there could be no dispute that the money was owed. I however felt that as Davis had given long and meritorious service—over 50 years I believe—that we could each settle the loan by paying what would amount to less than three thousand each.

They refused, Watson in particular saying the lender could enforce his security. I felt this was not only uncharitable given the nature of his service to the firm, but technically our fault, as Joyce should have cleared it before distributing what was in the estate. We had constructive notice of the debt, as the loan was made from one of the firm's clients and it was made through the firm.

I held to the view that Davis' grandchildren would be flabbergasted to know that more than five years after his death someone would turn up seeking to enforce security over the house that they now lived in. That did not hold sway, and I was told "well if you want to settle it do so." I certainly felt then a keen sense of betrayal, for while I had only worked with Davis for about ten years, Watson and Griffith each worked with him in excess of twenty-five years.

I chose to settle the debt myself because it was the right thing to do, and this principle has guided me throughout, even when doing so I would suffer a loss.

Herein lies another lesson: make sure you know who you are getting into bed with when entering a partnership. At the time that I accepted the offer such thoughts were far from my mind, but any advice that I would give to a young attorney now would be to make this of paramount consideration over and above any financial benefits, for whereas you may seek to bring a traditional marriage to an end, a legal partnership, as I have found out to my cost, can be a virtual noose around your neck.

As I have found out, doing what is right and principled can leave you facing challenges that seem to you unjust. There is no doubt that I would have done things differently if I had the chance, but I would still have taken the decision to try and keep the ship afloat. Just prior to his death in 2007 my friend Stephen had said to me that he was surprised that I had kept it going so long, because he felt that with the length of time then—five years—at recovering the debt it would already have come crashing down. That crash took nearly ten years to occur, and it must give tremendous satisfaction to those who kept rocking the boat.

What recommendations would I have to prevent such a mess occurring? It is clear that a more forceful judiciary would have assisted me, but by far the single most effective/pivotal circumstance that would have prevented this is a formal requirement that attorneys have their client's accounts audited at least once every two years.

The second suggestion of great importance is never to allow only one person where you are in a practice with others to have authority to sign cheques alone. This was how I found it, but I did not question it even though in every other organization I have been involved in two signatures were needed on every cheque. Clearly this would have led to questions have been asked when some of the payments were made by Watson to his wife which I am still trying to recover, and for which Smith had the audacity to file an affidavit on behalf of her to the effect that I waited so long she is surprised that I still wanted the money.

When I joined Cottle Catford I recall how when the auditors were in, even though I was not a partner, I would have to answer questions from the auditors with respect to some client who was under my portfolio. Cottle Catford, like most of the larger firms, had an annual audit and this had been carried out for years. However, when the auditors expressed concern about the accounts, their advice was simply ignored and as they were powerless to do anything about it, they simply walked away. Had it been a legal requirement for the accounts to be audited, many of the misuses that were perpetuated with respect to the funds as discussed in 151/152 would have been discovered by me much earlier. I know that such a recommendation would cause consternation within the profession and would be bitterly opposed. Whether it is ever adopted it will be too late to be of any help to me.

Still this same problem had occurred before at Cottle Catford, and though not there at the time, the financial implications ran until I became a partner when the revenue authority refused to allow claims to reduce income assessable to tax by writing of these losses as bad debts.. I have always felt that some of the persons who worked in the accounts department at the time were well aware of the mischief that Watson was up to, but chose to turn a blind eye. It has been sobering to me that over the last ten years, not one of them has expressed any concern or empathy with the situation that I am now facing, but as I have come to learn, that is the nature of the human being: Look out for 'number one'.

30

Requiem, Repast and Resurrection

WHILE PUTTING THE finishing touches to this book I received a disturbing message from Roger Smith in the United States on the evening of Wednesday October 14th 2015 that he had been trying to get in contact with his mother without success for over a day. His message to me was in response to one from me enquiring whether he and his mother had had a chance to follow up on the discussion she had with me on the night of Monday October 12th. That discussion centered on a matter that had been causing her much anguish for more than a year, and was directly related to actions of her brother-in-law Vernon Smith. After the call I immediately telephoned her residence, but there was no answer. The next day Roger called me to advise that he had reported his mother as missing to the police, and that his sister Tanya had brought forward her trip home from Sunday 18th to that day, the 15th, while he was arriving the following day. I was alarmed at the chain of events and feared the worst.

On the evening of October 24th I received a message from Roger and Tanya's elder brother Allan, who had arrived in the island by then, that they had been alerted by the police of the discovery of a body that they suspected was that of their mother. By this time rumours of the discovery were circulating on social media, and it was soon confirmed in the press. Due to its state of decomposition, formal identification of the body could not be confirmed until an autopsy was performed. The autopsy also determined that the cause of death was strangulation.

For the following three weeks after being informed first of the fact that Auntie Marcelle Smith had been missing and subsequently the manner of her death, I was unable to concentrate on several matters at hand. I found myself trying to suppress the rising anger in me because in my mind her last few months, even years, were dogged by the same evils that were befalling me because of the antics of one person in particular. I played over and over in my head our last conversation, trying to see if I had missed anything when she had called. At the time I was in the middle of watching my favourite picture *Murdoch Mysteries*, so I was somewhat distracted, but it was about 8:30 pm. *Murdoch Mysteries* is situate in Toronto, Canada, and tells the tale of a forward-thinking early twentieth century detective who solves murders by the use of scientific methods not common for that time. Unfortunately, life as we know it is a far cry from any TV drama, and I could only muse out loud hoping for the appearance of a Barbadian Murdoch to make sense of what on the face of it appeared to be a random act of violence.

Her death was the culmination for me of the misery I have endured these last fifteen years. It was by far the unkindest cut, and though she was not a blood relative, she played a role in my life for as long as I can remember. I grew up in her house while developing my love for cricket with her eldest son, and I will never forget her memory nor ever feel that she fell short of what is expected of an Aunt or an Uncle in our society who, while not a blood relative, is in a position of *loco parentis* to you. Any such person should be willing to offer the moral and spiritual guidance gained by being an older person, and she never failed in that regard with me. Her several calls always started by an enquiry as to my health or of that of my children, and by chance if the phone had been answered by one of them she would urge me to spend quality time with them, as one never knew how long you had. Knowing my interest in cricket and the total disdain the three all had for it, she would laugh when I related how the TV was tuned to some inane soap opera rather than a live sporting event.

As an individual you are never prepared for such a tragedy. Her call that Monday was in no way unusual, as it was one of many that I had received from her over the last few years, during which she listened to the frustrations I was feeling with the matters surrounding Cottle Catford. She urged me constantly to tell my story, and was looking forward to reading the completed version. Sadly, she never will have the chance, but at least I know she read the chapter that was of the most interest to her.

We had occasion to bond over a shared enemy—Vernon Smith. For the past three years she had watched helplessly as he diverted to his firm's accounts (accounts that he said in 151/152 that he owned) rent from a property owned by her husband and herself that used to be the family home in which I spent many an afternoon. Vernon's actions were typical Vernon, in that once he held a belief, however irrational, he carried on like a dog either in heat or with a bone between his jaws.

Just as in the case with his deceased friend when he refused to accept the ruling of the Trinidad Registrar, just as in the events happening in the BCA after the death of Sir Conrad Hunte when he refused to accept the stance of not only the Board, but of the general membership of the BCA as to when a successor should be elected, just as he refused to accept that a court had granted an injunction against the disposal of property owned by Delvina Watson and yet advised her (according to her sworn affidavit) that the order was not binding on her because it was improperly obtained, he now refuses to accept the order of the court appointing his sister-in-law—the wife of his brother—and his nephew as his brother's legal representatives.

These are just four immediate, clear instances that come to mind where he has acted as if he is above the law. His career is replete with these actions or antics, and I am sure there if I were to take a close examination of the profession many more would be revealed, while others would seethe with anger, making comments that decency prevents me from repeating here. I need only refer to the stinging criticism he received recently from the CCJ when costs were awarded against him on the grounds, amongst other reasons, that he perpetuated the delay in the matter rather than letting the matter come to an end as an illustration of how he prefers to practice law.

It was on this basis that he justified retaining in his possession under the guise of being his brother's attorney as much as $100,000, the proceeds of rent from a house he has no direct interest in. My last conversation with Auntie Marcelle, as did many over the last few years, centered on how to bring him to account. As she was preparing to comply with the court order appointing her and her son receiver of the affairs of her husband by filing a Statement of Affairs that would have included reference, it surely doesn't necessitate the incarnation of a Barbados Murdoch to wonder if her sudden disappearance and death just was not all too convenient.

Mindful that I live in a society that jealously guards against discussion of topics that are subjudice, it is not possible for me to discuss more of the events surrounding her death. Still the contents our last conversation encapsulated many of the themes in this book of about delays in the legal system and betrayal by persons who one would expect not to betray you. She did not deserve, whatever the bigoted views of others, the fate that befell her. May she rest in peace and rise in glory.

If some of the statements reported in the media are correct at this time, then there is a feeling amongst some of the prime ministers of the region, if not all, that there will soon have to be a funeral to commit to the earth the remnants of the West Indies Cricket Board. While the West Indies team continues to sink to newer lows on the field of play, making it difficult for supporters, however die-hard, to break up their night's rest to follow them in their exploits all around the world, this decline is not helped by the chaos reigning within the administration of the game in the West Indies.

The old maxim that when the head is bad then the body cannot be much better comes to mind, and some harsh criticism from many quarters, both from within the game, the region, and now most potentially damaging from the powerhouse of India, has been made against those charged with running the game in the region.

The prime ministerial sub-committee of CARICOM on cricket, a body that has evolved over the years as more and more crises have afflicted West Indies cricket, in a recently commissioned report into the governance structure of the Board, has issued a stinging criticism of the structure. The report outlines that the present structure has outgrown its days and has recommended that an interim Board be established to run the affairs of the WICB until regional consensus can be reached on what should replace it. It pulls no punches by saying that the present board of directors must resign at once.

While few will disagree that change to the WICB is needed, it will not come easy. I am sure that as politicians, prime ministers are well aware that one of the most difficult tasks in attempting to change any organization is to convince those in occupation that it is time to go. It is somewhat surprising thus to hear the wailing and expressions of offence at the comments of Dave Cameron, the president of the WICB, that a request for an early meeting with the sub-committee cannot be accommodated by the Board. What else did they expect?

The question I will leave for readers is this: If all the directors resigned *en masse*, who would replace them? It is not john public, nor the prime ministerial sub-committee, but the shareholders of the company who will have the responsibility to appoint new ones. In my humble opinion that is where any movement for change should start and that is with the shareholders who are the regional cricket authorities.

While actions of the directors of any company can come under scrutiny, and clearly some recent actions of the Board would fall into that category, it is as the bidding war for our Banks Beer shows— ultimately the call of the shareholders will decide. One thing is certain, and that is that despite whatever structure you end with, until all the stakeholders of the game start singing from the page as one of the dittys to promote the game goes: "all of we", then the resurrection and subsequent redemption of West Indies cricket will be far off.

There is a well-known saying that deaths of friends come in threes. I have suffered the loss of a dear Auntie, one of the things I am most passionate about is on its last legs, and now virtually my career and reputation have been destroyed and buried by the chain of events this book has described. Is it not fitting then that for me the third death in the conventional trilogy is the current judicial system?

I have experienced the judicial system now from every standpoint, something I would never have dreamed of when I entered the profession. As an attorney with a traditional solicitor practice, one daily encounters a level of bureaucracy from many government departments that would drive you cuckoo. For example, on the presentation of Letters Testamentary or Letters of Administration issued by the Registrar of the Supreme Court, which documents stipulate that the deceased died on such a date, you find yourself having routine matters held up because some clerical functionary wants sight of a death certificate.

Added to this is the pedantic view of some functionaries. One needs to be correct, especially with documents supposed to be valid for a lifetime, but a rose by any other name is still a rose, and if in the 21st century there are still individuals in a position of responsibility who feel that the wording of every single document must be akin to a photocopy of the precedent they have prepared, then heaven help us.

Such frustrations pale in comparison to what I have endured with my limited civil practice in the courts. Quite frankly I detest court, and have to summon the energy to attend because frankly on most occasions it is a waste of time. I have already described the chronic abuse of the system by some attorneys in delaying matters that they do not wish to come to an end.

I learnt with amazement that the current dispute over the ownership of Banks Holdings Limited had within a couple of weeks of having a decision in the High Court reached the Court of Appeal. How is this possible? What is so earth shattering about this case which is basically about two entities fighting over the carcass of another company for the purpose of maximizing its profits that it should be accorded such precedence over other matters affecting the daily life of other litigants? It is a disgrace, but then again who am I to complain? As I say in one of my chapters, I dun with that. If I am to be strung and quartered, so be it. If a blind man can see what is being done and the powers that be feel comfortable in giving every reason why not to do something about it, at least let me have my say. People may be advised to report me to the Disciplinary Committee, but to whom do I report those not doing what they should constitutionally do?

The profession, when I entered it, was with justification described as honourable. Youngsters could go and visit seniors and get advice, but it is now a cut-throat business that has degenerated into the trenches where 'you do this to me... well, I will wait until I catch you'. That in a way explains why I have been virtually left on my own to battle a single man who has openly told persons that he intends to make it as difficult as possible for Nicholls to get back his money, something that one of his disciples (I apologise for that blasphemy) said to me in a mocking tone in 2013, and he was not even a member of this profession when his leader had started his actions which appear to give him orgasmic pleasure.

In every instance that he is fighting to block me; I have a legal judgment, and yet every attempt at recovering the money is again the subject of challenge, often on grounds already disposed of, which is why I am so critical of the Chief Justice, as these matters now reside again in the Court of Appeal and should be disposed of summarily.

If Smith by his antics feels that he has broken my spirit, I refer him to what the Parisian who lost his wife in the latest terror attack said.

> "I will not give you the pleasure of letting you know that. I will not blame you for the many weeks that I have been unable to pay the 2 staff I currently have or the outgoings of a rented house, mine having long since been repossessed. You are now too deaf to hear the muttered insults and probably were too ignorant to understand same, but I know just as your funeral must one day come, whether before or after mine, that whereas my redemption will come, few other than your psychopathic followers will think favorably of you. As I have told you more than once you are a disgrace to the profession and to human beings."

My final word goes to all those clients who have been caught up in this debacle. It may not mean much, but I have been fighting and continue to fight to try and recover the millions due to me to repay you and my lenders. It has been a humbling experience, and one that I have suffered personal pain from. I apologise from the bottom of my heart, but hopefully the next generation will see what has happened to me as a warning to tread carefully, especially with your seniors.

Epilogue

January 1st 2016

THIRTEEN YEARS SINCE the end of the High Street Cottle Catford partnership, Allan Watson is holed up at an address in Atlanta, Georgia in the United States where he has been for the last three years, at least while an arrest warrant issued in April of 2015 lies somewhere on the desk of the fraud squad. Not only is the warrant lying there, but at least one other complaint was lodged about eighteen months ago, but the complainant was told that as he was out of the island they were powerless to act without a warrant.

The warrant, albeit for a different matter, has been issued and though the squad has been provided with information regarding his whereabouts obtained by me through the use of the US arm of G4S Security at some cost, he appears untouchable. I still have not figured out why. Is not my continued anger in light of the story I have told not only excusable, but justified when the same fraud squad that arrested me for alleged theft and money laundering at the behest of Barry Gale, seems unable or unwilling to act while the man who raped the coffers of Cottle with the assistance then of his Lady Macbeth and also diverted funds from clients to his coffers while at Gale's Hastings Attorneys, continues to be free?

While now she continues to fly to and fro to spend time with him with the full knowledge of her attorneys, I am deemed *persona non grata* in that country. Does this not reek of a conspiracy when at every turn the same suspects turn up to protect their interests? My memory of criminal law is that there can be a charge for aiding and abetting after the fact of a crime. Though my judgment against my partners was in a civil matter, as I was charged criminally for money missing from Cottle that they have been found liable for, it is not a far stretch that a criminal charge can follow. It is also not a far stretch that someone who continues to assist them in evading this judgment should face aiding and abetting charges.

The orders as set out in Appendix Ten make it clear the intent of the courts, yet Vernon Smith, in October 2014 with his cronies in tow, filed applications a year after the Court of Appeal dismissed an appeal from a judgment handed down in 2009, and as such the matter had to be functus. It has again delayed my ability to recover, which is synonymous with his type of practice, as the CCJ has alluded to more than once when they censured him.

Joyce Griffith is still in the island, due back in court at the end of January to again face an examination of how she will repay her debt, and will no doubt continue with the crying that she has suffered horrendously due to my actions. What actions? Trying to recover what she refused to repay while at the same time assisting the Watsons with hiding the assets that they had taken? She has never once been charged, and while I continue to try to eke out a day to day living from this mess, all she wails about is that it is my fault.

As a new year starts, I am drafting another letter to the registrar of the Supreme Court as I have done over and over since this debacle reached the courts. I can count twenty such letters over the last four years seeking help to try and dismantle the roadblocks that continue to be placed before me by the unethical manipulation of the judicial system to frustrate my attempts to recover the money taken from the Clients Accounts of Cottle.

While there is much truth in the saying that the definition of madness is doing the same thing over and over and expecting a different result, hopefully my writings will one day bear fruit, if only because the present registrar is the tenth (I think including persons who have acted) who has received these letters pleading for help. However, in the event that my actions are because I am now mad, at least my children and others will if necessary see the extent to which I have gone within the law to have this matter ended.

So where am I thirteen years on? To answer truthfully, in a far worse place than I was on December 31st 2002. As of December 31st 2015, the amount owed by Watson pursuant to the judgement is $1,102, 544.19 plus costs of $167,397.11, and the amount owed by Griffith is $735,943.40, plus costs of $158,368.25.

Costs for the appeal to the Court of Appeal estimated at $100,000 each are still to be assessed whenever I get the energy to do so. There are also other costs that will undoubtedly be added whenever the incessant filings for delays ultimately end, but will it make a difference? Delvina Watson herself owes now nearly $500,000, almost twice as much as the original judgment, because of non-payment since 2004.

Daily interest is nominally credited to me in the case of Watson in the amount of $145, and in the case of Griffith it is $97, while I estimate that each day that passes without repayment of the amounts that I have borrowed it runs between $500 and $750 dollars. One does not need to be Einstein to see my problem, and I no longer try to calculate the amounts owing, as I am sure the figure will undo all of Dr. Green's work.

I spent three hours of New Year's Eve giving a statement to the police, who felt compelled to investigate a second complaint by one Vernon Smith that I had threatened him. It is clear that Smith is not only going senile, but his lack of understanding of basic legal concepts despite the acquisition of initials Q.C., has led him to make a further jackass of himself. Let me make it clear that I have never threatened the jackass. If he thinks that after all I have done I am to look up to him then he is sadly misconceived, and my dying breath will be used to heap as much opprobrium on him to give a true picture of the person he is. Gale, Springer and Babb are not far behind.

The goodly inspector who took my statement, and I promised her not to mention her name, could not contain her mirth as I regaled her with the antics of Smith over the years. The two of us had a verbal tug of war over what would be recorded in my statement, which is now three pages in length, but was much shorter than it could have been to allow her to attend to New Year's festivities. As I have made it quite clear, Smith is a jackass, and for the second time he has sought to involve the police in comments I made in court surrounding his antics.

I will not divulge what I said, but I urged the goodly inspector to borrow some tapes of *Murdoch Mysteries* and observe how Detective Murdoch is able to solve many a crime and bring the true perpetrator to justice, and if Smith is unhappy that I have tarnished his name, then as he frequently tells people, he knows where the Law Courts are. Strange that a suit filed in 2005 against me by him for allegedly tarnishing a reputation he thinks he has (see Appendix Ten) has not come to trial.

I leave it to the reader to judge.

Smith first represented Delvina Watson in suit brought against her in 151/152. It is important to note that she does not defend the judgment; she has admitted she owed the money, yet twelve years later he is arguing that she has repaid the money by paying back clients' money that her husband gave her or used for the family's benefit to the same husband and Joyce Griffith nearly five years after they (Watson and Griffith) ceased being partners. But even if, under the Smith doctrine, as former partners they were entitled to the money that partners own clients' accounts, who is to repay the actual clients whose money it was? I guess that is where I became the jackass. He then argues when such a scenario is deemed nonsensical that I have waited too long to enforce the judgement and when this argument is thrown out, he promptly appeals it to the Court of Appeal where it has been stalled for over a year with the result that a person who has admitted they owed the money is now challenging my right to receive the money in the Court of Appeal.

Smith represented Griffith in Suit 1612/1613 until he withdrew, saying I have assaulted him. She loses at first instance as well as at Court of Appeal, at which he is not present, but returns in 2014 in that suit to represent firstly Allan Watson who fails to appear to answer a judgment summons, at which point an arrest warrant is issued for him.

Not satisfied with that, later in 2014 he then appears for Delvina Watson to object to my being granted a charging order over property jointly owned with her husband to settle the debt mentioned above. And what does he do? He argues a point as to the appropriateness of the judgement which should be clearly out of time as the appeal had been dismissed by the Court of Appeal over two years ago, and when it is pointed out that this was done, says he was not in those proceedings. A decision on this is outstanding for fifteen months. Unbelievable, as all the time interest is being added to my debt.

Then in 2015 Smith appears for Delvina and her husband who is still out of the island in all manner of preliminary points to simply stop the final hearing of a claim that money was again used by the two Watsons, during which he accuses me and my attorney Edmund Hinkson of a criminality.

Given all of that and comparing what he alleges are the defamatory words against him in his libel suit of 1123 of 2005 (Appendix 12) does anyone in their right mind not concur with me when I say to him in Bajan parlance "you want locking up"... whatever his crime is.

The End.

Appendix One

B.L.V. GALE, Q.C. LLB. (HON.)
Barrister & Attorney-at-Law
TELEPHONE (246) 427-9264
FAX NO. (246) 429-8056
E-MAIL bgale@aequus-chambers.com
VAT REG# 5402220155

CHAMBERS,
BLADES & WILLIAMS BUILDING,
TWEEDSIDE ROAD,
ST. MICHAEL BB11000,
BARBADOS, WEST INDIES

March 5, 2008

<u>PRIVATE AND CONFIDENTIAL</u>
<u>BY HAND</u>

<u>ATTENTION: MR PHILIP V. NICHOLLS</u>

Cottle Catford & Co
Attorneys at Law
Cnr 2nd Avenue & George Street
Belleville
St Michael

Dear Sir

    I act in association with Karen A Perreira, Attorney at Law on behalf of Elma Kathleen Inniss and Joyce Patricia Bowen, Power of Attorneys for John Patrick Connor and Hazel Sheila Connor respectively.

    I am instructed by my clients that Kynara Roett Banfield, Attorney at Law acting on behalf of Cottle Catford & Co, as Attorneys at Law for the Vendor in the sale of property known as "Golden Dawn", Lots 3 and 4 Lodge Hill, St Michael.

    I am further instructed by my clients that the sale and purchase of the property was completed in or around the month of December 2007 and proceeds of the sale were paid to the account of Cottle Catford & Co as Attorneys at Law on behalf of the Vendor.

    Further, I am instructed, that since the completion of the sale and purchase my clients have been making demand orally and in writing more particularly letters dated February 4, 2008 and February 23, 2008 requesting that Cottle Catford & Co issue a Completion Statement and payment of the balance of the proceeds of sale to my clients.

    My clients are particularly concerned over the non-payment of the balance of proceeds of sale in light of the fact that my clients are aware that the Real Estate Agent, Terra Caribbean was paid a commission on January 29, 2008 without the authorization of my clients or without my clients being provided with a Completion Statement.

Page 2   March 5, 2008

ATTENTION: MR PHILIP V. NICHOLLS

Cottle Catford & Co
Attorneys at Law
Cnr 2nd Avenue & George Street

Further, as was previously communicated to your office the said Real Estate Agent on collection of his cheque from Cottle Catford was informed by your Mr. Nicholls that the balance of the proceeds of sale would be made available to my clients on the afternoon of January 29, 2008. Yet no payments have been made to date.

I am further instructed by my clients that they received a telephone call from a person identifying themselves as Ms. Brewster in the Accounting Department at your office, who requested that my clients accept a cheque representing an amount equivalent to a couple of months rents at the Elderly Care Home for John Connor and Hazel Connor.

My clients find this unacceptable and have been advised that they are entitled to the balance of the proceeds of the sale.

On the 28th February 2008 a Completion Statement was finally sent to my clients but no cheque was enclosed for the monies due.

I am instructed to request from you a cheque in the sum of $861,423.64 representing the proceeds of the sale of the property within seven (7) days of the date of this letter hereof failing which I will take such further action against you to protect my clients' interest without further notice.

I look forward to your co-operation in having this matter settled amicably.

Yours truly

BARRY L.V. GALE, QC

cc: Ms. Marcia Stabler

Appendix Two

Cottle Catford & Co.
ATTORNEYS-AT-LAW

PARTNER
PHILIP V. NICHOLLS LL.B (Hons) UWI, LL.M (Manch)

ASSOCIATES
JULIE N. K. HARRIS HILL LL.B (Hons) UWI, LL.M Warwick
SHARRON C. GODDARD B.A. (UWI), LL.B (Hons) Buckingham

CONSULTANT
SIR NEVILLE V. NICHOLLS K.A. B.A. Econ (Cantab)

IN REPLY PLEASE QUOTE:
Our Ref: PVN\mb

29 September 2008

Mr. Barry Gale Q.C
Attorney-at-Law
Hastings, Attorneys-at-Law
Cnr. St. Matthias Gap & Highway 7
Hastings
CHRIST CHURCH

Dear Sir,

Re: Funds due John Connor et ux

I have for response our telephone conversation this morning which, to be frank, can only be described as muted. You indicated to me that you were now at the end of your tether with this matter and was exasperated at what you saw and perceived as my lack of professional courtesy in responding to your calls and letters on the subject. I explained to you that to the best of my recollection I have returned, or attempted to return all calls that were brought to my attention. At times I have had those calls returned on my behalf and this may relate principally to responding in writing because I have been advised that I am too emotionally involved in this matter to be the one responding. That point was made to me again today, less than 30 minutes prior to your call, in a conversation with Mr. Justice Williams whom, since May, has been trying to provide the sort of mediation role in the problems facing this Firm that all the Senior Practitioners in this island, including yourself, have refused and neglected to do despite my pleas for help.

In your conversation you first intimated and then accused me outright as "a thief of client funds". You further stated that I was using Mr. Watson as a "smokescreen" for the problems that I am facing. I do not know which allegation was the most unkind, the most callous, or the most unbecoming of a person whose present stature at the Bar has been built on a foundation of substantial assistance, work and contacts that were passed to you by a former late Senior Partner of this Firm.

When the current problem that I am facing arose, one that I have been facing repeatedly for the past six years, I attempted to convey to you some of the problems that I am facing. For you to now simply state that what I have been saying is merely an attempt on my part to use Mr. Watson as a "smokescreen" either suggests that the legal ability that you are given credence for is sadly lacking, or that you simply do not care.

P. O. BOX 63
ALPHONZO HOUSE
CNR. 2ND AVENUE & GEORGE STREET
BELLEVILLE, ST. MICHAEL,
BARBADOS, BB11000

TEL: (246) 435-2315
FAX: (246) 435-2270
EMAIL: lawcott@caribsurf.com

Cottle Catford & Co.

Page 2
29 September 2008
Mr. Barry Gale Q.C

Let me try and make it as simple for you as possible:- *The Partners of a Firm are collectively liable for the debts of the Firm.* I am therefore stunned that you could be so insultingly and abusively dismissive.

When the previous Partnership ended in December 2002 I took over a bank account that had less than $100,000.00. Payables stood nominally at approximately $4,000,000.00. We all know, however, that when receivables are set off the figure would be reduced, and that all Payables were not immediately due. Still, I am sure that even you would admit that the disparity between the two figures was startling. Unaudited accounts showed that the three Partners themselves owed the Firm, in the case of Mr. Watson approximately 1.75 million, in the case of Ms Griffith 1.25 million, and me the undersigned just under $1 million. There were miscellaneous fees due to be credited to their accounts of which only the fee for the Kingsland Estates' litigation was substantial and this was only settled years later at about $1.5 million. When apportioned the Kingsland Estates fee was applied to the amounts due by each Partner but, as stated above, these fees were only received in April 2006, four years after the Partnership ended. This meant that between December 2002 and April 2006, I had to find the funds to satisfy the clients' demands.

While all the Partners would have been jointly liable for the debts, as it became increasingly clear over this period that neither Ms. Griffith nor Mr. Watson would face their liability, I was forced to institute a series of legal actions against them and against Mrs. Watson who had, herself, spent over $300,000.00 in Cottle Catford clients' funds. These actions have been "defended" by a series of legitimate and mostly illegitimate means particularly at the hands of Mr. Vernon Smith Q.C, but with the connivance of your Partner, Leslie Haynes Q.C, the only purpose of which has been to stall, frustrate and erode at my attempts to recover the debts owed to the Partnership.

The result of this has been that I have been forced to keep borrowing to make up the commitments to clients. It has proven impossible for me to borrow quickly enough and enough money to cover the entire shortfall due from Mr. Watson and Ms. Griffith, with the result that the inevitable has happened where 'Peter has been paying for Paul'.

As for your admonition that I start a separate Clients account, this I did, and very quickly the claims on Cottle Catford outgrew this. The standard refrain from clients was and is that they are dealing with Cottle Catford and recognise no distinction between High Street or Belleville, far less who the present partners are.

So while I was being forced to pay others because of the defalcations of a present Associate, partner, or employee of yours, Lawyers, including your Partner were giving succor to Mr. Watson and using his services for direct benefit in their practice. I have lost count of the number of times your Partner has said that he would forward to me fees Mr. Watson earned in part-payment of his debt. This he has never done, leaving me to question whether the relationship between your Partner and my former Partner is really simply an employer/employee one. However I will reserve further comments on that relationship and, indeed, the present one for if and when it becomes necessary in another domain.

Cottle Catford & Co.
Page 3
29 September 2008
Mr. Barry Gale Q.C

The fact remains, however, that funds are due and funds that I am committed to repaying. Over the last three months I have seen refusals of requests by the traditional lenders to fund me any more on the basis that there appears to be no end in sight to my attempts at recovering the funds due from Mr. Watson and Ms. Griffith, something which even a blind man on a trotting horse can see is the root cause of this problem. Those who do not want to see that either have their own agenda or are just blinded to the truth.

So while I am under the barrel to your clients for $800,000.00 plus interest, they combined owe me just over two million dollars plus interest, with interest on three million for the years 2003 to 2006. In addition Mr. Watson and/or his wife owe an additional amount of just under $300,000.00 for funds that he allowed her to use from the Client funds, funds that I have had to repay, funds that every effort is made by Mr. Vernon Smith Q.C. at stopping me realize, but funds that you state are irrelevant towards my ability to repay the amounts due to clients.

Should you care to, searches will reveal that I have Mortgages over either my parents property or that of myself to the tune of nearly $2 million. I have unsecured loans also of about $300,000.00 and yet the net amount due by me to the Partnership stood at approximately $500,000.00. And you have the nerve to say that I have stolen the money?

I learnt from you today that Mr. Connor had passed. I was saddened that you saw it fit to so readily cast blame on me for causing or being party to his death, but at the same time you dismiss as totally irrelevant the status of Mr. Watson, your employee, Partner or Associate in the matter. Nothing has pained me more than the fact that the clients concerned or relatives of them are close personal friends of my parents. Do you think I have simply pocketed the money and gone off into the west? Trust me, when the final sordid story of Cottle Catford is told, whether it be by me, or, if I am not able to, by one of my close friends, the whole world will know the full story, including the part played by the whole Legal System and one or two Lawyers in particular who have blindly turned an eye to the problem, so that six years after, not only is it not solved, but the individuals who have caused the problem are freely practicing, and a Senior Member of this profession has the temerity to not only call me a thief but using the most vulgar language possible. If not for the fact that a lady was typing this I would reply similarly to you!

However, you have given a deadline and should I fail to meet it you will proceed as you must. I had indicated through my Attorney to Karen Perriera that placing a Judgment on record will make it all but impossible for me to attempt to raise the funds I need, but this apparently was me being difficult in not trying to deal with the issue. I am sure you will appreciate that in defending myself and name I will be at liberty to use what ever facts I deem relevant at that time.

Yours faithfully,

cc Sir Neville Nicholls
    Mrs. Yvette Lemonias-Seale
    Mrs. Dawn Holder-Alert
    Mr. Leslie Haynes
    Ms. Marcia Stabler

Appendix Three

HASTINGS ATTORNEYS-AT-LAW
Trident Insurance Financial Centre
Corner of St Matthias Gap & Highway 7, Hastings
Christ Church, BB15156, Barbados, W.I.
Telephone: (246) 228-9420/427-9264/435-2325
Facsimile: (246) 429-8056

Partners:
Barry L.V. Gale, Q.C, LLB (Hons)
Leodean Worrell, LLB (Hons)

Associates:
Jacqueline R. Chacko, BA (Hons), LLM
Laura F. Harvey-Read, LLB (Hons)
Taisha C. Corbin, LLB (Hons)

COPY

Ref: BG – Connor and Connor

22nd October 2013

The Commissioner of Police
Police Headquarters
Lower Roebuck Street
BRIDGETOWN

Dear Sir,

Re: Mrs. Kathleen Inniss re Mr. Philip Nicholls and Mrs. Hazel Connor and Mr. John Connor

We refer to the captioned and to the undersigned's letter of 30th July 2013 and set out below the payments made by Mr. Philip Nicholls in his attempt to repay the monies which he wrongfully appropriated from our clients in the sum BDS$861,672.00:

28th October 2008	$100,000.00
19th June 2009	$10,000.00 (this cheque was returned by the bank with "Refer to Drawer" stamped thereon)
10th September 2009	$10,000.00
29th October 2009	$5,000.00 (this cheque was returned by the bank with "Refer to Drawer" stamped thereon)
9th December 2009	$15,000.00
18th May 2010	$10,500.00
15th November 2010	$15,000.00
28th February 2011	$15,000.00
12th December 2011	$7,000.00
9th January 2012	$15,000.00
Total paid	$187,500.00

Mr. Philip Nicholls has failed and/or refused to pay any further payments towards the amount outstanding which now stands in the sum of BDS$674,172.00.

Appendix Four

17th April 2001

Mr. Allan Watson
Cottle Catford & Co.
No. 17 High Street
Bridgetown

Dear Mr. Watson

On my return to office on Tuesday 10th April 2001 I asked Rosalind, Doria and Alex to meet with me to ascertain their feelings towards the presentation we had received at Lex Caribbean on the 28th March 2001. As the Test Match and then my trip to Canada had intervened, I had not had the opportunity to discuss it with them prior to this.

As a result of my discussion with the three Associates, I have decided to write you as Senior Partner to ascertain where exactly you stand on the question of the merger with Lex. My discussions with the three have left me with the feeling that I may be somewhat premature in assuming that a merger has been agreed, contrary to the position suggested in previous discussions between us.

To allow us to proceed with confidence therefore, it is imperative that the Partnership make an unambiguous determination as to exactly where we stand. You will be aware that over the last six months I have tried to broker a deal that would see the firm merging with Lex to the benefit of all concerned, after being personally approached to join Lex as a Partner.

I am sure that, as someone who has his pulse on the local business community, you would be aware that the Lex offer can not remain on the table indefinitely. Therefore, in light of the presentation made to the Partners and the Associates at the meeting in March, I think that we must now make and communicate a clear decision in response to Lex's invitation to merge.

Time is of the essence and I would therefore appreciate your response as to how we are to proceed in the future within the next twenty four hours. I have a number of business meetings out of the office during this time but will make myself available at short notice to discuss this matter with you if desired.

Yours sincerely

Philip

Appendix Five

Cottle Catford & Co.
ATTORNEYS-AT-LAW

PARTNER
PHILIP V. NICHOLLS LL.B (Hons) UWI, LL.M (Manch)

ASSOCIATES
DORIA M. MOORE LL.B (Hons) UWI
ALEXANDRIA R. JULES B.A. (Hons), LL B (Hons) UWI

CONSULTANTS
SIR NEVILLE V. NICHOLLS K.A. B.A. Econ (Cantab)
ALLAN SLC. WATSON, BCH

IN REPLY PLEASE QUOTE:

Our Ref: PVN/jch

18 June 2003

Mrs Delvina Watson
Lot 2
Long Bay
St. Philip

Dear Mrs. Watson,

I am writing to you as a last resort with respect to your indebtedness to Cottle Catford & Co. I had a conversation with you earlier this year but neither that nor the several conversations I have had with Mr. Watson have lead to any reduction in the debt due to Cottle Catford & Co. by you. As at 12th June 2003, our books show the following deficit accounts:

A/c no. 30559 - Mrs. Delvina Watson et al - $259,256.52 o/d

A/c no. 3709 - Estate Muriel O. Weekes - $38,510.58 o/d

A/c no. 30365 - Estate Muriel O. Weekes - $8,862.83 o/d

These debts have been in our books for some years and in the case of account no. 30559, this debt appears to be as a result of an account that was being run as a personal bridging and/or chequing account by you and your husband.

As you know, the Partnership of which your husband was Senior Partner came to an end at the end of December 2002. At that time all moneys due to the Partnership should have been settled. Mr. Watson indicated at that time he was unable to settle his indebtedness and it was agreed that he would put in place plans to arrive at short, medium and long term solutions regarding financing his debt.

P. O. BOX 63
WARRENS GREAT HOUSE
WARRENS
ST. MICHAEL, BARBADOS

TEL: (246) 421-9618
FAX: (246) 421-9623
EMAIL: lawcott@caribsurf.com

Mrs. Delvina Watson 2 18 June 2003

During the last six months, I have been unable to get any concrete proposal from Mr. Watson regarding the repayment of this debt. In fact I can say without fear of contradiction, that since I insisted at the end of July 2001 that account 30559 be closed, not a cent has been repaid despite acknowledgments by Mr. Watson that the funds should not have been used in the manner that they were.

The situation that faces me in that over $300,000 in clients' funds has been utilised for payments for the benefit of you and Mr. Watson. Such use is illegal and could lead to disbarment of the Attorney who authorised same. Mr. Watson is well aware of this.

Within the last month Mr. Watson has indicated to me that he is unable to repay this debt which though large, is insignificant compared to the over $1,300,000 overdrawings he is charged with repaying. With this admission, I am left with no alternative but to seek to recover the money from the persons who have used it or for whose benefit it was spent.

Accordingly I am enclosing copies of cheques either made payable to you or in relation to the construction work done at your property in Hastings. The total of these cheques amount to $226,820.72. Additionally, mortgage payments were made to Globe Finance in the amount of $27,257.80, half of which ($13,628.90) may be attributable to you.

I must add that I have been finding it increasingly difficult to meet the existing demands to finance the deficit of the old Partnership and though I have been very patient in my actions to date, I am no longer prepared to allow the debt of other individuals to jeopardise my professional livelihood, especially when these individuals are making no effort to repay same.

Please let me have a firm response by Monday 30th June 2003 outlining:

1. What plans you have for repayment of this debt.

2. The length of time it will take to repay this debt; and

3. Whether you would be willing to sign an agreement acknowledging that you are indebted to Cottle Catford & Co.

Should I not hear from you by the 30th, I will consider myself free to take whatever action is necessary to recover these monies. Please act now and avoid potential embarrassment for us all.

Yours faithfully,

c.c. Mr. Allan Watson

Encs.

Appendix Six

COTTLE CATFORD & COMPANY

PAYMENTS MADE BY MR. PHILIP V NICHOLLS FOR THE PERIOD 2002 - 2007
DATED NOVEMBER 29, 2007.

2002

DATE	AMOUNT	RECEIPT NO.
1/25/2002	25,000.00	19018
3/15/2002	94.33	19456
3/22/2002	7,637.97	19190
5/2/2002	113.88	19579
5/7/2002	279.20	19305
5/29/2002	139.41	19649
6/19/2002	606.46	19808
7/31/2002	369.03	19903
8/8/2002	3,267.17	19919
8/13/2002	134.91	20027
8/20/2002	5,000.00	19934
8/21/2002	298.46	20046
8/22/2002	93.90	19943
9/20/2002	277.78	20134
10/10/2002	100,000.00	20185
10/21/2002	102.70	20288
11/20/2002	92.92	20359
12/9/2002	383.13	20110
12/31/2002	971.97	20570
Total	144,863.22	

2003

DATE	AMOUNT	RECEIPT NO.
6/16/2003	7,604.35	21298
2/7/2003	50,000.00	20683
2/26/2003	150.00	20840
3/11/2003	10,000.00	21250
3/12/2003	6,000.00	21254
4/7/2003	226.74	20915
4/9/2003	402.50	20919
5/9/2003	302.36	20950
5/16/2003	344.00	21168
5/26/2003	273.32	20979
5/27/2003	75,000.00	20753
6/5/2003	486.68	20995
6/8/2003	302.36	21509
6/13/2003	302.36	21426
7/7/2003	302.36	21460
7/21/2003	943.34	21497
7/21/2003	400.00	21495
8/25/2003	786.56	21749
9/29/2003	604.72	21591
9/29/2003	3,677.25	21595
10/17/2003	4,572.40	22020
10/21/2003	1,162.78	22024
Total	163,844.08	

2004

DATE	AMOUNT	RECEIPT NO.
1/19/2004	1209.00	22143
1/19/2004	257.99	22142
5/7/2004	1066.02	22574
6/18/2004	2000.00	22622
9/16/2004	355.34	22739
10/26/2004	5000.00	22759
11/29/2004	2368.02	23044
11/29/2004	131.98	23046
6/29/2004	175000.00	22567
Total	187388.35	

2005

DATE	AMOUNT	RECEIPT NO.
1/4/2005	60,000.00	23824
2/8/2005	1,160.00	23118
3/8/2005	2,878.60	23148
3/11/2005	1,500.00	23230
4/6/2005	164,892.50	23182
6/17/2005	25,000.00	23356
6/27/2005	18,000.00	23360
7/18/2005	9,000.00	23382
10/26/2005	500.00	23686
10/28/2005	1,600.00	23688
11/4/2005	400.00	23577
11/6/2005	300.00	23591
11/11/2005	300.00	23579
11/16/2005	2,500.00	23710
11/16/2005	381.35	23709
11/18/2005	2,000.00	23713
12/8/2005	1,405.00	23726
12/29/2005	85,000.00	23820
Total	376,817.45	

2006

DATE	AMOUNT	RECEIPT NO.
1/10/2006	5000.00	23830
3/3/2006	60,000.00	23870
3/5/2006	350.00	23869
3/15/2006	1000.00	23883
3/20/2006	2000.00	23798
3/24/2006	600.00	24003
3/24/2006	374.82	24004
4/6/2006	1000.00	23899
4/18/2006	3200.00	23908
5/9/2006	710.68	24049
5/22/2006	250.00	23922
5/31/2006	525.00	24069
6/6/2006	355.34	24084
6/15/2006	35000.00	24085
6/16/2006	600.00	23940
6/19/2006	1500.00	24086
6/20/2006	300.00	23943
6/26/2006	1600.00	23948
6/28/2006	580.00	23994
6/29/2006	844.00	24098
6/30/2006	1200.00	23953
9/6/2006	10000.00	24203
9/6/2006	5505.85	24202

2007

DATE	AMOUNT
4/23/2007	2,600.00
5/8/2007	425,847.14
5/8/2007	74,152.86
6/20/2007	433.33
8/14/2007	1,000.00
9/12/2007	3,000.00
9/15/2007	1,000.00
10/26/2007	1,000.00
10/30/2007	8,500.00
10/31/2007	3,000.00
11/7/2007	400.00
11/14/2007	3,000.00
11/15/2007	550.00
Total	524483.33

2006 Continued

DATE	AMOUNT	RECEIPT NO.
9/6/2006	32600.00	24211
9/7/2006	35000.00	24201
9/8/2006	1000.00	24173
9/11/2006	2000.00	24207
9/12/2006	1080.00	24177
9/18/2006	5750.00	24180
10/13/2006	6100.00	24256
6/6/2007	1600.00	24076
Total	217625.69	

Overall Total — Jan 25th 2002 - Nov 15th 2007

$ 1,807,772.31

Cheques 2003 - 2007

DATE	AMOUNT	CHEQUE NO.
5/27/2003	28009	708
11/2/2005	23000	146
1/24/2006	1000	247
5/29/2006	50000	204
6/5/2006	60000	193
6/6/2006	25000	205
4/23/2007	2000	226
4/30/2007	500	230
5/16/2007	476.26	239
7/4/2007	1000	216
7/26/2007	764.93	255
8/22/2007	1000	273
Total	192750.19	

Appendix Seven

Schedule "A"

Cottle Catford & Co
Payments made by Philip V Nicholls for the period November 15th 2007 to April 30th 2009

Date	Amount	Receipt No.
November 15th 2007	$ 3,000.00	24545
November 29th 2007	$ 800.00	24711
December 4th 2007	$ 1,000.00	24555
December 12th 2007	$ 300.00	24579
April 24th 2008	$ 487,203.97	18747
June 19th 2008	$ 266.04	24824
June 24th 2008	$ 1,250.00	24829
July 28th 2008	$ 1,250.00	24880
August 6th 2008	$ 2,000.00	24895
October 7th 2008	$ 11,000.00	24955
December 3rd 2008	$ 4,500.00	25025
January 27th 2009	$ 1,500.00	25100
January 27th 2009	$ 1,250.00	25101
February 17th 2009	$ 1,300.00	25128
February 27th 2009	$ 8,800.00	25139
April 4th 2009	$ 53,500.00	25209
April 30th 2009	$ 1,000.00	25215
Total	$ 579,920.01	

January 25th 2002 to November 15th 2007-$1,807,772.31
November 15th 2007 to April 30th 2009-$579,920.01

Total Payments-$2,387,692.32

Schedule "B"

List of persons Interest has been paid to and is payable to as at April 30th 2009

Names	Interest Amount
	$ 2,360.97
	$ 70,760.24
	$ 6,047.41
	$ 50,203.42
	$ 37,557.63
	$ 98,219.33
	$ 28,758.91
	$ 7,619.23
	$ 3,489.31
	$ 12,727.99
	$ 53,604.72
	$ 103,375.20
	$ 18,677.75
	$ 25,530.70
	$ 94,493.52
	$ 1,748.45
	$ 2,095.10
	$ 4,117.25
	$ 219.60
	$ 6,042.34
	$ 14,416.40
	$ 1,502.98
	$ 33,153.33
	$ 16,800.00
	$ 24,440.93
	$ 632.32
	$ 14,540.81
	$ 2,589.65
	$ 995.07
	$ 54,653.39
	$ 14,414.88
	$ 317,223.71
Total	**$ 1,123,012.54**

Appendix Eight

BARBADOS

IN THE SUPREME COURT OF JUDICATURE

HIGH COURT

Civil Division

Suit No: 1612/1613 of 2005

BETWEEN

PHILIP VERNON NICHOLLS	-	**PLAINTIFF**

AND

JOYCE GRIFFITH	-	**1st DEFENDANT**
ALLAN ST. CLAIR WATSON	-	**2nd DEFENDANT**

Before The Honourable Madam Justice Maureen Crane-Scott, Q.C.
Judge of the High Court
(In Chambers)

2009: May 15, 27;
     June 2, 22, 23, 29;
     July 13; 24
     August 10, 11, 18, 21;
     September 10, 11, 17.

Mr. Edmund Hinkson and Mrs. Julie Harris Hill of Cottle Catford & Co for the Plaintiff
The First and Second Defendants appearing in person

Order:

Consequent on the decision of the Court in relation to the 2 issues in dispute referred for the Court's decision relating to i) overdrawings and ii) David Bristow's fee, IT IS HEREBY ORDERED as follows:

1.) The Accounts of the former partnership of Cottle Catford & Co. between the Plaintiffs and the Defendants prepared by Mr. Carlyle Forde as contained in the following documents, namely,

 i. **Statement of Funds available at December 31, 2002 and Funds Received and Paid after December 31, 2002 (with Supporting Schedules)** updated as at August 26th 2009 and filed herein on the 8th day of September, 2009 and subsequently amended with leave of the Court on September 14, 2009 and filed herein on the 14th day of September, 2009;

 ii. **Updated Debit and Credit Account Working List** as at the 28th day of July, 2009, 2009 and filed herein on the 29th day of July, 2009;

 iii. **Detailed List of Funds received from Clients of the Former Partnership for 2003/2004** as at the 23rd day of July, 2009 and filed herein on the 29th day of July, 2009;

 iv. **List of Accounts to be placed in Contingency Liability Account** as listed in the *"Statement of Affairs following adjustment to Clients' Balances"* referred to at paragraph 2(ii) of this order;

 v. **Schedule of Clients balances paid by Philip Nicholls from funds received of $1,333,000.00** (other than those shown on the payments to Clients in 2003 and 2004" attached to the affidavit of Philip Vernon Nicholls filed with leave of the Court on September 14, 2009, having been certified by Mr. Carlyle A. Forde, Chartered Accountant and having been settled by the Plaintiff, the First Defendant and the Second Defendant, be and are hereby adopted as the settled Accounts of the Former Partnership;

2.) The undermentioned Accounts of the former partnership of Cottle Catford & Co. between the Plaintiffs and the Defendants having been certified by Mr. Carlyle A. Forde, Chartered Accountant which are set out in the following documents, namely,

i. **Partners' Capital and Current Account (Over-drawings)** updated as at the 26th day of August, 2009 and filed herein on the 8th day of September, 2009; and

ii. **Statement of Affairs following adjustment to clients' Balances** updated as at the 26th day of August and filed herein on the 8th day of September, 2009

having <u>not</u> been settled by the parties, but having, at their request, been settled by the Court, are amended by deletion from the account referred to at i.) of this paragraph of all references to the sum of $78,106.00 being the legal fees paid to Mr. David Bristow. In consequence of the said amendment, the total over-drawings standing in the name of the First Defendant are declared to be $441,576.00 while the total over-drawings of the Second Defendant are declared to be $661,541.00. The accounts of the former partnership identified at i.) and ii.) of this paragraph having been adjusted by the Court as aforesaid, shall be and are hereby also confirmed and declared as the settled Accounts of the Former Partnership;

3.) Judgment for the Plaintiff be and is hereby entered against the First Defendant in the sum of $441,576.00 certified in the accounts of the former partnership to be due by the First Defendant to the former partnership and to the Plaintiff together with interest thereon at the rate of 4 % per annum from the date of service of the Writ to the date hereof and at the rate of 8 % per annum from the date hereof until satisfaction;

4.) Judgment for the Plaintiff be and is hereby entered against the Second Defendant in the sum of $661,541.00 certified in the accounts of the former partnership to be due by the Second Defendant to the former partnership and consequently to the Plaintiff together with interest thereon at the rate of 4 % per annum from the date of service of the Writ to the date hereof and at the rate of 8% per annum from the date hereof until satisfaction;

5.) The client balances of the former partnership settled by the parties and certified in the amount of $407,622.00 and identified in the document entitled **Statement of Affairs following adjustment to Client Balances** referred to at paragraph 1(iv) of this Order shall be transferred to a Contingency Liability Account to be funded by the Plaintiff, the First Defendant and the Second Defendant in proportion to their respective shares in the former partnership and shall be operated on such terms and conditions as shall be approved by the Court. In this regard, there is liberty to apply;

6.) The reasonable professional fees, disbursements and expenses of Mr. Carlyle Forde, Chartered Accountant incurred in connection with this application shall be paid by the Plaintiff, the First Defendant and the Second Defendant in proportion to their respective shares in the former partnership within 21 days of the presentation by Mr. Carlyle A. Forde of his Invoice.

7.) The Plaintiff is awarded his costs of the application certified fit for one attorney-at-law to be agreed or taxed.

8.) There shall be liberty to apply generally.

Maureen Crane-Scott
Judge of the High Court

Approved

H.C.J.
17/9/2009

IN THE HIGH COURT OF JUSTICE

CIVIL DIVISION

BETWEEN:

PHILIP VERNON NICHOLLS   PLAINTIFF

AND

JOYCE GRIFFITH   FIRST DEFENDANT
ALLAN ST. CLAIR WATSON   SECOND DEFENDANT

ORDER

BEFORE the Honourable Madam Justice Maureen Crane-Scott Q.C. Judge of the High Court in Chambers on the 15th & 27th May 2009, 2nd, 22nd, 23rd & 29th June 2009, 13th July 2008, 10th, 11th, 18th & 21st August 2009 and 10th, 11th & 17th September 2009.

Entered on the 21st day of September 2009.

UPON the Parties appearing before the Judge for the hearing of the Plaintiff's Summons filed herein on the 30th day of April, 2009 AND UPON HEARING Mr. Edmund Hinkson and Mrs. Julie Harris Hill of Cottle Catford & Co. Attorneys-at-Law for the Plaintiff AND UPON HEARING the First and Second Defendants appearing in person.

Consequent on the decision of the Court in relation to the 2 issues in dispute referred for the Court's decision relating to i) overdrawings and ii) David Bristow's fee IT IS HEREBY ORDERED as follows:

1. The Accounts of the Former Partnership of Cottle Catford & Co. between the Plaintiff and the Defendants prepared by Mr. Carlyle Forde as contained in the following documents, namely:

    I. Statement of Funds available at December 31, 2002 and Funds Received and Paid after December 31, 2002 (with Supporting Schedules) updated

2009 and filed herein on the 14th day of September, 2009;

ii. Updated Debit and Credit Accounts Working List as at the 28th day of July, 2009 and filed herein on the 29th day of July, 2009;

iii. Detailed List of Funds received from Clients of the Former Partnership for 2003/2004 as at the 23rd day of July, 2009 and filed herein on the 29th day of July, 2009;

iv. List of Accounts to be placed in Contingency Liability Account as listed in the "*Statement of Affairs following adjustment to Clients' Balances*" referred to at paragraph 2(ii) of this Order;

v. Schedule of Clients' balances paid by Philip Nicholls from funds received of $1,333,000.00 (other than those shown on the payments to Clients in 2003 and 2003") attached to the Affidavit of Philip Vernon Nicholls filed with leave of the Court on September 14, 2009.

having been certified by Mr. Carlyle A. Forde, Chartered Accountant, and having been settled by the Plaintiff, the First Defendant and the Second Defendant, be and are hereby adopted as the settled Accounts of the Former Partnership;

2. The undermentioned Accounts of the Former Partnership of Cottle Catford & Co. between the Plaintiff and the Defendants having been certified by Mr. Carlyle A. Forde, Chartered Accountant, which are set out in the following documents, namely:

i. Partners' Capital and Current Account (Overdrawings) updated as at the 26th day of August, 2009 and filed herein on the 8th day of September, 2009; and

ii. Statement of Affairs following adjustment to clients' Balances updated as at the 26th day of August, 2009 and filed herein on the 8th day of September, 2009

having not been settled by the parties, but having, at their request, been settled by the Court, are amended by deletion from the account referred to at i) of this paragraph of all references to the sum of $78,106.00 being the legal fees paid to while the total overdrawings of the Second Defendant are declared to be $661,541.00. The Accounts of the Former Partnership identified at i) and ii.) of this paragraph having been adjusted by the Court as aforesaid, shall be and are hereby also confirmed and declared as the settled Accounts of the Former Partnership;

3. Judgment for the Plaintiff be and is hereby entered against the First Defendant in the sum of $441,576.00 certified in the Accounts of the Former Partnership to be due by the First Defendant to the former Partnership and to the Plaintiff together with interest thereon at the rate of 4% per annum from the date of service of the Writ to the date hereof and at the rate of 8% per annum from the date hereof until satisfaction;

4. Judgment for the Plaintiff be and is hereby entered against the First Defendant in the sum of $661,541.00 certified in the accounts of the former Partnership to be due by the Second Defendant to the former Partnership and consequently to the Plaintiff together with interest thereon at the rate of 4% per annum from the date of service of the Writ to the date hereof and at the rate of 8% per annum from the date hereof until satisfaction;

5. The client balances of the former Partnership settled by the parties and certified in the amount of $407,622.00 and identified in the document entitled Statement of Affairs following adjustment to Client Balances referred to at paragraph 1(iv) of this Order shall be transferred to a Contingency Liability Account to be funded by the Plaintiff, the First Defendant and the Second Defendant in proportion to their respective shares in the former Partnership and shall be operated on such terms and conditions as shall be approved by the Court. In this regard, there is liberty to apply;

6. The reasonable professional fees, disbursements and expenses of Mr. Carlyle Forde, Chartered Accountant incurred in connection with this application shall be paid by the Plaintiff, the First Defendant and the Second Defendant in proportion to their respective shares in the Former Partnership within 21 days of the presentation by Mr. Carlyle A. Forde of this Invoice

7. The Plaintiff is awarded his costs of the application certified fit for one Attorney-at-Law to be agreed or taxed;

8. There shall be liberty to apply generally.

Dated the 21st day of September, 2009.

_____
Dep REGISTRAR

Appendix Nine

PHILIP V. NICHOLLS

35 Plover Court, Inch Marlow, Christ Church, Barbados
Telephone: (246) 428-1931 • Fax: (246) 418-9087 • e-mail: nichls_p@caribsurf.com

September 30, 2001

Mr. Allan Watson
Ms Joyce Griffith
Cottle Catford & Co.
No. 17 High Street
Bridgetown

Dear Mr. Watson and Ms Griffith

Please accept this letter as my formal notice to resign from the Partnership and resign my position with Cottle Catford & Co. with effect from midnight on 31st December.

I have been associated with the firm since 1980, (working during the summers of 1980, 1981, 1982, 1983, 1984 and 1985, joining in a more continuous position on January 11th, 1987 and finally becoming a Partner since 1992) – a period of almost twenty-one years – and this is one of the most difficult decisions that I ever had to make. However, after long and careful consideration, I believe that it is the right decision which would augur well for both my growth in the profession of law and personally.

I hope that my leaving will also precipitate the major reorganization that the firm has recognized that it will need in order to survive in the millennium and I wish you every success. I would now like to make a few observations, many of which must be addressed before the date of my departure on December 31st 2001.

As you both know, the firm of Lex Caribbean approached me at the end of August 2000 with an extremely attractive offer to join that institution as a Partner. I could have immediately accepted this offer and secured the peace of mind that we all strive for with regards to our future financial security for ourselves and our family. However, I have always had a keen sense of preserving where possible Cottle Catford & Co. and because of my long association with Cottle Catford I felt that this was an excellent opportunity as an entity to attempt to broker a merger between the two firms, which could only be a win-win situation for both. I felt that I owed it to our many long serving staff since such a merger would bring much needed new life into our firm and guarantee its survival.

The offer made to me was attractive enough for me to just take it and walk away but I considered that a proposal to merge with Lex would be a lifesaver for Cottle Catford which needed some resuscitation, and Lex was willing to consider such a merger. Therefore, in the following months, I was frankly dismayed and disappointed that you did not appreciate the spirit in which I acted nor the benefits of this proposal made not just to me, but to the entire firm. From the beginning, you both immediately had reservations about it and were reluctant to consider the immediate and long-term benefits to Cottle Catford as a whole. However, it was my genuine belief that we had really no option if we wanted the core of Cottle Catford to survive long into the 21st Century.

In March of this year, you gave me cause to be fairly confident that we had been able to overcome the misgivings on your part and that and we were on the road to reaching a consensus on a merger. We had an important and crucial meeting with Lex, which introduced all the Associates to the idea of a potential merger. Unfortunately, for reasons not clear to me, we made no progress in formulating the proposed. Nothing significant transpired after the meeting with Lex and you seemed to have lost any interest in the proposed merger. After trying to ascertain from you by letter dated April 17th as to your intentions I was forced to give notice of my intention to leave by letter dated April 24th with my departure date being scheduled for 31st July.

Within a couple of weeks of that letter, there appeared to be renewed enthusiasm amongst both of you for the merger, an enthusiasm that was noted and commented on by Lex and thus the scheduled departure date of 31st July 2001 approached and eventually came and went with Lex and I in the firm belief that the prospects of a Merger were at hand.

During this period, an erroneous payment made by me precipitated a cash flow crisis in the firm. This error was fortuitous because unknown to me at that time, it revealed that we were carrying in addition to our over-drawings, debit accounts of approximately one million dollars ($1.0 m). To say that this realization stunned me is an understatement. I was on the verge of a physical collapse because, while I had always catered for the necessity of putting in place a restructured package to deal with our over drawings, I never for once contemplated that this would be exacerbated by such a deficit.

Knowledge of the debit accounts, or should I state the acute cash flow crisis, that the combination of the debit accounts and the over drawings was causing prompted me to examine critically all areas of our finances.

I feel that the personal debit accounts that are charged to you both need to be critically addressed immediately if only because of their size. Examination of the line items in these accounts reveal unacceptable charges for a typical clients account – I think they speak for themselves. Moreover, it is my view that you both need to redress them immediately since this situation poses severe consequences for all of us, including the personnel of the Accounts Department who did not draw them to the attention of one of the other Partners.

On another note, I refer to our Corporate Credit Card, the status of which I have also examined. The name of the Card speaks for it itself. Its use is presumed to be "corporate" only. It is a card to be used in the conduct of the affairs of the firm and while one is traveling on business for the firm. I really find it incredible that you, Mr. Watson could charge what appear to be **personal** expenses of upward of **US$20,000** to this card for the year to date and you, Ms. Griffith in excess of **US$10,000** and **BDS$14,000** for the same period. This is not what the card was meant for and these charges are in effect unapproved, substantial additional drawings for you both.

On August 6th 2001, I telephoned you, Mr. Watson in New York to advise you of the predicament that we were facing and the urgency of sourcing funds to cover the debit accounts. Knowing that our Bankers automatically debit charges to the Corporate Card to our Clients Account and the strain that this was having on our cash flow, I made the decision to place legitimate charges incurred on business trips to Washington and Miami on my personal cards. It was therefore very upsetting to see substantial charges occurring to Mr. Watson's card after the date of my telephone discussion with him and that personal charges on the said card continued to be placed after he returned home – all this during a difficult cash-flow time for the firm and while I was making the sacrifice not to use the card. To say that this was dispiriting is an understatement.

I have therefore come to the conclusion that in order to be able to repay my over-drawings I will need to obtain a substantial loan from a financial institution and in so doing, will have to satisfy them that I have the ability to service the monthly repayment for said loan. It is clear from the present position that I cannot use our accounts to do this and further, that our accounts would not satisfy the bank's criteria. I must now make other arrangements for employment in order to secure the required finance that I need. Rest assured that I would remain responsible only for those over-drawings and expenses which are properly mine. In this regard I am again requesting an urgent audit of our accounts and for a bill to be to delivered in respect of the Kingsland matters over which Mr.Watson has responsibility.

I have repeatedly pointed out to you both the urgent need not only for a formal audit of our accounts but also the Kingsland billings in order that we may clearly determine our financial situation. It is becoming tiresome to be urging fellow partners who are professionals to concur with this suggested action and it is baffling why this is being resisted or cannot seem to be done.

At our recent meeting *on the 26th September* the only consensus on a way forward was the decision that the firm needed to make a drastic cut in expenditure. In some ways, my leaving should contribute to cost reduction. I have communicated to you both the general feeling of the Associates as expressed to me and whilst I cannot and would not presume to speak for them I think your plans for reorganization should not be based around their presence.

I am acutely conscious of the fact that my departure will have a negative impact on the fortunes of the firm. I will not solicit any clients from Cottle Catford & Co. However, we must recognise that many clients will leave Cottle Catford and some may actively seek my services in the future. I therefore feel that it would be in the interest of the firm that my impending departure not be made public immediately and for some time thereafter. I am also conscious that we would have a lot of unraveling to do not only of entwined finances but also of my various clients. I am committed in this regard to work with you both to ensure that a smooth as possible transition is made over the next few months.

Generally, I enjoyed my tenure at Cottle Catford & Co. and again wish you every success in the future.

Yours sincerely

Philip V. Nicholls

Appendix Ten

WRIT OF SUMMONS
(O. 6, r. 1)

A81:090
(APPENDIX A Form No. 1)

DRAWN & PREPARED BY

Greaves

LISA R. GREAVES
ATTORNEY-AT-LAW
GLADSTONE HOUSE
PINFOLD STREET, BRIDGETOWN

IN THE HIGH COURT OF JUSTICE

20 05 . NO. 1123   CIVIL   DIVISION

BETWEEN

VERNON OLIVIER SMITH   PLAINTIFF

AND

PHILIP VERNON NICHOLLS   DEFENDANT

ELIZABETH THE SECOND, by the grace of God, Queen of Barbados:

TO THE DEFENDANT   [name]   PHILIP VERNON NICHOLLS

of [address]   ALPHONZO HOUSE
CORNER 2ND AVENUE & GEORGE STREET
BELLEVILLE SAINT MICHAEL

THIS WRIT OF SUMMONS has been issued against you by the above-named Plaintiff in respect of the claim set out on the back.

Within *8 days* after the service of this Writ on you, counting the day of service, you must either satisfy the claim or return to the Registry of the Supreme Court, Law Courts, Bridgetown the accompanying ACKNOWLEDGMENT OF SERVICE stating therein whether you intend to contest these proceedings.

If you fail to satisfy the claim or to return the Acknowledgment within the time stated, of if you return the Acknowledgment without stating therein an intention to contest the proceedings, the Plaintiff may proceed with the action and judgment may be entered against you forthwith without further notice.

Issued from the Registry of the Supreme Court this   7th   day of   June   20 05.

Note:— This Writ may not be served later than 12 calendar months beginning with that date unless renewed by Order of the Court.

IMPORTANT
Directions for Acknowledgment of Service are given with the accompanying form.

STATEMENT OF CLAIM

1. The Plaintiff is and was at all material times an attorney-at-law and a solicitor registered to practise in Barbados and carrying on such practice of an attorney-at-law under the firm name Smith & Smith whose office is situate at "Gladstone House" Pinfold Street in the city of Bridgetown in Barbados.

2. The Defendant is an attorney-at-law registered to practise in Barbados and carries on such practice under the firm name of Cottle Catford & Company, attorneys-at-law whose office is situate at Alphonzo House, Corner of 2nd Avenue and George Street Belleville in the parish of Saint Michael in Barbados.

3. On or about the 16th day of March 2005 the Defendant wrote and published, or caused to be written and published the following words contained in a typewritten letter (hereinafter referred to as "the letter") which are defamatory of the Plaintiff:

"In your attempts to frustrate my legitimate attempts to recover these funds you deliberately chose the most infuriatingly obstructive Attorney at the Bar and the one whom you know to have a personal vendetta against me to represent your wife, thereby making it impossible to reach any civilized dialogue on the matter. In fact he has increased my costs to date and I fully intend to add those to my judgment.

"As a result he has been giving his vindictive mouth free reign to publicize the problems of which you are aware but has created the impression that I am the **sole** cause of these problems."

"I further advise that unless you and your wife instruct Mr. Smith to desist from breaching Attorney/Client privilege as he had frequently done by making statements to my father, and secure his commitment in WRITING to do so as well as his undertaking to my satisfaction that he will furnish me with the name of the individuals to whom he has spoken of this matter and clear up **ALL ASPERSIONS CAST AGAINST ME BY FRIDAY MARCH 18, 2005, I WILL PROCEED WITH THE PUBLICATION OF THE ADVERTISEMENT IN THE NEWSPAPER AS I WILL NOT ALLOW MY REPUTATION TO BE SULLIED BY YOUR DELIBERATE INACTION.**

4. These words referred to and are understood to refer to the Plaintiff.

PARTICULARS

(1) Paragraph 1 is repeated.

(2) The Plaintiff is the attorney-at-law on record acting for Mrs. Delvina Watson, the wife of Mr. Allan St. Clair Watson in the matter of the High Court judgments obtained by the Defendant.

5. The letter was dictated by the Defendant to a typist or for transcription by a typist, in the Defendant's employment whom the Plaintiff cannot at present identify.

6. The letter was then sent by hand in an envelope addressed to Mr. Allan St. C. Watson, Attorney-at-Law at his office situate at Equity House Pinfold Street in the city of Bridgetown.

7. At all material times the Defendant knew that the Plaintiff was the legal advisor and consultant to the said Allan St. Clair Watson and was representing his

- 3 -

wife Delvina Watson in a matter of the High Court judgments obtained by the Defendant.

8. In their natural and ordinary meaning the said words meant and were understood to mean:

(a) That the Plaintiff as an officer of the Supreme Court of Barbados was and is acting improperly and unprofessionally by deliberately obstructing the Defendant as a judgment creditor from recovering funds owed to him.

(b) That the Plaintiff was and is acting vindictively and with improper motive in his duties as an officer of the Supreme Court by carrying on a vendetta against the Defendant contrary to section 45 of the Legal Profession "Code of Ethics".

(c) The Plaintiff was and is guilty of conspiracy in acting with Mr. Allan St. Clair Watson and Delvina Watson to deprive the Defendant of the funds owed to him and obstructing the course of justice.

(d) The Plaintiff was and is in breach of the "Attorneys-at-Law Code of Ethics" by defaming the Defendant and casting aspersions on the Defendant's character and professional reputation.

(e) The Plaintiff was guilty of breaching his attorney-at-law/client privilege by divulging his client's secrets and confidences.

(f) The Plaintiff was not a suitable person to practise as a registered attorney-at-law in Barbados.

9. The said words were calculated to disparage the Plaintiff in his said profession and business.

10. In consequence the Plaintiff's reputation has been seriously damaged and he has suffered distress and embarrassment.

11. Unless restrained by the Honourable Court the Defendant will further write or publish or cause to written or published the said or similar words defamatory of the Plaintiff.

AND the Plaintiff claims:

(1) Damages for defamation;

(2) Interest on such damages pursuant to section 35 of the Supreme Court of Judicature Act chapter 117A of the Laws of Barbados at such rate and for such period as the Honourable Court deems just;

(3) An injunction restraining the Defendant whether by himself, his servants or agents or otherwise from further publishing or causing to be published the said or similar words defamatory to the Plaintiff.

(4) Costs.

Dated the 7th day of June 2005.

L. Greaves
LISA R. GREAVES
Attorney-at-Law for the Plaintiff

This Writ of Summons was issued by Lisa R. Greaves, Attorney-at-Law in association with Mr. Hal Gollop, Attorney-at-Law whose address for service is "Gladstone House" Pinfold Street Bridgetown, Attorneys-at-Law for the Plaintiff who resides at "Veronda" Brownes Gap Hastings Christ Church.

Drawn and Prepared by:

Attorney-at-Law of
Inn Chambers
Pinfold Street
Bridgetown
BARBADOS, W. I.

BARBADOS

No. 1123 of 2005

IN THE HIGH COURT OF JUSTICE

CIVIL DIVISION

BETWEEN:

VERNON OLIVIER SMITH   PLAINTIFF

AND

PHILIP VERNON NICHOLLS   DEFENDANT

DEFENCE

1. The Defendant admits paragraphs 1 and 2 of the Statement of Claim.

2. The Defendant admits that he wrote the words complained of in paragraph 3 of the Statement of Claim in a letter dated 16th March, 2005 addressed to Mr Allan Watson, a former Partner with the Defendant in the law firm of Cottle Catford & Co.

3. The Defendant denies that the said words bore or were understood to bear any meaning defamatory of the Plaintiff in that their proper meaning can only be ascertained when the entire letter and previous correspondence passing between the Defendant and Allan Watson are examined.

4. Further or in the alternative, the words complained of in paragraph 3 of the Statement of Claim were published on an occasion of qualified

Allan Watson along with Ms Joyce Griffith are former Partners of the firm which Partnership ceased on the 31st December, 2002.

(2) Mr Allan Watson, the husband of Delvina Watson, who is the Defendant/Judgment Debtor in High Court Actions 151 and 152 of 2004 brought by the Defendant as Plaintiff. As an Attorney-at-Law, the said Allan Watson signed the Acknowledgment of Service for the Delvina Watson in the aforesaid suits.

(3) The Plaintiff claims to be acting for the said Delvina Watson in the said High Court Actions 151 and 152 of 2004, but to date, has not officially informed the Defendant of this fact.

(4) The words complained of were contained in a letter dated 16th March, 2005 addressed to the said Allan Watson marked "PRIVATE AND CONFIDENTIAL" and pertained to the matter of the attempts of Philip Nicholls, Partner of Cottle Catford & Co. to recover funds owing to Cottle Catford & Co. by the said Delvina Watson being funds advanced to her by her husband, a former Senior Partner of Cottle Catford & Co. from the firm's clients' accounts.

(5) In the premises, Mr Philip Nicholls and Mr Allan Watson had a common interest in the subject matter of the letter complained of, and Mr Philip Nicholls wrote the letter complained of in the reasonable protection of his own legitimate interests to Mr Watson who had a like interest in receiving it.

(6) In the premises, the words complained of are protected by an original qualified privilege.

5. Paragraph 4 of the Statement of Claim is denied in that all the words complained of do not refer to the Plaintiffs

7. The Defendant makes no admission as to the formal representation of Delvina Watson by the Plaintiff and denies any knowledge that the Plaintiff is representing Allan Watson in any form or fashion.

8. The Defendant denies paragraphs 8, 9 and 10 of the Plaintiff's Statement of Claim and states further that in relation to paragraph 8 (c) of the Statement of Claim, that the Plaintiff, despite stating that he is the Attorney for the said Delvina Watson has

   (i) refused by letter of 16th February 2005 to accept service of documents on behalf of his purported client;

   (ii) sought and obtained by ex-parte application a Stay of an Order granted by the High Court of this Island to serve the said Delvina Watson by advertisement in the press consequent on the Plaintiff's refusal and the Defendant's inability to find the said Judgment Debtor, thereby further delaying the Defendant's attempts at realizing an undefended judgment obtained over a year ago.

9. Paragraph 11 of the Statement of Claim is denied. The Defendant has no present intention of publishing any of the words of which complaint is made in this action or any words to similar effect. It is further denied that there are any grounds upon which an injunction should be granted.

10. Further, or in the alternative, pursuant to Section 6 of the Defamation Act, 1996, it is alleged that the circumstances of the publication of the words complained of were such that the Plaintiff was not likely to suffer harm to his reputation.

Dated the 14th day of July, 2005.

Attorney-at-Law for the Defendant

Appendix Eleven

ATTORNEYS-AT-LAW

PARTNER
PHILIP V. NICHOLLS LL.B (Hons) UWI, LL.M (Manch)

CONSULTANTS
SIR NEVILLE V. NICHOLLS K.A. B.A. Econ (Cantab)
ALLAN St.C. WATSON, BCH

ASSOCIATES
DORIA M. MOORE LL.B (Hons) UWI
ALEXANDRIA R. JULES B.A. (Hons), LL. B (Hons) UWI

IN REPLY PLEASE QUOTE:

Our Ref: PVN/jch

28 March 2003

FirstCaribbean International Bank
Warrens
St. Michael

Attention: Mr. W. Mark Strang

Dear Sirs,

Re: Your letter of 14th February 2003 on the subject of Cottle Catford & Co.

I have for reply your above-captioned letter.

I make no apology for the delay in responding despite your repeated demands in your letter under reference for an urgent response. This delay has been for a number of reasons but by and large because of my desire to:

(a) allow a period of time to elapse between the receipt of your letter and my response as one should never been too hasty to respond to a letter that may provoke an unwise reply; and

(b) collect the necessary information to allow for an informed response to a number of your ludicrous and unsubstantiated charges.

With respect to (a) I think it only appropriate that I should point out to you a fact that you are apparently unaware of, judging by the tone of your letter and by the fact that you indicate that your association has been with CIBC. This Firm has been in existence for over one hundred years and has during that time, been of service to Barclays Bank as its main legal counsel in Barbados. As our services have been retained over the years, we may be forgiven for thinking

P. O. BOX 63
WARRENS GREAT HOUSE
WARRENS
ST. MICHAEL, BARBADOS

TEL: (246) 421-9618
FAX: (246) 421-9623
EMAIL: lawcott@caribsurf.com

FirstCaribbean International Bank	2	28 March 2003

that there was or has been a general satisfaction with the level of service being rendered by our Firm to the Bank. It should therefore strike one as strange that we would deliberately set out to harm the interests of a client for whom we have acted for over 100 years.

It strikes me as passing strange that someone, who is generally unknown in the professional or business world in Barbados, could be so bold as to make the level of public disparaging remarks that you make in your letter of such an established firm, which would continue for the immediate future to be one of the Attorneys for FirstCaribbean, if only by default.

I must confess that it was with a degree of astonishment that I received what can only be described as your unprofessional, baseless and potentially libelous letter of 14th February.

Several charges were laid in your letter, which charges I will deal with later. However just as you appear to have taken the liberty of sharing our correspondence with others, I have taken that liberty as well. All of the persons with whom I have shared the correspondence including one of our consultants, Sir Neville Nicholls, whom I understand as Chairman of the Securities Exchange Commission, has chaired meetings that you have attended, have expressed disappointment and surprise that such a letter could be written by a professional person.

As Chairman of the Disciplinary Committee of the Barbados Bar Association, it distresses me that the disparaging remarks that you make of our legal competence are being made by someone who though not admitted to practice law in Barbados is holding himself out as entitled so to do. Should you have been admitted to the Bar, questions may be raised as to whether your comments could be considered as a breach of the Code of Ethics which bind all Attorneys licenced to practice in Barbados and which would justify a complaint from the Attorney to whom the remarks were directed. As you are not registered to practice, I would be failing in my duty as Chairman, if I did not draw to the relevant authorities your flagrant flouting of the law in holding yourself out to be an Attorney whilst not licenced to practice.

I now turn to some specific points raised in your letter.

Acting as counsel with respect to the merger agreement

Any first year law student would recognise that a client is free to choose the Attorney of his choice. The staff at Cottle Catford are no different. I therefore take strong exception to this totally ridiculous statement in paragraph two of your letter under reference and challenge you to identify the person or persons who have complained that Cottle Catford was unhappy that they were not retained by Barclays to act on their behalf in the merger. On several occasions

Cottle Catford have complained with justification, that as the Firm dealing with a significant portion of Barclays work in the Island, it had not been officially informed of the state of affairs of the merger after it was made public. To this end, I enclose a copy of a letter dated 8th November 2002 addressed to Mrs. Sandra Applewhaite by the undersigned and draw reference not only to the date of the letter, but to paragraphs four and five therein which contradict your assertion.

Advice to Barclays Branches

Cottle Catford over the last 10 years has given Barclays Bank advice on a variety of subjects. Much of this advice has been rendered without charge and by way of responses to telephone inquiries from various branches to our Mrs. Gale who has in turn consulted respective Attorneys before answering the Bank.

In light of the serious legal consequences that would have followed from the change in any status of Barclays, Cottle Catford, as any prudent Attorney-at-Law would do attempted to ascertain the correct status of Barclays. These attempts were made both verbally and by letter in an attempt to highlight the problems we envisaged would arise as a result of a merger. Despite repeated requests we were never favoured with a definitive response until your sarcastic letter of 14th February and your subsequent letter of 28th February.

In paragraph four of your letter of 14th February, you refer to your letter of 14th October. It is my belief that the letter to which you refer was a circulatory letter that was distributed to the legal profession on that day to advise of the birth of FirstCaribbean. Let me reiterate, AT NO TIME was Cottle Catford favoured with a copy of this letter. This we found incredulous when we heard of its existence through the legal grapevine, as we had work in progress at hand for Barclays Bank. The non-receipt of your letter and many reports of a vesting order prompted our letters of 8th November and again of 24th January seeking clarification on the status of FirstCaribbean, especially as verbal requests were not being productive. You will note in our said letter of 24th January and I refer you to paragraph one of page two, that our opinion therein was expressed to be conditional on the possibility that there may be a vesting order in favour of Barclays. It is therefore disingenuous to say the least of you to conclude that in giving our honest opinion we were in any way acting detrimental to the interests of our client (Barclays Bank) or in a manner deliberately designed to cause them harm.

Vesting Order SI 2002 No. 115 dated 10th October 2002

In your letter of 14th February, you refer to the above-captioned Vesting Order and chide us for not being aware of same prior to your letter of 14th February.

While we will accept the premise that we should have had this come to our attention prior to 14th February in the normal course of events, we do not accept for the reasons alluded to below that in this case we can be considered negligent for not being aware of same. As we had been constantly asking verbally and in writing for information on the merger from the Bank which information was then only known to the Bank and counsel dealing with the merger, it is our opinion that if FirstCaribbean had its house in order this information which was subsequently circulated in a letter dated 28th February some four and a half months after the legal change took effect, would have been communicated to all relevant parties in greater detail than we understand was communicated in your letter of 14th October.

The date of the Statutory Instrument that contains the Vesting Order is October 10th. However this would not have been the actual published date as this would not have occurred for at least a few weeks after 10th October most probably in November. In addition, unless we were actually looking out for this Instrument, in the normal course of events it would be sometime before it came to someone's attention in the Firm. With the then impending Christmas season and our subsequent move of premises, our lack of sight of this document cannot be viewed as a sign of incompetence that you are alleging.

On this subject however we must go further. The Vesting Order refers to "a Share Transfer Agreement made on the 26th day of July 2002 between Barclays Bank Plc, CIBC Caribbean Limited and CIBC West Indies Holding Limited". We have never seen this agreement nor for that matter have many people.

In our respectful opinion the Vesting Order that you refer to is of no use to us in determining the validity of your statements about the status of FirstCaribbean without sight of the agreement referred to therein.

It is our understanding that the contents of this agreement are one of the most closely guarded secrets at FirstCaribbean and as such few persons have had sight of same. As such we would not expect that you would wish make a copy available to us. However as we were never informed of this agreement nor made privy to its contents, we are of the view that you are out of place in condemning us for taking a reasoned legal stance with which you do not agree and which we have indicated may differ if what you allege in the agreement were confirmed.

FirstCaribbean International Bank　　　　　5　　　　　　　　　　28 March 2003

In light of the above, we can only describe your purported legal opinion on page two of your letter of 14th February as to the correctness of our legal opinion as without merit. Whilst we have the utmost respect for Dr. Carmichael's opinion, as the letter of 14th October was never received by this Firm, it is difficult for us to understand what relevance his vetting of it has in relation to the problems raised by us.

We must therefore state that until we **either have sight of the agreement referred to in the Vesting Order for us to make our own determination or are given a letter from local counsel confirming that your interpretation of the agreement is correct**, together with a letter of indemnity from FirstCaribbean indemnifying us against any future claims for any proceedings done contrary to our advice, our continuing to prepare documents as you have requested is done merely to facilitate innocent customers of the Bank.

It follows that without sight of the agreement we are in no position to review and rescind the advice we have given former Barclays operations or lawyers of their clients and for reasons we have stated before, we think it is the height of impertinence for you to so suggest.

Retainer

Your letter of 14th February rejects our request for a retainer to act on your behalf on the basis that CIBC has never paid one. The fact that you make such a statement shows a level of understanding about retainers that is appalling in someone who holds himself out to be an Attorney-at-Law.

A retainer is paid to secure the legal services of an Attorney-at-Law or firm of Attorneys. It is not paid as a gift or in lieu of fees. As we were retained by Barclays up to the end of 2002, it meant for instance that we could not accept work, as we were offered, from your favourite people - outside counsel - on behalf of disgruntled workers of CIBC and Barclays. Our inability to do so was despite the fact that we were not acting on the merger. Not being retained means that we would be free to accept such a request in the future, although given your opinion of the Firm, that would not worry you.

Public perception of FirstCaribbean it that it is the merged entity of Barclays and CIBC. However as more details come to light, especially comments like "CIBC has never paid annual retainers for legal firms in the region and has had quite satisfactory service from its external counsel", one needs to question whether we are dealing with a merger of two institutions or a buy out by CIBC of Barclays. In this case, we venture no opinion on the subject as we have not seen the agreement, however as we are aware of the high level of dissatisfaction amongst some members of Barclays staff, this may be a true indication of what has actually happened. Your statement already quoted also appears to indicate that the merger picture that you are so desperately trying to sell may not be all that clear.

Libellous Statement

The final page of your letter again contains libelous statements of me in particular, the Firm in general and our Mrs. Ann Gale and although we have not yet ruled out further legal action if you continue with the spreading of your disparaging comments about the Firm, we are forced now to respond to place your statements in perspective.

Mrs. Gale has been a valued employee of this Firm for over 30 years. During that time she has built up considerable ties with all branches of Barclays Bank and has worked with a number of Attorneys both within this Firm and who have been practicising in Barbados during this period of her work. She has never sought to qualify as an Attorney-at-Law, but in my opinion and in the opinion of those more qualified than me, she has more experience and expertise in matters pertaining to mortgage and conveyancing transactions than most Attorneys in Barbados. Mrs. Gale has been distressed at the contemptuous manner in which the Firm has been treated in this matter especially as this has impacted on our ability to provide the service that you are so keen to achieve. On more than one occasion when she has discussed the merger with the undersigned, Mrs. Gale has stressed that it is not the fact that we are not working on the merger that has caused her dissatisfaction, but the manner in which information regarding the merger is being transmitted to the Firm that is causing the resentment.

Our Mr. Nicholls, Mr. Watson and Mrs. Gale have complained about this fact ad nauseum without response from members of your staff. To be fair to the Barclays staff some have responded stating that they are unable to shed any light. Late last year our Mr. Nicholls spoke to your Ms. Holder with whom he studied, pointing out the constraints under which we were working. Still no information was forthcoming until your most recent letter of 28th February.

Future Work

As we conclude it is evident to us that there is little prospect of a long-term relationship between FirstCaribbean and Cottle Catford continuing unless there is a willingness on the part of both parties to meet and find a way forward. However until you instruct us otherwise and as long as we obtain the letter of indemnity as requested, we will be prepared to continue working on your behalf but within the following constraints:

FirstCaribbean International Bank

28 March 2003

1. Payment of all out of pocket expenses prior to the incurring of these. In this regard we will submit our invoice for same. Until payment for such expenses is received, we will be unable to proceed with the matter further. It is therefore in your hands how quickly a matter can proceed.

2. The settlement of all invoices for fees and expenses within 30 days of their issue. All outstanding invoices will attract interest at the rate of 1.5% per month.

3. Any requests for information pertaining to any subject other than routine enquiries about matters in hand will not be entertained unless in writing and will be subject to a charge.

4. We will no longer process routine requests for the forwarding of title deeds on behalf of the Bank on receipt of an undertaking from the Attorneys to whom they are being forwarded without charging the Bank for same.

All the above changes are necessary as a result of your decision not to renew our annual retainer as we cannot continue expending time for which they will be no corresponding income.

We are available to meet at a mutually convenient time should you desire.

Yours faithfully,

c.c. Mr. Michael Mansoor - Chairman, FirstCaribbean
Mr. Charles Pink - CEO, FirstCaribbean
Chancery Chambers - Dr. Trevor Carmichael Q.C.

Encs.

Appendix Twelve

hand delivered on Feb. 11, 2011

PHILIP NICHOLLS & ASSOCIATES

ATTORNEYS - AT - LAW

Principal
Philip V. Nicholls LL.B (Hons) UWI, LL.M (Manch)

Associate
Sharron C. Goddard B.A. UWI, LL.B (Hons) Buckingham

Consultants
Sir. Neville V. Nicholls K.A.B.A. Econ (Cantab)
Dr. Sharon B. Le Gall LL.B (Hons) UWI,
LL.M (Osgoode), Ph.D (Cantab)

PVN/Tb

February 10, 2011

Mr. Hal Gollop
Attorney-at-Law
Harford House
Roebuck Street
BRIDGETOWN

Dear Hal

<u>Re SCS No 1123 of 2005 and 1057 of 2005 Vernon Smith and Philip Nicholls and Sharon Carter</u>

I refer to the hearing before Mr. Justice Olson Alleyne(ag) on Monday 7th February, 2011, which had been requested by me to have the above captioned suits against myself and my former employee Ms Carter both of whom you know are Attorneys at this bar dismissed for want of prosecution by your client a Queens Counsel at the same bar.

Prior to the hearing you approached me and offered your hand in friendship as a colleague with respect to settling the matter, a gesture that was greatly appreciated by me, and gave your undertaking to the Court for yourself and your client that the appropriate measures would be done to see that the matter is put to bed. I welcomed your personal undertaking to this effect.

In a spirit of compromise, and to put an end to this unsavory part of a wider malaise that is still afflicting me with respect to the Affairs of Cottle Catford, I did not insist on a formal ruling from the Court but noted the comments of his Lordship that the matter will be taken off the list. For that reason also, I made no comment about the undertaking given by your client and will only say now that as it was given by you he and I had no hesitation in accepting it. However, as your client has over the last nearly ten years told several persons including counsel representing me and also my parents that he would do all within his power to bring a Resolution to the troubled Affairs of the Partnership but has proceeded to do the exact opposite over these years, that has added to the present predicament I am in. I could only have wished that he had listened to the comments of a Judge when she asked why he does not keep out of the Affairs of Cottle Catford.

You, and most Members of the Bar who have any calling of over five years, know of the terrible predicament that I have faced over the years as a result of the actions of my Former Partners at Cottle Catford who have been found liable to him by the Courts of this

P.O. BOX 93W, SEASTON HOUSE, HASTING, CHRIST CHURCH, BARBADOS BB15159
Tel: (246) 435-8171 Fax: (246) 228-0801

Page 2
February 10, 2011
Mr. Hal Gollop

country with interest and costs for almost $2,000,000 dollars (two million dollars) in September 2009 after the partnership dissolved at the end of 2002. To this day I have never recovered a cent but have had to find the resources to settle claims from clients of the former Cottle Catford and to this day am still facing claims and indeed disciplinary charges because of the inability of Cottle Catford to settle clients funds.

Your Client has from early known of these problems yet has done all within his power, to forestall all and any attempts by the undersigned to recover these moneys from his former Partners. In particular, the subject matter that lead to this suit, namely, the amount of money due from Mrs. Watson, the wife of the former Senior Partner who had advanced it to her from around the year 2000, and who, despite repeated requests, had failed to repay same at the end of the Partnership forcing the undersigned to obtain an undefended Judgment in 2004 against her. Your client acknowledged service of the Writ.

Needless to say, that that money has long since had to be repaid by me because up to this day it has not been fully repaid by Mr. or Mrs. Watson and every attempt by me to recover same was frustrated by his antics. With this history for your Client to file a suit alleging defamatory comments in a letter that I wrote concerning my efforts to recover this money and I quote from his Reply filed on July 12th 2005 at Paragraph 4 -

> "that Neither Ms. Joyce Griffith nor Mr. Allan Watson has or has an interest in or an entitlement to the debt for which Mrs. Delvina Watson was being sued by Cottle Catford"

and yet in April 2007 for your client to so calmly write a letter to me after an order from Madam Justice Cornelius that the funds be repaid by the end of April 2007 stating that he had paid their one third share to the said Griffith and Watson as former Partners and worst still file receipts for payment on the Court file which receipts the then Registrar has written and said were not officially done is beyond belief given the statements in the Court proceedings.

It should be known that these payments that Ms Griffith in 2009 on later examination before Madam Justice Cornelius admitted were never made by Mrs. Watson as alleged by your client is surely behavior that the Disciplinary Committee would find borders on if it is not unethical practice the same accusations he accused me of making and so tarnishing his reputation. Whether it is or is not it is behavior unbefitting of one with the letters Q.C behind his name .

Your Client has thereafter continued to frustrate every opportunity by me to get settlement of this and indeed the wider claims for settlement of the Partnership debt with the situation now that I am on the verge of bankruptcy, the stress has played no small part in the end of my marriage, the Bank has foreclosed on my house, and is threatening the property of my parents because of my inability to

Page 3
February 10, 2011
Mr. Hal Gollop

recover the funds from these two to repay them whom I had borrowed from to settle pressing CLIENT Claims.

Your Client must have been aware of the stress his actions have caused or has been indifferent to same not only on me but my wider family and parents in particular. What he does not know but may well guess but not care for is the loathing and contempt that I feel towards him – A man that as a child I referred to as Uncle but one now I am ashamed to admit that I know.

I will not even mention the minor details of the costs of this matter that I incurred in obtaining advice from Counsel in UK nor that which he has caused Ms. Carter by this suit.

If he were man enough he would apologise for his actions but he has never said a word and I expect that men will give birth before he does. In closing, I will just state that he is unwelcome at any matter associated with any Member of the Nicholls family as long as he refuses to acknowledge the harm that he has done and I for one will embarrass him if I ever see him around any such event.

I am copying this letter to persons who have an interest in the matter as I deem fit.

I look forward to receiving the Relevant Notices of Discontinuance.

Yours sincerely,

Philip Nicholls
PHILIP NICHOLLS & ASSOCIATES

About the Author

PHILIP VERNON NICHOLLS was born on October 6th 1960, the first of three boys of Neville and Yvonne Nicholls. Stephen is a financial analyst and Christopher an oncologist, while Philip followed in the footsteps of his father in becoming an attorney-at-law. His mother was a teacher for many years at the former Girls Foundation and Queens College, and was on staff at the University of the West Indies when Philip also joined the Faculty of Law there as an Associate Tutor ,something he did for over 20 years.

His early education was at the Merrivale Preparatory School, also known as Mrs. Carrington's school, where his two brothers were all schooled before the three of them entered Harrison College. After Harrison College he entered the Faculty of Law at the University of the West Indies, Cave Hill Campus from where he graduated with an Upper Second Class Degree in Law before completing his professional Legal Education Certificate at the Norman Manley Law School in Jamaica in 1985. From there he read and obtained a Master's in International Business Law from the Victoria University of Manchester in 1987. He was called to the Bar in Barbados in 1986 and joined the firm of Cottle Catford in January of 1987 as an associate attorney-at-law.

He was admitted as a partner of the firm from January 1st 1992 and remained as a partner of the firm until he closed it on October 30th 2009.

He is a former president of Pickwick Cricket Club, and served on the board of the Barbados Cricket Association between 1988 and 2005, the last five as honourary secretary. He has also sat on several other boards in the island, and was the last president of the Canada Barbados Business Association. He has served as chairman of the Disciplinary Committee of the Bar Association and the Barbados Hockey Federation, and currently sits on the Complaints Committee and Rules Committee of the Barbados Cricket Association.

He has three daughters, Carissa and twins named Anya and Edaynah, but is no longer married to his former wife Beverley, who is also an attorney-at-law.

Made in the USA
Charleston, SC
02 December 2016